Ethnic and Racial Minorities in Advanced Industrial Democracies

Recent Titles in
Contributions in Ethnic Studies

Creative Awakening: The Jewish Presence in Twentieth-Century American
Literature, 1900-1940s
Louis Harap

The South African Society: Realities and Future Prospects
Human Sciences Research Council

In the Mainstream: The Jewish Presence in Twentieth-Century American
Literature, 1950s-1980s
Louis Harap

Dramatic Encounters: The Jewish Presence in Twentieth-Century American
Drama, Poetry, and Humor and the Black-Jewish Relationship
Louis Harap

The Politics of Racial Inequality: A Systematic Comparative Macro-Analysis
from the Colonial Period to 1970
J. Owens Smith

How Minority Status Affects Fertility: Asian Groups in Canada
Shivalingappa S. Halli

Religion, Intergroup Relations, and Social Change in South Africa
Human Sciences Research Council

Latino Empowerment: Progress, Problems, and Prospects
Roberto E. Villarreal, Norma G. Hernandez, and Howard D. Neighbor, editors

Contemporary Federal Policy Toward American Indians
Emma R. Gross

The Governance of Ethnic Communities: Political Structures and Processes in
Canada
Raymond Breton

Latinos and Political Coalitions: Political Empowerment for the 1990s
Roberto E. Villarreal and Norma G. Hernandez, editors

Conflict Resolution: Cross-Cultural Perspectives
Kevin Avruch, Peter W. Black, and Joseph A. Scimecca, editors

Ethnic and Racial Minorities in Advanced Industrial Democracies

Edited by
Anthony M. Messina,
Luis R. Fraga,
Laurie A. Rhodebeck,
and Frederick D. Wright

Contributions in Ethnic Studies, Number 29
Leonard W. Doob, Series Editor

GREENWOOD PRESS
New York • Westport, Connecticut • London

Library of Congress Cataloging-in-Publication Data

Ethnic and racial minorities in advanced industrial democracies /
   edited by Anthony M. Messina . . . [et al.].
      p.   cm.—(Contributions in ethnic studies, ISSN 0196-7088 ;
   no. 29)
    Rev. papers presented at the Conference on Ethnic and Racial
   Minorities in the Advanced Industrial Democracies, which was held at
   the University of Notre Dame, in Dec. 1987.
    Includes bibliographical references and index.
    ISBN 0-313-27259-X (alk. paper)
    1. Ethnic relations—Case studies—Congresses. 2. Minorities—
   Population—Case studies—Congresses. 3. Industry—Social aspects—
   Case studies—Congresses. I. Messina, Anthony M. II. Conference
   on Ethnic and Racial Minorities in the Advanced Industrial
   Democracies (1987 : University of Notre Dame) III. Series.
   GN496.E837   1992
   305.8—dc20   91-26374

British Library Cataloguing in Publication Data is available.

Library of Congress Catalog Card Number: 91-26374
ISBN: 0-313-27259-X
ISSN: 0196-7088

First published in 1992

Greenwood Press, 88 Post Road West, Westport, CT 06881
An imprint of Greenwood Publishing Group, Inc.

Printed in the United States of America

The paper used in this book complies with the
Permanent Paper Standard issued by the National
Information Standards Organization (Z39.48-1984).

10 9 8 7 6 5 4 3 2 1

Contents

PART I: IMMIGRATION POLICY AND ETHNIC TOLERANCE

PART II: MINORITIES, POLITICS, AND THE STATE

PART III: POLITICAL CONSCIOUSNESS, ORGANIZATION, AND
PARTICIPATION

Figures and Tables

FIGURES

TABLES

Series Foreword

Contributions in Ethnic Studies focuses upon the situations that develop when peoples from different cultures and with different goals come together and interact either productively or tragically. The modes of adjustment or conflict are various, but usually one group dominates or attempts to dominate the other. Eventually some accommodation is reached: the process is likely to be long and, for the weaker group, painful. No one scholarly discipline monopolizes the research necessary to comprehend these intergroup relations. The emerging analysis, consequently, is inevitably of interest to historians, social scientists, psychologists, and psychiatrists.

The fourteen chapters in this book, as its title suggests, concentrate upon the problem of ethnicity in many of the industrial democracies of the West or those with a Western orientation. Included are least once are the ethnic situations in France, Germany, Great Britain, Israel, the Netherlands, New Zealand, Spain, and the United States. The scope is thus wide and restricted.

The authors of each chapter pursue their own interests, which they believe provide insight into the ethnic problem at hand. Historical backgrounds are discussed when they seem relevant and necessary. Quantitative data, of the kind available from questionnaires and public-opinion surveys, appear. Successful and unsuccessful efforts and "solutions" to improve relations between ethnic groups are reported. The vocabulary employed to name the basic concepts and categories varies; references are made to theories, models, hypotheses, policies, "common threads," and schools of social science. Many relevant disciplines and major authors are cited, as the long list of references at the end of the volume demonstrates. Views ranging from those of Marxists to those of Ronald Reagan are noted.

The very heterogeneity and variety of these case studies reflects the state of the art as well as your struggles and mine to comprehend ethnicity. There is no standardized way to investigate ethnic problems, to describe them, to conceptualize them, and to induce them to give rise to generalizations. The editors of this volume have not dogmatically forced their contributors to follow a stereotyped format; they know how pleasing but misleading that would have been. Of course their Introduction is a guide to ethnicity in "democratic" settings; and the very valiant, most helpful Conclusion offers a tidy, stimulating summary of the major contributions of each study.

Again, it is evident that the problems of ethnicity cannot be resolved through simple formulas. Somehow the particular situation at hand must be analyzed and appraised; only then can sensible proposals be promoted. This book, by sweeping across the advanced industrialized countries, is a valuable source for theorists and policy-makers to consult.

Leonard W. Doob

Preface

Social science scholarship on ethnic and racial minorities in the advanced industrial democracies has always been quite extensive. Indeed, since the 1980s, a mini-explosion of academic research on the condition of recently settled, immigrant minorities in Western Europe has added a considerable number of volumes to the existing literature (Başgöz and Furness 1985; Brubaker 1989; Hammar 1985; Miller 1981). This volume seeks to break new ground in the study of ethnic and racial minorities in two respects. First, the collected essays survey a broad range of countries, but only those that share a similar set of economic, political, and social institutions and a liberal democratic, constitutional tradition. Previous works focused only on two or three countries (Glazer and Young 1983) or, somewhat inappropriately, compared the condition of minorities across countries that are at very different stages of economic and political development (Brass 1985; Fried 1983; Greenberg 1980; Sowell 1983). A central assumption of this volume is that ethnic and racial minorities in the advanced industrial democracies, in spite of their obvious differences, share a common context that qualitatively differs from that of Third World and communist countries. Second, the volume brings together the work of two groups of scholars who rarely collaborate: those whose work primarily focuses on long-established (e.g., African Americans) or ethnoregional (e.g., Spanish Basques) minorities and those who study recent immigrant populations (e.g., Asians in Britain).

This book is based on revised papers presented at the Conference on Ethnic and Racial Minorities in the Advanced Industrial Democracies, which was held at the University of Notre Dame. The conference was primarily funded by the Ford Foundation and co-sponsored by the Department of Government and International Studies, the Institute for Scholarship in the Liberal Arts, and the African American Studies Program of the University of Notre Dame.

The following chapters are not organized around a single theme. Neither do they share an explicit perspective on the condition of minority populations in the advanced industrial democracies, nor do they necessarily agree about how, if at all, this condition is likely to change in the foreseeable future. Rather, in bringing these essays together the editors wish to prepare the intellectual groundwork for other comparative volumes of this kind and, more important, stimulate empirical researchers to scrutinize further the arguments and observations presented in the introductory and concluding chapters. These may be interpreted as intellectually untidy objectives. While the editors do not fully accept this verdict, we willingly acknowledge that we have accepted a certain degree of untidiness in the conceptualization and organization of the volume in an attempt to analyze a broad and complex subject. The interested reader, we anticipate, will judge our effort for what it is: a modest, and, we hope, thoughtful, attempt to expand the parameters of existing social science paradigms concerning the socioeconomic and political location of ethnic and racial minorities in the advanced industrial democracies.

Anthony M. Messina, Luis R. Fraga, and Laurie A. Rhodebeck shared the responsibilities of editing equally.

Ethnic and Racial Minorities in Advanced Industrial Democracies

Introduction
Anthony M. Messina and Luis R. Fraga

Among the most perplexing dilemmas confronting the advanced industrial democracies are those that spring from the persistence of conflict among their majority populations and ethnic and racial minorities. Problems of economic disadvantage, political equality, and social harmony continue to exist in virtually all these societies, despite the construction of various constitutional settlements, power-sharing agreements among ethnic communities, and the enactment, in many countries, of anti-discrimination and equal opportunity statutes since the early 1960s. The persistence of ethnic and racial conflict raises an obvious question: Is such conflict a permanent feature of the advanced industrial democracies?

The origins of minorities in these societies are certainly varied (Heckman 1983, 12-21). Ethnoregional and ethnoterritorial minorities in Belgium, Canada, Spain, and Switzerland, for example, were long-established and often politically autonomous prior to the founding of the modern state. African Americans in the United States, on the other hand, were forcibly transplanted to North America as a result of the seventeenth- and eighteenth-century slave trade. In contemporary Britain and France, former colonial peoples are relatively recent immigrants who are part of the legacy of overseas empire and post-WWII decolonization. Moreover, most recently settled, and often without the rights of full citizenship or permanent residence, are various Third World minorities in countries such as Austria, France, the Netherlands, the United States, and Germany. Most of these new minorities were actively recruited by governments and private employers during the 1950s, 1960s, and the early 1970s to satisfy the demand for cheap, unskilled labor in the booming economies of the advanced industrial democracies (Castles and Kosack 1973).

Although the various minority groups in the advanced industrial democracies can be differentiated on the basis of their origins and, therefore, by the timing of their entrance into the economic, political, and social hierarchies that obtain in these societies, most currently suffer limited social mobility, political disadvantage, and restricted access to material well-being. They are united as well in that they very often have been the recipients of governmental policies that directly or indirectly have effected or perpetuated these conditions (Owens Smith 1987). For these reasons it is important that the study of ethnoregional/ethnoterritorial minorities not be divorced, as it has been for so long, from the study of the conflicts arising from the settlement, whether forced or voluntary, of Third World immigrants in the industrialized democracies. Moreover, it is important for two additional reasons. First, unlike the 1960s and early 1970s when most immigrant workers could not claim citizenship in the advanced industrial democracies, millions of these workers and their families in the 1980s acquired citizenship and are now permanently settled in their host countries (Hammar 1985; Rogers 1985). Like traditional ethnic and racial groups, these new minorities are politically conscious and increasingly well organized (Miller 1981). Second, at a juncture in the historical evolution of the advanced industrial democracies when color and ethnicity remain relevant variables in the formulation and implementation of public policy (Piore 1979; Rogers 1985), and when new ethnic and racial conflicts have been superimposed over the old, it is appropriate to examine the condition of all minorities who are defined by the mainstream society, and who define themselves, by their ethnicity or race. As the chapters in this volume by Grove, Safran, Klass, and Shingles remind us, ethnic and racial disadvantage persist among minority groups with both recent and long historical claims to citizenship.

THE ADVANCED INDUSTRIAL DEMOCRACIES

For reasons of analytical clarity, the chapters in this volume consider only the advanced industrial democracies, and our analysis is therefore appropriately confined to these societies. Ethnic and racial conflict is not exclusive, of course, to the advanced industrial democracies. To the contrary, such conflict poses great problems as well for political governance and the integrity of the state in socialist or formerly socialist countries like the Soviet Union and Yugoslavia and in many nations of the Third World. Nevertheless, a central assumption of the volume is that ethnic and racial minorities in the advanced industrial democracies, despite their significant differences, operate in a common economic, political, and social context that is qualitatively different from those of Third World and former communist countries (Esman 1977). In particular, the organization of their economies, their core political institutions, and their central decision-making processes set the advanced industrial democracies conspicuously apart from other societies.

The advanced industrial democracies specifically include only those countries whose economies have reached a very high, if unspecified, level of industrialization; that is, these societies are not primarily agricultural. A large majority of their populations are employed in manufacturing or advanced service industries and are residentially concentrated in urban areas. Moreover, the technologies that dominate and penetrate virtually every aspect of these societies are among the most sophisticated.

A second defining characteristic of the advanced industrial democracies is that their politics are organized around and mostly realize the principles of public contestation and the right of the individual to participate (Dahl 1971). In these societies elections are frequent, competitive, and open; well-organized political parties exist and operate freely; and basic civil liberties and human rights are protected by government and constitutionally guaranteed. Included among the advanced industrial democracies are such countries as Belgium, Canada, France, Germany, Italy, Japan, the Netherlands, Spain, Sweden, the United Kingdom, and the United States.

ETHNIC AND RACIAL CONFLICT IN THE ADVANCED INDUSTRIAL DEMOCRACIES

Throughout much of the 1960s, numerous scholars and policymakers argued that powerful trends were sweeping across the advanced industrial democracies that were seriously weakening both the scope and the intensity of ethnic and racial tensions in these societies. Although the argument took several forms, implicit in each was the assumption that the industrial democracies were following a common trajectory that was gradually eroding the foundations of non-class, primordial group solidarities and, hence, the potential for ethnic and racial conflict.

According to one view, the tremendous prosperity generated during the post-WWII period was facilitating the more equitable distribution of material resources across economically backward regions and disadvantaged groups. Unlike earlier periods when the economic progress of ethnic and racial minorities often precipitated majority-minority group conflict over fair shares, in the new age of affluence, majority populations endorsed the advancement of minorities since, they, too, were experiencing substantial upward mobility relative to their previous position. Indeed, so great was the prosperity generated in the advanced industrial democracies that it was spilling over into the less economically developed countries. Guest workers from Greece, Morocco, Portugal, Turkey, and elsewhere, recruited to satisfy the demand for labor during the full-employment, boom years of the 1950s and 1960s, were embraced by the advanced industrial democracies as valuable contributors to the prosperity of the domestic economy. Implicit in this welcome, of course, was the expectation that most guest workers would return to their home countries once the demand for labor slackened. Hence, at the height of the boom, issues related to the long-term integration of these new minorities into the industrial democracies were neglected (Hammar 1985, 293).

A second argument, also economically deterministic, was often advanced by scholars writing within a Marxist framework and intellectual tradition. According to this view, the increasing polarization of class conflict and the decreasing political salience of non-economic cleavages within the advanced industrial democracies were inexorably eroding traditional ethnic bonds and identities in favor of class solidarities and identities (Nimni 1989). According to this perspective, ethnic and racial conflict were inevitably declining not because social conflict had significantly diminished within the advanced industrial democracies, as the affluence school argued, but, rather, because the nature of such conflict had been transformed. Indeed, a number of Marxist scholars went so far as to argue that the persistence of any form of politicized ethnicity was ultimately reactionary and, hence, an impediment to the eventual emergence of proletarian socialism (Rothschild 1981, 24).

In a third view, ethnic and racial conflict was perceived as declining in the advanced industrial democracies as a consequence of the systematic intervention of the state in defense of minority group rights and interests. In particular, the adoption by the state of compensatory legislation to remedy the effects of past discrimination or to satisfy the long-standing claims of minorities for greater cultural and linguistic autonomy was perceived by many as a significant strategy to ameliorate majority-minority group relations. Prominent examples of such efforts include the passage of numerous equal opportunity laws in the United States during the 1960s and the policy of linguistic and educational devolution in Belgium (Glazer 1987; De Ridder and Fraga 1986). In the latter example, the practice of consociational democracy, or "segmented pluralism," appeared to demonstrate how the state could successfully intervene to manage fundamental ethnic cleavages in society without seriously undermining its own legitimacy (Lijphart 1977a). In Belgium and other consociational democracies the state was believed to respect and even preserve ethnic group differences, but not at the expense of polarizing the whole of the political community.

Proponents of a fourth view, on the other hand, argued that the forces of modernization, such as the expansion of the economic market, the spread of communications and transportation, mass education, and the development of the modern state, had so diffused a set of rational, maximizing behaviors throughout society that ethnic and racial group identifications and, hence, majority-minority group conflict, had been significantly transcended. In a modern society, it was stressed, norms are instilled that are based on "universalistic achievement criteria," to the exclusion of norms that preserve culturally specific solidarities (Rothschild 1981, 19). In such societies, "the characteristics of individuals, on the one hand, and their choices and decisions, on the other, determine where individuals will be located in the social structure" (Berger and Piore 1980, 3). As a result, to the extent that it persisted in the advanced industrial democracies, ethnic and racial conflict was seen as an irrational legacy of the premodern era. Moreover, the maintenance of ethnic and racial identification was viewed as counterproductive to the economic, political, and social advancement of minorities.

As we now know with the benefit of hindsight, of course, ethnic and racial conflict in the advanced industrial democracies did not appreciably diminish during the late 1960s, 1970s, and 1980s (Esman 1977; Brass 1985; Zarinski 1989). Neither the experience of prolonged prosperity, the decreasing salience of many non-economic cleavages, the active intervention of the state, nor the irresistible march of modernization significantly undermined traditional patterns of majority-minority group conflict. If anything, such conflict has escalated in many of the industrial democracies during recent years (Rudolph and Thompson 1989; Messina 1989a). Why, then, does ethnic and racial conflict persist?

In a particularly comprehensive response, Lijphart (1977b) cites eight plausible explanations for the resurgence of ethnic conflict in the industrialized democracies:

1. *The transition-integration balance.* Ethnic conflict has increased as a consequence of the rapid expansion in social transactions, for example, social communication and trade, among diverse groups. Such transactions were stimulated by the ongoing process of modernization. Greater and more intense interaction among different ethnic communities has diminished their capacity to co-exist peacefully as perceptions of threat to their cultural integrity increase.

2. *The increasing "horizontalization" of "vertical" ethnic groups.* Modernization has led to a degree of horizontalization among previously vertical ethnic groups by creating significant economic inequalities among various groups and regions. These new inequalities foster feelings of superiority in the more-favored groups and of resentment among the less-favored groups.

3. *The expanding scope of state intervention.* The growth of the economic and social-welfare responsibilities of the state during the postwar period has significantly exacerbated the problem of perceived inequalities among ethnic groups. Specifically, state intervention in the economy and civil society make it more likely that unequal results among groups will occur by chance and, in the event of deliberate action by the state to equalize differences among groups, that such intervention will be perceived as unfair and discriminatory by the dominant group(s).

4. *The increasing displacement of ethnic conflict.* Ethnic conflicts have resurfaced in the advanced industrial democracies as a result of the decreasing salience of ideological conflict along the left-right cleavage. Traditional ethnic tensions had never disappeared; rather, they had only been temporarily displaced by more salient economic, political, and social conflicts.

5. *The new wave of democratization.* All of the manifestations of the new wave of democratization that have swept across the industrial democracies

since the early postwar period, in particular increased group mobilization and group penetration of the policy-making process, have fostered politicized ethnicity. To the extent that mass and relatively unstructured political participation increased governmental immobility, demands for ethnic autonomy have accelerated.

6. *The growth of postbourgeois values.* The decline of material and the rise of postmaterial values and the concomitant shift from elite-directed toward elite-challenging activities among Western publics have fostered ethnic solidarities and ethnic militancy. For individuals who consciously identify with a particular ethnic group, the aspirations to belong and to achieve intellectual and aesthetic self-fulfillment, in their view, are best realized within the context of a self-governing ethnic community.

7. *The principle of self-determination.* Ethnic demands and ethnic group cohesion have been reinforced in recent decades by the principle of self-determination. The universal appeal and widespread acceptance of this principle across societies has influenced many ethnic minority communities to challenge the authority of national governments and the legitimacy of contemporary territorial boundaries.

8. *The demonstration effect of ethnic demands.* The example set by militant ethnic groups has encouraged previously passive groups to be more demanding. The domino effect of this process has increased the overall scope of ethnic conflict in the advanced industrial democracies.

Although Lijphart's theses were primarily inspired by specific cases of ethnonational and ethnoregional conflict, at least six of these theses (3 through 8) also apply to other kinds of majority-minority group conflict both within and outside of Western Europe. The expanding scope of state intervention during the postwar period and the new wave of democratization, for example, undoubtedly influenced the struggle over African American civil rights in the United States during the 1960s.

Lijphart's eight theses for ethnic conflict can be collapsed into three macro-explanations: the effects of modernization, the influence of the "end of ideology" (Lipset 1964), and the domino effect (Table I.1). Grouping the eight theses in this manner reveals the central assumptions upon which they are founded. First, virtually all of the theses, excluding those grouped under the domino effect, have an economic dimension. Specifically, they assume that the major structural changes that have occurred in both the domestic and international economy during the postwar period have negatively affected majority-minority relations in the advanced industrial democracies. Second, and most important, the theses collectively imply that the recent surge in ethnic conflict has been precipitated by the successes rather than the failures or shortcomings of the advanced industrial democracies. Paradoxically, as the economies of the industrial democracies have become more modern, integrated, and affluent, and as their politics have become less ideological along class lines

Table I.1 Explanations for Ethnic Conflict

Modernization	End of Ideology	Domino Effect
Transition-Integration Balance	Expanding State Intervention	Principle of Self-Determination
Horizontalization of Ethnic Groups	Displacement of Ethnic Conflict	Demonstration Effect
	Wave of Democratization	
	Growth of Post-Materialism	

and more democratic, conditions have been created that have led to greater ethnic conflict. Finally, an important assumption underpinning virtually all the theses is that ethnic conflict in the industrialized democracies is more or less inevitable. The scope, intensity, and severity of ethnic conflict may vary from country to country, depending on local conditions, but the forces for conflict exacerbated by the trends identified in Table I.1 exist and are at times transformed by the continuing social, economic, and political development of the modern nation state.

While Lijphart's eight theses do not cohere into a single, consistent view of why ethnic conflict has surged in the advanced industrial democracies, it is nevertheless possible to construct a schema which represents the essence of his macro-perspective, as demonstrated in Figure I.1. This macro-perspective is informed by two implicit views about the general nature of conflict within the industrial democracies. First, the influences of modernization, the end of ideology, and the domino effect are represented in Figure I.1 as being relatively independent of one another. At no point do they intersect and, presumably, the absence of one or two of these influences diminishes, but does not completely eliminate, the potential for ethnic conflict. Second, Lijphart's explanations for ethnic conflict are not integrated into a broader view of or explanation for other kinds of conflict in the advanced industrial democracies, and particularly class conflict. Although Lijphart implies in his essay that the increasing horizontalization of ethnic groups fosters class tensions both within and between groups, his eight theses collectively assume, on the whole, either that class conflict does not exist within the industrial democracies or that such conflict does not significantly intersect with or impact ethnic conflict. The end-of-ideology thesis in particular purports that class conflict is not a significant problem for the advanced industrial democracies. Moreover, only in the instance of the domino effect does ethnic conflict feed the forces that initially

Figure I.1 Ethnic Conflict in the Industrial Democracies

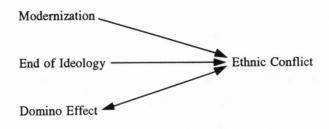

nurtured it. Ethnic conflict has no apparent influence, for example, on the
ongoing process of modernization or the trends associated with the end of
ideology.

An alternative model, Figure I.2, which purports to explain ethnic and
racial conflict and which implicitly subsumes a number of Lijphart's theses, has
been offered by Richmond (1988). Although short on detail, Richmond's model
improves upon Figure I.1 in three ways. First, Figure I.2 explicitly recognizes
that ethnic conflict is linked to the declining autonomy of the nation-state in the
international political economy. In Richmond's model the emergence of the
ubiquitous multinational corporation and the resultant creation of oligopolistic
markets fuel global inflation by restricting economic competition. Governmental
policies aimed at curbing domestic inflation inevitably precipitate mass
unemployment which, in turn, inflames class conflict. As economic and
political conditions deteriorate, traditional, bureaucratic and charismatic political
authority are severely undermined and are "challenged by leaders claiming to
represent oppressed classes and ethnic minority groups" (Richmond 1988, 7).
The ultimate result is a legitimation crisis of the state and increased majority-
minority group competition and conflict.

Second, Richmond's model suggests that ethnic conflict is inevitably
exacerbated when the burdens of structural economic adjustment are
disproportionately borne by the lower classes. In Figure I.2, the reaction of the
majority population to economic dislocation are expressions of nationalism,
racism, authoritarianism, and political conservatism. Ethnic minorities, on the
other hand, respond to economic crisis with increased sentiments for separatism
and ethnic solidarity and a propensity for political deviance and radicalism.

Third, Figure I.2 appropriately portrays the state as instigating and
often perpetuating ethnic and racial tensions. In Richmond's view, the state is
never a "benign or neutral arbiter" of conflict in the advanced industrial
democracies (Richmond 1988, 7). In defending the existing social order the

Figure I.2 Conflict in the Industrial Democracies and the International System

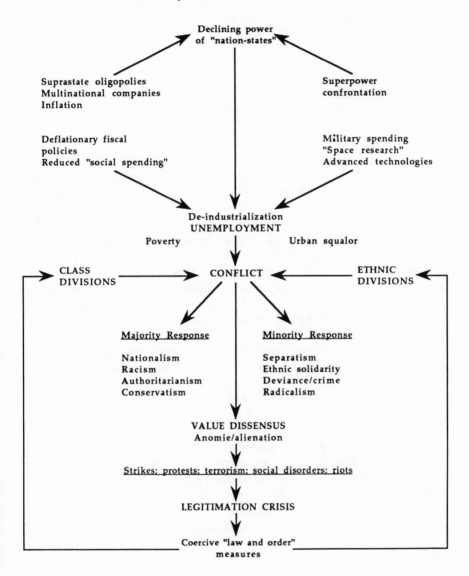

From Richmond (1988, 6).

state will often pursue coercive law and order measures that reinforce class and ethnic divisions, thus further alienating disadvantaged groups. Such a view of the state is not only consistent with the prevailing literature on the subject (Gamble 1988; Nordlinger 1981) but, moreover, concurs with many of the essays in this volume and much of the prominent scholarship on the nature of ethnic and racial conflict in the advanced industrial democracies (M. Heisler 1986).

TOWARD A PARADIGMATIC MODEL OF ETHNIC
AND RACIAL CONFLICT

Although they share some common ground, juxtaposing the Lijphart and Richmond models of ethnic conflict illuminates their obvious differences. As we emphasized above, for Lijphart it is the march of economic, political, and social progress in the advanced industrial democracies that, paradoxically, has heightened ethnic and racial tensions during recent decades. Ethnic conflict is an unfortunate and unintended by-product of modernization, the end of ideology, and the domino effect in the industrial democracies. For Richmond, on the other hand, majority-minority group conflict is deeply embedded in the political institutions and socioeconomic structures of the advanced industrial democracies and in the international political economy in which they interact. Although these structures too are largely impersonal, they are ultimately sustained by a concrete state which, in its defense of the existing socio-economic and political order, often pursues policies that are injurious to ethnic and racial minorities. In rationally responding to injury and disadvantage, ethnic and racial minorities cohere as a community, thus facilitating the deterioration of majority-minority group relations.

How, if at all, can these different perspectives be reconciled? We suggest four modifications to each model that will make them more comprehensive and will allow them to converge substantially. First, each model should incorporate a historical dimension that attributes proper weight to the origins of majority-minority group relations and, specifically, to the set of historical circumstances that initially shaped these relations. Of course, origins do not structure majority-minority group relations forever; these relations are inevitably and significantly transformed as economic, political, and social conditions within and across the industrial democracies change. Former slave minorities, for example, eventually acquired full citizenship in the advanced industrial democracies as these societies developed economically and became more politically progressive. Nevertheless, the pattern of contemporary ethnic conflict is still structured in many countries by the origins of majority-minority group relations (Steinberg 1981). In the specific example of slavery, its divisive legacy is difficult to overcome even where, as in the United States, the socioeconomic system that spawned slavery has been undergoing considerable change since the mid-19th century.

A second modification is suggested by the work of Joseph Rothschild (1981, 137-171). For Rothschild, a politics of ethnicity and race, and hence ethnic competition and conflict, are cultivated by the emergence and the political activities of ethnic entrepreneurs who rally minorities, or members of the majority, in defense of their collective interests. According to this view, ethnicity and race continue to structure conflict because ethnic leaders and would-be leaders perceive that making group-based claims on the state yields positive outcomes, given that the liberal state is extremely vulnerable to organized group pressure (Schattschneider 1975). Once mobilized and organized by ethnic leaders, minorities are likely to cohere further, especially if they perceive themselves as sharing a common economic condition. In these circumstances, solidarity among minorities arising out of economic disadvantage, or in the case of the majority out of advantage, stimulates even greater mobilization and individual recruitment. The ultimate result is the hardening of ethnic boundaries and, with the active instigation of ethnic entrepreneurs, the indefinite politicization of ethnicity and race.

A third modification to the Lijphart and Richmond models is the explicit recognition of the dynamic quality of ethnic and racial conflict. Put simply, ethnic and racial conflict in the advanced industrial democracies is not and never has been static. Its foundations, whether economic, political, or cultural, are always in flux, even when the nature and the composition of the groups in conflict remain relatively constant. Demands made by ethnic and racial minorities can vary from equal opportunity to full incorporation into the mainstream to substantial autonomy, if not secession. The demands can focus on political equality or material equality. The demands can focus on language or education. As a result of this variability, the state can rarely adopt a definitive solution to ethnic conflict. Indeed, state policies aimed at combatting the current causes of majority-minority group conflict will not only prove ineffective after a relatively short period, but they may feed new, emerging causes.

Lastly, we suggest that both the Lijphart and Richmond models should be located within the broader framework of societies organized by and oriented toward markets. The existence and pervasiveness of a market economy in the advanced industrial democracies, founded on capitalist principles, is self-evident and requires little further comment. Somewhat less obvious is the organization of contemporary politics into a market. What are the main features of this political market? They are essentially four: the existence of a mass electorate, political competition between at least two political parties for the votes of this electorate, a set of formal and informal rules governing this political competition (Gamble 1974, 6), and an asymmetrical distribution of resources among groups with competing, and often incompatible, interests.

This final modification implies that there is something about the way the industrial democracies are economically and politically organized and externally linked to and integrated into the international political economy that preserves and even promotes traditional ethnic and racial identities (Esman 1977; Rothschild 1981), distributes economic uncertainty and adjustment along ethnic and racial as well as class lines (Berger and Piore 1980), and pits ethnic and racial subgroups against one another in a competition for finite economic and political resources.   Specifically, at both the domestic and international levels competitive economic and political markets operate that simultaneously foster ethnic and racial solidarities, reward politicized ethnic and racial assertiveness (Rothschild 1981), *and* use ethnic solidarities and assertiveness against ethnic and racial minorities during periods of economic and political uncertainty and adjustment. Viewed from this perspective, the market is never neutral for ethnic and racial minorities in the advanced industrial democracies. It is both an arena of opportunity where organized minority groups can often achieve significant economic and political gains, and a perpetuator of conflict and an allocator of disadvantage.

Two propositions follow from this final modification. First, although ethnic and racial conflict will often diminish during a prolonged period of prosperity in the domestic and international economy, prosperity itself will not automatically reduce conflict and disadvantage (Owens Smith 1987). Several of the essays in this volume, that is, those by Safran, McDonald and Engstrom, Shingles, and Laponce, suggest that political elites in the industrial democracies must adopt explicit and sustained initiatives to reduce conflict and disadvantage, and, that even then, both will often intensify once economic uncertainty returns. Second, although the status of minorities in the advanced industrial democracies remains fluid, it is nevertheless likely that ethnic and racial conflict will indefinitely persist so long as the internal organization of these societies and their position in the international political economy remain relatively unchanged. Specifically, so long as the market, both economic and political, is invested with considerable authority to resolve major conflicts of interest and to allocate important economic and political outcomes, ethnic conflict in the industrial democracies will prove intractable. From this proposition it does not necessarily follow that ethnic conflict can be significantly reduced only by abolishing economic and political markets in the advanced industrial democracies. Rather, the latter proposition simply recognizes the limitations of the market for resolving conflict and diminishing ethnic and racial disadvantage.

PLAN OF THE BOOK

The organization of the fourteen chapters in the present volume follows the logic of our theoretical concerns and orientation. Part I--chapters 1 through

4--considers the general status of the new ethnic and racial minorities in the advanced industrial democracies and the social conflicts that are often engendered by a liberal immigration regime. These chapters survey the experience of immigration, for both immigrants and hosts, in four of the largest immigrant-receiving countries: Britain, France, Germany, and the United States. Part II--chapters 5 through 8--examines the relationship of ethnic and racial minorities to the state and to mainstream political institutions, including political parties. The chapters by Grove and Klass primarily focus on ethnic minorities as "receivers" of public policy, while the McDonald and Engstrom and Studlar and Welch chapters examine the impact of electoral rules and other structural arrangements on the representation of minorities in local government. Not surprisingly, both of the latter chapters conclude that electoral laws and constituency definition and size do affect the chances of minority candidates to win local office in Britain and the United States.

Part III--chapters 9 through 11--primarily concentrates on the dimension of ethnic minorities as political actors operating and being transformed by their participation within a broad political market. A common thread running throughout the chapters by Shingles, Ortiz, and Rath and Saggar is that ethnicity can be utilized as a tool or resource in politically mobilizing and organizing minority populations. These chapters confirm the importance of ethnic entrepreneurs in securing access for minorities to policy-making arenas and in elevating issues of particular concern to minorities on the political agenda of the industrial democracies. Finally, in Part IV--chapters 12 through 14--the contributions of Clark, Schmidt, and Laponce consider the manner in which the demands for territorial autonomy and/or basic rights are raised by ethnic minorities and politically channelled and acted upon by the state. These chapters suggest that ethnic minorities are not simply receivers of public policy but, rather, that they possess a considerable capacity to shape it and, in some circumstances, to alter the configuration of the state.

Part I

**Immigration Policy
and Ethnic Tolerance**

1

The Consequences of Immigration Policies for Immigrant Status: A British and French Comparison
Gary P. Freeman

These days nearly everyone, of whatever political persuasion, agrees that states have the right to control their borders, to set conditions for entry and exit, to demand passports and visas, and to regulate and control access to citizenship. It was not always so (Dowty 1987), but it seems likely that all states will for the foreseeable future develop an increasingly complex network of rules and regulations in the matter of immigration. Given that this is so, is there anything we can say about the implications that the choice of particular kinds of immigration rules may have for the eventual status and experiences of immigrants and for the nature of immigrant-host relations?

In debates over immigration policy, it is often claimed that the strictness, selectivity, and general tone of the immigration policy process affects the likelihood that immigrants will be able to adapt to their new surroundings. Advocates of a tough immigration policy often support their position by claiming that it is essential to exercise mastery over the entry of immigrants if one wishes to create a climate in which those who come in are able to adapt to their new circumstances. On the other hand, those who oppose tight immigration controls often stress that such measures send an unmistakable message to native citizens that immigrants are undesirable or at least may be potentially threatening. Such policies, they claim, undermine the possibility of a peaceful integration of immigrants into the national community. A racially selective control policy, many have argued, is necessarily inconsistent with domestic laws and programs that seek to establish strict equality of all persons regardless of race or national origin. Finally, the choice between an immigration of families for permanent settlement and a temporary immigration of workers is also often discussed in terms of its supposed consequences for domestic relations among immigrants and natives.

Despite the important role these arguments have played in the actual process by which immigration policies have been devised, there has been little research into the real consequences of immigration policy for the situation of immigrants once they have arrived. Even more surprising, there has been little written about the logically prior question of the linkages between the two sides of immigration policy: the regulation and control of entry and exit, on the one hand, and the management of the living conditions of immigrants, on the other. Instead, scholars have tended to treat the two sets of policies as separate and distinct. In other words, there is a significant disjuncture between the language with which public discussion of immigration policy is carried out and the scholarly investigation of public policies toward immigrants.

This chapter will seek to bridge this gap through a comparative case study of French and British policies toward immigration control and toward the domestic situation of immigrants. The data will be drawn from the entire period from the late nineteenth century to the present. The analysis will concentrate, however, on the postwar era, years in which these countries have experienced considerable conflict both over the appropriate immigration policies and, internally, between immigrants and the indigenous population. I begin by discussing the possible connections between those policies directed externally to the limitation, regulation, and control of entry and exit and those policies having to do with the living conditions, rights, and status of immigrants once they have arrived. These relationships will then be studied empirically through a comparison of the experience of Britain and France.

PRELIMINARY DISCUSSION

It may prove useful to distinguish between immigration regimes, immigration policy, and immigrant policy. By immigration regime I refer to the laws, agencies, procedures, techniques, practices, and goals that constitute the framework, machinery, and operation of immigration policy in a particular country and time. The idea of a regime is appropriate because it emphasizes the extent to which immigration policy is a complicated, multidimensional phenomenon directed toward multiple goals and employing a variety of means.[1] It is based on formal legal arrangements that are publicly and clearly acknowledged, but it includes the more nebulous values and practices that develop informally around institutions. It does not assume that a conscious, well-articulated regime will always exist. Some sort of immigration regime has been in place in the two countries under discussion since at least the early nineteenth century, but regimes may be marked by informal, inchoate, and confused structures.

Immigration regimes consist of two types of policies. In what follows, immigration policy refers to the regulation and control of entry and exit of persons to and from the national territory; the term *immigrant policy* is reserved for those laws and programs relating to the social, cultural, and political status of foreigners and their interactions with the native population (Hammar 1985). Although immigration and immigrant policies are a complex mix of programs, it is useful for the purposes of this chapter to distill these nuances in order to permit a reasonably clear and parsimonious analysis. Toward this end, I will treat immigration policy as having only three relevant dimensions: its liberality, its selectivity, and its position on permanence of settlement. We may conceive of these as dimensions rather than dichotomies. Policy may be more or less liberal or restrictive; more or less selective in terms of nationalities, ethnicity, education, or skill level, and so forth; and more or less committed to either permanent settlement or temporary migration. Immigrant policy, on the other hand, may be thought of as being indirect or direct (Hammar 1985). Indirect policies are those that assume that immigrants' needs for such things as housing, medical care, and education for their children will be met by including them in the normal distributive systems of the host country. Direct immigrant policy, by contrast, is built upon the assumption that special measures are necessary: particularistic benefit programs, affirmative action policies, anti-discrimination laws, and the like. Another relevant aspect of immigrant policy is whether it is designed to encourage the integration of migrants into the national society or to insulate and cordon them off to prevent assimilation.

The task of this chapter is to explore the ways in which the two principal dimensions of immigration regimes--immigration policies and immigrant policies--are connected and to what effect. Hypotheses about these connections can be gleaned both from the academic literature on immigration and from a reading of the national political debates that have occurred wherever immigration has been an issue.

I propose to concentrate on five questions:

1. *Is there any evidence that a laissez-faire approach to controls is related to domestic conflict and hardship for immigrants?* It is ironic, perhaps, that when states take a very tolerant attitude toward the entry of foreigners, they are often criticized for failing to care properly for the housing, education, health, and general living conditions of those who come in. Liberality at the border seems often to be combined with neglect or exploitation at home.

2. *Can a restrictive control policy founded on ethnic or racial considerations be made consistent with domestic policies that treat all persons fairly?* This is one of the most commonly asserted linkages between external control policies and social conditions domestically. If the state adopts discriminatory rules to regulate entry, how can it then creditably establish color-blind policies at home?

3. *Is it possible to protect the rights of immigrants while at the same time pursuing a control policy explicitly directed toward short-run economic goals?* If immigration policy is organized around the pursuit of economic growth, efficiency, cheap labor, and other common economic goals, is it likely to be possible to run an immigrant policy that significantly improves the living conditions, rights, and privileges of immigrants? Is there, in other words, a contradiction between the economic role of immigrants in the economy and the desire of some persons to achieve equal status for them in the social, cultural, and political spheres?

4. *Does citizenship matter?* On its face it would seem obvious that immigrants who arrive bearing the rights of citizenship would be in a more favorable position than those lacking them. Citizenship implies the right of settlement, the security of immunity from expulsion, as well as the opportunity to participate fully in the political process. The circumstances under which immigrants enjoy citizenship and the consequences it has for their status are questions of fundamental importance.

5. *What is the difference for the experience of immigrants if they are admitted on temporary work permits or are granted permanent immigrant status?* One hears arguments for both options. Generally it is conceded that immigrants admitted for permanent settlement are fortunate, but some argue that a well-run system of temporary immigration can also be sensitive to the interests and needs of migrants.

Britain and France make especially interesting cases from the perspective of exploring these five questions. They are two of the principal countries of immigration in Western Europe. As the narrative will show, immigration policy has taken a number of twists and turns in the two countries over the last century and a half. Immigration policy in both countries has alternated between laissez-faire and direct intervention. Immigrant policies have been in turn indifferent, solicitous, integrative, and insular. The authorities in the two countries have admitted immigrants under a number of different statuses and conditions. The majority of immigrants to Britain, especially since World War II, have enjoyed citizenship rights in the United Kingdom as residents of New Commonwealth countries. A smaller but important stream of guest workers and non-citizen immigrants have also entered the country. French immigration is more diverse still. France is a country with a tradition of immigration for settlement. Since 1945 it has admitted large numbers of immigrants from colonies, former colonies, and overseas dependencies who have either held citizenship rights or have been treated as if they held them and, in the fifties and sixties, a wave of foreign workers who have held temporary work permits. Both of the policy variables that are the focus of our analysis-- immigration and immigrant policies--provide an admirable range of differences between the two cases and over time in each of them. Moreover, the same is true of the nature of immigration itself.

THE EVOLUTION OF IMMIGRATION REGIMES

France

France has had four immigration regimes since the late nineteenth century: 1825-1919, 1919-1944, 1945-1974, and 1974 to the present. From about 1850 until the First World War, foreigners were free to move in and out of France and to take up residence without controls (Prost 1966). A law adopted in 1893 merely required foreigners to register with the police, and although a decree in 1899 permitted towns to set limits on the number of foreigners who could hold jobs in public works, it was rarely invoked. The long-standing problem of depopulation and an ideological commitment to free trade were probably the most significant factors contributing to this era of liberalism (Bonnet 1976; Perotti 1985; Spengler 1979; Mauco 1984).

Innovations during the First World War opened the second stage of French policy. Facing severe shortages of manpower, the Ministry of Armaments began to recruit workers from the colonies. About 222,000 non-European workers came to France, but as a consequence of a deliberate policy of repatriation only about 6,000 remained by 1920 (Prost 1946, 537). In 1917 the government began to require foreigners to carry identity cards for the first time. This tentative move toward stricter regulation did not prevent a boom in immigration after the war, nor was that its intention. From 1921 to 1926 the foreign population rose by 66 percent. This growth was actively facilitated by the government and by a new commercial recruitment agency, the General Immigration Society (SGI), established in 1924 by agricultural and coal industry employers (Cross 1983). Between 1924 and 1931 it established a de facto monopoly over organized immigration and supervised the introduction of some 50,000 workers (Prost 1946, 538). The government was not idle, however. It negotiated pacts with a number of countries to secure workers and it intervened in immigration matters to channel workers into jobs not directly competitive with natives, to reduce competition among employers for scarce labor, and to mollify the governments of sending countries with respect to living conditions of their nationals (Cross 1983, 12, 70).

As domestic unemployment soared with the onset of the depression in France in 1931, the state sought to halt new entries and discard redundant immigrants. There had been 120,000 new entries of foreigners in 1930, but there were only 25,000 in 1931. New legislation in 1932 permitted the establishment of quotas limiting the numbers of foreigners allowed to work in particular economic sectors and provided for a program of assisted repatriation. The two decades after World War I were, in summary, marked by a pragmatic policy of laissez-faire largely in the hands of industry followed by a more interventionist state pursuing essentially protectionist policies in a reactive and unplanned way. [2]

At the conclusion of World War II it appeared that a new immigration regime organized around permanent settlement would be established. In November 1945, a major immigration ordinance was adopted establishing a work and residence permit system for foreigners wishing to follow an occupation in France. The National Immigration Office (ONI) was given a formal monopoly over the recruitment and admission of foreign workers. Permits could be valid for different periods and could stipulate whether the individual had to work in specified activities or was free to move from job to job. With de Gaulle's support, a Ministry of Population was created and for a moment it looked as if a seriously coordinated policy was in the works. Instead, conjunctural labor market conditions pushed the government toward a policy of temporary immigration to be tied closely to labor market needs (G. Freeman 1979; Miller 1986; Sauvy 1946).

But this policy turned out to be observed primarily in the breach. The ONI apparatus never established control over the flow of immigrants to France. The state was relegated to a secondary but by no means insignificant role. Besides negotiating labor pacts with sending countries, it gave its official stamp of approval after the fact to thousands of individuals who entered the country and took jobs outside official channels. The procedure, which was called regularization, was the admission by the government that it accepted illegal and spontaneous immigration. From 1947 to 1967 France pursued a casual immigration policy. The rationale that lay behind this non-policy of apparent indifference was spelled out by a 1973 working party from the Organization for Economic Cooperation and Development (OECD), and at various times by government officials themselves (OECD 1973, 54; Minces 1973, 37, 136). The chief reason that steps had not been taken to master immigration was that the perceived benefits from an uncontrolled flow of workers outweighed the costs.

The factors that led to a dramatic shift in policy in 1974 were the political embarrassment generated by scandals associated with immigrant living conditions, the growing anger of sending governments over the treatment of their nationals, the emergence of racial and ethnic tensions and the growth of extremist nationalism, the tendency of ample cheap labor sources to discourage productivity-enhancing capital intensification, the evidence that supposedly temporary workers were not in fact temporary at all, and, perhaps most important, the striking shift in the sources of immigration to non-European countries.

It took the government six years (1968-1974) to take the steps necessary to rearrange the French immigration regime. An initial policy paper appeared in 1969 (Calvez 1969). Circulars issued in 1972 linked the granting of work and residence permits, announced measures to end clandestine immigration, and made immigrants responsible for securing adequate housing for themselves. In July 1974 the new Giscard d'Estaing administration announced a temporary suspension of all new immigration for work. At the same time a major expansion of immigrant policy was launched. One may say that since 1974 the effort to halt new entries for work has been relatively successful. As few as 1,000 workers per year have received work permits since 1975. On the other hand, rather sizable numbers of immigrants already in the country have had their situations regularized, the families of persons already admitted have been allowed to join them, and family members have then subsequently entered the labor force.

The state has taken stern measures to crack down on clandestine immigration. One indication that a gradual victory is being won is the fact that by 1983 72 percent of total admissions were through regular channels, whereas the figure in 1968 had been only 18 percent (Perotti 1985, 18). In October 1981 the new Socialist government toughened the sanctions that could be imposed on employers who hired workers without permits. The current penalty is two to twelve months in jail and\or a fine of 2,000-20,000 francs. The government also announced an amnesty for undocumented immigrants to extend from September through December 1981. Altogether, nearly 150,000 persons came forward and 132,000, or 88 percent, received papers (SOPEMI 1985, 22).

Efforts directed toward encouraging legal immigrants to go back home have borne little fruit. A program of assisted repatriation (*aide de retour*) was instituted in 1977. Its centerpiece was a grant of 10,000 francs to foreigners willing to leave the country. Only about 100,000 persons took advantage of this offer and many of these were Spanish or Portuguese people whom the government did not wish to drive away (Verbunt 1985, 144).

Great Britain

One may demarcate the history of British immigration into four regimes: 1826-1919, 1919-1962, 1962-1971, and 1971 to the present. Before 1826 the British government made little effort to regulate the entry of foreigners. The king enjoyed a royal prerogative to expel any aliens who incurred his displeasure. Parliament had enacted a number of minor aliens acts, usually in time of war, that extended the state's power to deny entry to persons posing security threats, but these were quickly retracted after each emergency passed. The first serious peacetime legislation was embodied in the Aliens Act of 1826 and the Aliens Restriction Act of 1836, but even these laws were enforced only halfheartedly.

The impetus for a more consequential policy was a substantial influx of Jews, mostly fleeing persecution in Russia, which reached 120,000 between 1875 and 1914 (Foot 1965, 86). Back-bench pressure led to the Aliens Act of 1905, giving the government the power to restrict entry of "undesirable" aliens, placing the implementation of policy in the hands of immigration officers at ports of entry and providing for the deportation of aliens convicted of crimes. Despite this, the dominant approach in this period was an enthusiasm for free immigration, a stance that was consistent with the ideology of free trade and the commitment to the rapid expansion of British industry around the globe. The chief source of anti-immigrant fervor was the threat of nihilist, anarchist, and other types of dangerous subversives (Foot 1965, 85). It should be remembered that aliens legislation was never intended to apply to that vast number of persons who inhabited the British Empire: all of these were subjects of the Crown and exempt from its provisions.

The second British immigration regime dates from 1919 with the passage of the Aliens Restriction Act. It modified a 1914 act by the same name that had been another wartime emergency measure. The 1919 act established a more normal and routine framework for controls in peacetime. The basic thrust of this legislation remained unchanged until 1971. The act gave immigration officers the discretion to deny entry to aliens for cause. Entry permits were limited to three months unless the applicant possessed a work permit or had visible means of support. The Home Secretary inherited the Crown's prerogative to expel aliens who endangered the public good. This new legislation was both effective and unnecessary. Prolonged and deep unemployment meant that the only aliens seeking entry to Britain in the twenties and thirties were female domestics. Instead, the government concentrated on encouraging emigration. Between 1919 and 1930 two million people emigrated from Britain (Layton-Henry 1984, 89).

The Second World War and its aftermath had profound consequences for the British immigration experience, but did not result in a change in the basic legal framework for nearly two decades. There was, first, some pressure for immigration from war-torn Europe. A number of resettlement schemes were tentatively undertaken by the Attlee government after 1945, but they were not sustained (Tannahill 1958). Existing aliens legislation was sufficient to control immigration from the continent. The second development was the first arrivals of immigrants from New Commonwealth countries. These individuals possessed British citizenship and all the rights that pertained thereto. They were not subject to the various pieces of aliens legislation that we have been discussing. As immigration from non-Commonwealth areas was not a major factor between 1945 and 1971, the aliens law is only a minor detail.

The postwar immigration was the direct, if unforeseen, consequence of empire and decolonization. Within the empire, Britain sought to support a policy and ideology of political and economic equality and openness. This required both free trade and free movement of labor. It also meant that all members of the empire, and later the Commonwealth, were subjects of the Crown and entitled to the protection and privileges of such status. The right to move from any of the Commonwealth nations or dependencies to the mother country was an anchor of this ideology. In fact, few exercised this option at first. But in the late forties small but growing numbers of non-European New Commonwealth citizens began to come to Britain seeking work. There was an estimated net immigration of only 2,000 New Commonwealth citizens (West Indians) in 1953, but by 1955 the number had grown to 42,650 (from India and Pakistan in addition to the West Indies) and remained at that level for three years (Layton-Henry 1984, 23).

In 1962 the Conservative government decided to put an end to the idea that the full rights of British citizenship could be extended to all persons living within the Commonwealth. How quickly thinking had changed on this matter may be seen by considering that as recently as 1948 Parliament had in the British Nationality Act enshrined the twin concepts of citizenship of the United Kingdom and Colonies and citizenship in the former colonies that were now independent countries. Persons in both statuses were British subjects and Commonwealth citizens. Just fourteen years later, the government moved to correct its mistake by stripping Commonwealth citizens of their right of freedom of movement to Britain. The purpose of the 1962 legislation was transparent: to limit the entry of non-white, non-European immigrants from the New Commonwealth countries. To avoid the explicit stigma of racism, however, the Act applied to blacks and whites alike and erected a voucher system that was ostensibly linked to labor market conditions. The decision at first sparked sharp partisan conflict, with the Labour party solidly opposed at final passage, but within three years Labour had come around to accepting the necessity of controls (G. Freeman 1979; Layton-Henry 1984).

The voucher system was relatively effective in the narrow sense that it sharply curtailed the number of new entries for work. Official statistics show that between July 1962, when the Commonwealth Immigrants Act went into effect, until December 1968, only 77,966 voucher holders were admitted, but 257,220 dependents came in. Between 1969 and 1977 the total number of persons from the New Commonwealth countries who arrived for permanent settlement was 318,521. Of these, 259,646 were dependents and only 58,875 were male workers. The trend has continued downward: 1,700 work vouchers were issued to men in 1982 and only 23,000 dependents were admitted. In 1984 total immigration from the New Commonwealth countries and Pakistan was only 24,800 (Anwar 1986, 9).

Two sets of legislation were passed in the period between 1962 and 1971. One, the Immigration Act of 1968, dealt with the crisis in Kenya provoked by the expulsion of Asians holding British passports. The Act stripped such persons in East Africa and elsewhere of the automatic right to enter and settle in Britain unless they had a substantial connection to Britain by birth, naturalization, or descent. A quota system was implemented to reduce the flow of passport holders without such a connection. The law was the first of its kind to employ the idea of patrials, based as it was on criteria designed to trap non-whites in the net of controls while allowing the white descendants of British emigrants in the Commonwealth to enter the country freely. On the other side of the coin, race relations acts were adopted in 1965 and 1968. This outlawed some forms of racial discrimination and erected a framework of committees and boards to promote harmonious community relations (Layton-Henry 1984, ch. 9).

The 1971 Immigration Act ended the distinction between aliens and Commonwealth citizens and ushered in the fourth immigration regime. The goals of policy were to eliminate any lingering preferential treatment of New Commonwealth citizens, maintain strict controls over the immigration of aliens, but permit the entry of those persons living in the Commonwealth who were of British descent. To accomplish this, distinctions were made between patrials and non-patrials, and UK passport holders and Commonwealth citizens. A patrial is anyone who has a parent or grandparent born in the United Kingdom (in 1971 the vast majority of such persons were white). Patrial passport holders must queue up for entry vouchers. Patrial Commonwealth citizens also enjoy free entry and the right of abode. Non-patrial Commonwealth citizens without a grandparent born in the United Kingdom must have a work permit to enter.

This legislation has had the intended effect of clarifying the government's position, but it hasn't changed much the numbers of new immigrants coming into the country for work because these had been well under control since 1962. The most important source of new immigration was the big stream of dependents of those already settled who joined their family members. There were only 5,800 dependents from the New Commonwealth admitted between July 1 and December 31, 1962. The number roughly tripled to 17,816 in 1963, rose to over 30,000 in 1965, reached a peak of 44,539 in 1967, and didn't fall below 17,000 annually until 1971.

With the terms of entry apparently settled, public attention has turned more or less exclusively to the question of those immigrants already in Britain. The only major legislative initiative that has altered the immigration regime since 1971 is the new Citizenship Act of 1981.[3] With its adoption, all the pieces of the framework are in place. The overblown concept of British citizenship has been cut down to size. Three categories of citizenship were created: (1) British citizens (those with a close personal connection with the United Kingdom either because their parents or grandparents were born, adopted, naturalized or registered as citizens of the United Kingdom or through permanent settlement in the United Kingdom); (2) citizens of British Dependent Territories (those who are British citizens because of their own or their parents' or grandparents' birth, naturalization, or registration in an existing dependency or associated state); and (3)   British Overseas Citizenship (a largely formal category with few privileges). Most fundamentally, the law moves Britain away from the concept of jus soli toward that of jus sanguinis, as not all persons born in the United Kingdom will henceforth be considered citizens or have the right of abode if their parents are of uncertain status.

IMMIGRATION CONTROL AND IMMIGRANT POLICY

Drawing on this brief sketch of the French and British immigration experiences, what generalizations can we make about the linkage between immigration control and immigrant policies?

1.   Laissez-faire or liberal immigration policies have been associated with poor living conditions for immigrants and have, periodically, seemed to provoke outbursts of anti-immigrant protest and violence. One would have to say, therefore, that the argument that controls are a necessary precondition to decent immigrant policies and immigrant living conditions seems confirmed in a double sense. First, one doesn't see immigrant policies at all without some relatively self-conscious and usually restrictive immigration regulation policy. If governments aren't managing entry, it's very unlikely that they will try to intervene positively into the daily lives of immigrants. Immigrant policies are secondary and derivative. Secondly, there is more than a modicum of evidence to suggest that the indigenous population does take some solace in the fact that the government has taken entry under its control. The open-ended nature of an unregulated policy seems to generate fear among the public at large and creates a climate suitable for exploitation by anti-immigrant political entrepreneurs.

There is evidence from both cases to support these contentions. From the late fifties until 1968 a "spontaneous" control policy was associated in France with the development of appalling immigrant living conditions. Only after controls were imposed did a more active immigrant policy develop. These were in part a fig leaf to cover the new, discriminatory control policies, to be sure, but they were also part of a general response to what was coming to be seen as a crisis (G. Freeman 1979, 85-98). As Verbunt notes, "The 1974 immigration stop was said to be necessary because of the calamitous social conditions that uncontrolled immigration had brought about, and this argument was strengthened by fears of growing unemployment" (1985, 154). Britain after 1962 is another case in point: when Labour came around to supporting controls the party explicitly tied them to a more generous immigrant policy (*Immigration from the Commonwealth*, 1965). This was, as in France, a legitimating strategy, but the fact is that very large numbers of new entrants would have placed strains on the system of reception and on the race relations structure. Perhaps more important, putting on controls had the salutary effect of stifling the wildest and most irresponsible claims of opponents who were no longer able to conjure up credible scenarios of unending waves of aliens.[4]

Were individual immigrants better off after controls than before? One would think they had less competition in jobs for which they were suited. On the other hand, controls are often only imposed during economic downswings, which would be associated with special hardships for those immigrants already on board and who choose to remain. Because spontaneous immigration tends to be tolerated only during economic expansions, immigrants who come into a country during such periods may be relatively well off despite the absence of a state-supported social infrastructure to receive them. The result is that it is hard to sort out what is causing what. One can say that governments spent more, did more, and generally acted more concerned about domestic conditions after controls were imposed. In other words, insofar as immigrant policy is concerned, there can be no doubt that it is more likely to be mounted, once some element of order has been established at the border.

2. Can an ethnically restrictive policy be consistent with a fair-minded domestic policy? Is it possible to protect the rights of an immigrant population that has entered under a racially restrictive control policy? We have to start with the observation that all immigration policies are ethnically restrictive, if not in theory then in practice. Once one moves from the situation in the early nineteenth century when there were literally no controls over entry to a contemporary system that regulates entry, one inevitably finds selectivity or preference on the basis of ethnicity or nationality. Of the two cases, the British is the most overt in this respect. The 1962 Commonwealth Immigrants Act affected, in the vast majority, only non-European residents of the New Commonwealth. The 1968 act was even more direct: it explicitly stripped non-European British passport holders of their rights of entry. The 1971 act, with its introduction of the concept of patriality, inserted discrimination into the heart of British aliens legislation. French policy is less enshrined in legislation, but practically equally transparent. Since at least 1968 a series of papers, circulars, decrees, and other administrative acts have shifted immigration preference from non-Europeans. Official discussion of these policies has been starkly explicit. Non-Europeans, especially Arabs, cannot be assimilated and must, consequently, be excluded or kept on a temporary footing.

What became of immigrant policy after discrimination was admitted into regulatory policy? In Britain a wave of race relations legislation was passed creating the most extensive system for the protection of the civil rights of immigrants that exists in any European nation. Still, the government was on record that non-whites were a problem and might find it difficult to assimilate. One could certainly argue that the latter effectively undermined the former (Layton-Henry 1984, 122-144). There was not much special effort on the social policy front, either. Britain never really developed direct immigrant policies, although its urban policy came over time to be increasingly associated with immigrant problems (Scarman 1981, 157-175) and special measures were introduced with respect to housing and education (Jones 1977). France passed only a weak race relations act that was limited in scope, but mounted a much more active immigrant policy, largely direct. After 1981 these domestic efforts were even more forceful, though the Socialists did not undo the immigration control policies of previous governments (G. Freeman 1979, 168-172; Verbunt 1985, 145-154).

As far as immigrant-host conflict is concerned, neither country has a good record, and it is almost impossible to argue that conflict has ebbed and flowed as a result of policy changes. In fact, policy has typically responded to changes in the level of conflict, not shaped it. Britain had worse outbreaks of immigrant protest and rioting after discriminatory legislation was passed than it did before. Does this mean that controls failed to defuse a growing social problem or does it mean that discriminatory controls exacerbated the problem? I suspect that the negative effects of racially selective controls outweighed the presumably positive effects of slowing down the pace of entries. France has seen the Front National emerge as a serious national political force nearly a decade after policy turned against Arab and African immigration between 1968 and 1974 (Schain 1987). If there is a connection between immigration policy and the intensity of anti-immigrant agitation, the history of the Front National suggests that government policies based on racial selection encourage nativists rather than reassure them. One has to conclude that the linkage between social conditions and periodic shifts in immigration and immigrant policy is tenuous at best.

3. What evidence is there with respect to the radical argument that it is impossible to treat immigrants decently, equally, and fairly while at the same time running an immigration policy designed to augment the regime's economic policy? Of our two cases, only the French have tried to tie immigration to economic needs in a consistent and systematic way. The British probably should have, given what their European competitors were doing, the labor needs of the British economy in the fifties, and the vast resources of labor at Britain's disposal in the Commonwealth. But, as I have argued elsewhere, they never did (G. Freeman 1979). The French, on the other hand, have seen the economic possibilities in immigration for a long time (Spengler 1979, 194-217; Cross 1983; Sauvy 1946). The result of these very different approaches to the economics of immigration is that only the French case is really pertinent to the question. Having only one case, it is not easy to generalize.

Nonetheless, a few comments are in order. There are essentially two models of an economically motivated immigration policy. The first is that of the guest worker program and the second is that of a spontaneous, laissez-faire system of more or less free immigration. A real guest worker program requires active and forceful administrative oversight and a detailed legislative foundation. The theory of a guest worker program is that by closely regulating the entry of workers and by insisting that they remain in the country only so long as their work permits are valid, it is possible to have only the numbers and types of workers that the economy needs and to avoid additional costs associated with permanent or long-term, family immigration. Mounting a guest worker program is an ambitious undertaking and, in point of fact, no country can claim to have done so in a completely satisfactory way. The evidence is strong that guest workers tend to be highly resistant to the kind of cyclical manipulation that the program's planners had foreseen (Miller and Martin 1982; Bendix 1987).

Given that guest worker programs require the mobilization of considerable governmental resources and don't usually pan out, it is not surprising that many countries are drawn to the laissez-faire alternative. This may sound, on first encounter, to be imputing more intention than the facts suggest. Isn't a laissez-faire policy simply what transpires when governments fail to develop any explicit and self-conscious approach to immigration control? And does such a posture deserve the appellation "*policy?*" Closer examination reveals that it is not so easy to carry out a laissez-faire immigration policy, especially one that produces large economic benefits for the host society. Ironically, a country gets the most economic benefit from immigration when its government is able to do nothing; that is, when it is able to resist pressures either to slap on controls or to ameliorate living conditions. States may undertake certain active policies, especially in the area of recruitment, but in most respects an economically exploitative immigration policy is a loosely coordinated set of non-decisions and refusals to act. Controls reduce labor supply and drive up labor costs. Policies to achieve equal status for immigrants reduce their economic utility because it is impossible to extract the maximum economic advantage. The whole point of bringing in immigrants is, apart from the sheer need for labor, that they are cheaper, more mobile, more malleable than native workers (Castles and Kosack 1973, 57-115). Hence, if measures are undertaken that make them less mobile and malleable, they are also less useful. If immigrants must be paid the same wages, provided the same social benefits, and accorded the same rights in the workplace: if, in other words, they enjoy a status more or less equal to that of indigenous workers, it is probably rational for the employer to shed labor and move to capital intensification. In this sense, the radical contention of inconsistency between immigrant rights and economic objectives is a truism.

What are the conditions under which states are able to operate economically oriented, laissez-faire immigration policies? It seems clear that the more insulated, autonomous, and independent policymakers are, the more capable they are of running such policies. It is fashionable these days to refer to this capacity as "relative autonomy" (See Braybrooke 1985). One factor that seems to enhance autonomy is whether policy is made by administrators or legislators, that is, whether the policy process is quiet, hidden, and discretionary, or open, debated, and public (Hammar 1985, 279-281).

A major difference between the immigration policy processes of France and Britain is the greater extent to which British policy has been formulated in the public arena and embodied in major legislative acts. French policy changes have taken the form of administrative decisions to exercise existing powers more or less strongly, or to interpret existing legislation more or less strictly. The apparent weakness of Parliament in the Fifth Republic, as well as the long period of rightist control of the executive, enabled French officials to act with remarkable impunity as far as public opinion or the political opposition were concerned. France, then, was much better positioned than Britain to conduct an economically oriented immigration policy, and did so. British policy, on the other hand, was conducted out in the open, in the Parliamentary arena, and it was the focus of sharp public interest. This was a chief reason that British policymakers acted as if their hands were tied very early on (G. Freeman 1979, 115-119). But even the French encountered obstacles along the path to a laissez-faire policy. I have recounted elsewhere the way in which French officials slowly and painfully felt their way toward a more effectively enforced system of controls (G. Freeman 1979, 85-98; cf. Tapinos 1975).

The conclusions I would draw from these episodes are twofold. First, despite the undeniable fact that migrants have been grievously exploited in many European countries in the last several decades, the evidence is that the normal processes of public opinion and electoral democracy preclude the most extreme forms of exploitation. This means that while the radical position that an economically derived policy is incompatible with the protection of immigrant rights and status is true, it is also true that the framework of constitutional democracy in Europe is incompatible with a doggedly economic immigration policy. Governments have wanted to implement such policies, but they have drawn up short of their objectives. The immigrants protest, liberal sympathizers complain, anti-immigrant groups stir the waters, the home governments intervene on behalf of their nationals, and the rules and regulations of the modern welfare state prevent the grossest forms of exploitation. One sees instead cycles of exploitation, where real economic benefits are produced most often in the earliest stages of immigration, before public attention has gotten aroused. Memories being short, new cycles are sometimes begun after a hiatus of a decade or so. The upshot of all this is that while the radical critique is valid insofar as it identifies a basic contradiction between economic exploitation of immigrants and the protection of their rights, it misses the point. In the struggle between these two incompatible goals, the latter seems usually to win out, at least sufficiently to reduce the economic advantages of immigration for the regime below the level that had been expected (Freeman 1986).

4. I have already touched on the significance of citizenship and the right of permanent residence, both factors that have been hypothesized as

important determinants of status. I may briefly note here that on the evidence in these two cases citizenship is less fateful than one might have expected. This is in part a consequence of the fact that at least at the outset citizenship rights are not exploited by immigrants in politically potent ways. It takes a while to learn the means to employ political resources effectively. But it is also because those immigrants without citizenship are able to use the language of rights more effectively than might have been anticipated. There is a convergence, then, so that the fact of citizenship is ultimately less significant than predicted.

5. In the same way, while it is obviously preferable to hold a right of permanent settlement rather than being in a temporary status, the inability of governments actually to institute a guest worker system means that this difference in legal status is less determinative of economic status than one would have predicted, though I must stress that neither of the two countries under consideration should be thought to have attempted a full-fledged guest worker program.

CONCLUSION

The late twentieth century is likely to be remembered by historians as a period in which immigrants and refugees were at the center of political controversy. Indeed, they will probably be seen as a manifestation of the character of the relationship between the industrial countries and the Third World. The dominant trend of policy since the nineteenth century has been toward increasing state controls over population movements. Discussion of these matters has tended to be from the point of view of the needs, interests, and prerogatives of national states. How one immigration policy or another does or does not contribute to national economic growth or to social cohesion and harmony are legitimate and vital issues. Nonetheless, it is proper as well to begin to think systematically about the possible impacts of one or another policy on the living standards and opportunities of those individuals who move across borders. Such a perspective is not only attractive because of its possible contribution to improving the situation of an increasingly important segment of the world's population, but also because it is obviously in the interest of states themselves to see that the two sides of their immigration policies are more carefully coordinated.

Migration to Advanced Industrial Democracies: Socioeconomic and Political Factors in the Making of Minorities in the Federal Republic of Germany (1955-1988)

Barbara Schmitter Heisler

The movement of people from economically less developed regions to the advanced industrial societies has been a major feature of the world capitalist system in the post-World War II period. While large-scale transnational migration is not a new phenomenon, post-World War II migrations have differed from previous transnational population movements. They have been more pervasive and varied, involving large numbers of migrants and a large variety of both host and sending countries.

There are considerable differences between sending countries on the one hand and receiving countries on the other. For example, among the countries of origin we find countries with a long history of emigration (Italy, Mexico, Spain, Portugal, Greece) and others that had little experience with sending their citizens abroad (Turkey). Countries of destination include such classic immigration countries as the United States and Canada as well as countries that had in the past been primarily emigration countries rather than immigration countries. The latter include the majority of Western Europe's immigration countries, with the possible exception of France.[1]

As a consequence, the characteristics of the migrant populations and their legal conditions in the host countries have also varied. Migrants have included large numbers of illegal or undocumented as well as legal immigrants. The latter include permanent immigrants, temporary guest-workers, and seasonal contract workers. Migrants have left their countries of origin to seek greater economic opportunity or to flee from political persecution.[2] Although the vast majority of transnational migrants have been relatively unskilled, a small minority have been skilled and professional workers.[3]

The new scale and pervasiveness of post-World War II migrations has not only generated a large and growing body of literature, it has also contributed to a theoretical reorientation on the consequences of transnational migration in the modern democratic state. The once-dominant assimilationist perspective pioneered in the United States by Park and Gordon (Park and Burgess 1921; Gordon 1964), which focused primarily on cultural differences between newcomers and native populations and studied the effects of ethnic or racial differences on the process of assimilation, has been largely replaced by more structural perspectives that have focused on the incorporation of newcomers into the economic institutions--or more specifically into the labor markets--of the host society. Rather than projecting their eventual assimilation or integration into the host society, structural theories have tended to emphasize the long-term institutionalization of initial labor market segregation and continued sociopolitical inequality between newcomers and host society populations.

These newer perspectives include deductive macro-theoretical Marxist and neo-Marxist approaches (Portes and Walton 1981; Petras 1981; Castles and Kosack 1973) and several inductive middle-range models of immigrant incorporation, such as the split labor market (Bonacich 1973), middleman minorities (Turner and Bonacich 1980; Zenner 1983), immigrant entrepreneur (Light 1984; Light 1986) and immigrant enclave (Wilson and Portes 1980). By drawing attention to the effects of larger structured inequalities between sending and receiving countries on the one hand and to differences in the process of labor market incorporation on the other hand, these perspectives have made significant contributions to understanding the processes of migration and migrant incorporation and settlement in the host society. Yet they are not without their own limitations, limitations that I believe present some difficulties when applied to the Western European case.

First, macro-theoretical perspectives have tended to see economic and political relations between senders and receivers as zero-sum, relatively fixed and immutable. Economically and politically powerful receivers determine the rules for economically and politically weak and dependent senders. This relationship, in turn, determines the fate of immigrants themselves in the host countries, where they play the role of an industrial reserve army of labor and serve as a capitalist device to control the native working class. While this model can be fruitfully applied to some cases, in particular to the relationship between the United States and Mexico, Central American countries, and Caribbean countries and to a lesser degree to the early stages of European migrations, sending countries have not been as powerless in most European cases, as this literature postulates. The relations between senders and receivers have not only varied between individual pairs of senders and receivers, they have also changed over time. The degree to which immigrants are exploited has varied from host society to host society and has changed as migrants have improved their legal and socioeconomic positions both individually and collectively over time (Heisler 1985).

Developed primarily from empirical observations made in one society, the United States, the theoretical usefulness of the middle-range model of immigrant incorporation is also limited. These models presuppose the presence in the host society of certain historical, structural and/or legal conditions and assume specific characteristics of the newcomers themselves. Although they have found some applicability in other advanced industrial societies where similar conditions exist--for example in the Netherlands and the United Kingdom (e.g., Boissevain and Grotenberg 1986; Ward and Jenkins 1984)--the empirical realities of several European cases do not fit well into this model. Finally, both perspectives have focused primarily on the incorporation of newcomers into labor markets and have tended to see the dimensions of social and political incorporation as epiphenomenal or inconsequential.

Although we can observe numerous similarities in the patterns of immigration and immigrant incorporation in advanced industrial democracies--in Europe and the United States--similarities that can be analyzed and interpreted within above theoretical models, we should not overlook less obvious yet significant differences between the United States and European societies on the one hand, and differences between European societies, on the other hand. There has been a marked tendency to focus on the similarities inherent in transnational migrations to advanced industrial democracies: ethnically or racially distinct newcomers generally occupy low socioeconomic positions, they generally encounter discrimination and prejudice from host society institutions and populations, their children are less likely to succeed in school (Castles and Kosack 1973; Piore 1979; Castles 1984). Few attempts have been made to examine inherent differences.

POST-WORLD WAR II EUROPEAN MIGRATIONS

The purpose of this chapter is not to engage in a detailed critique of the merits and/or shortcomings of existing theories but rather to explore new directions. Just as the new structural models of immigrant incorporation were developed from observations of processes of immigrant incorporation in the United States, I believe that we can gain new insights on some of the consequences of migration in advanced industrial democracies and perhaps develop additional models by more closely examining the European case or, more specifically, European cases.

To do this we must first move away from the unidimensional economic or labor market perspective that has been the hallmark of existing structural perspectives to include social and political conditions of contact. Second, we must examine the factors that structure the process of economic, social and political incorporation. Two factors in particular have set the Western European case apart, creating somewhat unique conditions of initial contact: (1) the structure and pervasiveness of the mature European welfare state and (2) the legal conditions of immigration.

In the following pages I begin by briefly discussing these factors. I will then turn to examine data from a representative survey of immigrants in the Federal Republic of Germany that illustrate considerable differences in the patterns of economic, social and political incorporation between nationalities. Finally, I will interpret these differences in the light of the different constraints and possibilities inherent in the European experience.

Factors that Have Shaped the European Experience

Although migrants have occupied inferior labor market positions--which have been frequently accompanied by an absence or restriction of civil and political rights--in Europe they have also benefited from the range of economic and social rights extended to all workers in the mature welfare state. This means that, while the majority of immigrants engage in unskilled work and generally occupy low socioeconomic positions, such positions are not necessarily equal to the positions of unskilled immigrants in the United States. Access and participation in unions, the inclusion in health and unemployment benefits, the availability of subsidized housing and child benefits, and so forth, do not only provide a modicum of well-being but also shape the possibilities for present and future social and political efficacy and action.

The origin of European migrations in systems of temporary contract labor based on bilateral agreements between host and sending countries has provided the latter with access to institutional and organizational means that permit them to shape the conditions of settlement of their citizens. Within the original framework of a contract labor system sending countries were encouraged to set up their own network of organizations aimed at providing social services to their citizens while abroad. Although the structure and pervasiveness of these networks and their activities vary from case to case, they have come to play a vital part in many immigrant communities.

Sending countries have a strong interest in insuring the continuous flow of remittances. Yet as immigrants remain abroad for extended periods and become settlers rather than migrant workers, they tend to reduce or even halt their remittances. To insure their continued flow, sending countries must insure the long-term allegiance of their citizens and maintain their commitment to eventual return. The networks of sending country organizations permit sending countries to engage in daily activities designed to promote allegiance, reinforcing the migrants' natural tendencies to maintain social and political distance from the host society. This supports the "myth of return" that is at the center of the prevailing climate of temporariness that has been one of the hallmarks of post-World War II migrations in Europe. In this fashion sending countries contribute to shaping the attitudes and actions of all participants--migrants and their families as well as host society institutions and policies (B. Heisler 1986).[4]

While both factors are present in all European cases, setting them apart from the United States, their long-term effects may vary from host society to host society depending on host society immigration and naturalization policies, differences in labor market conditions and the structure of social and political institutions, differences in recruitment procedures, and political relations with the countries of origin. Thus, although the overall experiences of European societies are similar when compared to the United States and although their policies have further converged in recent years (Hammar 1985), there are continuing differences between them.

For example, naturalization, generally considered an important non-economic factor in facilitating the process of incorporation, is relatively easily available in the Netherlands, Sweden, and France, but remains a privilege rather than a right in Germany and Switzerland. Immigrants are also eligible to vote and be elected in local elections in Sweden and the Netherlands. Although the integrative effects of the extension of the vote in local elections have not been ascertained and the importance of the relative ease of naturalization may be exaggerated--migrants today do not appear overly eager to naturalize even where this option is available--both have important symbolic meanings that may influence the behavior of immigrants. When analyzing return rates of the same nationalities in three host countries--Switzerland, the former Federal Republic and the Netherlands--Pennix found that return rates of the same nationalities varied with the relative restrictiveness of the host society policies toward immigrants (Pennix 1986).

In addition to differences in immigration policies, there are also considerable differences in employment and labor market conditions and the structures and responses of social institutions in the European democracies. Although the vast majority of migrant workers have occupied semiskilled and unskilled positions in industrial production and services, their relative sectoral distribution and skill levels differ from host society to host society. For example, a larger proportion of immigrants are employed in services in Switzerland and France than in Germany, affecting their distribution of skill levels and with it their unemployment rates. The opportunity to open small businesses, a prerequisite for the immigrant entrepreneur or middleman minority model, is subject to laws and regulations that in some host societies make it exceedingly difficult for foreign nationals to own small businesses.

Directly related to differences in sectoral distributions are differences in union structure and employee representation at the workplace. Outside the workplace we find structural and institutional differences in the nature and organization of social and political institutions and the delivery of social services (e.g., housing, education, welfare).

Finally, diverse sources and patterns of recruitment have shaped the ethnic composition of the immigrant population and continue to shape the ongoing relations between sending and receiving societies. Some host countries (the Netherlands, France and the United Kingdom) recruited immigrants from their former colonies as well as from southern Europe and the European periphery. Others (Germany, Sweden, and Switzerland), recruited exclusively from southern Europe and the European periphery. As a consequence, Algerians are the largest group in France but are hardly present in other host societies. The process of settlement and the nature of incorporation of Algerians is shaped not only by their insertion into the French labor market and by their access to social and welfare rights, but also by ongoing Algerian-French relations. Turks, while present in the Netherlands, Sweden, Belgium, and Switzerland, are the largest group in Germany, which has been host to 80 percent of Turks working abroad. The Turkish government has concentrated its efforts on that country. Although the majority of Italian migrants are not in Switzerland, the majority of immigrants in Switzerland have been Italian, and Switzerland has been the country of destination for Italian migrants for close to a century. Italians are also a strong presence in Germany, Belgium, the Netherlands, and France. Because Italy is a member of the European Community, Italians are free to move between member states. In Switzerland, which is not a member, Italian workers have confronted more restrictive conditions. The Italian state has directed much of its efforts toward that country.

Although a systematic examination of these differences and their consequences for the incorporation of newcomers requires a large-scale comparative analysis of several host countries, the necessary data are not available. To make some small steps toward a different inductive approach, I will examine data available from one host society, the former Federal Republic of Germany. While this approach does not permit comparison of host societies, it does make possible comparisons of similarities or differences between immigrant nationalities in terms of their relative positions along several indicators of labor-market and social incorporation in one society. Although the purpose of the following analysis is primarily exploratory, it may shed some light on the complexities involved in the process of immigrant incorporation and the creation of new ethnic minorities.

THE CASE OF THE FEDERAL REPUBLIC OF GERMANY

Next to Switzerland, Germany stands out among European labor importers in that its policies concerning immigrants have been characterized as comparatively restrictive. Immigration was initiated as a strictly temporary solution to labor shortages beginning in the mid 1950s. Between 1955 and 1968 the West German government concluded bilateral labor recruitment agreements with Italy, Greece, Spain, Portugal, Yugoslavia, Turkey, and Tunisia. After a slow start in the 1950s the flow of migrants developed rapidly in the 1960s until it was unilaterally halted by the West German government in 1973. The halt did not apply to family reunification, so that migration continued throughout the 1970s and 1980s, further increasing the size of the immigrant population and changing its demographic characteristics.[5] At present the vast majority of the immigrant population in Germany has acquired a modicum of legal security. Yet the German government continues to refuse to legally recognize them as permanent immigrants.

The data reported here are drawn from a 1980 national survey of immigrant workers and their families contracted by the Federal Ministry for Work and Social Order (Merhländer et al. 1981). The purpose of the survey was to gather information on and to analyze the social, cultural, and economic situation of foreign workers and their families. The sample includes the nationalities from major recruitment countries--Italians, Greeks, Spaniards, Portuguese, Yugoslavs, and Turks--providing rather detailed information on several socioeconomic characteristics of these groups.[6]

In 1980, at the time of the survey, the immigrant population of the former Federal Republic stood at almost 4.5 million, representing 7 percent of the total population.[7] Among the six major nationalities recruited, Turks were the largest contingent, representing one-third of the total immigrant population. Yugoslavs and Italians were the second and third largest groups, each representing 14 percent of the total. Greeks, Spaniards, and Portuguese were smaller, yet sizable fractions (6.6, 4 and 2.5 percent, respectively).[8]

Given the fact that all nationalities were recruited to fill low socioeconomic positions in the industrial and service sector and arrived within a relatively short time period between 1955 (the date of the first recruitment agreement) and 1973 (the end of recruitment), we should not be surprised that the majority still occupied relatively low socioeconomic positions in 1980.[9] While this expectation is generally born out by the data, the data also indicate (1) considerable differences in the labor market position between immigrant nationalities and (2) varying degrees of correspondence between the relative labor market and social positions of several of the nationalities.

Let us examine several indicators of the nature and degree of incorporation of each nationality in terms of their labor market characteristics and social and political position. The former consist of data on skill levels, type of employment, and union membership. The latter data reflect several social and political factors that condition the contacts between newcomers and host societies outside the workplace. These include housing, leisure activities and organizational life.

Given the exploratory nature of this discussion, I have limited my observations to males--keeping in mind that there are significant differences between males and females along all variables, that is, females, especially females who are not in the labor force, are considerably less integrated than males.

Labor Market Position: Work Organization, Skill Distribution, and
Union Membership

As indicated above, all nationalities came to the Federal Republic under
similar circumstances, as temporary migrant workers recruited to fill vacant
positions at the bottom of the labor market, and thus faced similar structural
conditions.[10] In 1980, the vast majority of immigrants (76.9 percent) surveyed
were employed in the manufacturing sector, while a relatively small proportion
were in services (13.2 percent, including transport, which employs the largest
number within the service sector) and an even smaller one in extraction (3.1
percent). The remainder were in technical occupations (2.3 percent) and others
(3.8 percent).[11]

Although a sizable minority (21 percent) among immigrants were
employed in small work organizations (up to fifty employees), most (40.1
percent) were employed in relatively large organizations, employing more than
500 employees. While the data indicate only minor differences in sectoral
distribution among nationalities, the differences were more pronounced in the
size of workplaces. Only 29.8 percent of Yugoslavs, but 61.4 percent of
Portuguese, worked in large companies, while about 40 percent of Turks,
Italians, and Greeks were so employed (Merhländer et al. 1981, 110).

The vast majority of immigrants were workers (92.2 percent), while
only a small minority were *Angestellte* (white collar workers). Among the
sample of male workers, 30.3 percent were skilled, 42.4 percent semi-skilled,
and 27.3 percent unskilled.[12] There were significant differences across
nationalities (Table 2.1). Although Turkish males were the least skilled (18.3
percent skilled, 35.2 percent unskilled), they were closely followed by Italian
males (22.2 percent skilled, 35.0 unskilled). In comparison, Yugoslav males
were the most skilled (53.6 percent) followed by Spaniards (39.7 percent),
Greeks (35.7 percent), and Portuguese (35.1 percent).

Table 2.1 Skill Level of Male Foreign Workers by Nationality

Skill Level	Total	Turks	Ital- ians	Greeks	Portu- guese	Span- iards	Yugo- slavs
Skilled	30.3	18.3	22.2	35.7	35.1	39.7	53.6
Semi-Skilled	42.4	46.4	42.8	49.2	44.0	35.9	34.1
Unskilled	27.3	35.2	35.0	15.1	20.9	24.5	12.3

Source: Merhländer et al. 1981, 124.

Compared to many other host societies such as Switzerland and France, union membership among immigrant workers was fairly high. Almost half (44.6 percent) of immigrant workers surveyed reported that they were union members. For men alone, the percentage was 50.7 percent. A breakdown by nationality reveals that Portuguese men were the most organized (70.7 percent were union members), Yugoslavs followed by Italians the least organized (38.0 and 43.6 percent were union members, respectively), while union organization among Turks and Spaniards and Greeks was 57.5, 57.7, and 53.0 percent respectively (Table 2.2).

According to German law, the works council--elected by workers in workplaces employing more than five workers--is charged with insuring the equal treatment of all employees. For this reason one would assume that immigrants should have an interest in knowing about and participating in works councils. The survey reveals that a surprisingly large number of the respondents were ignorant of the existence and/or function of works councils in principle and at their place of work in particular. The degree of information varied by nationality (Table 2.3). Looking only at men (women were, as might be expected, were less informed), Yugoslavs were the least informed about the role of the works council, and they most frequently indicated that they did not know of the existence of a works council in their place of work, whereas Portuguese, Greeks and Italians were among the more informed nationalities. Among male workers who reported knowledge of the existence of a works council, Italians expressed most satisfaction with works council representation of their interests, followed by Yugoslavs and Turks. Spaniards, Greeks, and Portuguese registered the least satisfaction.

Table 2.2 Percentage of Union Membership by Nationality (Men Only)

Nationality	Percent Members
Portuguese	70.7
Spaniards	57.7
Turks	57.5
Greeks	53.0
Italians	43.6
Yugoslavs	38.0
Total	50.7

Source: Merhländer et al. 1981, 214.

Table 2.3 Opinions Concerning Works Councils (Men Only)

Nationality	Sufficient Interest Representation	Not Sufficient	Undecided
Turks	35.7	44.0	20.3
Yugoslavs	37.5	31.4	31.1
Italians	40.1	38.5	21.4
Greeks	30.5	48.8	20.7
Spaniards	33.8	45.3	20.9
Portuguese	20.0	51.8	28.2
Total	35.5	41.6	22.9

Source: Merhländer et al. 1981, 197.

Social Indicators: Family Reunification, Language, Housing, and Leisure

Among the major changes in the composition of the immigrant population over the period from 1968 to 1988 was the increased presence of families. The survey clearly shows that the vast majority of married immigrants were accompanied by their wives (80 percent). Yet the survey also reveals some variation between the different nationalities: Yugoslavs are the least likely to be accompanied by their wives, married Greek men are virtually always accompanied by their wives, and Turks, Italians, and Spaniards fall somewhere in the middle.

Language skill is generally considered an important prerequisite for integration at the workplace and in the society at large. The majority of immigrants surveyed reflected positively upon the need to know German, but the various nationalities tended to emphasize different reasons (Table 2.4). Thus, from among four possible answers--(1) to take advantage of one's rights, (2) to get along in daily life, (3) to have better contact with the native population, and (4) to improve one's chances at work--Turks and Italians appeared most concerned about their rights, while Yugoslavs and Greeks appeared most concerned about getting along in daily life.

As for their actual knowledge of the language, the majority (79.1 percent) answered in the affirmative. Men, as expected, were more likely to know German, whereas women who did not work were the least likely. By nationality, Yugoslavs were the most knowledgeable, Turks the least. As for language proficiency, 31.9 percent indicated that their knowledge was "good to

Table 2.4 Reasons for Learning German

Reasons	Nationalities						
	Turks	Yugoslavs	Italians	Greeks	Spaniards	Portuguese
To Increase Professional Chances	9.2	14.1	17.9	14.8	16.2	14.6
To Secure One's Right	24.1	22.6	22.3	23.1	22.2	20.5
To Have Better Contacts with Germans	16.5	17.2	19.2	16.3	16.4	21.1
For Everyday Life	20.9	26.7	20.0	23.9	23.0	24.0
Because Children Speak German	5.3	4.2	6.0	5.3	5.7	4.6
To Watch TV, etc.	18.3	12.5	14.2	12.4	13.4	12.2
To Receive a Permanent Permit	5.3	2.4	0.2	4.0	2.7	2.3

Source: Merhländer et al. 1981, 485.

very good." Portuguese reported the least proficiency (only 10.2 percent chose "good to very good"), followed by Spaniards (27.9), Turks (28.7) and Italians (29.5). According to their own estimation, Yugoslavs and Greeks appeared the most proficient, choosing "well to very well" at the rate of 40.2 and 40.5 percent respectively. At the opposite end, answers in the category "badly and very badly," represented 16.5 percent of the total. Portuguese and Italians reported this category more frequently than others.

Housing segregation has been a common consequence of mass migration. Despite concerns expressed by many analysts, compared with the United States housing segregation is less severe in Germany. Overall, housing segregation is more prevalent in large cities than in small towns. It also varies somewhat between cities. The survey considered housing concentration and segregation in terms of neighborhood and dwelling unit. Neighborhood segregation was somewhat less pronounced than segregation by apartment buildings. Thus, 40.6 percent of the immigrants stated that they lived in neighborhoods with a majority of foreigners (Table 2.5), whereas 44.1 percent stated that they lived in apartments where the majority were other immigrants (Table 2.6).[13] Portuguese and Turks were the most segregated in terms of both neighborhood and dwelling, whereas Spaniards and Greeks were the most integrated and Italians and Yugoslavs ranked in the middle.

Segregated living arrangements do not appear to be a preferred choice for the majority of immigrants. Only a small minority stated that they would prefer to live only with other foreigners. While the vast majority had no preference, 35 percent among Turks, 34.5 percent among Spaniards, and 31.4 percent among Italians stated that they actively preferred living with Germans. Yet Turks and Greeks also most frequently indicated a preference for living with other foreigners (10.5 and 9.1 percent respectively).

Leisure contact, another indicator of the degree of incorporation, varied along with housing. Almost half of the migrants reported some leisure-time

Table 2.5 Percent Living in Neighborhoods with a Majority of Foreigners

Turks	49.7
Portuguese	42.1
Yugoslavs	36.2
Italians	34.8
Greeks	34.4
Spaniards	29.3
Total	40.6

Source: Merhländer et al. 1981, 478.

Table 2.6 Percent Living in Houses with a Majority of Foreigners

Portuguese	56.2
Turks	49.6
Italians	42.2
Spaniards	39.5
Yugoslavs	39.6
Greeks	34.5
Total	44.1

Source: Merhländer et al. 1981, 477.

contact with Germans. As in the case for housing, the degree of leisure contact was greater for those who had been in Germany for a longer period. There were also differences by nationality, with Turks having the least contact, followed by Portuguese, Yugoslavs, and Italians. Spaniards indicated the most contact. Those with no contact most often mentioned their lack of knowledge of German as the main reason, although prejudice and rejection on the part of the majority population were also mentioned.

About one-quarter (24.9 percent) of the immigrant workers interviewed indicated that they were members of voluntary organizations. Among these the majority were members of foreign organizations, while only 14.2 percent participated in German organizations. Unfortunately, data on membership by type of organization (foreign versus German) and nationality were not available.

As expected, few immigrant workers interviewed expressed the intention of applying for German citizenship (6.6 percent). Although the variation between nationalities was insignificant, Portuguese followed by Spaniards were least interested, whereas Greeks and Italians indicated slightly more interest. Turks were in the middle (Table 2.7).

ANALYSIS AND DISCUSSION

The patterns of contact emerging from the above data do not lend themselves to easy generalization. They indicate considerable variation between nationalities as well as several apparent inconsistencies and contradictions within the patterns of some nationalities. Among the six nationalities, Turkish immigrants presented the most consistent pattern: in terms of both labor market and social indicators, they were clearly the least integrated. Although somewhat more integrated than Turks, Italians emerged as the second most segregated in terms of their labor market positions and moderately segregated in terms of the social indicators. While Greeks, Portuguese, and Spaniards occupied

Table 2.7 Percent Intending to Seek German Citizenship

Greeks	7.6
Yugoslavs	7.3
Italians	7.0
Turks	6.2
Spaniards	5.3
Portuguese	4.6
Total	6.6

Source: Merhländer et al. 1981, 554.

intermediate positions in the labor market, Spaniards and Greeks appeared more integrated in the social realm while Portuguese workers were socially the second most segregated. Yugoslavs, who were by far the most skilled, were also the least unionized and revealed contradictory response patterns in terms of the social indicators. They most often left their wives behind and appeared relatively segregated in terms of housing patterns and leisure activities. Yet they also revealed the greatest language proficiency and were most interested in acquiring German citizenship.[14]

While the emerging patterns of Spaniards and Greeks were more consistent, they presented their own small puzzles. This was particularly true for Greeks, who in the social realm were second to Turks in preferring housing with other foreigners, but were, next to Spaniards, the least segregated and, next to Yugoslavs, the most interested in German citizenship.

The pattern displayed by the data on Turks clearly reflected the conception that the problem of immigration in the former Federal Republic of Germany was primarily a Turkish problem (Andereggen 1986; Wallraff 1987). It also fit well into structural theoretical frameworks. Coming from a semiperipheral country, Turks occupied the lowest socioeconomic positions and encountered severe discrimination and hostility. Yet these frameworks could not account for the considerable variations between immigrant nationalities or the apparent inconsistencies or contradictions between the labor market and the social and political location of some nationalities in 1980. In particular they could not explain the comparatively low degree of overall incorporation of Italian workers.

Since all nationalities encountered the same labor-market and institutional structures, the differences and contradictions may have been due to characteristics inherent in the immigrant nationalities themselves. These may have included cultural differences, differences in skill levels at the time of immigration, as well as differences in the structure of the immigrant community itself. For example, assimilation theory would suggest that different nationalities' cultural characteristics--in particular the cultural distance between their culture and that of the host society--affect the ease of a group's assimilation. While Turks were culturally the most distant and hence would be expected to have been least incorporated, it is relatively difficult to rank the remaining nationalities in terms of cultural distance. Italian culture is surely no more distant from German culture than is Spanish or Greek culture. Yet Italians were noticeably less well incorporated into German economic and sociopolitical life.

The majority of all nationalities came from rural, non-industrial regions of their respective countries of origin. Most received primary education and almost half had received some form of vocational training before migrating. While the percentage of those with vocational training was somewhat higher among Yugoslav and Portuguese men (52.4 and 64.2 respectively), the percentages of the two most integrated groups--Spaniards and Greeks--was very similar to that of the two least integrated--Turks and Italians (between 41 and 45 percent) (Merhländer et al. 1981, 32). Thus, differences in education and vocational training at the time of emigration do not account for the low degree of Turkish and Italian integration.

This suggests that we take a closer look at the "temporary but permanent" dimension of migration. At first glance, the effects of temporariness appear obvious: the survey data indicate an almost universal opposition to naturalize among all nationalities. Yet, while the overwhelming majority of immigrants (including even the second generation) was opposed to naturalization, those who also expressed the intent to return represented a considerably smaller majority. In addition, "intent to return" varied considerably from nationality to nationality (Table 2.8). More than 90 percent of Portuguese migrants expressed such an intent (93.3 percent), followed by Spaniards (87.9 percent), Yugoslavs (86.7 percent), and Greeks (83.6 percent). Only 78.3 percent of Italians and 59.9 percent of Turks expressed this intention.

Table 2.8 Percent Intending to Return to Country of Origin

Portuguese	93.3
Spaniards	87.9
Yugoslavs	86.7
Greeks	83.6
Italians	78.3
Turks	59.9
Total	75.1

Source: Merhländer et al. 1981, 545.

Thus, although Turks clearly stand out as being the least inclined to return, Italians again rank second.

Contrary to expectation, the legal security enjoyed by Italian citizens did not seem to function as an integrative device. The ability to move back and forth without losing work and/or residence permits provided Italians with a built-in flexibility that permited them to be truly "permanent but temporary" residents, simultaneously reducing incentives to improve their socioeconomic positions in the host society.

As indicated above, immigrants in Europe were subject to the policies of their countries of origin. Locally these were expressed and organized within sending country organizational networks. Italy has a long history of sending its citizens to work abroad, and the Italian state has developed an extensive network of organizational structures--including semiprivate, private, and public organizations--that provide a host of services for Italian migrants abroad. These organizations have made it virtually unnecessary for Italian immigrants to participate in host society institutions (Schmitter 1984). The Turkish state has been ineffective in this regard and has been hindered by continuous political turmoil at home, turmoil that also migrated to the immigrant community in Germany.

Thus, even though Italians and Turks were the two most segregated nationalities in terms of their socioeconomic characteristics, the two sending countries have different capacities to influence their citizens abroad. These different capacities and the two sending countries' different political relations with Germany are likely to shape the patterns of incorporation or exclusion of their citizens. Turks, the least integrated, the most culturally different, the least inclined to return, may well be on their way to becoming a permanent ethnic minority. Despite the fact that the labor market and social indicators have placed Italians in a similar position, their similar labor market and social position reflect different host-sending country political relations. These permit Italians to remain an itinerant group with significant rights but relatively low attachments to and identification with the host country. Turks, who showed the least inclination to return, are also not likely to be granted the same freedom of movement in the near future.[15] In their case, the reality of their low labor market position and low degree of social integration are more likely to define the nature of their longer-term incorporation.

3

Public Acceptance of Racial and Ethnic Minorities: A Comparative Analysis
Marilyn Hoskin and Roy Fitzgerald

Among the questions that confront governments in first-world democracies, few are as vexing as how they deal with foreigners wishing to become permanent residents. All of these nations have experienced both economic gains from foreign labor and the tensions that arise when support for general immigration goals conflicts with concrete socioeconomic measures to ease absorption into the host society. Significantly, all have utilized restrictive immigration controls during the period since 1945. That the debate continues across virtually all advanced industrial societies indicates that the issue is chronic. More important, scholars studying it believe that the challenge it poses to democratic norms and processes is unparalleled in this century (Miller 1981; Dahrendorf 1967; G. Freeman 1979; among many).

The twin issues of immigration and integration are fundamental to the definition of any nation's political character because they reflect so many of its vital functions: maintaining a national identity, facilitating economic growth, cultivating political responsibility, sustaining a harmonious if variegated social structure. Since all host nations must reconcile policy toward new or recent immigrants with these functions, there is some logic to studying the issues within a common if general analytical framework. Most comparative studies have employed such a comprehensive approach (Castles and Kosack 1973; G. Freeman 1979; Power 1979; Bryce-LaPorte 1980; Klasen and Drew 1973; Miller 1981; Kubat 1979). In so doing, they have been able to observe some fairly universal patterns: the economic basis of emigration and immigration, reactive rather than long-term governmental policy, citizen concern with large influxes of immigrants.

In casting the broadest analytical net, however, this research approach has also revealed but not explained internation variations, for the simple reason that including larger numbers of countries limits the number of national-level factors that can be examined. Thus differences in historical experience or sociodemographic elements of size, economic base, and other factors can only be used speculatively if the research is globally framed. To determine whether such factors cause variations in immigration experiences or policy, comparisons need to be made more selectively, among two or more nations whose similar contexts allow commonly based questions to explore variations in outcome. The "most similar systems" approach is basic to intermediate-range comparative theory in providing an appropriate test of whether important variables (particular policies, experiences, consequences) are plausible functions of common systemic properties, or whether their explanation must be sought in other factors (Przeworski and Tuene 1970). On a more pragmatic level, the approach is appealing because it avoids the over-stretched comparisons needed to accommodate a range of vastly different nations.

    This analysis starts from the assumption that historical and economic tradition and population size are major systemic factors that influence the scope of a nation's immigration program and the assimilation it ultimately achieves. By making such an assumption, we rule out the comparison of states such as the United States or Canada (founded and defined by immigrants) to nations with only relatively recent experience with immigration (Britain, Germany). It also precludes comparing geographically large, economically diverse nations to smaller, densely populated states. We begin with a relatively crude differentiation between large, historically receptive nations and small and historically reluctant nations, and do not attempt initial comparisons between categories. Instead, we focus on Britain and the former Federal Republic of Germany as examples of the "small and reluctant immigration nation" category. Because their traditions and geo-economic situations are similar, comparison of specific dimensions of immigration can be made with some confidence.

    We also assume that historical tradition, political culture, official policy, and public opinion on this issue, like others, are interrelated (Almond and Verba 1963; Erikson, Luttbeg, and Tedin 1988). Clearly, historical events or conditions are at some point prime movers in the process of responding to public demands and framing policy, but over the longer term the direction of the relationships can be reversed. We thus examine these elements for consistency rather than causal direction.

    Our analysis begins by documenting briefly those historical factors whose similar occurrence in Britain and Germany is basic to our argument that similar systems should, in theory, exhibit similar policies and social outcomes. We then turn to an examination of actual policy toward those who have entered the country and remain in it even without citizenship. From this discussion we offer hypotheses as to how fully foreigners are likely to be accepted in the two nations. Finally, using public opinion data from both nations, we examine public acceptance of immigrants and the implications that it may have for ethnic and racial integration in each country.

IMMIGRATION TRADITIONS

Britain and Germany were largely contributors to the widespread population movements of the nineteenth and early twentieth centuries. Esser and Korte thus note that "in many respects the present situation in Germany is unprecedented" (1985, 165). Rees begins his essay on Britain with the observation that "the United Kingdom has primarily considered itself a country of emigration" (1979, 67). Neither nation had the economic or political appeal that lured large numbers of Europeans to North America. Perhaps as important, many scholars agree that regimes in both nations discouraged potential immigrants by their staunchly nationalistic and isolationist postures (Dahrendorf 1967; Gerrard 1971).

Given these beginnings, it is not surprising that early experiences with immigrants were negative in both nations. The only significant number of non-Irish immigrants attracted to Britain before 1920 were European Jews who were a poor fit for the labor needs of the time. Since they tended to concentrate residentially (in East London) and in particular industries (garment making, shoes, tobacco), they were sufficiently visible to inspire the first campaign to limit or control immigration. Despite a symbolic commitment to open immigration, Parliament responded to racist appeals by adopting the restrictive Aliens Act of 1905.

In Germany, the initial entry of Polish immigrants was marked by restrictions and forced assimilation. At first, Poles were recruited only for work during the agricultural season; when it became evident that they were essential to industry as well, the government responded by prohibiting the teaching or use of Polish (Reimann and Reimann 1979). During both twentieth century wars, this hostility expanded to the use of forced labor, inhumane treatment, and massive relocation. In both cases, then, early experiences with immigration inspired nationalistic opposition and laws that, in turn, served as the basis for further restrictive traditions.

If early experiences were dominated by nationalistic exclusion, those of the postwar period were defined by economic needs. Both nations faced severe labor shortages as a result of war casualties and turned to foreign manpower to fuel their recovery. Britain recruited European Voluntary Workers (including a large percentage who were displaced persons or former prisoners of war), but offered them no permanent residence. Work permits were limited, housing and wages were minimal, and after 1947 family members were not permitted. Not surprisingly, a large number of these workers left England for the United States or other Commonwealth nations (Cheetham 1972).

The British experience was repeated some ten years later in the Federal Republic of Germany. Initially, the postwar labor shortage was muted by the stream of refugees from former German territories. When the erection of the Berlin Wall cut off that supply in 1961, the government of the Federal Republic worked with governments in southern Europe, Turkey, and North Africa to facilitate the recruitment of workers from those nations. By 1973 over two million foreigners entered the Federal Republic of Germany as guest workers. Although their workplace conditions were safeguarded by general union provisions, such workers had little long-term security. Work and residence permits were granted for short terms and the workers faced at least the threat of job and residence permit loss in times of recession. More important, permanent residence and citizenship were never encouraged, since official policy expected that foreign workers would rotate in and out of the Federal Republic. Work force "guests" were clearly seen as an instrument of the state and its need to keep the economy in balance (Rist 1978; Reimann and Reimann 1979; Mehrlaender 1979). Nonetheless, by 1973 political leaders recognized that rotation was not occurring; large numbers of foreigners were becoming de facto permanent immigrants. At that point, recruitment of new workers was banned, but guest workers with jobs were allowed to stay and continue to bring their families. Still, leaders in all three major parties expressed confidence that the number of foreigners would stabilize or decline as Germans gradually replaced them in the economy.

During the 1961-1972 period, British attention turned from the problem of European immigrants (who obliged their hosts by migrating again) to that of economic migrants from Commonwealth members. Until 1962, Commonwealth citizens were entitled to enter Britain with their families, work, and settle permanently if they so desired. Both government and private employers encouraged migrants from the Caribbean basin, India, Pakistan, and British East Africa (Rees 1979; MacDonald 1972). Like its German counterpart, the British government began in 1962 to utilize employment vouchers (matching skills with job openings) to restrict entry, and that provision virtually stopped the flow of Blacks from the Caribbean. Although the voucher system was phased out in 1972, the number of legitimate immigrants had by then tripled from its 1961 base, and higher birth rates within those groups had insured that their percentage in the population would increase.

The similarities between the British and German immigration traditions are thus striking. In both cases nationalistic regimes defined their boundaries restrictively, allowing very limited population movement during a period of industrial growth when other nations were attracting large numbers of new citizens. In both, early experiences with immigrants were negative or harsh. In both, a long period without immigration was followed by a period of labor shortages and a subsequent rash of hastily devised recruitment programs. For both, the recognition that foreign workers were unlikely to return to the homeland came late--too late to reduce the number of foreigners by restricting entry. For both, the problem of regulating entry of immigrants was quickly overshadowed by the more current problem of reconciling non-nationals into the host society. At this point, the problem facing both nations is not that of the initial recruits, whose expectations for steady if dead-end employment have been met. Rather, both need to address questions of education, jobs, and social integration for the generation born without citizenship in their host nations. For this issue we examine the nexus between immigration and integration policies.

IMMIGRATION AND INTEGRATION POLICIES

Changing Policy Expectations

Despite obvious differences in the way foreigners entered the two nations (recruited as temporary labor in the Federal Republic of Germany; allowed into Britain by virtue of Commonwealth citizenship), the similarities in their approaches to migrant populations are striking. First, both nations have displayed an official naivete about the presence of ethnic and racial minorities in their otherwise homogeneous societies. Before the unification of the two Germanys the FGR's population was 7 percent foreign, virtually all of those who resided in Germany for ten years or more, and one-third were under the age of twenty-one. Still, most official documents begin with a specific statement that Germany is not an immigration nation. In Britain, numerous observers note an official deaf ear to issues associated with racial tension. Ashford characterizes the official position as one of simple neglect (1981). The more conservative analyst Philip Norton argues that a cultural desire to work things out, coupled with an integral acceptance of established authority, has allowed officials to assume that like all other issues, this one will be resolved as long as overall concerns of British society are addressed (1984b).

Harder to document but perhaps more revealing is a generally patronizing orientation toward immigrant minorities in both nations. Although both feel some sense of moral obligation toward their resident minorities (Britain toward former colonial subjects, Germany toward those uprooted to serve the German economy), the obligation may well be linked to a historically evident feeling of superiority that easily translates into condescension or contempt. In neither case does the government define the issue of minority integration as one central to its own definition of democracy. If the minority issue is defined as minor or nonexistent (as noted above), minorities themselves can hardly be seen as integral concerns.

Perhaps as important as generalized expectations of policy have been the changes in expectations that have developed over the past two decades. At the outset both systems were quite specific about the future of their ethnic minorities, but with different messages. Britain actively encouraged the immigration of Third World labor who, under British law in the early 1960s, would be eligible for free entry, movement, and citizenship. West Germany brought in foreign workers with only short-term residence guarantees and no hint that naturalization was a possibility. Interestingly, that divergence in the terms of entry of large minority populations in the two nations was followed by a convergence in policy in the years after the mid-1960s.

Simply stated, Britain increasingly tightened its restrictions on entry and redefined its categories of Commonwealth-based citizenship, with the effect that poor immigrants were effectively excluded. Work permits were mandated in 1962 and the unskilled category was abolished in 1965. A new act passed in 1968 strictly limited Asians as a category, and the Race Relations Act of that year delegated integration programs to local governments. The controversial British Nationality Act of 1981 narrowed Commonwealth citizenship (Butler and Kavanagh 1984; Ashford 1981). What had been a relatively friendly climate for immigrants thus turned quite quickly into a situation in which foreigners assumed the position of the country's most unwanted group (Rees 1979). Since immigrants qualified for British social welfare benefits, few specific integration programs were initiated.

In the former Federal Republic, the initial restrictive policy that mandated only temporary residence permits was gradually replaced by a system that renewed permits as long as the guest worker had a job. By permitting that change, the government implicitly accepted the idea that steady workers could stay as long as they wished. Moreover, longer residence invariably brought greater numbers of family members, and the federal government facilitated entry of that category (Rist 1978). In addition, the special needs of guest worker children were addressed by at least some state educational systems (Rist 1978). Finally, a number of language and adjustment programs designed specifically to aid ill-prepared foreigners were developed, mostly at the state and local level (Hoskin and Fitzgerald, 1987). By the mid-1970s, both nations' governments recognized that foreigners were there to stay but left their integration to generalized or local programs.

Policy Components: Rights and Representation

As noted above, the Federal Republic of Germany modified its original restrictions on residence, effectively guaranteeing the right to remain to those who have been there a long time; by 1985 86 percent of the work permits granted were unrestricted. With residence permits foreigners are entitled to the full array of economic and social benefits built into the German system (a guarantee won by German labor unions who did not want industry to undercut German labor). As David Conradt has noted, residence led to economic security, insuring that "they do not constitute a subculture of poverty in the Federal Republic" (Conradt 1982, 70). In Britain, patrials (those from Commonwealth members) are also entitled to the extensive range of welfare benefits (public housing, social security, and education, including youth vocational employment). Since the sluggish state of the British economy has meant a high unemployment rate among foreigners, they are not as prosperous as their German counterparts, but neither are British nationals as prosperous as German citizens.

Where important differences do exist is in the area of political rights. Germany offers no widespread program for facilitating naturalization. Under these circumstances, formal rights of political expression and organization are understandably underutilized. During the 1980s Liselotte Funcke, Commissioner for Foreign Residents, repeatedly argued that the small number of applications for citizenship (under 40,000 annually) stemmed from the fact that requirements were too difficult and officials too discouraging (*Deutsche Nachrichten* September 1986). The government officially denies that naturalization might be a positive force in integrating guest workers with its position that "naturalization should not be an instrument for the promotion of integration but rather should stand at the end of a successful integration process" (Federal Ministry of the Interior, *Record of Policy and Laws Related to Foreigners in the Federal Republic of Germany*, 1985). Esser and Korte conclude that this stance has "created a lasting insecurity concerning future life in the Federal Republic of Germany, and this in turn affects the everyday life of immigrant families" (1985, 189).

In Britain, the system for granting citizenship is not as restrictive as that in Germany. Virtually all who enter are eligible for citizenship application at some point. Distinctions do exist, with first preference being given to patrials, second to the Irish, third to nonpatrials from Commonwealth countries, fourth to European Community nationals, and fifth to other aliens. Although immigrants' active participation in British politics has not been encouraged (Ashford 1981; MacDonald 1972), it is important that there is no official expectation that immigrants will remain non-citizens forever.

However extensive their socioeconomic coverage under government programs, foreign workers can hardly be said to be well represented until they find direct expression through organized political processes, and in neither nation has there been significant progress in this regard. Given their numbers and permanence in both nations, however, we might expect that these workers would receive considerable attention from political leaders, but that has not been the case. We noted in an earlier analysis that parties in Germany have been split on this issue on ideological grounds: the Social Democrats see the issue partly in terms of worker rights but recognize the hostility toward foreigners within labor unions. The Christian Democrats and Free Democrats appreciate the utility of foreign labor to the economy but have little interest in improving the workers' social status (Hoskin 1985). Faced with such contradictory cues, all three have displayed a preference for responding to specific questions over developing a comprehensive position. Reimann and Reimann characterize party positions as "a policy of indecisiveness, postponing a real solution to the dilemma" (1979, 76). Daniel Kubat describes the resulting set of policies toward foreigners as "at base a patchwork sum of separate group demands" (1979, 36). Finally, two corollaries are worthy of note. One is that in the absence of party advocacy, the task of representing guest workers has fallen mainly to churches, charitable organizations, and labor unions (Conradt 1982). A second is that the lack of a central political concern has a spillover administrative effect of dispersing responsibility for issues important to foreigners over dozens of federal and state agencies, thereby diluting the chance that one unit will become a powerful champion of their interests.

In Britain the policy-making picture is strikingly similar. British policy is a creature of mixed goals, since the hosts exhibit "a pervasive ambivalence between patronizing and fearing the once colonized," producing policy that is "a curious amalgam of colonial nostalgia and refusal to notice growing racial tensions within British society" (Ashford 1981, 235, 237). As in Germany, both parties initially agreed that stricter immigration controls might resolve or prevent domestic problems. That consensus supported various immigration and nationality laws between 1961 and 1981. Also as in Germany, apparent consensus was partly a product of internal division within the parties. For the Conservatives it was a split between those with anti-immigrant views and those fiercely loyal to the Commonwealth bond; for Labour the tension was between its vague ideological support of the underdog and the obvious public hostility to that specific dog (Ashford 1981, 237-238). In fact, Labour initiated an official voluntary repatriation program and supported wider use of deportation. As Ashford notes, the Race Relations Act of 1965 seemed to inspire "a consensus to do little or nothing about growing racial problems within the country" (1981, 239). The absence of party initiatives on immigrants is reflected in the fact that an entire volume, *Law and Order in British Politics* (Norton 1984b), includes no discussion of the electoral dimensions of this issue. Some observers, such as Dunleavy and Husbands, go so far as to argue that one reason partisan dealignment occurred in Britain during this period is that divisive issues such as race have never been lively aspects of traditional two-party competition, leaving voters with no party-defined choice on these issues (1985, 17).

In sum, policy is ill defined and reactive in Britain as well as Germany. Rose even uses the same language: "Legislation on race relations in Britain has been characterized by a series of *ad hoc* responses to specific immediate and political controversies" (quoted in Ashford 1981, 244). The only major difference appears to be that where in Germany neither party has taken a particularly strident position on the impact of foreigners, leaders of both British parties have embraced alarmist positions and proposed radical cutbacks in immigration. This difference may be traced simply to inflammatory figures in Britain during this time (Enoch Powell) or to the fact that Germany's own firebrands (Franz Josef Strauss) were directing their vitriol at other targets. In both cases, however, the predominant pattern is one of strikingly similar circumstances and responses. Finally, it is significant that scholars have warned that the immigrant issue is straining the democratic capabilities of each nation. Mark Miller noted that "by history and socio-cultural tradition, the Federal Republic would seem the least prepared to accommodate a large alien population over the long run" (1981, 103); Douglas Ashford is even more pessimistic in his conclusion that the race relations issue in Britain "raises the most profound doubts about the effectiveness of the two-party system and parliamentary politics" (1981, 233).

PUBLIC ACCEPTANCE AND ITS ROOTS

Hypotheses

The comparisons presented thus far lend encouragement to the proposition that examining similar systems is helpful in revealing a common political pattern with respect to immigrant integration. To carry this line of inquiry one step further, we may now generate specific empirical hypotheses about how the mass publics in each country view the integration of immigrants:

1. Given similar histories of limited and/or negative experiences with immigrants, public sentiment in both nations will be predominantly negative toward foreigners living there.

2. Given the general sentiment and the unwillingness of the major liberal parties (Labour in Britain, the Social Democratic party (SPD) in Germany) to take positions favoring immigrant integration, public hostility will cut across party and ideological lines.

3. Sentiment should be more negative in Britain than in Germany, for two reasons: the more strident positions taken by British leadership, and the greater affluence enjoyed by West Germany during the 1961-1984 period.

4. In both nations the socioeconomically advantaged and the young will be more integrationist in their views, as they are less threatened by the presence of foreigners.

Data and Measures

Although a study of this kind would ideally have identical survey instruments administered simultaneously in the two nations, there is no single data set meeting these criteria. Instead, we utilize as many sources of data as possible to chart patterns of opinion in each nation, and draw necessarily cautious comparisons between the two *sets of patterns* rather than between *measures*.

For West Germany, the data are those from the National Social Surveys conducted in 1980 and 1984.[1] Both surveys included questions on political attitudes and standard demographics and both included four questions asking respondents how strongly they agreed or disagreed with statements about integrating guest workers socially, politically, and economically. In addition, we refer where relevant to poll data from the Allensbach Institut for Demoskopie and the EMNID Institute. For Britain the data sources are more varied. Since the process of closing the immigration door started more than a decade earlier in Britain than in Germany, we include data from the 1970 Political Change in Britain study directed by David Butler and Donald Stokes. Where appropriate, we refer to data from earlier parts of that study (1964 and 1966), analyzed in Donley Studlar's work on racial voting (1977, 1978). We also analyze data from the British Social Attitudes study of 1984, a study which is modelled after the American and German Social Surveys and which includes questions on political and racial attitudes.[2]

The measures of our key variable--attitude toward the integration of foreigners into the host society--are not identical and may even tap slightly different dimensions of the attitude we seek to analyze. The German items present four provocative negative statements about the treatment or behavior of guest workers. Two are concerned with policy (when economic times are hard, they should be sent home; they should be denied all political rights), and two relate to personal behavior (they should adjust their lifestyles in Germany; they should marry only within their own groups). For all items respondents placed their own views on a seven-point agreement-disagreement continuum. The summed measure is a multidimensional variable tapping overall attitude toward foreigners.

In all three British election surveys (1964, 1966, 1970), respondents were asked if they agreed with the statement that there were too many immigrants in Britain, then asked to reveal how strongly they held that opinion. We combine the two variables into a single summary measure of strength of opinion. The 1984 survey, on the other hand, asked respondents how they would feel about marrying a member of a minority group, how they would feel about having a boss who was a member of a minority group, and how they classified their own views in terms of racial prejudice. The summed score provided our second measure of integrationist attitude.

The measures we use do raise questions of strict comparability. One set of British questions is more similar to the German questions in that it asks respondents to agree or disagree with a policy position. Since the other set taps personal feelings about socially sensitive issues, it is more direct but also less likely to identify extreme cases. Those who do fall at the anti-integration end of the scale are undoubtedly more negative than those who simply favor anti-guest worker policies in Germany. For our purposes, however, the comparison of sets of patterns rather than individual items is appropriate, and by tapping basic attitudes our measures indicate the directions we seek in this analysis.

General Attitudes toward Foreigners

We hypothesized that lack of an immigration tradition and the otherwise homogeneous political culture in both states should be expected to produce generally negative reactions to foreigners. Table 3.1 presents the breakdown on individual questions at our base data point (1970 for Britain, 1980 for West Germany) and in 1984. Note first the initial set of comparisons. In 1980 West Germans responded fairly uniformly across the four rather diverse items. More than half agreed that foreign workers should be limited in their political, cultural, and economic freedom, and almost as many thought they should marry only other foreigners. Only a third wanted foreigners to enjoy German society when jobs were tight. On the overall measure, fully a third of the respondents could be categorized as "nonreceptive." Similarly, the 1970 British questions reveal that citizens held predominantly negative feelings. Only the variation in intensity muted the fact that 85 percent of the sample thought too many immigrants were in the country. Almost half of the British sample fell into the hostile category of the overall measure.

These patterns represent interesting variations from data collected earlier. In the 1964 and 1966 British data, identical questions revealed that fewer respondents held negative attitudes. In West Germany, on the other hand, earlier patterns indicated more ambivalence and non-concern than outright hostility. The questions were not as strongly worded as those asked in 1980 (asking how things were with guest workers and whether they should enjoy job mobility); nonetheless, the percentages who thought the guest workers would be a problem (36 percent) in one Allensbach survey did not approach the 80 percent of the British whose assessments were negative. The comparisons with earlier data in West Germany indicate a lessening of fear and hostility over time--a pattern that contrasts with the increase in negative judgments seen in the British data (Hoskin 1985).

The 1984 data extend this pattern. Among Germans in 1984 there is a small but consistent decline in negative opinion across all items, and the percentage in the receptive category increases distinctly. In a remarkably short period, then, empathy for foreigners increased. The 1984 British discrimination variable is a composite of three direct questions to the respondent. As the table indicates, only a very small percentage admit to being very prejudiced, but a third describe themselves as "a little prejudiced" and more than half would be personally opposed to interracial marriage. The measures are too different to

Table 3.1 Attitudes Toward Immigrant Minorities in Germany and Britain

German Attitudes Toward Foreign Workers 1980			British Attitudes Toward Immigrants 1970	
Guestworkers Should:	**Agree**	**Disagree**	**Attitude**	**Agree**
Adjust Lifestyles in Germany	66	21	There are Too Many Immigrants in Britain	85
Be Sent Home If Jobs are Tight	52	33	*Feels Strongly*	50
Be Forbidden All Political Activities	51	36	*Feels Fairly Strongly*	34
Marry Only within Their Own Groups	45	42	*Doesn't Feel Strongly*	16
Summary Measure			**Summary Measure**	
Receptive	31		Receptive	26
Mixed/Moderate	36		Mixed/Moderate	28
Hostile	33		Hostile	46
n = 2995			n = 1531	

1984		1980	
Guestworkers Should:	**Agree**	**Attitude**	**Agree**
Adjust Lifestyles in Germany	61	React to a Minority Boss:	
		Mind a Lot	12
		Not Mind a Lot	76
Be Sent Home If Jobs are Tight	41	Marry a Minority:	
		Mind a Lot	29
Be Forbidden All Political Activities	47	*Not Mind a Lot*	47
		Self--How Prejudiced:	
Marry Only within Their Own Groups	34	*Very*	3
		Not Much	63
Summary Measure		**Summary Measure**	
Receptive	39	Receptive	26
Mixed/Moderate	35	Mixed/Moderate	28
Hostile	26	Hostile	46
n = 3004		n = 1675	

Note: Entries are percentage figures.

compare directly, but we should note that a significant proportion of Britons give responses which are directly and unequivocally discriminatory. In both nations, then, the early data reveal a relatively large core of citizens voicing discriminatory opinions, supporting the hypothesis that similar systems have produced at least directionally similar attitude patterns. We hypothesized that the general economic climate would condition response to foreigners in otherwise similar systems, and that aggregate relationship is clearly evident in these data.

Roots of Public Sentiment: Economic and Political Factors

Survey data allow us to examine individual-level effects of economic and political factors on attitudes toward foreigners. In theory, the people who face the greatest job threat from foreign labor should be most resistant to their presence. Our data, however, indicate that unemployment (real or feared) is not related to hostility (Table 3.2). Among West Germans, the group experiencing job insecurity at least once during the previous ten years was actually more receptive to foreigners than those with no unemployment experience. Moreover, this pattern became stronger in the economically sluggish period between 1980 and 1984. In Britain, contrary to popular perceptions that fear of job competition is at the root of dislike of foreigners (Power 1979), there were no differences associated with employment security in either 1980 or 1984. Although there is a greater system-level, aggregate hostility in less prosperous Britain, an individual-level source is not evident. It is possible that those most threatened by foreigners are not those actually out of work (from all types of jobs) but those in the job strata foreigners occupy (the unskilled and semiskilled occupations). As the data in Table 3.2 indicate, in West Germany occupational hostility does exist, consistent with class-based resentments found in earlier studies (G. Freeman 1979; Gaugler et al. 1978; Wallraff 1985). Still, that hostility level is lower in 1984 than in 1980. In Britain, on the other hand, opinion on immigrants does not vary greatly among occupational classes. British workers appear reluctant to face off against other workers, suggesting that ideological consistency may be greater in Britain than Germany. In documenting this difference, we are reminded that the German Social Democrats, troubled by the electoral failure of strident class appeals, moderated their ideological programs in 1959. It is thus plausible that system divergence in this respect has produced a difference in opinion.

Turning to political sources of opinion, we should recall our earlier observation that party leadership in both systems has been timid in staking out clear and distinct positions on issues involving foreign workers. To see if, despite this void, public opinion toward foreign labor is shaped by partisan or

Table 3.2 Economic Sources of Opinion Toward Foreign Workers (Percent)

	Germany		Britain	
	Unemployed		Fear Job Loss	Unemployed
	1980	1984	1970	1984
Receptive	42	46	28	38
Hostile	27	20	47	36
	n=156	n=181	n=279	n=429

Germany							
	Unskilled, Semi-skilled		Skilled		Self-Employed		White-Collar Professional
	1980	1984	1980	1984	1980	1984	1980	1984
Receptive	22	24	26	34	27	42	39	51
Hostile	43	39	32	31	38	26	23	15

1980 n = 2925   1984 n = 1320

Britain

	1970 Subjective Class		1984 Occupation			
	Working	Middle	Manual	Skilled	Service	Professional
Receptive	26	26	33	39	32	39
Hostile	46	44	31	24	30	27

n = 1326   n = 1440

ideological positions, we examine political links to opinion with the data in Table 3.3.

Although there is a relationship evident in the 1980 data, it is small, tied to variations associated with minor parties, and mild compared to variations within parties. The differences are greater in Britain than West Germany, but the distributions within parties indicate why none has rushed to champion the issue: only the Conservatives could even identify a party position. In 1984 this pattern is continued. Only the West German Greens held a clear position on guest workers, and the differences between the SPD and Christian Democratic

Table 3.3 Partisan Support and Opinion Toward Foreigners (Percent)

Germany	1980				1984			
	CDU	FDP	SPD	Greens	CDU	FDP	SPD	Greens
Receptive	21	37	33	61	25	35	38	70
Hostile	38	30	31	17	36	27	30	10
			n=2338				n=2174	

Britain	1970			1984		
	Conservative	Labour	Other	Conservative	Labour	Other
Receptive	18	27	33	33	41	36
Hostile	52	45	37	29	27	21
		n=1517			n=1393	

Union (CDU) actually decreased in the 1980-1984 period. In Britain, the majority that underlay the Conservative position in 1980 disappeared in 1984, and Labour exhibited deep divisions as well. If there is any ideological intensity on this issue, it exists only within factions of one or more of the parties rather than as a catalyst for the membership as a whole.

What emerges from this analysis is two patterns worthy of note. One is that most of the popular theories about why people resent foreigners find little support in either Britain or the former Federal Republic of Germany. Economic hardship, occupational threat, and traditional party-based stands all fail as strong predictors of opinion. The second is more generic. With the exception of a healthier economy in West Germany and possibly stronger ideological forces in Britain, the two systems exhibit similar socioeconomic and political features and similar patterns of opinion. That suggests to us that the basic political elements we have described (political history, demographic makeup, general ideological alignment, and governmental structure) appear sufficiently important to produce similarities in policy and opinion.

Change in Opinion: Generational Factors

Immigration scholars have often observed that the greatest facilitator of integration of new groups is time. Even where ethnic differences are great, the lure of mainstream life persuades successive generations to adapt, with the

Immigration Policy and Ethnic Tolerance

Table 3.4 Age and Opinion Toward Foreigners

Germany	18-35		36-55		55+	
	1980	**1984**	**1980**	**1984**	**1980**	**1984**
Receptive	50	53	29	35	17	23
Hostile	20	19	32	27	55	51
	1980	n= 2925	1984	n = 2967		

Britain	18-35		36-55		55+	
	1970	**1984**	**1970**	**1984**	**1970**	**1984**
Receptive	35	44	25	35	17	32
Hostile	35	21	46	28	60	32
	1970	n = 1689	1984	n = 1603		

youngest foreigners most likely to blend in with their host society peers. If that reasoning is correct, we should anticipate that younger age groups in each host society will feel more comfortable with foreigners. If the relationship is this straightforward, we should witness no major differences across national boundaries.

Table 3.4 presents the most clearly defined relationship in our analysis. In both nations hostility is monotonically related to age. In West Germany, an aging generation of 1960s liberals makes the middle-age category decidedly more receptive than it was even four years prior; this pattern also holds in Britain. The only exception we find is in the youngest cohort, where the increase in receptivity is small. Still, that group was clearly the most liberal in earlier years, so its base was not likely to change as dramatically as that in other age categories. Age and the related concept of getting used to a group with time are hardly unique to these nations. In these instances, however, these elements appear to counteract more negative forces at work.

CONCLUSION

We began this chapter with the objective of determining whether a similar systems approach would be useful in examining variations in immigration outcomes in two nations with similar geographic, historical, and economic circumstances. Our review of those circumstances generated hypotheses that overriding system similarities should predict similar public policies and opinion. Our analysis of policy and popular sentiment has revealed several patterns worthy of note.

First, common traditions of immigration history and economic circumstance appear to be more influential in defining current patterns of opinion than factors often assumed important by many political scientists as they compare political culture and policy (age of the democracy, grounding in constitutional traditions, and the like; Almond and Verba 1963; Dahrendorf 1967). For both Britain and West Germany, the distrust of foreigners associated with early history discouraged later immigration and gradually created a national climate in which generally negative opinion could and did flourish. That their respective constitutions safeguard the rights of residents is, apparently, less central to the native populations than a legacy of opposition to immigration.

As important as that basic tradition, however, are those that serve to mute it. Specifically, economic health emerged as a major factor that defines how key actors (parties, leadership, interest groups) treat this issue. Interestingly, economic health, even though it impacts differently on various groups within the society, appears to have an overall national effect: hostility is greater in Britain, across classes, than in Germany. Irrespective of governmental goals or policies of integration, resistance to foreigners is likely to persist as long as the economy remains sluggish. Since both nations compared here have had restrictive immigration histories, it is impossible to tell if a positive tradition would temper the effects of a poor economy. What we can say, however, is that negative immigration histories appear to encourage hostility even where economic conditions have been relatively prosperous, as in West Germany. Such traditions exist as very powerful factors influencing popular and leadership attitudes.

Third, we should note that whatever it lacks in elegance as a social science variable, time (and its associated individual variable of age) appears to play a major role in this issue. It might still be true that effective leadership would obviate the need for such lengthy periods of acceptance, but in both states studied here time appears to be making up for at least some of the leadership void. Even in Germany, where children of guest workers are not encouraged to assimilate into citizenship, the younger cohort of Germans is more receptive to the needs of those with whom they have grown up than older generations.

Finally, it is easy to see the specter of democratic failure in the fact that political leaders avoid direct resolution of this issue or the fact that the public can be so ambivalent to the plight of foreign residents. To be sure, neither case examined here would qualify as a model new home for the world's tired and poor. Still, it should be remembered that despite negative historical traditions and non-courageous political leaders, other system characteristics (constitutional safeguards, basic respect for some categories of human rights) appear to allow time to make its positive impact on the mass public's acceptance of foreigners. Although traditions and economic conditions may retard eventual integration, basic structural features and political norms appear to work as long-term facilitators of this process.

4

Sociopolitical Context and Ethnic Consciousness in France and the United States: Maghrebis and Latinos
William Safran

The condition of ethnic minorities in industrial democracies depends on a number of factors: the history and patterns of settlement; the circumstances surrounding the building of the state; formal institutional arrangements and actual modes of government; the international context; the number and relative strength of ethnic communities and the relationship among them; the relations of the state to society and to the culture that informs it; the definition of the *nation* and, by derivation, of nationality and citizenship; and the values attached to political, socioeconomic, and cultural pluralism.

The present study attempts to compare the relationship between majorities and minorities in France and those in the United States in terms of some of these factors by focusing on their most numerous and most rapidly growing ethnic groups: the Maghrebis, or North African Arabs, in France and the Latinos, or Hispanics, in the United States. While attention will be directed most specifically at Algerian and Mexican natives and their offspring, the existence of categorical differences between immigrant and native-born minorities is acknowledged. It is obvious, too, that there are differences between long-settled and recent immigrants with respect to socioeconomic status, cultural-linguistic assimilation, and identification with the mores and values of the majority. However, the differences among ethnically related people are far from precise. A gross labeling (as of Harkis and Beurs in France and of Chicanos and Mexicans in the United States) tends both to suggest distinctions between subminorities and to obscure the relationship between them.[1]

A comparison of France and the United States is appropriate because of the many characteristics they share. Both have for many generations been countries of immigration and have acquired their present territorial shapes by adding--by means of conquest or treaty--pieces of adjoining lands. Each country has attempted to create a nation by welding diverse ethnic strains into a homogeneous and more or less coherent society. Each has been committed to the proposition that membership in the national community is not a matter of race or descent but rather the product of an act of will: the voluntary acceptance of a common language and, above all, a commitment to common political values such as republicanism and constitutional government (Huntington 1981, 14, 25, 29; Schnapper 1987, 361-365).

To be sure, the Jacobin ideology in France and the faith in the efficacy of the melting pot in the United States co-existed with certain unpleasant realities: in France, the periodic emphasis (in particular by the political Right) on an "organic" view of French society composed of "our ancestors the Gauls"; and in the United States, the occasional tendency to define membership in the American nation in White Anglo-Saxon Protestant (WASP) terms--and the continuing difficulty of integrating Blacks into the mainstream. In France, the official commitment to the welcoming and absorption of minorities was punctuated by the xenophobia and the anti-semitism of the Dreyfus affair, the racism of Vichy, the hostility to indigenous ethnics immediately after World War II, and the anti-immigrant sentiments that have been spreading rapidly since the 1970s and have been exploited by the extreme-right Front National.

In the United States, anti-immigrant and anti-minority sentiments have been reflected in the Know-Nothing movement in the mid-nineteenth century, the Chinese Exclusion Act at the end of the century, the xenophobia of the 1920s and 1930s, and the internment of Americans of Japanese ancestry during World War II. By and large, however, the assimilative machinery was successful in both countries. From the mid-nineteenth century through the early twentieth century, the descendants of Irish, German, Jewish, Polish, and Italian immigrants to the United States were made into Americans, and the offspring of Belgian, Italian, German, Portuguese, and Polish immigrants--and of the "indigenous" Alsatian, Basque, Breton, Catalan, Corsican, Flemish, and Occitan inhabitants of the Hexagon--were transformed into French men and women. The major instruments of this transformation were the respective national public school systems; the attraction of progressive, and generally "superior," cultures; and the cooptative capabilities of expanding economies that promised employment and upward mobility.

To the extent that ethnic consciousness still existed, it was--for the majority of descendants of minorities--often little more than an awareness of their origins (or, in customary American terms, their nationalities). The ancestral languages--now often demoted to the status of mere dialects--were no longer transmitted, and what remained of ethnic culture had been so watered down and trivialized that little more was left of it but vague nostalgia about the old country (*le pays*) or home village, fragments of ethnic vocabulary, and a few folk festivals and culinary traditions (Gordon 1964; Dinnerstein and Reimers 1975).

CHALLENGES TO THE MELTING POT IDEOLOGY

After World War II, the melting pot model and the interpretations of majority-minority relations implicit in that model were challenged in both the United States and France. The postwar influx of immigrants into both countries--they had been brought as cheap laborers into an expanding economy--was so sudden and massive that it threatened to overload the economic integration machinery, in particular with the onset of industrial stagnation and the growth of unemployment after the mid-1970s. The relegation of the Maghrebis and most Latinos to the inferior part of what has come to be described as the dual economy sharpened their perceptions of a relative deprivation and fortified their ethnic consciousness.

These immigrants also challenged the cultural assimilation machinery. Immigrants from Mexico, Puerto Rico, and Cuba settled in such densely clustered communities in the American Southwest, New York City, and in south Florida, respectively, that they could maintain ethnic community institutions, Spanish-language newspapers, and ethnically ascriptive social relations and resist quick Americanization. In France, the pattern of Maghrebi settlement has been less territorially coherent (except for thickly inhabited communities in Paris, Lyon, Marseille, and elsewhere); however, the Maghrebis have been considered culturally far less "digestible" because of their non-European language, culture, and religion.

For both Algerians and Mexican Americans, the appeal of the majority political culture--and of the majority elites as role models--was much weaker than it had been for the more manageable European ethnic minorities in France and the United States. The image of French civilization and the credibility of its *mission civilisatrice* had been tarnished by the misbehavior of many French citizens during World War II and the cruelties perpetrated by French soldiers during the war in Algeria, the global influence of the French language had declined, the humanistic elements of French culture were being gradually displaced by scientific-technical components that were transnational in nature, and the development of the European Community and other regional transaction patterns put in question the belief in the economic self-sufficiency of the French nation-state. Moreover, the contagion of Third World independence movements infected the ideologies of the French elite, in particular that of the democratic Left: the increasing acceptance of the idea that the politicization of tribal consciousness was legitimate--and not necessarily reactionary--contributed to a reawakening of Breton, Occitan, Jewish, and Basque ethnic assertiveness and weakened the Jacobin armor of the majority (Safran 1984). One of the manifestations of that development was the weakening of Gaullism and Marxism, the two ideologies that had been most intimately associated with the Jacobin idea of the nation-state and the opposition to ethnic pluralism.

The image of the United States had suffered, too: the war in Vietnam and the support of Latin American dictators put in question the commitment of the United States to the spread of democracy, while continued discrimination against African American and other minorities raised doubts about the absorptive capacity of U.S. society. The American majority has had more resistant cultural and linguistic equipment than its French counterpart: the English language has become a global idiom, and American mass culture and technology have continued to spread widely. Nevertheless, France has had a more coherent public policy approach to language and culture than has the United States. French republican governments inherited the concern of Bourbon monarchs with the national cultural patrimony and the official status of the French language and continued to be preoccupied with the protection and dissemination of that language. In the United States, in contrast, education has been left to subnational authorities; cultural matters, literature, art, and the theater, to the private sector (and occasionally to local governments); and language (at least until recently), to the marketplace.

The greater permeability of the cultural armor of the majority at state and local levels has made it easier for Latinos to maintain their culture and to secure public legitimation of it in the United States than has been possible for Maghrebis in France. Bilingual election ballots, public notices and driver license tests in Spanish, English as a second language, ethnic-minority curricula in public elementary schools, and Chicano studies programs in universities--all these are phenomena for which there are no Maghrebi equivalents in France. It would be difficult to imagine candidates for the National Assembly or municipal councils (even in such heavily Arab towns as Aix-en-Provence or Sarcelles) making campaign speeches in Arabic or for official documents to be issued in any language other than French.

The relative openness of the Anglo majority to Hispanic culture must be attributed not only to traditions of American institutional pluralism but also to the fact that the American majority is far less hostile to Latinos than the ordinary French person (belonging to *la France profonde*) is to the Maghrebi. Public opinion polls conducted in the past ten years have shown consistently that North Africans are considered by a heavy majority to be the least desirable ethnics; that Italians, Jews, Portuguese, and Spaniards (in descending order) are considered more acceptable than Maghrebis; and that Algerians are more undesirable than Tunisians or Moroccans (*Le Point* 1983; Schnapper 1985/86).

To be sure, the Latinos, like the Maghrebis, are the subjects of negative stereotypes and are considered to be less desirable ethnics than the Irish, the Poles, the Germans, and the Jews. A poll conducted in 1981 revealed that 58 percent of whites (and 71 percent of African Americans) felt that immigrants were taking jobs away from Americans, and in a poll of March 1982, 66 percent of respondents thought that English immigrants were good for the country, whereas 62 percent had the same positive feelings for Irish immigrants, 59 percent for Jewish, 46 percent for Black, 44 percent for Chinese, but only 25 percent for Mexican, 17 percent for Puerto Rican, and 9 percent for Cuban immigrants (Harwood 1983). There is a growing feeling among Anglos that Latinos are competing unfairly for their jobs, housing, and places in schools; this feeling is particularly strong in such places as Miami, where Cubans are often equated with drug pushers and the central high school has been referred to as "Havana High." Like Maghrebis, Latinos (especially Mexican Americans) are often thought of as belonging to a less democratic culture and a more hierarchical social system and of keeping their women in subordinate roles (Mora and Del Castillo 1980; Schmitt 1974).

However, the Latinos are not demonized so much as the Maghrebis, or Arabs, who are accused of befouling low-cost housing projects, celebrating their feasts noisily, and contributing to the lowering of school standards and who are said to be criminals, scabs, petroleum extortionists, fanatics, and terrorists (Aissou 1987, 36). A petit-bourgeois French provincial is quoted as saying: "I am voting [Jean-Marie] Le Pen [the leader of the *Front National*] because I have been burglarized four times. This place [has become like] Beirut" (Aissou 1987, 39-40). Nevertheless, there is no categorical association of Latinos in the United States or Maghrebis in France with criminality (except for supporters of the *Front National*), and there is no clear proof that ethnic stereotyping plays a determinant role in criminal convictions (Holmes 1984; Schnapper 1985/86). The French majority does not wish to expel the Maghrebis, nor does the American majority wish to expel the Latinos; both majorities acknowledge the contributions of their large (and relatively young) ethnic underclass of menial workers to the productive process and to the social security funds.

In each country, the larger minority has become a metaphor for its most numerous component. Thus, attitudes toward the 1.6 million Maghrebis in France are generalizations of attitudes toward Algerians, of whom there are more than 800,000; and the attitudes toward the estimated 20 million Latinos in the United States (as of 1987) are generalizations of attitudes toward the more than 14 million immigrants or descendants of immigrants from Mexico or those whose forebears had been nationals of that country (i.e., the Chicanos). That has meant that the indigenous majority in France has been unable to make precise distinctions among Algerian, Tunisian, and Moroccan immigrants, between Arabs and other Muslims, and between Arabic-speaking Maghrebis and the 600,000-800,000 Beurs, the second- or third-generation descendants of Maghrebis, whose language and much of whose culture is French, and whose identification with the majority would be even stronger if that majority were more tolerant of them. It has meant that the American majority has been unable to make clear distinctions between newly arrived Mexican *obreros* and partly Americanized Chicanos and among Mexicans, Cubans, Puerto Ricans (of whom there are more than 1 million and who account for about 15 percent of the population of New York City), and other Latinos. Because of these misidentifications and because of their incomplete acceptance, these minorities live in an ethnocultural twilight zone: just as the Beurs are "no longer Maghrebi but not quite French" (Aissou 1987, 8), so the Chicanos are no longer Mexican but not quite American.

However, Latinos in the United States are in a much stronger and more secure position than are Maghrebis in France. The Latinos are Roman Catholic and therefore members of one of the three "American" religions--in a country where no religion has been officially established--and their churches can hardly be distinguished from other houses of worship. The vast majority of Maghrebis are Muslims, members of an exotic faith that is considered fundamentalist and intolerant and that claims more than mere religious obedience; its mosques are not generally accepted as part of the traditional urban landscape of France--a country once considered "the eldest daughter of the [Catholic] Church"--where the cathedral is still the centerpiece of every town. Furthermore, while Catholic churches attended by Latinos have sometimes fostered integrationist attitudes, many mosques and Koranic schools in France, often led by imams brought in from North Africa, have tried to nourish sentiments of Arabité (Arabism) that imply a rejection of French values.

Some French people, in particular those who had been sympathetic to the idea of an Algérie Française, resent the presence of the Maghrebis because it serves as a constant reminder of France's military defeat by Algeria, the country of origin of half of the Maghrebis; others, because that presence feeds the guilty conscience of those, in particular within the intellectual community of leftist bent, who opposed France's colonial involvements; and still others, because France continues to be exposed to the economic and political pressures of Arab oil-producing countries. In contrast, the Anglo majority has no bitter memory of--nor, more than a century after the Mexican war, a guilty conscience about--a conflict with Mexico, the major sending country of Latinos, and one that has been relatively powerless. Whereas to Latinos themselves, the Mexican war is a matter of history (regardless of how often the injustices of the Treaty of Guadalupe Hidalgo are evoked), for many Maghrebis the Franco-Algerian war is a matter of personal experience and relatively recent memory. In their polemics vis-à-vis the majority, Maghrebis, in particular Algerian-born intellectuals, derive a degree of moral strength from the claim that the French occupation of Algeria resulted in a deculturation of the natives. Before that occupation, 40 percent of Algerian males had been literate, but gradually the male population was reduced to illiteracy (Aissou 1987, 23). There is no such history (or mythology) available to the Latinos, in particular to those--and they account for the majority--who had come voluntarily to the United States as workers in the hope of expanding chances of upward mobility for themselves and their children.   For these reasons, Latinos are more integrated psychologically into U.S. society than Maghrebis are into French society, and there is no serious doubt about their political loyalties (De la Garza 1985).

Unlike Maghrebis of Algerian origin, Latinos of Mexican origin have no problem serving in the armed forces of the United States; on the contrary, the proportion of Latinos in U.S. uniform is greater than that of Anglos, and their fighting has not been against Mexicans but Germans, and more recently against Koreans, Vietnamese, and Iraqis.

Another trump card of the Latinos is the fact that they are not the major scapegoats of the majority. African Americans are, at present, more numerous than Latinos; since they are less "meltable," and since their presence is more obvious and therefore more threatening, they act as deflectors of Anglo fears and prejudices. The very existence of the Black buffer can make the Latinos feel at once relatively less disprivileged and more optimistic about prospects of social acceptance and upward mobility. By contrast, the Maghrebis have no significant ethnoracial underclass below themselves, for, historically, a large proportion of the 500,000 to 700,000 Blacks, for the most part originating from French overseas departments in the Caribbean and elsewhere, resident in the Hexagon have been *embourgeoisé* and *francisé*. There are indications that the growing number of legal and illegal uneducated Blacks from sub-Saharan Africa is contributing to old-fashioned anti-Black racism, which, in turn, tends to moderate anti-Maghrebi prejudices. Conversely, the conspicuous presence of Maghrebis makes the Jews--once regarded as unassimilable "orientals"--appear to be an authentic component of French society, one that even the political Right (other than the extremist Front National) now regard as based on Judeo-Christian values (Club de l'Horloge 1985, 205).

POLITICAL SOCIALIZATION AND POLITICAL BEHAVIOR

A most important difference between the two communities is the far greater extent of Latino political socialization. There are many more third- and fourth-generation Latinos in the United States than descendants of Harkis, naturalized French army veterans of North African origin, in France. Unlike the children of Maghrebi immigrants, who are referred to as *"immigrés de la deuxième génération,"* second-generation Latinos are more readily accepted as Americans. They learn from the behavior of politically more Americanized Latinos who have entered the middle class and who in some cases have achieved positions of political power. Younger Chicanos (whose parents were, for the most part, semiliterate) have become active on local levels, especially since the 1960s, and they have been considered particularly important by Democratic party organizations (De la Garza and Vaughan, 1984, 290-307). These Latinos express themselves politically without relinquishing their ethnic concerns--and without being apologetic about such concerns; their electoral participation is significant, especially since the expansion of the Voting Rights Act in 1975, and they freely engage in ethnic lobbying without raising suspicions about their political loyalties. In France, by contrast, ethnic voting and clearly political lobbying by ethnic organizations are considered uncivic, if not subversive, even for "indigenous" ethnics such as Bretons, and offensive to the Jacobin sensitivities of the French elite. Such acts would be considered even less acceptable for Maghrebis, who enjoy much less national legitimacy. It would, therefore, be difficult for a person who is openly identified as a Maghrebi to appeal to non-ethnic French voters for support as a candidate for election.

For all these reasons, Maghrebis in France do not resort as much to overt political pressure as do Latinos in the United States. They tend to prefer the intellectual-polemical approach: French-educated Maghrebi academicians, social researchers, journalists, and novelists are active in explaining the peculiar situation of their fellow ethnics to the more sensitive elements of the public at large and in assuring them that Maghrebis are quite civilized, that Islam is compatible with modernity and democracy, and that Maghrebi culture can make a positive contribution to the culture of France.[2] In these efforts, which are directed at national audiences, Maghrebi intellectuals are joined by a growing number of French colleagues.[3]

On local community levels, particularly in neighborhoods and low-rent housing projects heavily populated by Maghrebis, one finds a growing number of voluntary associations, some of them subsidized from municipal budgets, that help Maghrebis to adjust to their surroundings, promote interethnic understanding, and organize neighborhood ethnic folk festivals. But in France there have been few sustained local efforts to get Maghrebis to register and vote--of the kind that exist in connection with Latinos in the United States. During the 1980s, Maghrebi leaders set up an organization, the Association France-Plus, whose major aims were to get as many of their fellow ethnics as possible registered so that they could vote in the presidential elections of 1988 and, ultimately, to put up their own candidates in future elections. An example of official reactions to such efforts was a circular sent by the Minister of the Interior to mayors calling upon them to listen to the demands of the Beurs (*Le Point* 1988; Safran 1989c).

Owing to the federal structure of U.S. politics and the corresponding regionalization and localization of electoral politics, there are now several large cities with Latino mayors, a substantial number of Latinos in state legislatures, and a growing contingent of Latino members of the U.S. Congress--the ten Hispanic Representatives as of 1987 constituted a large enough group to make up a Congressional Hispanic caucus (Welch and Hibbing 1984). In recognition of the contribution of Latinos to his election (via the electoral votes of Texas), President Carter named more than one hundred of them to federal positions. In 1987, over 11 percent of the New York City police was Latino--a proportion hardly imaginable for Maghrebis in the Paris police. There are no Maghrebi political parties in France that would be analogous to La Raza Unida and other regional parties that periodically exerted political influence in the American

Southwest, and there has been no attempt to construct, on a national level, ethnically balanced tickets that include Maghrebi candidates. At this time, there are barely a handful of Maghrebis in the national parliament in Paris, relatively few Maghrebi civil servants, and although the number of Maghrebi city councilors is growing, not a single mayor of a sizable town. According to a 1985 poll, only 37 percent of the French accept--and 53 percent reject--the idea that some day there would be a prime minister of Maghrebi origin (*SOFRES* 1987). A further breakdown of these statistics shows that opposition was lowest among sympathizers of the Left (50 percent), higher within the "republican" Right including Union pour la démocratie française (62 percent) and Rassemblement pour la République (65 percent), and highest among supporters of the Front National (83 percent).[4] It is safe to predict that such a prime minister would be a secularized Maghrebi with a Gallicized name.

Even this kind of speculation is unrealistic, since the estimated 800,000 Maghrebis who are entitled to vote account for only 2 percent of the total electorate (Malet 1987, 69). They tend overwhelmingly to be leftists, because the Left in France has been more responsive than the Right to their needs. The Left has a guilty conscience with respect to the Maghrebis, in much the same sense that the liberals in the United States may have a guilty conscience with respect to the Latinos and African Americans. The status and the very presence of these minorities are seen as the consequence of colonialism; and their treatment does not accord with the Left's ideals about equality and social justice. In neither country does the Right have a guilty conscience--when it should have it: In both the United States and France, the business community (which has supported right-wing parties) imported cheap Mexican and Algerian labor in order to avoid having to spend the money for (more costly) labor-saving machines (Moulin 1985, 42).

Maghrebis opt for the Socialist party (PS) rather than the Communist party (PCF). The PS has been more sympathetic than the PCF to the ethnic cultural concerns of Maghrebis, more open to the idea of dual nationality, and more interested in economic insertion than in rapid cultural assimilation (Giordan 1982; Marangé and Lebon 1982). The Maghrebis have had greater difficulty in relating to the PCF because it had little understanding of their ethnic claims (which according to orthodox Marxist doctrine were based on false consciousness) and even less tolerance for the Islamic elements of Maghrebi consciousness. Furthermore, PCF officials, especially on local levels, have reflected the xenophobia of the indigenous working class that has been competing with the Maghrebis for jobs, housing, and social benefits and that has shown signs of transferring its electoral support from the PCF to the Front National.

The Right has been viewed as even less sympathetic to Maghrebis. The Front National is frankly racist: ideally it favors the expulsion of Maghrebis and other "undesirable" minorities; failing that, it opposes their naturalization.

The Gaullist party (RPR) is officially anti-racist, but its Jacobin ideology leads it to oppose the perpetuation of the distinct ethnic identity of Maghrebis and to favor their complete cultural assimilation. However, the RPR as a whole has been afraid of losing voters to the Front National; therefore, it has increasingly advocated tough "law and order" attitudes toward Algerians and a tougher citizenship code, that is, a more restrictive approach to naturalization, and during the presidential elections of 1988 it transparently appealed to the xenophobic electorate. Within the Giscardist Union pour la démocratie française (UDF), the centrist ally of the RPR, there are politicians who welcome the Maghrebi presence and even countenance a degree of ethnocultural pluralism, but the UDF is highly fragmented and must compete with the RPR for the votes of less tolerant right-of-center French citizens.[5]

In the United States, in contrast, there is no political party with serious electoral prospects that caters openly to racist voters. On the contrary, both major parties appeal to Latinos for their support because it can make a difference in electoral outcomes. Yet although Latinos have more political power than Maghrebis, they are more divided ideologically. The majority of Mexican Americans have been Democrats and have been more likely to vote a straight Democratic ticket than have Anglos (Cain and Kiewiet 1984). But their electoral participation has not been as high as that of Anglos and has been relatively lower than that of Cuban Americans, who tend to be politically conservative. Arriving in the 1960s as political refugees, earning a much higher median income than Mexican Americans, and being strongly anti-Communist, Cuban Americans have tended to vote Republican. Although the Cubans (of whom there are, at 1989 estimates, 800,000 to 1,000,000) constitute a relatively small part of the Hispanic community, their number is increasing rapidly, their rate of naturalization is greater than that of Mexican Americans, their voting turnout is higher, and their political influence in south Florida is often decisive (Portes and Mozo 1985).

Both Latinos and Maghrebis have tried to compensate for their weaknesses--internal fragmentation in the one case, and institutional and ideological constraints in the other--by making alliances with other ethnics. The results have been mixed, and the prospects of success are uncertain. Jesse Jackson's efforts at constructing a "rainbow coalition" were impeded by mutual resentments between Latinos and Blacks, by distrust on the part of Jews and other white ethnics, and by the improbability of Jackson's nomination as the Democratic presidential candidate. He seemed to make some headway in the spring of 1988, when many--perhaps half--of the Mexican American and Puerto Rican (but not Cuban) voters supported him for the nomination; but many other Latinos supported Michael Dukakis, either because he was viewed as more electable or because they were impressed by his fluency in Spanish, a language he occasionally used in addressing Latino audiences. In France, SOS-Racisme, a movement for fighting racism established in 1984 by Harlem Désir, a second-generation Maghrebi, succeeded in organizing big interethnic solidarity marches. These were reminiscent of the U.S. civil rights demonstrations of the early 1960s; indeed, the slogan of SOS-Racisme, *touche pas à mon pote* (Don't Harm My Buddy) paralleled the slogan We Shall Overcome of the U.S. civil rights movement. However, the political prospects of that movement are weak for a number of reasons: lack of funds, low voting turnouts by Maghrebis, and interethnic tensions (e.g., between Maghrebis, Jews, Corsicans, and Occitans). Moreover, both Jackson and Désir are widely distrusted for demagogic tendencies and for wishing to exploit for personal ambition the resentment of ethnic minorities against discrimination.

Political involvement of ethnic minorities is a function of the degree of identification with the country in which they live. Both Mexican and Algerian immigrants, in particular illegal ones, frequently return to their countries of origin. They send remittances to their kin who remained behind, thereby contributing to the upward mobility of the recipients (DiNardo 1985), maintaining cultural ties to their mother country, and keeping alive the "myth of return." That myth, however, has been more constraining to Maghrebis than to Latinos. To many Algerians, the adoption of French citizenship is a form of betrayal to a "colonialist" country, while to Cubans, opting for life in the United States implies identification with a freer regime than that of the country they left and one that might some day liberate their native island. That explains why, between 1962 and 1978, only 9,449 Algerians opted for French nationality (Malet 1987, 75), whereas the vast majority of Cuban immigrants resident in the United States for more than ten years have become citizens and entered the political fray--although the notion of a Cuban diaspora was not abandoned (Benenson 1986).

Despite the fact that the political socialization of Latinos of Mexican origin has been easier and their acceptance by the majority has been greater than has been the case for Maghrebis of Algerian origin, the sense of grievance of the former has been at least as great as that of the latter. Both groups have articulated their feelings of relative economic deprivation and their resentments over the imperialist behavior of their "host" country toward their countries of origin. But the Latinos' resentment has been greater than the Maghrebis'. Whereas the Maghrebis settled in France of their own volition, the forebears of many Latinos did not; like the Corsicans, who found themselves part of France when their island "acceded" to French sovereignty, the Latinos' ancestors, especially in the Southwest and West, found themselves subjects of the United States when the Mexican lands on which they lived were conquered. Many Chicanos still consider New Mexico and parts of Colorado, Texas, and California their territory on which their culture, language, and values flourished until these were challenged and "inferiorized" by the Anglos. Latinos are aware of the fact that after the Treaty of Guadalupe Hidalgo of 1848, leaders of the conquered Mexican communities shared in the decision-making processes of the

Southwest and played a major role in its development until they were displaced by Anglo settlers (De la Garza and Vaughan 1984). Latinos are continually given proof of their long-established presence in the very Spanish names of cities, rivers, counties, and even states. Most Anglos accept these names, which antedate American independence, as natural elements of the American reality, much as they accept Mexican food and Spanish architectural styles in the southwestern regions and in Florida. Moreover, the Spanish language is taught in virtually all U.S. high schools. In France, non-ethnics may like to eat couscous, but there is no city or region with an Arabic name, and there are few *lycées* in which Arabic is taught, let alone promoted as a desirable option among modern languages. All this explains why Maghrebis' ethnicity is less situational, and their ethnic boundaries are less permeable than those of Latinos (Padilla 1984).

THE PUBLIC POLICY CONTEXT

The different institutional and historical contexts of the United States and France have different effects on the official position of the Latinos and Maghrebis and on the attitudes of the majority toward them. However, there are comparable socioeconomic developments in both countries that have had a chilling effect on the maintenance of an ethnoplural society as well as on the prospects of ethnic integration. The scarcity of jobs other than perhaps low-paying service jobs in both countries, the growing scarcity of places in schools, the pressures on governmental budgets--all these make it increasingly difficult for governments at national and local levels to pursue policies of economic insertion *or* cultural assimilation. This has been particularly true under the conservative rule of the Republicans in the United States and the Gaullists in France, both of whom have exploited the backlash of majority voters who resent the "otherness" of ethnic minorities as well as their desire to integrate. Both the Reagan and the Chirac supporters have resented the cultural differences of the large minorities in their countries and have equated these differences to "moral relativism";[6] at the same time, they have been hostile to measures designed to reduce these differences: affirmative action, bilingual education, school integration, and the enforcement of equal protection laws.

Maghrebis have relied much less than Latinos on policies of affirmative action for gaining entry into the mainstream, in part because of the widely held view that the provisions of the French constitution and the legislation flowing therefrom adequately guarantee the rights of all citizens. Measures of affirmative action (*discrimination positive*) were embraced, selectively and hesitantly, under two presidents of the Fifth Republic. Thus in 1959 and 1961, ordinances were issued to facilitate the recruitment of Muslim expatriates from Algeria; under laws passed by the Socialist government between 1981 and 1986

naturalized citizens were given the same political rights as native-born ones
(discussed later), and foreign workers were granted union rights on practically
the same basis as French workers; and in 1987, the Chirac government promised
measures to speed up the integration of repatriates (including Muslim ones) into
the French economy. However, there have been no systematic, American-style
efforts in France to recruit minority students and faculty to schools and
universities on a preferential basis and no allocation of government funds
dependent on progress in such recruiting. (Premier Chirac appointed a minister
for human rights, but the concerns of that official did not specifically extend to
entitlements of ethnic minorities.) Most of the French elite continues to believe
in the operative validity of the Napoleonic principle of non-ascriptive recruitment
("careers open to talent"); moreover, university admissions criteria are still
largely set on a national level, at which it would be difficult for Maghrebis to
exert effective pressure. Under these conditions, it would be unthinkable to find
a Maghrebi parallel to the suit brought by Hispanic organizations and supported
by Mexican American political leaders against the state university system of
Texas for failing to provide proportionally equal access for Mexican Americans
to public universities. There are no Maghrebi study programs in French
universities that would be analogous to the Chicano studies programs found in
a number of U.S. universities--programs that might, for instance, revolve around
the sociology of the Algerian ghettos in Marseille, Algerian poetry of protest,
or patterns of discrimination. There are, of course, specialists and study groups
on Maghrebi problems--they may be connected with the National Center for
Scientific Research (CNRS) or other "roof organizations"--but these tend to
address themselves to a relatively narrow academic clientele. The reason for
that absence is threefold: (1) the high degree of centralization of the educational
curriculum, (2) the notion that only French majority culture must constitute the
standard educational curriculum, and (3) the conviction that those aspects of
Maghrebi culture that will survive the French assimilation process are by
definition in the realm of folklore, not culture.[7]

Both France and the United States believe in the efficacy of their public
school systems as mechanisms of assimilation, and both have thrown their
school doors wide open to children and grandchildren of Maghrebi and Latino
immigrants. But in both countries there are tendencies toward a dual school
system that parallels and sustains the "dual economy": With the flight of
children of the bourgeois majorities from the public schools in working-class or
slum areas to private schools that are often parochial, public schools are
increasingly becoming the training grounds for Muslim Maghrebis and Roman
Catholic Latinos (Hammet and Proux 1984). On the one hand, the secular
curriculum of these public schools helps to "modernize" the attitudes of these
minorities and to prepare them for cultural assimilation; on the other hand, the
relatively inferior quality of schooling tends to undermine the prospects of the

socioeconomic integration of the minorities and to sharpen their ethnic consciousness.

MAJORITIES AND MINORITIES

The degree of cordiality shown by the majority to ethnic minorities has depended in some measure on the extent to which the minority's policy concerns have coincided with those of society at large. To the extent that Latinos and Maghrebis have been part of the disadvantaged classes, they have shared a number of domestic policy preferences with the poor in general: an expanded welfare state, progressive taxes and other measures of income redistribution, and job protection. For that reason, they have tended to support left-of-center political parties.

There have been a number of domestic issues on which the views of these minorities have diverged from those of the respective majorities: thus Latinos have been less supportive of pro-choice (i.e., legalized abortion) than Anglos (Cain and Kiewiet 1984); and Maghrebis have been more indifferent toward free choice in education, that is, the private parochial schools, than the general French population. Although both the Latinos and Maghrebis are more secularized than their ethnic *confrères* in Latin America and North Africa, respectively, the vestigial religious sensitivity has been important enough to make a difference. In both cases, there have been two domestic issues on which these minorities have taken positions at variance with those of the majority: language and naturalization. Latinos have tended to favor bilingualism, that is, state support of the Spanish language as an additional medium of instruction to English in public schools and as a language of choice for voting and commerce, and Maghrebis have favored governmental subsidization of instruction in Arabic.

With respect to foreign policy, too, there are elements of divergence. Both minorities have been more sympathetic toward the Third World and more critically sensitive toward their countries' imperialist behavior than the majorities. Maghrebis have been more tolerant of the price-gouging behavior of OPEC and more critical of Israel than of the Arab states on the Middle East conflict, although in this instance the Maghrebis have been more closely identified with the government position than has the French public at large. To the extent that Latinos have been concerned with foreign policy--and according to some scholars that concern has not been large (De la Garza 1985)--Latinos have been much more critical of U.S. government policies regarding Latin America, and especially Central America, than the average American. However, on this issue the Latino community has been polarized: the Cuban immigrants and their offspring, and the more recent political refugees from Nicaragua, who are overwhelmingly middle class and anti-Communist, have pushed for a hard line against the Castro and Sandinista regimes (Richardson

1986). Both the Latino and the Maghrebi minorities have favored more generous immigration laws, more flexible approaches to the regularization of the status of illegal immigrants, quicker and easier naturalization, and equal treatment of naturalized citizens. On this issue, France has been more liberal than the United States, in particular since the installation of the Mitterrand presidency. Dual citizenship has been more readily accepted in France than in the United States; moreover, under laws passed in 1981, the stigma of second-class citizenship has been removed from naturalized citizens: they can now run for any political office, including the presidency of the republic. Such liberality seems paradoxical, in view of the widely accepted reference in France to "immigrants" (*immigrés*) or "foreigners" (*étrangers*) (Grillo 1985) rather than, as in the United States, "minorities."

ETHNICITY AND LANGUAGE

The public at large in both the United States and France has considered a common language a major ingredient in the glue that bonds a diverse society. Hence, support for bilingual education has not been overwhelming in either country. It was widely believed that immigrants as well as indigenous ethnic minorities would opt quickly for the majority language in recognition of its intrinsic superiority and utility. In the United States bilingualism does, however, have a certain historical legitimacy: In the first half of the nineteenth century, laws in Pennsylvania were published in German and English; in 1849, a California statute provided that "all laws, decrees, and . . . regulations . . . shall be published in English and Spanish"; and until 1867, Louisiana published its laws in French and English (*Harvard Law Review* 1987). In the early twentieth century, the Supreme Court struck down several attempts by state legislatures to prohibit the teaching of school subjects in any language other than English (Meyer v. Nebraska 262 U.S. 390 1923); and basing its action on the "equal protection" clause of the Constitution, the Voting Rights Act incorporated a provision forbidding states to interfere in the citizens' participation in voting on the grounds of inability to understand English in its 1975 expansion. In 1968, the Bilingual Education Act was passed, providing federal financial assistance for local bilingual projects, including courses in English as a second language (San Miguel 1984). The American Ethnic Heritage Act of 1972, the Equal Education Opportunities Act, and subsequent laws passed on the federal and state levels and sanctioned by the Supreme Court (Lau v. Nichols 1974), protected the rights of ethnic minorities to the use of their own language. By 1980, 500,000 non-English speakers, most of them Latinos, are said to have benefited from these measures (*Time* 1980).

In the United States, the declarations periodically issued by state legislatures that English is the official language have had little more than symbolic value. In the Hexagon, by contrast, the French language has been "official" since 1539, when François I promulgated the Ordinance of Villiers-Cotterets, which required that all judicial acts be published in the language of Ile-de-France. Since then (and in particular since the Third Republic), the purity and the uniform use of the French language have been promoted by the national public school system inaugurated in the 1880s by the Ferry laws, by the Académie Française; by a number of voluntary associations and ministerial advisory councils "for the defense of the French language," by decrees mandating the use of French in scientific activities supported by the government, and by the appointment of a secretary of state for concerns of French-speaking communities (*francophonie*). Until the last decade or so, the use of any language other than French as a medium of instruction or public administration was discouraged, forbidden, and often punished--except in the case of ethnic minorities who were not expected to remain in France, for example, the children of Polish industrial workers in the interwar period who were given governmentally financed supplementary instruction in the Polish language (Malet 1987, 35).

The French government's preoccupation with language is a reflection of the fact that the humanistically educated have long dominated the French political elite, and this preoccupation is part of a long tradition of the state's role as custodian of the country's culture. The contrasting U.S. official indifference regarding the purity, correct usage, and development of the English language must be attributed to a number of factors: the decentralization of responsibility for education under the federal system, the importance of the market in matters of culture, and the non-humanistic (and non-intellectual) background of the American political elite, exemplified in no small measure by the relatively modest literacy of many U.S. presidents.

Yet curiously, public policies in the post-1980 period have not corresponded to these traditions. In France, cultural and linguistic pluralism has come to be increasingly tolerated by the official authorities and--since the advent of a Socialist government in 1981--affirmed by such measures as the legalization of private radio stations, many of which broadcast in ethnic minority languages (including Radio Beur, an Arabic-language station in Paris with a powerful transmitter); bilingual street signs in regions heavily populated by ethnic minorities; government subsidization of instruction in regional ethnic languages; and even the permission to use these languages in registry offices, banks, and the courts (Safran 1985). What has been most relevant for Algerian immigrants has been a relaxation of requirements in recent legislation and in current legislative proposals regarding the mastery of the French language for candidates for naturalization. Conversely, in the United States the campaign to make the English language the only official one has been spreading from state to state.

There are simple explanations for this paradox. In France, bilingual policies do not carry a great risk, notwithstanding the arguments of dogmatic

Gaullists, conservative newspapers such as *Figaro*, and right-wing political formations that any concession to minority languages threatens the embattled French language and weakens its resistance to U.S. cultural imperialism (Lagorce 1982). Official bilingualism extends by preference to those languages that are "native" to the Hexagon, that have been demoted to the status of peasant dialects, that have a steadily declining number of speakers, that do not benefit from an infusion of foreign cultural-linguistic support, and that do not threaten the dominance of French: Alsatian, Basque, Breton, Corsican, and Occitan. Some French intellectuals want to extend bilingual support to Arabic; others, among them those harboring a professional interest in or a romantic fascination with Islam, even propose a dual-language track of education for French public schools and have even suggested that indigenous "Gallic" French pupils learn Arabic (Berque 1985). Still others want Arabic to be an alternative language of instruction for Maghrebis in order to foster Maghrebi cultural ghettoization, a diaspora sentiment, and a "myth of return." But in the view of most cultural pluralists, bilingualism--to the extent that it is furthered at all--is not intended for Maghrebis, nor, for that matter, other non-territorially based (*communautaire*) minorities, but rather for the indigenous, regionally concentrated ethnics. As a case in point, the National Council for Regional Languages and Cultures, which was established in 1985 to promote cultural-linguistic pluralism, had only one North African (a Berber, not an Arab) representative among its more than forty members. In any case, that Council did not meet under the Gaullist government of Chirac.

In the United States, no great need had been felt to protect the position of English in relation to the languages spoken by minorities that entered the country between the mid-nineteenth and the early twentieth centuries: German, Italian, Yiddish, and Japanese. But there has been a growing fear that English is being threatened by the Spanish language, whose speakers have been multiplying rapidly--as a consequence not only of natural increase but also of continued massive immigration: Unlike France, which froze large-scale legal immigration in the mid-1970s and made illegal immigration more difficult, the United States continues to let thousands of Latino immigrants into the country legally (in particular under the Immigration Reform and Control Act of 1986) and lacks adequate means to prevent illegal immigration. However, it is unclear how the "U.S. English" laws can be implemented and how the spread of Spanish can be halted--in view of the fact that Spanish is the most frequently selected foreign language in American schools. The significance of the legislation in question is, therefore, more symbolic than practical. The displacement of Spanish by English among Latinos is a gradual and voluntary matter: it is largely a consequence of their increasing acceptance and their insertion into the U.S. social and economic mainstream. The symbolism of the legislation may, however, have an opposite, and unintended, consequence: it may sharpen the resentment of Latinos and enhance their ethnocultural consciousness, including maintenance of Spanish.

The spread and use of minority languages are influenced not only by government policies but also by socioeconomic developments. Here a comparison of France and the United States reveals a contradictory situation: In France under Chirac the partial degovernmentalization of culture, a policy under which the support of libraries, theaters, art, and the mass media would become increasingly the responsibility of private patrons and market forces, has led to a more intensive use of French (if not English) and a corresponding neglect or reduced use of ethnic minority languages, including Arabic. In contrast, the increased official interest in the legitimation of English in the United States has been occurring in step with a rapidly growing use of Spanish on radio and television and in advertising and product labeling.

ETHNICITY AND NATIONAL IDENTITY

Some two decades ago, a growing number of U.S. social scientists began to question both the feasibility and the desirability of the melting pot. They wondered whether the American cultural pressure cooker, while producing loyal U.S. citizens dedicated to common political values, did not also produce the kind of homogeneity that made for boredom and undermined creativity. To some, the embrace of cultural pluralism resulted from the conviction that political consensus could easily co-exist with ethnoculturally diverse interests; to others, that embrace was little more than a romantic nostalgia--born of a disenchantment with the dry, functionally based social relations of industrial civilization--for the warmth of an old-fashioned (and idealized) community. To still others, it was a manifestation of political realism; a recognition of the fact that millions of inhabitants of the United States wanted to be recognized as Americans *and* as Blacks or Hispanics.

As was pointed out at the beginning of this essay, a similar questioning has occurred in France, due largely to the presence of a large Maghrebi community, many of whose members, despairing of the prospects of being melted into standard French men and women, have insisted on being both French *and* Maghrebi. Whereas only a generation ago the existence of minorities was denied, it is now acknowledged. Whereas French society was once described as culturally homogeneous (if politically dissensual), it is increasingly seen as culturally varied (if politically consensual). Whereas the French nation was once depicted as one and indivisible, it is now viewed as pluralistic. There is no doubt that institutional, economic, intellectual, and social pluralism as well as a pluralism of elite structures and lifestyles have been growing and that the ethnic diversification of French society has contributed significantly to that development. However, there is no consensus about how this diversity should affect the relationship between nation and state. It is in this respect that France and the United States have differed sharply.

To put the difference simply: the United States is a largely functional construct, superimposed upon civil society without dominating it, whereas the French state is an awesome, virtually omnipotent entity, developed by absolute monarchs before there was a French nation. Once created and centralized, the state helped to shape the nation, to dominate it, and to define its culture. Whereas the American state has largely confined itself to political mobilization-- to the use of constitution, flag, rhetoric, and socioeconomic opportunities in order to secure the civic commitment of its inhabitants--the French state has been a cultural mobilizer: it has equated political loyalty with undivided cultural allegiance. Whereas once that allegiance was equated with religious, that is, Catholic, orthodoxy, it came later to be equated with cultural-linguistic monism. The fusion of *état* and *nation* has implied a fusion of citizenship and nationality. There is no French equivalent for the "hyphenated American." Immigrant as well as indigenous ethnic minorities "are asked to abandon their differential claims. . . other than their customs, which they may maintain . . . privately" (Tibon-Cornillot 1984, 41). But in a country in which the state has taken a strong hand in elevating one majority culture and delegitimating or suppressing other cultures and where voluntary associations have by turns been outlawed, officially recognized, and subsidized, the private promotion of minority cultures is virtually impossible. Because "France is dominated by the non-recognition, on an explicit level, of cultural differences" (Tibon-Cornillot 1984, 42), one customarily speaks of a French person of Italian, Breton, Jewish, Corsican, or Maghrebi "origins," *d'origine italienne, bretonne, juive, corse,* but not of his complex, actual, and culturally meaningful identity, *appartenance.* The remark of President Mitterrand that "we are French [and] our ancestors [were] Gauls, and Romans, and a little German, a little Jewish, a little Italian, a little Spanish, increasingly Portuguese . . . and I ask myself if we are already a little Arab [as well]" (Solé 1987) was intended to be flattering to the Maghrebis, but it made no concession to cultural pluralism.

There are French intellectuals and politicians who would favor a disjunction of state and nation and, as a corollary, of citizenship and nationality and who speak of the easy association of two parallel forms of citizenship: the political and the cultural (Colin 1984; 1986; Gallissot 1986; Kettane, 1986). Some of them look upon the United States--and the heterogeneous nature of its society--as a model for a functional approach to national identity in France; they romanticize the apparent ease with which a modern, culturally fused society is continually being created out of a diversity of various ethnocultural strains (Malet 1987; Cazemajou and Martin 1983). Others view the United States as a counter-model: one in which the presence of millions of Latinos with their distinct culture leads to the bastardization of American national culture, if not ultimately to the disintegration of the state. Still others point out that whereas Latino culture can be comfortably fused with the culture of the majority in the United States just as Italian and Breton cultures have complemented the majority culture in France, Maghrebi culture cannot co-exist with that culture: rather than providing a valuable ingredient into any future French culture, the culture of the Maghrebis pollutes, disfigures, and indeed negates it (Club de l'Horloge 1985; LeGallou and Club de l'Horloge 1985). Moreover, there is a systemic difference between the two countries. In the United States, the federal nature of the government makes for a decentralization of the minority problem in that it permits each state to determine its own approaches to assimilation and accommodation, such that a pluralism of policies contributes to the maintenance of a plural society in the country as a whole. In France, by contrast, there is a systemic contradiction, *mixte contradictoire* (Tibon-Cornillot 1984, 45): an increasingly pluricultural society that continues to be governed by a unitary state.

In both countries there are voices emanating from the dominant elements of society that express fear that the number of Maghrebis in France and Latinos in the United States is now so large that it threatens the respective country's political unity. But in neither country is that threat a serious one. In France, the threat of terrorism and economic extortion is ever present, but few Maghrebis are involved in it. The Maghrebi population is not growing so fast as it did during the 1960s and early 1970s, especially since legal immigration was stopped in the aftermath of the oil crisis. The Maghrebis already in the country are geographically dispersed, and there is no adjacent Arab country to which Maghrebis could attach themselves and hence no danger of separatism. In the United States, separatism is, theoretically, a more distinct possibility, but the government would not tolerate a physical detachment of any part of its territory. In any case, it is highly unlikely that Latinos would work for such a detachment, since most of them are already too Americanized and too habituated to U.S. political values and economic advantages to be seduced by Mexico. The prospect of the maintenance of the Spanish language by the Latinos (albeit a partially Americanized form of it) and of the Arabic language by the Maghrebis (albeit partly *francisé*) on a more than vestigial or "peasant" level is not unrealistic because each has a respectable literary tradition, a cultural elite, and a home breeding ground outside the United States and France that may function as continued sources of cultural infusion. However, the Islamic emphasis of Arab elites sent from abroad has a diminishing appeal for the secularizing Maghrebi working class, and the relationship between Latin American intellectuals and native U.S. Latinos, especially Mexican Americans, is not close. The possibility of the establishment of bilingual regions in the United States is greater than in France, but it is counteracted by the dominant position of English and the cultural attrition of second- and third-generation Latinos, and especially of the Latino elite, a situation that makes most Americans--except, perhaps, in Florida and the Southwest--relatively relaxed about the number of speakers of Spanish.

CONCLUSION

This preliminary comparative study suggests that there is a certain convergence between the United States and France regarding the condition of ethnic minorities: whereas in France one finds a greater receptivity to the idea of a plural society, in the United States one detects a growing concern with the cultural impact of minorities, and in particular Latinos, on society. The study also suggests that, on balance, the combined historical, sociopolitical, institutional, and ideological context of the United States is more favorable than that of France for the survival of ethnic pluralism, and hence that the ethnocultural future of the Latinos is brighter than that of the Maghrebis.

There are a number of unanswered questions. Will an enlargement of the role of Latinos in the political process and more significant public policy gains serve to escalate their ethnocultural demands in the future, or to reduce them? To what extent does the cultural bias of a society, and especially of its elite, affect the particularistic cultural demands of ethnic minorities? Does the humanist tradition of French society and of its elite make it more, or less, resistant to the impact of other cultures than the technological emphasis of American culture? To what extent will the working-class condition of Maghrebis enhance their ethnoreligious consciousness or weaken it--by transforming their Islamic orientation from a theological to a sociological one? Will the partial breakup of the barrio and the *embourgeoisement* of an increasing number of Latinos contribute to an interest in Hispanic higher culture or, on the contrary, leave only a fossilized folklore? Does the presence of another large ethnic minority that is racially more distinct and less likely to "melt" into the majority enhance, or reduce, Latino or Maghrebi ethnic consciousness? Will the growth of institutional pluralism and the enlargement of the civil rights of the individual lead to an enlarged ethnic consciousness, increased ethnic mobilization, and a greater assertion of demands for community rights and hence contribute to the development of ethnoplural society, or do the opposite? The answers to these questions go beyond the limited scope of this chapter; they might, however, emerge from an extension of the universe of comparison beyond the two complex ethnic groups and the two countries dealt with here.

Part II

Minorities, Politics, and the State

5

Did Minority Gains Begin to Disappear in the 1980s? A Four Nation Study
D. John Grove

Did the economic gains of ethnic minorities from 1950 to 1970 begin to disappear in the 1980s in the advanced industrial societies? This chapter examines the argument that between-group differentials reemerged in the 1980s because of a lack of political support for equal opportunity strategies, which have contracted sharply in recent years. One reason for this, I believe, is that those people who are paying a disproportionate share of the social costs are now beginning to resist any further reform measures. But who has gained and lost during the post-World War II period of economic expansionism and social reform? Unfortunately, there are no systematic comparative studies that have assessed the social costs of reform in advanced industrial societies.[1] Therefore, we must turn to theory as a starting point for a more in-depth analysis. The two most influential approaches--the so-called cultural mobility and cultural reproduction arguments--do provide opposing predictions about the likelihood of ethnic change and who gains or loses from it.

In order to assess which theory fits ethnic trends, I have chosen four economically advanced multiethnic societies that have implemented social policies designed to equalize opportunity structures (both welfare state and affirmative action varieties), and have published ethnic data over time. The countries and groups are: Canada (British, French, German, Italian and Ukrainian), Israel (Ashkenazic and Sephardic Jews; unfortunately, Arab data have not been consistently published over at least a fifteen-year period), New Zealand (European and Maori) and the United States (Black, Chicano, Chinese, Indian, Japanese, and White). This sample includes most of the industrialized countries that have systematically collected ethnic socioeconomic data during the post-World War II period.

If ethnic differentials have declined in the 1950 to 1970 period and then reemerged in the 1980s, then the question is whether the reversal in trends is due to the uneven social costs of those changes. In order to assess this argument, I will evaluate the educational, occupational, and income trends in the four sampled countries and what groups have gained or lost by those changes. Socioeconomic data from 1950 to 1980 for each group have been collected and will be the basis of the analysis.

CONTENDING POSITIONS

The Mobility Model

In the 1950s, governments in the four sampled countries began to subscribe to equal opportunity strategies as a way of providing the education necessary for increasingly more difficult jobs and as a method of weakening the ascriptive allocation of roles that limits aspiring ethnic minorities from converting their educational resources into socioeconomic mobility (Erikson, Goldthorpe, and Portocarero 1982; Lenski 1966; Tyree, Semyonov, and Hodge 1979). The core adaption process within the mobility model is assimilation: as ethnic groups acquire educational skills and become more occupationally mobile, they will economically advance (Gordon 1964, 77; Park 1921, 3). Educational systems attempt to equalize opportunities for all groups by molding different ethnic backgrounds to accept the beliefs and values of the dominant group (Key 1963, 316; Merton 1949, 117).

The mobility approach makes few explicit statements about the matching of jobs to persons. Once individuals are acculturated into the mainstream through education, occupational and economic mobility is then mainly determined by family background, personal characteristics, and levels of educational attainment for all ethnic groups--the status attainment model (Sewell and Hauser 1975).

The fruits of a more competitive, assimilated, market-orientated system should accrue to employers because they now maximize profits from a larger labor pool where well-educated disfavored groups now enter previously excluded jobs (Becker 1957). This results in unequal beneficiaries within the dominant group (employers gain and workers lose) and proportional benefits to those educated discriminated groups that can take full advantage of altered opportunity structures.[2]

The Reproduction Model

Theories of cultural reproduction differ from mobility approaches by claiming that the main function of any educational system is the reproduction of the culture and social values of the dominant groups in society. They also differ from Marxian theories in that they contend that the reproduction of social hierarchies has become more dependent on cultural assets than on inherited wealth. The cultural reproduction thesis assumes that schools not only reinforce the dominant groups' culture by turning it into a form of capital (cultural capital), but the content of school curriculum reflects the knowledge of the dominant group (Bernstein 1971). This creates problems for minorities because there is a discontinuity between home and school, and the rewards are based on individuals' participation in the culture and social values of the dominant group (Bourdieu 1977).

Dominant groups who inherit cultural assets through primary socialization capitalize on their cultural resources by exchanging it for educational credentials and desirable jobs, and in turn, transmit it to their offspring. Educational systems, and more specifically teachers, play a critical role in encouraging and helping the inheritors of cultural resources, while weeding out those groups whose relationship to status culture is more distant. Thus education simply certifies the cultural advantages of the dominant group. In order to legitimate this process, equal opportunity strategies are designed to spread education so that teachers can independently evaluate members of disadvantaged groups to see if they have the requisite cultural goods (Murphy 1982).

Cultural capital thus becomes a major factor in entwining the student into social networks that facilitate both the getting of a job and advancement within it (Bourdieu and Boltanski 1978; Granovetter 1974). In order to obtain managerial, well-paid primary jobs a student must acquire the appropriate educational credentials and cultural stock. Then entry ports between better-paid primary jobs and subsistence-level secondary jobs become convenient cultural screening places where monopolistic closure, through rules governing occupancy of jobs, is used by inheritors of cultural capital to segmentalize the labor force (Edwards 1979; Grove 1986). The consequence of this cultural screening is that ethnic minorities become disproportionately represented in low-wage, labor-intensive jobs (Bonacich 1973; Haex and Wolf. 1976).

This means that ethnic inequalities will persist, because the inheritors of high culture will seek to limit the privileged access to high-paying primary jobs to those who have acquired cultural capital and will allow dominant-group workers to monopolize the supply and recruitment of labor (Bonacich 1978). Thus cultural elites and dominant-group workers benefit by the perpetuation of the three-tiered system.

In sum, the difference between the two approaches lies in the direction of change and who benefits from it. The cultural mobility thesis contends that anti-discriminatory policies will help dominant-group employers and educated non-dominant groups, thus promoting greater equality between ethnic groups. Cultural reproduction theories, on the other hand, argue that equal opportunity strategies simply reinforce the advantages of the dominant group (both employers and workers) and restrict the upward mobility of minorities, thus perpetuating the ethnic division of labor. In the former model, dominant-group workers are the major losers, while in the latter case, it is all those minorities who do not acquire cultural capital that lose.

EVIDENCE FROM THE FOUR CASES

The sample includes Canada and its bilingual/bicultural policy of supporting parity for English and French speakers and equality of education for all ethnic groups; the United States and its Civil Rights Act, which forbids discrimination in employment and public accommodations; and two of the more successful welfare state systems in the Middle East (Israel) and Oceania (New Zealand). In reviewing the literature on socioeconomic mobility in the four countries, we found evidence that interethnic inequalities have declined, but apart from the United States, and one economic study, there are no studies that have identified the beneficiaries from these egalitarian trends. Although these four cases are not identical, the underlying question of whether redressing unequal ethnic wealth is a zero-sum structure (where one group's gains can mean another's loss) is sufficiently similar to warrant comparative analysis.

The most comprehensive studies are in the United States, where there is a lively debate about how effective affirmative action programs have been in elevating the economic position of Black and Hispanic Americans (Darity and Myers 1980; Farley 1984; Freeman 1973; Hoffman 1979; Lazear 1979; Smith and Welch 1978; Reich 1981). A number of studies show that although discrimination is still the major cause of the lack of Black and Hispanic mobility (Duncan 1967; Lieberson 1980; Nelson and Tienda 1985), there has been a moderation of societal discrimination that has improved the chances for societal mobility by the well-educated Black, Hispanic, and Oriental American population (Bonacich and Modell 1980; Featherman and Hauser 1976; Farley 1984; Hirschman and Wong 1981). A more recent study shows that Black advancement from 1979 to 1984 began to slip and Hispanics were worse off in 1984 compared with 1967 (Grove and Hoshino 1989). Reich (1981) also disputes that these trends will be long lasting and argues that workers will be the major beneficiary of any short-term decline in discriminatory practices.

In Canada, under the bilingual/bicultural program, French Canadians were the first group to receive discriminatory compensation, while the other three major ethnic groups (Germans, Italians, and Ukrainians) are protected by anti-discriminatory legislation. Studies show that there has been a substantial reduction in the income gap between French and English workers from 1961 to 1981 (Boulet 1980; Boulet and Levalee 1983; Lacroix and Vaillaincourt 1981).

Grove and Hoshino (1989), on the other hand argue that these gains began to disappear from 1979 to 1983.

In the two welfare state systems, there are also some encouraging signs of greater ethnic equality. Studies that have evaluated the effectiveness of the Israeli welfare policy of gradually assimilating immigrant groups show that the income gap widened between the two major ethnic groups--Jews from Asia or Africa and Jews of European or American origin--during the 1950s and early 1960s but declined in the 1970s (Remba 1973; Semyonov and Kraus 1983) and then began to increase again in the 1980s (Grove and Hoshino 1989).

In reviewing a similar policy in New Zealand of assimilating the Maori population into the European culture, we could find only two studies that had evaluated ethnic income differentials over time, and they show that urban Maoris have made some progress between 1951 and 1966 (Collette and O'Malley 1974, 150), but in 1980 some of those gains disappeared (Brosnan 1982; Brosnan and Hill 1983; Grove and Hoshino 1989).

METHOD

The two indexes that have traditionally measured income inequality between groups, the Theil index and Lieberson's (1976) net difference measure, cannot disaggregate by percentiles to show the gains and losses of particular income groups. The Grove-Hannum (1986) measure, however, is sensitive to decomposed gradations of distance in group comparisons, and can therefore be used to measure the gains and losses by percentile. The Grove-Hannum measure is expressed in two parts, an intergroup inequality measure that is simply a ratio of mean incomes (it compares the distributions in an average sense through the ratio of mean incomes) and a crossover measure (the difference between a distance-type measure that detects any discrepancies between two distributions, and an inequality-type measure) which can determine the gains and losses of particular income groups when the cumulative distributional curves intersect.[3]

The distributional benefits within groups will have to be analyzed by two different measures. The relative gains and losses within non-dominant groups should be judged in comparison with those comparable income groups within dominant groups that they are trying to catch up with. More specifically, I will use the change in the Grove-Hannum inequality scores in order to measure the magnitude and direction of gain/loss by a particular group. A positive sign of inequality means a loss and the negative sign means the gain for the disadvantaged groups.[4] I decided to adopt Reich's (1981, 120-121) threefold division of the top 10 percent, middle 50 percent, and bottom 40 percent as our criteria for income groups. Since there are no external reference groups to assess the gain and losses within dominant groups, I will simply use the Gini coefficient as an overall measure of income concentration. The Gini coefficient indicates the extent to which any one segment within the dominant community is paying a disproportionate share of the costs of change.

I have collected a reliable income data set from census and government publications in the four multiethnic societies (see Grove and Hoshino 1989, for a description of some the data). Census classifications allocate individuals to their respective categories on the basis of their preferred cultural affiliation or common ancestry (self-classification).

In measuring educational changes between groups I applied Lieberson's (1976) index of net difference ND, a measure of ordinal differentiation, to educational attainment for each group.[5] ND scores indicate the degree of differentiation between two opposing probabilities of group or rank advantage. The educational attainment data is comprised of primary (1-8 years), secondary (9-12 years) and higher education (13 + years) for each group over four ten-year time periods--1950, 1960, 1970, 1980 (see Grove 1985 for a description of data).

In measuring between-group occupational differentials, I decided to use Gibbs's (1965) modification of Duncan's dissimilarity index.[6] The absolute standardized measure of differentiation (ASMD) controls for structural effects by treating all occupations as if they were of equal size. As a measure of occupational differentiation it can be interpreted as the proportion of individuals who would have to change occupations in order for the ethnicity ratio to be the same in all occupations. The occupational data on the fifteen ethnic groups is taken from census surveys from 1950 to 1980 and is comprised of the number of individuals in professional, managerial, clerical, sales service, agriculture, and production jobs.

FINDINGS

1950-1980

Has education restructured the ethnic division of labor in industrial societies? Table 5.1 shows that in most cases educational (NDs) and occupational (ASMDs) differentials have declined over time, with a few instances of ethnic leapfrogging. Oriental Americans have overtaken the educational attainment levels of American whites (ND scores move from + to -). The average ND scores for the eleven pairwise comparisons steadily declined from .22 in 1950 to .18 in 1980, and the average ASMD scores decreased from .331 in 1950 to .222 in 1980. Now the question is whether this reduction in occupational segregation is related to increased educational attainment levels of minorities. When we calculated the educational and occupational changes between groups in the periods 1950-1960, 1960-1970, and 1970-1980 and then pooled these change variables (see Bornschier, Chase-Dunn, and Rubinson 1978, 659 and Hannum and Young 1977 for a discussion of pooled cross-sectional designs), we found a statistically significant relationship at the .05 level between educational changes in time t-1 ($\triangle$NDT-1) and occupational mobility between groups ten years later ($\triangle$ASMDt, r = .41, n = 32). In other words, increased educational attainment in industrial societies is related to mobility within the ethnic division of labor.

There are two cases however, where the ethnic division of labor has become more hierarchical and specialized. Educational advancement of New Zealand Maoris has not kept pace with that of their European counterparts (NDs have increased), and consequently, from the period 1966-1980 upward occupational mobility for Maoris slowed down (ASMDs scores rose). Europeans are increasingly overrepresented in professional and managerial jobs, while Maoris are overconcentrated in production sectors. Similarly, Mexican

Table 5.1 Educational and Occupational Differentials

| | Indices of Dissimilarity | | | | | | | |
	Education NDs				Occupations ASMDs			
Canada	1950	1960	1970	1980	1950	1960	1970	1980
French/British	.26	.24	.22	.09	.182	.138	.062	.062
German/British	.21	.16	.10	.26	.292	.162	.138	.106
Italian/British	.26	.24	.19	.03	.310	.405	.261	.192
Ukrainian/British	.30	.22	.17	.04	.316	.201	.151	.106
Israel		1960	1970	1980		1958	1970	1980
Oriental/Western		.44	.38	.31		.311	.299	.200
New Zealand	1956	1966	1970	1980	1956	1966	1976	1980
Maori/European	.16	.18	.23	.31	.460	.372	.372	.408
United States	1950	1960	1970	1980	1950	1960	1970	1980
Indian/White	.26	.31	.17	.26	.424	.382	.296	.198
Black/White	.22	.22	.17	.15	.393	.430	.397	.347
Chicano/White	.27	.30	.23	.26	.305	.301	.330	.348
Chinese/White	.08	-.16	-.12	-.11	.348	.292	.220	.275
Japanese/White	.18	-.07	-.08	-.13	.282	.218	.136	.196

Americans have not progressed educationally, which has meant limited upward occupational mobility (ASMDs increased). By 1980, Chicanos were more disproportionately represented in unskilled labor than in 1950.

To what extent have these social changes affected income mobility? Table 5.2 shows the income inequality scores by year (I) broken down into lower, middle and upper income groups (LI, MI, UI), the crossover factor (C) in the overall pairwise comparisons, and the Gini scores (G) for each ethnic group. The data show that the income gap between groups for each of the four industrial societies has declined (I scores are reduced), which has had a redistributive effect within groups. In the case of Canada and Israel, the income convergence between groups has had an equalizing effect (Gini scores have declined) within both dominant and non-dominant groups, while in the United States and New Zealand the reduction in income inequalities has been unevenly distributed within all groups (Ginis have risen). Four groups--German and Ukrainian Canadians, and Chinese and Japanese Americans--have overtaken (the I scores go from + to -) the economically more advanced position of the British Canadians and American whites. In all four cases the income crossovers started at the bottom and then spread to the top and middle categories, although in the case of the Ukrainian Canadians, in 1980 the overlap of incomes occurred only at the bottom.

To determine whether the equalization of income between groups is related to changes in educational and occupational differentials, I pooled the cross-sectional data and ran partial correlations. The correlations show that changes in the ethnic occupational hierarchy at time t-1 ($\blacktriangle$ASMDt-1) are unrelated to changes in ethnic income inequalities ten years later, t(r$\blacktriangle$ASMDt-1. $\blacktriangle$It $= .22$, N $= 32$). However, when I correlate changes in educational attainment between groups in time t-1($\blacktriangle$NDt-1), controlling for changes in occupational mobility in time t-1, with changes in income mobility between groups ten years later we find a robust relationship (r $\blacktriangle$NDt-1. It $\blacktriangle$ASMDt-1 $= .48$, p $< .01$, n $= 32$). Thus increased educational attainment levels of minorities are related to subsequent ethnic income changes between groups.

I can now examine who has benefitted from these changes. If we simply subtract the pairwise I scores (in Table 5.2) in 1950-1960 from those in 1980 for the three income groups (top, middle and bottom) and then divide by the population percentile, we will then have a comparable measure of how each income group has progressed.[7] When I disaggregated these overall I scores, I found that upper-income minorities in Canada and Israel, and the Oriental Americans all made two to four times the average gains (for example, UI Francophones are calculated the following way: -.14/-,.039=3.5). A different style of catch-up is experienced in the United States with the middle-income Blacks, Chicanos, and Indian Americans who have made the most gains (one to two times the average gains), with upper-income groups in fact losing ground. In New Zealand, it is the lower-to-middle-income Maoris who have made

Table 5.2 Income Inequality between and within Groups

		Is	LI	MI	UI	C	Gₓ	G_y
			Between Groups				Within Groups	

		Is	LI	MI	UI	C	G_x	G_y
Canada								
British/French	1960	.0569	.0028	.0393	.0147	0.0	.390	.371
	1970	.0352	.0033	.0218	.0101	0.0	.412	.405
	1980	.0171	.0022	.0163	.0007	5.2	.348	.353
▲I, 1960-80 =		-.0398	-.0026	-.023	-.014			
British/German	1960	.0261	-.0022	.0187	.0097	8.7	.390	.369
	1970	-.0401	-.0060	-.0267	-.0074	0.0	.412	.407
	1980	-.0087	-.0071	-.0016	.0000	2.7	.348	.331
▲I, 1960-80 =		-.0348	-.0049	-.0599	-.0097			
British/Italian	1960	.0611	-.0038	.0419	.0231	6.3	.390	.343
	1970	-.1151	-.0258	-.0771	-.0122	0.0	.412	.367
	1980	.0052	-.0021	.0069	.0003	22.0	.348	.346
▲I, 1960-80 =		-.0559	-.0017	-.0350	-.0228			
British/Ukrainian	1960	.0353	-.0024	.0238	.0140	7.1	.390	.361
	1970	-.1376	-.0155	-.0973	-.0249	0.0	.412	.404
	1980	-.0047	-.0064	.0016	.0002	27.4	.348	.334
▲I, 1960-80 =		-.04	-.004	-.0222	-.0138			
Israel								
Western/Oriental	1960	.2412	.0407	.1504	.0501	0.0	.360	.357
	1970	.1039	.0163	.0679	.0197	0.0	.305	.298
	1980	.1122	.0188	.0804	.0129	0.0	.307	.309
▲I, 1960-80 =		-.129	-.0219	-.07	-.0372			
New Zealand								
European/Maori	1950	.1761	.0566	.1007	.0188	0.0	.221	.265
	1960	.1437	.0261	.0769	.0408	0.0	.353	.332
	1970	.0355	-.0119	.0321	.0152	20.2	.390	.330
	1980	.1198	.0262	.0671	.0264	0.0	.469	.484
▲I, 1950-80 =		-.0563	-.0304	-.0336	.0076			

Table 5.2 continued

		Is	LI	Between Groups MI	UI	C	Within Groups G_x	G_y
United States								
White/Black	1950	.2396	.0449	.1701	.0245	0.0	.405	.478
	1960	.3009	.0596	.2028	.0385	0.0	.348	.403
	1970	.2317	.0194	.1526	.0597	0.0	.491	.483
	1980	.1785	.0197	.1092	.0496			
▲I, 1950-80 =		-.0611	-.0252	-.0609	.0251			
White/Indian	1950	.4167	.0653	.2872	.0641	0.0	.405	.485
	1960	.3543	.0788	.2412	.0343	0.0	.348	.458
	1970	.2653	.0284	.1801	.0569	0.0	.475	.493
	1980	.1613	.0196	.0977	.0439	0.0	.491	.503
▲I, 1950-80 =		-.2554	-.0457	-.1895	.0202			
White/Chicano	1950	.2175	.0313	.1482	.0380	0.0	.405	.433
	1960	.1501	.0279	.1034	.0187	0.0	.348	.371
	1970	.1550	.0101	.1040	.0409	0.0	.475	.452
	1980	.1333	.0096	.0801	.0437	0.0	.491	.471
▲I, 1950-80 =		-.0842	-.0217	-.0681	.0057			
White/Chinese	1950	.0654	-.0050	.0559	.0145	7.7	.405	.381
	1960	.0603	.0134	.0481	-.0011	2.1	.348	.378
	1970	.0155	.0015	.0177	-.0037	1.5	.475	.485
	1980	-.0073	-.0017	-.0045	-.0010	2.5	.491	.489
▲I, 1950-80 =		-.0727	-.0033	-.0604	-.0155			
White/Japanese	1950	.0648	-.0004	.0496	.0156	6.5	.405	.386
	1960	.0004	-.0052	.0068	-.0012	48.6	.348	.340
	1970	-.0498	-.0092	-.0348	-.0058	0.0	.475	.456
	1980	-.0073	-.0017	-.0045	-.0010	2.6	.491	.489
▲I, 1950-80 =		-.0721	-.0013	-.0541	-.0146			

Notes: I=Intergroup inequality; LI=Bottom 40 percent; MI=Middle 50 percent; UI=Top 10 percent; C=Percentage of crossover between groups; G_x=Gini index for dominant groups; G_y=Gini index for minority groups.

Absolute change in income inequality (▲I)=I_t-I_t-1.   For example, ▲I for British/French = I_{80}-I_{60}. The average change for each upper, middle, and lower income group is divided by the population decile.   Thus ▲I for the bottom income group= ▲I in bottom 40%/4.

progress while the upper-income group also lost ground. Table 5.2 shows that most of the income gains within disadvantaged groups were made during the 1950-1970 period, and the next ten years show little progress for minorities. This, of course, is the time when political support for further social reform began to contract.

Now, if we compare these results with the within-group Gini scores (Gx and Gy in Table 5.2) we can then make some judgments about the social costs of these group gains for income classes within dominant groups. In the case of Canada, upper-income gains of ethnic minorities have not been at the expense of any income class within the dominant British group, since income concentration (Ginis) within the British community has diminished. Similarly, in Israel, no one income category within the Western Jews has paid a disproportionate share of the costs of the mobility of the upper-income Oriental Jews (Ginis for Western Jews declined). This is not the case for New Zealand and the United States where dominant-group Ginis have risen sharply. The median income ratios for both dominant New Zealand and Europeans and American whites shows that lower-to-middle-income groups within the dominant groups have suffered.

If little economic progress was made during the 1970-1980 period, then who had benefitted by the slowdown? To answer this question we must use more current, yearly data that take us beyond 1980. In Canada, Israel, and the United States, household and family income surveys are conducted every year on a limited number of ethnic groups,[8] and these give us some indication of the 1980 trends. Unfortunately though, the New Zealand census is the only ethnic income data that are published there.

I applied the Grove-Hannum (1986) measure to these income surveys and the overall results are decomposed into convergent and divergent periods in Table 5.3. In Canada the differences in family income between Francophone and Anglophone declined from 1960 to 1979, and then began to increase from 1980 to 1984. This reversal is mainly due to the lack of income gains by the top 10 percent of the Francophones ($I = .021/.004 = 5.2$.). This same group ten years earlier had been the major reason why French-speaking Canadians were beginning to catch up with their English counterparts. These results differ somewhat from Israel, where the reversal in differential trends between Western and Oriental Jews occurred in 1976, and the reason for this is the income slippage of middle-income Orientals (.027), and to some extent the bottom 40 percent (.018) between 1976 and 1982; these same groups made gains from 1967 to 1976. Upper-income Orientals, however, did make steady progress during the late 1970s and early 1980s (-.094).

In New Zealand the reversal in trends occurred between 1970 and 1980 when all three income groups within the Maori community failed to keep pace with the Europeans. Since upper-income Maoris made only marginal gains in the 1950-1970 period, this meant a substantial loss over the thirty year period.

Table 5.3 Intergroup Income Convergence and Divergence

	Overall Changes $\blacktriangle I$	Average Gains/Losses of Income Groups		
		$\blacktriangle$ Bottom 40%	$\blacktriangle$ Middle 50%	$\blacktriangle$ Top 10%
Canada: British French				
1969-79	-.033	-.0017	-.0382	-.128
1979-84	.004	.004	.0016	.021
Israel: Western/Oriental				
1967-76	-.141	-.027	-.1674	-.278
1976-82	.012	.018	.0274	-.098
New Zealand: Maori/European				
1950-70	-.1406	-.1712	-.1372	-.036
1970-80	.0848	.0952	.0700	.112
United States:				
(a) White/Black				
1967-78	-.021	-.0145	-.0248	-.031
1978-84	.017	.0065	.024	.026
(b) White/Hispanic				
1972-79	-.0226	.0063	-.0252	-.0915
1979-84	.0227	.0198	.0186	.0539

The steady decline in Black/white differentials in America also stopped in 1978, resulting in widening racial inequalities in the early 1980s. This is due to the lack of income mobility of the middle-to-upper-income Blacks. The more limited data on Hispanics shows that they have not been able to make any gains on whites from 1979 to 1984, mainly due to the losses of the upper-income groups.

CONCLUSION

Despite the achievements of ethnic minorities in higher education and occupational mobility, which have enabled them to make relative income gains from 1950 to 1970, ethnic income differentials have emerged in the early part of the 1980s. The reason for the fall and rise of ethnic differentials varies from country to country. The beneficiaries within those minorities who have made substantial progress in catching up with dominant groups from 1950 to 1970 are the same income groups that lost ground in the 1980s. In Canada the upper-income Francophones have caused the rise in the wage gap; in Israel, it is the middle-income Oriental Jews who have suffered; in the United States, the relative decline of American Blacks is due to middle-to-upper-income groups; while in New Zealand all segments of the Maori community slipped. Thus, this evidence does not support the neoclassical thesis that employers are the first to benefit or suffer by group progress, nor does it support the Marxian thesis that workers will be the beneficiaries or sufferers of group changes.

Also, this evidence does not support the contention that the reappearance of ethnic inequalities in the 1980s is due to the resistance by those income classes within dominant groups who have suffered form social reform measures. There are, of course, numerous reasons why inequalities have widened, and they appear to have little to do with the possible zero-sum structure of reform. Obviously, this complex process needs monitoring.

It is true that income inequalities in the 1980s were less than they were in the 1950-1960 period. This evidence, coupled with the gains of many of the upper-income groups, is supportive of the cultural mobility thesis. There is, however, a nagging question of whether these trends are simply two steps forward and one step backward. Or will the two steps forward affect too many entrenched class interests and therefore produce in the 1990s a further step backward? This question will have to wait for the published data in ten years.

Bad Politics and Bad Social Policy:
A Half-Century of Isolation
Gary Klass

Much of contemporary social welfare theory describes how American social welfare policies have been shaped by forces hostile to the interests of the poor and disadvantaged: a business elite that seeks to regulate social protest and labor markets (Piven and Cloward 1977), special interest groups such as the American Medical Association, a racist white middle class, a middle class that adheres to an anti-government political ideology (Wilensky 1975), or a middle class that eclectically endorses governmental programs targeted on groups with a positive social image (Rochefort 1986). It is true that such interests have resisted purposive social policy change designed to enhance social equality. It is also true that these forces have often prevailed and that under the Reagan administration they enjoyed something of a heyday. But this theory says little or nothing about the role and influence exercised by those who have represented the interests of the poor and disadvantaged.

The thesis of this chapter is that the self-interests, political beliefs, prejudices, and social images of those who aspire to defend the interests of the poor have shaped the most distinguishing and dysfunctional features of the American welfare state. The forces arrayed against the welfare state, I argue, have succeeded in large part because of the ineptitude of their opposition.

It is the tendency to define common citizenship interests as the narrow community interests that most clearly distinguish the American welfare state from that of most other industrial democracies. While other nations have assumed the burdens of the welfare state by establishing universal citizenship rights to minimum levels of health care, income security, employment security, and housing, American government assumes the same burdens--establishing the principle that it is proper for government to provide such benefits--without expanding the scope of citizenship rights. The result is an American pork-barrel welfare state that targets social welfare benefits to clientele groups rather than out of a respect for the rights and entitlements of citizenship. It is an arbitrary and capricious welfare system that is politically insecure and that does little to remedy the persistence of poverty while it fosters further isolation and disintegration.

The theories of two separate schools of social science thinking, one from sociology, the other from political science, provide the basis for a general interpretation of the causes and consequences of this uniquely American social policy pattern. On the political science side, the interpretation draws from the anti-pluralist theories of minority faction government and policy-making advanced by E. E. Schattschneider (1935, 1960), Grant McConnell (1953, 1966), and Theodore Lowi (1979). On the sociology side, it draws upon the integrationist theory of social welfare policy design of T. H. Marshall (1964), Richard M. Titmuss (1968, 1974), and Chaim Waxman (1983). The two schools share a critique of the pervasive fragmentation, decentralization, and disintegration of American social policy. Together, they provide a basis for an interpretation of the causes and consequences of the peculiarities of the American social welfare policy that differs substantially from conventional left, liberal, and conservative social welfare theory.[1]

For political scientists, the concern is primarily with the political institutions and processes that produce bad social policy. Schattschneider, McConnell, Lowi and others argue that undemocratic (though pluralist) political institutions typically subvert diffused public interests, preserve the status quo power arrangements of a multitude of special interest elites, and impede the formulation of comprehensive and effective social policy. In Lowi's interest-group-liberalism formulation, the primary mechanism of plural-elite control involves the delegation of public authority, through the enactment of ambiguous legislation by the Congress, to bureaucratic elites and congressional subcommittees that have been "captured" or co-opted by special interests. The politics of special-interest domination of the policy-making process is essentially a patronage politics that diverts the attention and resources of government away from broad and consequential redistributive social policy and emphasizes distributive pork-barrel benefits. Schattschneider argues that special interests seek to restrict the scope of political conflict by preventing the organization of countervailing interests and by keeping policy issues from exposure to the public arena.

The concerns of the sociologists focus more on the consequences than the causes of social policy and on the narrower realm of social welfare policy. The recurrent theme of Marshall and Titmuss is that the development of the welfare state in Europe has corresponded to a progressive articulation of expanded citizenship rights. The enactment, in the twentieth century, of comprehensive and universal citizenship rights to minimal levels of employment security, income maintenance, housing, and health care represents a final achievement of the democratic and egalitarian principles. Titmuss and Waxman, in particular, emphasize the integrative effects of universal social welfare rights that transcend class, ethnic, and religious societal cleavages. Waxman recommends comprehensive and universal social welfare as a more effective anti-poverty strategy than the prevailing American emphasis on means-tested and targeted social welfare programs. Social policy structures that transcend class lines would serve to eliminate the stigma commonly attached to welfare in the United States and reduce the isolation of the poor that fosters a separate culture of poverty. He argues the choice between integration and isolation should serve as the "operational index for the evaluation of social policy [and that] . . . the most effective means of breaking the vicious circle, the stigma of poverty, is by creating and implementing policies and programs that will lead to the integration of the poor with the non-poor, rather than their further isolation" (1983, 128, 118).

Although the two schools advance a broad critique of contemporary liberal social policy, it would not be correct to classify either as a form of conservative social theory. Lowi, for example, consistently criticizes contemporary interest-group liberalism as a fundamentally conservative political force resistant to comprehensive social policy initiatives, redistribution, and positive social change. Similarly, Waxman's criticisms of the American welfare state consistently argue for a more expansive national role in assuring at least minimal levels of social welfare security. Yet each is in the tradition of Lockean-Liberal political thought, a tradition that many libertarian conservatives would claim as their own. Each stands opposed to the exercise of discretionary bureaucratic power--Lowi and McConnell, because it is undemocratic; Titmuss and Waxman, because it imposes a stigma on welfare recipients--that fosters isolation and perpetuates poverty. Each advocates a broader governmental role to achieve positive social change, yet each seeks to limit arbitrary governmental intrusion into citizens' lives and condemns dysfunctional disruptions of marketplace incentives.

What follows is a history of American social policy designed to illustrate the insights offered by these two schools of thought. This is an eclectic (and perhaps oddly so) interpretation of history based on five general themes:

1. American social policy is isolationist in that it emphasizes distributive rather than redistributive policy goals, decentralized and fragmented program structures, and the targeting of social policy benefits to discrete social groups.

2. This isolationist social policy is both cause and effect of a political philosophy and political strategies that stress group isolation, solidarity, and self-determination and that assume that majoritarian social values are inherently hostile to minority group interests.

3. This isolationist political philosophy seeks to secure minority group benefits through enhanced administrative discretion rather than enhanced

citizenship rights, and seeks to avoid the resolution of policy issues in public arenas where majoritarian values may prove decisive.

4. This emphasis on group solidarity and self-determination generally serves the interests of the group representatives themselves and the least disadvantaged group members to the detriment of the public interest and the interests of the disadvantaged.

5. Isolationist social policies stigmatize the poor, exacerbate social conflict, delay integration, and fragment broader constituency support for comprehensive and universal social welfare.

INTEGRATION, ISOLATION, AND THE NEW DEAL

In 1935 and for decades before, the United States was a nation of three great impoverished classes: immigrant industrial labor in the Northeast; farmers in the Midwest, West, and South; and the Negro, primarily in the rural South. Within a generation, New Deal social policy would firmly entrench most of the first two classes in the ranks of a new and expanded middle class. For industrial labor, middle-class status was a consequence of a long process of integration and of a social policy strategy that reflected, encouraged, and at times forced that integration. For the American farmer, isolationist social policy was responsible for an enhanced, if somewhat precarious, status.

The period from the end of Reconstruction to the beginning of the New Deal had marked the beginning of the phenomenon of American social policy exceptionalism and the corresponding absence of effective class-based socialist political organizations in the United States. At this time most European nations were taking the first steps on the road to welfare statehood--in the case of Bismarck's Germany, with the expressed intent of integrating a divided nation. Social insurance programs were established and agrarian and working-class political parties began their gradual rise to power. For conservative historians, this was an era of classic American laissez-faire social policy reflecting a popular commitment to the principles of limited government, free enterprise, and rugged individualism. Such interpretations, however, take great care to overlook the expanded use of governmental power to suppress labor unrest, to regulate the economy and foreign trade to the disadvantage of American farmers, and to impose an oppressive serfdom on southern Blacks.

An alternative explanation points to the failure of the victims of the new American exceptionalism to overcome ethnic, racial, religious, and regional conflict--conflict exacerbated by carefully targeted social programs. The best illustration of this was the Civil War disability pension program and the extensions of the program enacted by Republican Congresses in the 1880s and in 1890. The Pension Bureau, the Grand Army of the Republic (G.A.R.), and Republican congressmen formed a classic iron triangle that by 1890 had created what the G.A.R. itself called the most liberal pension measure ever passed by any legislative body. G. John Ikenberry and Theda Skocpol estimate that by the turn of the century the program provided monthly pensions to one out of every three native-born men in the North, all presumably disabled by war injuries, and constituted over one quarter of the federal budget (1987, 195). Immigrants and Southerners derived little benefit from the program. For farmers, the program provided a convenient excuse for Republican congressmen who supported the high tariff policies that were undermining the farm economy.[2]

Racial and religious cleavages produced two systems of separate schooling: parochial schools in the North and segregated schools in the South. The isolation that resulted continues to handicap American efforts to achieve education equality. Exacerbating these conflicts was the rise of machine politics that, according to Piven and Cloward, did much to suppress "working class consciousness" among industrial labor:[3]

> Big City machines were able to win and hold the allegiance of workers by absorbing their leaders and by conferring favors and symbols that sustained the loyalties of workers on individual, neighborhood, and ethnic bases. This not only prevented the emergence of industrial workers as a political force directed to class issues, but it actually freed political leaders on all levels of government to use police, militia, and troops against striking workers without jeopardizing working-class electoral support. (1977, 106)

Pre-New Deal politics and social policy established the precedents for the targeting and isolation that subsumed common citizenship interests to narrower constituency interests and that define the character of American social policy exceptionalism to this day.

The end of unrestricted immigration after the turn of the century, the gradual integration of immigrant groups into American culture, and the inability of machine politics to deal with the problems of the Great Depression set the stage for the New Deal. The social policy consequences--Social Security retirement and disability, unemployment insurance, a national minimum wage, and new federal government protection of the rights of organized labor, in particular, represented confirmation of citizenship for industrial labor and a broadened understanding of citizenship rights.

The new rights of citizenship, however, were restricted to those who were considered citizens. Social Security and labor legislation specifically did not include agricultural workers, a group that included vast numbers of American Blacks. Conventional welfare state social programs from which Blacks might have received disproportional benefits--comprehensive national health insurance, a system of family allowances are examples--were not (and have yet to be) adopted. The unemployment insurance and public assistance components of the Social Security Act (Aid to Dependent Children (ADC), Aid to the Blind, and Old Age Assistance) were purposively decentralized, to the continuing disadvantage of Southern Blacks (Ikenberry and Skocpol, 1987). Public assistance benefits would not be provided on the basis of claims to national citizenship, but were conditioned on state and local residence.

Nor did the enhanced rights of citizenship have much of an effect on the status of American farmers. For the farmer, the agricultural policies of the New Deal conferred the status not of interdependent citizen but of dependent client. The principle was to use government to preserve and restore the culture of the family farm by facilitating the organization of agricultural interests and granting them autonomous control over both their markets and the dispersal of tax and expenditure subsidies. For political scientists, McConnell (1966) and Lowi (1979) in particular, American agriculture came to epitomize a new and disturbing trend toward special-interest government.

For both the farmer and the industrial laborer, the New Deal entailed new governmental protections against the unrestrained forces of the marketplace. But the protections offered the industrial laborer were of a substantially different form than those granted the farmer. For labor, the New Deal protections came in the form of social rights that fundamentally transformed the balance of power between capital and labor. New Deal labor policy, including here the Taft-Hartley Act, represented a permanent social policy consensus, an understanding of the rights of both capital and labor. Specific laws defined the rules that would regulate and shape the conflict between capital and labor, and the essential elements of these new arrangements would remain largely unaltered by subsequent policy changes. Whether business or labor would gain the greater advantage in subsequent conflicts did not in itself justify a change in the rules.

Had it not been for the timing of the "switch in time that saved nine," the farmer and the industrial laborer would have been in the same boat. Had the Supreme Court not invalidated provisions of the National Industrial Recovery Act (in Schecter Poultry Corporation v. U.S.), American industrial policy would have taken on many of the same characteristics as American farm policy. And, as Lowi repeatedly insists, had the Court applied the Schecter standard against ambiguous delegation of legislative authority thereafter, farm policy would not have devolved into the system we have today.

In contemporary political terminology the farmer was empowered--even as the agricultural economy became dependent on government subsidies and on the exercise of governmental authority to regulate markets. Authority to regulate the dispersal of the new farm spoils was placed in the hands of a new kind of political machine: the iron triangles of co-opted federal bureaucracies, organized farm interests, and compliant congressional subcommittees.

In the end, every segment of the agricultural economy, with the possible exception of catfish farming, acquired a tailored set of subsidies and market controls that were regularly redesigned to meet new market circumstances. Any "rights" created by the new farm policy would be impermanent, commodity-specific, and granted at the discretion of individual iron triangles. Corn growers would be given the so-called right to a payment-in-kind one year, the right to above-market-price crop loans the next year, and the right to export subsidies the next. The so-called rights of dairy producers, lemon growers and mohair sheep ranchers were entirely unique. Apples and oranges were never mixed.

For the industrial laborer, the New Deal meant the eventual decline of his ethnic political machine and the discretionary welfare and employment benefits that the machine provided. While the laborer achieved independence of ethnic machine welfare, the farmer traded dependence on an unstable market place for dependence on the capricious policies of the new agriculture machines.

The new rights for industrial labor were the basis for a strengthened commitment to the national Democratic party, a commitment that entailed support for the tax increases required to fund the new rights. For the farmer, New Deal policies resulted in a new anti-government political philosophy that would turn against any politician who committed the crime of being in office during a downturn in the commodity markets--be it caused by good weather or bad, the trade policies of other nations, or the policies of his own iron triangle.

Whether New Deal-style farm policy brought the farmer economic prosperity or eventual economic collapse can be debated by those who enjoy a good discussion of free market economics. For some farmers, at least, the New Deal meant a great deal of money. For the larger number driven from their farms, it represented an integration of sorts. For those who remained, it would mean a strange isolation from American society, politics, and government.

This isolation is best illustrated in recent congressional testimony of farm lobbyists and the wives of now-destitute farmers. New agricultural subsidies and market controls are needed, they argued, because farmers are too proud to ask for welfare. Not too proud to ask the rest of society to pay for the ever-increasing subsidies or to pay higher prices for farm products, but too proud to be treated as common citizens.

THE LEGACY OF THE GREAT SOCIETY

The tension between integration and isolation in American politics reached the breaking point in the mid-1960s. The most important legislative accomplishments of the Great Society era, particularly in the early years of that era, were a consequence of the integrationist impulse of the civil rights movement. The Civil Rights Act of 1964, the Voting Rights Act of 1965, the Elementary and Secondary Education Act of 1965, and in certain respects, the Food Stamp Act of 1962 each reflected a new, though brief, American commitment to integration and a desire to extend citizenship to the impoverished class neglected by the New Deal.

By 1965, the United States appeared to be on the verge of mature welfare-statehood. Passage of the Civil Rights and Voting Rights acts seemed to assure that the poor would be better represented in all levels of government and that Blacks would soon be assimilated in the mainstream of American society. Medicaid and Medicare seemed to many, and certainly to their opponents, to be the precedents for a comprehensive and universal entitlement to health care. In subsequent years Aid to Families with Dependent Children (AFDC) and Food Stamp eligibility requirements would be increasingly standardized and less arbitrary. In ensuing years, Blacks registered significant gains in income. Proposals for a guaranteed income and negative income tax, similar in some respects to a European-style family allowance program, would be advanced.

Although the American welfare state would continue to grow, it would not be consolidated. While the United States soon surpassed all other nations in the raw number of social welfare and anti-poverty programs, it lagged well behind in the enactment of comprehensive and universal guarantees of citizenship rights to income security, health care, and employment. Instead of consolidation, new programs brought fragmentation and decentralization as the nation embarked on a course that would lead to the development of a large number of narrowly targeted and uncoordinated programs. The strategy of committing resources to a large number of "itty-bitty" programs rather than comprehensive and universal social policies that had begun with the War on Poverty Community Action Program continued throughout the Nixon, Ford, Carter, and even the Reagan administrations.

Instead of national health insurance, Congress enacted Medicaid for the poor, Medicare for the elderly, black-lung benefits for coal miners, and a variety of community and regional health service programs, such as the National Health Service Corps and the Neighborhood Health Center program, each targeted to serve the special needs of particular areas and groups. These programs were in addition to previously established programs that provided tax deductions to the middle class, separate national health services for veterans and native Americans, and the Hill-Burton Act construction subsidies for medically underserved areas. In the Supreme Court's Bakke decision, affirmative action was justified as a means of improving health care services in minority communities.

Among the education programs designed to break the cycle of poverty were Head Start and Follow Through, Work-Study and Upward Bound, and various college loan and grant programs. Largely to compensate for the ineffectiveness of compensatory education programs, Congress created a series of employment training programs. Nathan Glazer (1986) has compiled the following list of their initials: ARA, MDTA, JC, NYC, WIN, JOBS, CEP,

PEP, CETA, PSE, STIP, HIRE, YEDPA, PSIP, PICs, YCCIP, and YIEPP. JTPA was added later, under the Reagan administration.

In addition to Food Stamps there were the school lunch, milk and breakfast programs, Meals on Wheels and senior citizen nutrition programs and the Special Supplemental Nutritional Program for Women, Infants, and Children. The Reagan administration added the Special Dairy Distribution Program (i.e., the cheese give-away) and, later, the Temporary Emergency Food Assistance Program.

Three federal black-lung benefit programs created in the 1970s are good examples of the pork-barrel social welfare that epitomizes post-1965 American social policy: the 1969 Federal Mine Health and Safety Act, creating the Social Security black-lung program; the 1972 Black Lung Benefits Act, establishing a similar Department of Labor program; and the 1977 Federal Mine Safety and Health Act, providing health care and rehabilitative services.

Together the three programs represent a combination of workman's compensation, disability insurance, sickness pay, pension, and health insurance plans for the nation's coal miners. To be classified as "totally disabled" under the Labor Department program or just "disabled" under the Social Security program, miners need not be unable to work in other non-mining activities. The 1977 reforms prohibited the agencies from arranging their own x-rays to verify claims and established several presumptions that would enable claimants to receive benefits in the absence of sufficient proof of disability. Any respiratory ailment would be presumed to be black-lung disease. A deceased miner was presumed to have had black lung, without medical examination, if he had been employed in the mines for more than twenty-five years and his widow provided an affidavit certifying that he had suffered respiratory ailment (Sundquist 1986, 531-532; Committee on Labor and Education 1979).

There is, of course, no principle other than political expediency that justifies the substantial differences in rights or entitlements accorded pre-1973, pre-1977, post-1977, and post-1981 victims of black lung; to say nothing of the lack of similar entitlements for iron-ore miners suffering from red lung, textile workers suffering from white lung, uranium miners, or even the steelworkers who unloaded the coal as it entered their plants. In total, the benefits enjoyed by the American coal miner would compare favorably with the universal occupational disability, sickness, and health care rights enjoyed by all workers in a country like the Netherlands, except that the coal miner's benefits are more like perquisites than rights, and their continuation depended directly on the continued political influence of a few Appalachian congressmen serving on the key congressional subcommittees.

Consider the position of these congressmen when, in 1981, the new Reagan administration proposed substantial cutbacks in the Social Security and Supplemental Security Income disability rolls, to be accomplished through a national audit of already certified disability claims and more stringent enforcement of eligibility criteria. For the black-lung programs, the administration proposed an increased coal tax and elimination of the presumptions for new claimants. Much like the machine politicians described by Piven and Cloward, who could send the police after striking workers without fear of losing their working-class electoral support, the Appalachian congressmen were given the opportunity to maximize their own political support by going along with the Reagan budget proposals, perhaps to avoid the threat of the administration lending assistance to their opponents in the next election, while devoting all their efforts to preserving black-lung standards. Similarly, the United Mine Workers now have an incentive to shift their resources to the protection of black-lung programs and less incentive to contribute to broader labor union efforts to secure adequate occupational injury protection.

Small programs survive by remaining unobtrusive. Unfortunately for some coal miners, the 1977 presumptions resulted in a substantial increase in program expenditures. When the economy prospered and revenues were rising-- that is, as the need for social welfare decreased--the coal miners and other narrow community interests prospered. Conversely and perversely, when the economy faltered, revenues declined and deficits soared, these program expenditures became matters of a broader public interest. The conflict between national interest and community interests and the absence of broad-based constituency support for targeted social programs was exposed as program expenditures became matters to be decided in public arena forums--in the congressional budget committees rather than the relatively isolated appropriations and authorization committees where the programs were created.

If isolationist social welfare proved to be a bad political strategy, it was at least equally bad social policy. The War on Poverty, the liberal expansions and conservative retrenchments in the Nixon, Ford, Carter, and Reagan administrations all had one fundamental commonality: they left the structure of the nation's public assistance programs intact, a structure imposed in 1935 at the behest of conservative southern legislators who sought nothing more than to perpetuate the stigma of poverty and race and the isolation of rich and poor, Black and white.

ISOLATING THE CHILDREN: THE FAILURE OF WELFARE REFORM

Between 1959 and 1969, the nation's poverty rate fell from 22.4 to 12.1. The most dramatic declines were recorded for Blacks after 1965. More than half of Black Americans lived in poverty in 1965; in 1969, less than a third did (see Table 6.1).

Since 1969, the year President Nixon proposed the first comprehensive welfare reform measure to Congress, the national poverty rate has actually increased. It has increased despite a significant decline in poverty among the nation's elderly. The elderly poverty rate has been cut in half and has been below the national rate since 1982. As the status of the nation's senior citizens improved, the poverty rates for Black children have steadily increased.

The decline in the elderly poverty rate represents one of the most significant achievements in the history of American social welfare policy. In 1970 and 1971, the Congress enacted significant increases in Social Security benefits. In 1972, it enacted a portion of the Nixon welfare reform proposals, primarily those components of the plan that directly affected the elderly. The Supplemental Security Income (SSI) program effectively guaranteed the elderly, blind, and disabled a minimum income as a matter of right (cf. Lowi 1979, 228). Social Security benefits were increased 20 percent and cost of living adjustments were enacted. Subsequent benefit increases were no longer matters of political discretion, a discretion that tended to tie benefit increases to the election cycle.[4] But welfare reform was not in the cards for those who relied, or could not rely, on the remaining components of the income maintenance system. Three presidents tried and all three failed. Black children were the losers.

By the end of the Johnson administration, the critical flaws in the public assistance foundations and the need for reform were apparent to liberals and conservatives alike (Leichter and Rodgers 1984, 44-45). Welfare reform promised to correct most of the shortcomings. Family disincentives would be eliminated by extending public assistance coverage to two-parent families in every state. Work disincentives, through a negative tax on earnings assuring that work, would be compensated. Program consolidation and extended coverage of intact families and single persons would eliminate many of the gaps and overlaps and the vertical inequities. Federal minimum benefit standards would eliminate interstate variation, horizontal inequity, and some of the administrative duplication. Because family size and earnings (under the Nixon Family Assistance Plan) would be the primary eligibility and benefit-level criteria, bureaucracy and administrative discretion would be reduced.

Table 6.1 Percentage Difference Changes in Poverty Rates

	1959-1969	1969 Rate	1969-1984
All Persons	-10.3	12.1	+2.3
Persons 65+	-9.9	25.3	-12.9
All Blacks	-22.9	32.2	-.5
Black Children	-22.6	39.6	+6.8

Source: U.S. Bureau of Census 1959-1984.

There were several problems with each of the welfare reform proposals. Because reform was not a family allowance plan, it would still target poor people, leaving both an element of work disincentive that earnings taxes would not fully correct and some of the social stigma and isolation. To standardize benefits across the states without an enormous increase in program expenditures would require a reduction in the benefits of existing welfare recipients in the wealthiest states in order to extend benefits to those who were falling through the gaps and to increase payments to families in the nation's poorest states. Subsequent experimental evaluations indicated that reform would increase work disincentives for those who would be added to the rolls and, perhaps, for recipients in low-AFDC states, and raised questions about the impact of reform on family stability. A way would have to be found to correct the dependency incentive created by the Medicaid program.

Although not a universal social welfare program, welfare reform would have gone a long way toward establishing a national citizenship right to a guaranteed income, reducing isolation, and targeting and creating a broader constituency support base. As a side benefit, federalizing AFDC and general assistance would have produced substantial state and local government expenditure savings. Whether or not benefits provided sufficient income security would be a matter to be decided in Congress, not in fifty state legislatures and Congress. Gone would be the arguments of state legislators that generous benefits would serve only to attract welfare recipients from other states. The interests of various segments of the nation's poor--the elderly, the disabled, women with children, two-parent families, southern poor, and northern poor--would no longer be in conflict. It would be more difficult to apply stereotypes of welfare mothers and food stamp cheats to a program that embraced a broader and more varied clientele (Hamilton and Hamilton 1986, 304-305).

Unfortunately, these political opportunities, as well as the opportunity for extended coverage and increased payments for recipients in the poorest states, however, were all "birds in the bush"; to attain them, some current recipients would have to forego some of the benefits they had in hand. Those who have something to lose are inevitably those that have been most successful in the past; those who have the most to gain, the most powerless. This is true of tax reform, regulatory reform, and welfare reform. With welfare reform, the interests of the northern poor and the social work bureaucracy were pitted against the interests of the southern poor. The interstate variation in existing welfare benefits had been a consequence of the relative powerlessness of the southern poor in both the Congress and their state legislatures. In the Congress, they would be represented by conservative legislators who cared little about the benefits they had to gain; while the northern poor were represented by liberal legislators who could be trusted to protect their existing entitlements at all costs. The northern poor (those who were already covered under existing programs) also had the organizational resources of the National Welfare Rights Organization.

There have been many explanations of the failure of welfare reform.[5] Weak presidential leadership, the unanticipated and confusing program evaluation results, the sometimes conflicting goals inherent in any attempt to reform welfare, and the general inability of Congress to reform anything are frequently cited.[6] Few of these factors would have been determinative, however, if it had not been for the perplexing northern-liberal resistance to reform. In addition to the conflicting interests of northern and southern poor, one other factor accounts for their opposition.

In the summer of 1965, the contents of the Moynihan report were leaked to the press. Moynihan's thesis was that "equality of opportunity" civil rights laws alone would not suffice to correct the disastrous effects of "three centuries of unimaginable mistreatment" on Black family life. Citing 1960 census figures indicating that nearly a quarter of all Black families were headed by women, nearly a quarter of all Black births were out of wedlock, and half of all Black children would reach the age of eighteen without the continual presence of a father in the home, the report described a "tangle of pathology" involving desertions, illegitimacy, and welfare dependency.

In the fall of 1965 (after the Watts riot, Moynihan would stress), Moynihan went from civil rights celebrity to villain. He was attacked as a racist and fascist at a November planning session for the White House conference, and civil rights leaders demanded that family issues be stricken from conference agenda. The report, it was said, placed too much emphasis on pathology and blamed victims for the consequences of racism and oppression.

Among the more dubious consequences of the Moynihan report was the creation of a new sociology subfield dedicated to providing a Black perspective on the Black family. For the next two decades, research on the Black family was devoid of ethnocentric statistical comparisons and exploitative dwellings on the pathology of family disintegration.[7] An extensive literature praised the newly discovered, presumably non-isolated, "attenuated nuclear family" and the "attenuated extended augmented family." Illegitimacy would be interpreted "not as a sign of generational acceptance of pathological behavior, but [as] a respect for life at its conception" (Johnson 1978, 30), a pertinent sociological insight, perhaps, until one begins to think of the social policy implications. The image of the independent, self-confident, single Black mother fulfilling the needs of her children and the pluralistic society that this literature promoted was assuredly a middle-class construction, reflecting the social status of the scholars who advanced it.[8]

By the time welfare reform was proposed, white liberal concern for welfare dependency and family disintegration was generally recognized as another manifestation of the "blaming the victim" disorder. Indeed, the symptoms of the disorder were broadened to include "blaming the welfare system." Thus Elizabeth Wickendom listed among her reasons for opposing the Nixon welfare reform the fact that it "is based on the false premise that the causes of poverty lie within the poor themselves and, by derivation, within the welfare 'system'" (Moynihan 1973, 323). The only thing that made poor people poor, it was insisted, was a lack of money and political power. That welfare reform was the key to enhancing the political power of the poor went largely unrecognized.

For a while, the new sociology could avoid criticism on the contention that everything was fine in the Black family. Recall that the Black poverty rate was in rapid decline from 1965 to 1969, a period that saw a substantial increase in AFDC rolls. Indeed, the poverty rate for Black children not in single-parent female-headed families continued to decline, from 29.8 percent in 1968 to 17.6 percent in 1978, and in 1988 it remained only a few percentage points above the poverty rate for all children. In 1988, there were nearly one million fewer two-parent-family Black children living in poverty than there were in 1968. Unfortunately, they were replaced by an additional million children from Black female-headed families. In 1989, more than half of all black children under the age of six were living in poverty.

As welfare reform floundered in the U.S. Congress, welfare recipients were steadily losing ground in the state legislatures. Throughout the 1970s inflation steadily eroded AFDC benefits in almost every state. AFDC benefits declined by a third in constant dollars by 1987, while the benefits accorded the elderly by Social Security and SSI generally kept pace with inflation. By 1989, the social welfare program most successful in reducing poverty among children was the survivors insurance component of Social Security (Ozawa and Alpert 1984). In 1971 California and New York established new work-fare requirements and Congress enacted the "Talmadge Amendment," establishing workfare requirements far more stringent than those envisioned under Nixon's plan. And the children who would suffer the most as a consequence of the failure of welfare reform were not Black but Latino. Florida, Arizona, New Mexico, and Texas, among the wealthiest of the Southern states, continued to rank among the lowest AFDC states in the nation.

Perhaps the most isolationist and anti-integrationist expression of the new philosophy on the Black family was the largely successful effort of the National Association of Black Social Workers to put an end to transracial adoption. In 1972 NABSW attacked transracial adoption as a form of cultural genocide, a position the organization defends on the grounds that Black children raised in white families "suffer severe identity problems" and "do not develop the coping mechanisms necessary to function in a society that is inherently racist" (Merrit 1985). The direct effect of the NABSW position has been the near eradication of transracial adoption. Between 1971 and 1975, the number of transracial adoptions fell from 2,574 to 830 and continued to decline afterward--this at a time when 40 percent of the nearly 100,000 children waiting for adoption are Black and when mounting evidence on the effects of transracial adoption has yet to identify anything but beneficial consequences for the children involved (Simon and Alstein 1981).

The policy change was accomplished entirely through administrative discretion in child welfare agencies that NABSW consistently branded as racist. And the policy persists despite numerous federal court decisions to the contrary (for summaries see National Coalition 1984). A comparison of the decline in transracial adoptions before and after the NABSW declaration with the increases in adoption resulting from Father George Clements's One Church--One Child program in Illinois indicates that over a similar length of time, the NABSW position was twice as harmful to the chances of a Black child being adopted as Clements's program was helpful (Committee on Labor and Human Resources 1985).

For their crude and distorted misunderstanding of the purposes of the Moynihan report and welfare reform, the anti-pathologists have a lot to answer for. They were wrong to place the blame for the culture of poverty, or the onus for correcting it, on the Black community. They were wrong to suggest that recognizing the existence of social disorganization precludes one from acknowledging its causes. In the end, the advocates of a new Black perspective on the Black family achieved only one of their expressed aims, Black self-determination. Perhaps Moliere, Swift, or Dante could do full justice to the achievements of the new sociology over these two decades. One can only wonder what economics has done to merit the title "dismal science."

AFFIRMATIVE ACTION: CIVIL RIGHTS, MINORITY RIGHTS, OR STATES' RIGHTS?

In T. H. Marshall's formulation (1964), citizenship rights in Western democracies developed in stages: first, early definitions of civil citizenship rights to own property and to defend property rights before impartial courts; then political rights, involving primarily the extension of the franchise; and finally social welfare rights. In the United States, the development of citizenship rights has followed a unique and uneven pattern. At the time of the founding, a broad range of American citizens enjoyed civil and political rights substantially in excess of anything found in the European continent. Yet it was not until the passage of the Civil and Voting Rights acts, well after European nations had evolved into full-fledged welfare states, that meaningful civil and political rights were accorded to the full American citizenry.

No policy more clearly manifests the fundamental change in public philosophy that occurred after 1965 than the American reinterpretation of Civil

Rights Act to accommodate the principles of affirmative action. The new public philosophy has been succinctly summarized by two Carter administration appointees to the Civil Rights Commission, Blandina Cardenas Ramirez and Mary Frances Berry. Dissenting from the Reagan appointees' position on affirmative action, they insisted that "Civil rights laws were not passed to give protection to all Americans, [but] out of a recognition that some Americans already had protection because they belong to a favored group; and others, including blacks, Hispanics and women of all races, did not because they belonged to disfavored groups" (*New York Times* 1985). The proposition that different groups of Americans are, or can be, accorded separate, but somehow equivalent, protection of the law is not entirely new to American politics. The idea that the standard of "separate but equal" can be employed to the benefit of the disadvantaged is more original.

Affirmative action policies involving race and sex preferences clearly conflict with the principle that social equality can best be attained through an enhanced respect for common, rather than alienable, citizenship rights. One common criticism, that conventional forms of affirmative action serve to exacerbate white male prejudice, minority stereotypes, and a psychology of inferiority among members of protected classes, is consistent with the contention that targeted social policies foster stigma and isolation. Affirmative action also threatens to fragment constituency support and public respect for other redistributive social policy efforts.

By Waxman's "integration and isolation" standard, some forms of affirmative action might be recommended, such as vigorous color-blind enforcement of non-discrimination laws, or a national commitment to a full-employment policy. Alvin Schorr (1986, 48) argues that affirmative action in the form of "minority conscious recruitment, bias-free assessment of qualifications, remediable preparatory programs, and monitoring of employment and enrollment patterns" is consistent with integrationist social policy goals.

Much of the political science minority faction theory, with a slight modification, is directly applicable to contemporary affirmative action politics. The modification involves Lowi's contention that special-interest power is facilitated by the enactment of ambiguous statutes in Congress that delegate discretionary power to co-opted bureaucracies. In the case of the Civil Rights Act, however, there is no such ambiguity. In Johnson v. Transportation Agency, Santa Clara County, Justice Scalia noted that the act was written "with a clarity which, had it not proved so unavailing, one might well recommend as a model of statutory draftsmanship." If one adds ambiguous interpretation of explicit statutes to Lowi's theory, affirmative action becomes an almost classic case of special-interest social policy.

The rules of interest-group liberal policy-making are well stated in a series of Supreme Court affirmative action decisions. Race-conscious remedies were permitted as long as the penalties imposed on unprotected "favored" groups were "moderate," "flexible," and "gradual." As is typically the case with special-interest policy, benefits could be secured only in so far as the competing interests were diffuse. Affirmative action thus does not supersede the seniority rights of organized labor. It is permissible to punish a large pool of applicants, each a little, to provide affirmative action benefits to members of a protected class, but it is not permissible to fire clearly identifiable individuals to accomplish the same ends. As an analogy, consider the special-interest benefits granted California citrus growers, who are permitted to (in effect) fix prices on produce grown for the fresh fruit market, where consumers directly bear the costs, but not on produce sold to citrus processors, where a few multinational corporations would bear the costs.

In the Johnson case, moreover, the Court added still another permutation to the old notions of a civil right. For the first time, the Court decided that the real intent of the Civil Rights Act was to create a state right--a right for state and local bureaucrats to impose affirmative action group-preference policies as a matter of administrative discretion. Only in rare and egregious cases of discrimination--the Alabama State Troopers, for example--has the Court required that racial or sex preference affirmative action be imposed. More often, it simply permits it, in the Johnson case, without evidence that any discrimination had occurred and in spite of a finding that the agency had not discriminated. The effect is to absolve bureaucracies that wish to provide compensation to protected classes of any responsibility to identify and acknowledge previous discriminatory practices or to seek to end them. Moreover, the unwillingness of the Court to require compensation or punishment for less than egregious cases of discrimination assures that remedies for subtle and institutional racism will be provided only by those employers who are predisposed to aid women and minorities. Yet it is they who are least likely to be guilty of subtle and institutional racism.

Affirmative action is clearly a redistributive and, in many respects, an integrative social policy. Nevertheless, while many affirmative action practices are redistributive and integrative and contribute to social equality, it is not clear that they will remain so. It is possible that the future beneficiaries of affirmative action will increasingly be made up of the sons and daughters of previous beneficiaries. The large Black underclass may become an unaffected excuse for maintaining second-generation affirmative action benefits for the Black middle class. Minority contract set-asides will serve less and less to encourage the creation of new minority enterprises and increasingly as "iron triangle" special-interest subsidies, as well-established minority firms contribute heavily to political action committees that, in turn, support influential politicians favoring program continuation. In the end, affirmative action may do little more than lend temporary legitimacy to old-fashioned graft and spoils.

THE REAGAN REVOLUTION

> Virtually every American who shops in a local supermarket is
> aware of the daily abuses that take place in the food stamp
> program. (State of the Union Address 1982)

By design or happenstance, the Reagan administration pursued a
strategy of exploiting prejudice against social welfare constituencies in the
interest of a conservative policy agenda that consistently exacerbated the worst
features of social policy isolation.   Much like a boxer who keeps a disabled
opponent from falling to the canvas with one hand while pummeling his or her
face with the other, the Reagan administration sought to destroy the American
welfare state by reinforcing its structural defects.   Many elements of the Reagan
agenda appeared incongruous and contradictory to those who would seek to
discern an underlying logic of social welfare program design.   There was,
however, an underlying political strategy to this agenda, a strategy that
consistently fostered greater fragmentation and isolation of social welfare
constituencies.
        On its face, the Reagan administration stance on affirmative action was
simply another example of indecisive presidential leadership unable to resolve
internal policy conflicts.   On one hand, the administration followed the advice
of two secretaries of labor to keep intact the Johnson administration executive
order governing affirmative action hiring policies of the federal government and
government contractors.   It did not seek reconsideration of existing minority
contract set-aside legislation and offered only sporadic challenges to new
congressional set-aside initiatives.   On the other hand, the Justice Department
and the Reagan appointees to the Civil Rights Commission continually
challenged the fairness, constitutionality, and legitimacy of race-conscious hiring
practices.   The effect was to keep the most poorly legitimized Great Society
program in place and to exploit it as a focus of popular discontent with liberal
social policy and as a source of constituency fragmentation.   The Reagan attack
on the nation's social welfare programs consistently sought to pare program
expenditures to the bone marrow while retaining the fundamental isolationist
structure of the American welfare state.   Among the administration's key initial
social policy objectives cited by Martin Anderson, former domestic policy
advisor, was that of not proposing welfare reform (Albrecht 1982).
        The attack began with the submission of the first Reagan budget.   While
the president argued that public assistance should benefit the "needy, not the
greedy" and that welfare recipients abused federal largess and avoided work,
David Stockman prepared new program eligibility requirements for AFDC,
Medicaid, and food stamps that had the direct effect of increasing the work
disincentives of each of these programs.   The budget reserved its most drastic

cuts for public assistance programs and treaded lightly on the social insurance programs that disproportionately benefited the middle class. Within these public assistance programs, the cuts targeted the working poor for reduced benefits.

The logic of using welfare abuse as an excuse for increasing work disincentives and of classifying welfare recipients who do earn some outside income as "greedy" and those who do not work at all as "needy" is impenetrable only if one is trying to discern an underlying strategy of social welfare program design. As a political strategy, the logic is consistent. The Reagan social policy agenda served to foster a more restrictive welfare system with narrower and more segmented program constituencies, to isolate the underclass from the working poor, and to place each at the mercy of market forces and state legislatures. Serious welfare reform posed a threat to the conservative political agenda. Converting the food stamp program into a cash grant guaranteed income--the obvious solution to welfare abuse Reagan had such a problem with--clearly would not have served conservative political interests, although it would have been perfectly consistent with the individualism and self-reliance the administration espoused. The peculiar stigma of food stamps was both preserved and exploited. To the extent that the Reagan administration attack on the American welfare state succeeded, it did so not because social welfare expenditures had grown so large as to warrant a welfare backlash, but because the constituency support for social welfare programs was narrow, fragmented, and small. It was least successful in paring expenditures from those programs that were reformed in 1972--Social Security and Supplemental Security Income.

THE PROSPECTS FOR INTEGRATION

Much of what is truly exceptional about the American welfare state can be traced to a public philosophy that seeks to pursue the cause of social justice and equality through a disintegrative politics and isolationist social policy--a political agenda modeled on pre-New Deal machine politics and post-New Deal farm politics. It is a public philosophy that assumes that social equality is a minority interest, that racism and hostility to the poor are inherent and irremediable, and that citizenship rights and democratic processes are inimical to the interests of the poor. Throughout most of U.S. history, minorities, the poor, and the disadvantaged were the recognized victims of isolationist social policy strategies that subsumed citizenship rights to community interests and resisted integration in an effort to preserve racial and parochial cultural values. In contemporary times, the same policy strategies are pursued in the alleged interest of the same victims, rationalized under the banner of new academic theories of role models, community empowerment, self-determination, economic self-determination, and cultural pluralism. There may be understandable reasons for the rise of this public philosophy, but it persists only because it is self-perpetuating.

Despite the impediments to integration that may be inherent in the American political system, there are several reasons to suggest that there is some hope for a universalist social policy agenda grounded on a greater appreciation of citizenship rights. First, there is some evidence that the foundations of interest-group liberal politics are weakening (McFarland 1983, 1987). The rise of Republican conservatism in the Reagan era, while not in itself a factor conducive to an expanding welfare state, does represent a shift toward greater ideological cohesion and coherence in American politics. Cohesive parties, in theory, should serve to undermine pork-barrel politics.

The rise of countervailing public interest groups and the successes of tax reform, deregulation, education reform as well as the environmental, anti-drug, anti-drunk driving and anti-child abuse movements attest to the responsiveness of American politics to majoritarian politics and may indicate a weakening of the interest-group liberal state and its public philosophy. Admittedly, all of this has occurred in policy realms having little to do with race, poverty, or social welfare. Nevertheless, it suggests that the structural proclivity of American politics to distributive politics is not unassailable.

The increasing awareness of the separation of Black middle-class and Black underclass interests may contribute to a shift from race-conscious to poverty-conscious social policy as it becomes increasingly more difficult to justify benefits for the more advantaged of minority communities on the basis of trickle-down benefits that might accrue to the disadvantaged. Also promising are indications that social policy debate in the United States is beginning to open up and is becoming more receptive to universalist arguments. For most of the period after 1970, debate was dominated by conflicts between those who sought to defend existing entitlements and those who distrusted any governmental social welfare efforts. Four books (Schorr 1986; Wilson 1987; Garfinkel and McLanahan 1986; and Anderson and Pickering 1986) have advanced detailed versions of an alternative political and social policy agendas grounded on the principles of citizenship rights and universality. Each incorporates specific policy proposals derived from recent empirical poverty research. In each case, the authors seem to have independently discovered the same social policy logic, usually without reference to the works of Marshall, Titmuss, or Waxman.

Each of these works argues for some form of a national full-employment policy and some form of family allowance program. Garfinkel and McLanahan and Schorr propose turning income tax exemptions into a refundable income tax credit as a no-cost strategy for initiating a family allowance program. Wilson and Garfinkel and McLanahan propose a comprehensive child-support assurance program. Anderson and Pickering, Schorr, and Wilson address their works to questions of race, racial isolation, and racism as much as questions of poverty. Each of these three works argues for a new approach to racial politics in America, emphasizing a commitment to principles of national community, integration, and "common ground" politics.

In general, the works share with Waxman, Marshall, and Titmuss a common criticism of means testing--that it isolates and stigmatizes the poor--and argue that universalist reforms (Schorr calls it "mainstreaming") make sense both as an effective strategy for dealing with poverty and as a political strategy that will broaden constituency support for social welfare. Throughout all of these works there is a consistent implication that a confluence of events involving an end to Reagan-era politics, new empirical findings about poverty and social policy, and an impending collapse of old and tired academic dogmas about race and the family have created a rare opportunity for what Wilson calls the "hidden agenda" of American politics.

Time will tell. What is clear is that until a commitment to integration is restored, efforts to address the pathologies of poverty in America will be hopelessly mired in confusion and ambivalence. The iron triangle of bad politics, bad social policy, and bad social science will continue to be the most intractable feature of the cycle of poverty.

7

Minority Representation and City Council Electoral Systems: A Black and Hispanic Comparison
Michael D. McDonald and Richard L. Engstrom

Electoral systems are far from politically neutral mechanisms. Different systems can have vastly different political consequences. The choice of one or another system, therefore, is often the subject of debate and controversy. Given that electoral systems are, in Giovanni Sartori's words, "the most specific manipulative instruments of politics" (1968, 273), the controversy is of more than simply academic interest.

AMERICAN MUNICIPAL ELECTORAL SYSTEMS

One of the most persistent electoral system debates in the United States is concerned with whether to use at-large or district (ward) systems for the election of city councils. The at-large format places electoral decisions in the hands of a citywide plurality or majority. District systems divide a city into a number of geographical units with approximately equal populations and allow the voters in those units to elect, by plurality or majority vote, the council member(s) from those geographical areas (Lyons and Jewell 1986).

The at-large format has been, for many years in the United States, one of the structural features recommended for municipal governments by the municipal reform movement. Election at-large, the reformers have argued, would eliminate the seamy side of "ward politics" from city council decision making. Decisions would not result from logrolling or vote trading among representatives with only segmental, neighborhood interests. Rather, the decisions would reflect the interest of the entire city (Judd 1988, 91-93). With this argument as the frame of reference in the debate, the municipal reformers have had great success at having the at-large format adopted. Approximately 60 percent of the municipalities in the United States with populations above

2,500 elect their entire council at-large; another 27 percent select a portion of their council in this fashion (Featherman 1988, 6).

Whether decisions made by at-large councils are truly of higher quality than those made by councils elected under a district format is not something readily documented. Numerous definitional and measurement problems remain to be resolved before such generalizations about decision-making consequences can be accepted. Another consequence of the choice of format, however, has been documented impressively and forms the basis of the other side of the debate. That is the tendency for racial minorities to be more underrepresented when council elections are conducted at-large rather than with districts, an underrepresentation which not infrequently takes the form of total exclusion from the council (Engstrom and McDonald 1986).

This difference in minority group representation between at-large and district systems is not difficult to understand, given that racially polarized voting is common in American cities and that minority voters tend to be residentially segregated. When voting is divided along racial lines, the racial composition of an electorate is a major determinant of whether majority or minority race candidates win. In the at-large context, a citywide minority's vote is submerged by the majority vote; the result is the election of only a small number, perhaps zero, minority candidates. This is especially true when rules and procedures precluding "single-shot" or "bullet" voting (discussed later in this chapter) are added to the at-large format (Engstrom and McDonald 1987). District systems, on the other hand, often reflect the racial segregation in American cities, and therefore some districts in which minority group members constitute a majority of the voters are likely (Lyons and Jewell 1988). Minority race council members are most likely to be elected from these "majority minority" districts.

This minority representation side of the debate is associated with a second generation of reformers. This set of reformers, many of whom are Black or Hispanic, advocate changing municipal elections from the at-large to the district format. At-large elections, they argue, discriminate against minorities by diluting the minority voting strength--that is, they make it more difficult for minority voters to convert their votes into the election of representatives of their choice. The district format, they argue, is more equitable inasmuch as a council elected through districts is likely to be more representative, at least descriptively, of a city's population. This latest reform generation has concentrated much of its effort toward the judiciary, using either the equal protection clause of the Fourteenth Amendment or, more recently, the Voting Rights Act as a medium for contesting the validity of at-large arrangements (see Engstrom 1985a, 1985b).

The racial representational effect of at-large versus district elections has been impressively documented (Davidson and Korbel 1981; Engstrom and McDonald 1981, 1982; Heilig and Mundt 1983; Karnig and Welch 1982; Mundt and Heilig 1983). Indeed, that evidence has been so strong that we have elsewhere suggested that "few generalizations in political science appear to be as well verified as the proposition that at-large elections tend to be discriminatory toward Black Americans" (Engstrom and McDonald 1986, 207).

The same cannot be said about the electoral system consequence for Hispanic representation. Some case studies of particular cities have highlighted gains in Hispanic representation following the adoption of the district system (Thomas and Murray 1986; Brischetto, Cotrella, and Stevens, 1983; Fraga 1988). Broader comparative studies, however, have produced only the most modest evidence of a linkage between electoral formats and the election of Hispanics (Fraga, Meier, and England 1986; Karnig and Welch 1979; MacManus 1978; Taebel 1978). The usual explanation for the absence of such a linkage is that Hispanics are less acutely residentially segregated than Blacks and, therefore, are not similarly advantaged by geographically based district systems (Karnig and Welch 1979, 474; Lyons and Jewell 1988; Taebel 1978, 151).

Reported below are the results of another, more recent analysis of the effect of city council electoral systems on the election of both Blacks and Hispanics. The analysis provides further confirmation that at-large elections, in contrast to district elections, are an impediment to the election of Blacks to councils in majority white cities. Unlike the previous comparative/cross-sectional studies, however, this analysis also finds a similar electoral system consequence for Hispanics in cities in which Hispanics are a minority.

DATA BASE AND ANALYTIC DESIGN

Information concerning election systems and the election of blacks and Hispanics to the city councils was collected through a telephone survey of city clerks' offices during February and March of 1982. The survey included the largest central city within every Standard Metropolitan Statistical Area in the United States, as determined by the 1980 Census of Population (N = 317). Data on the electoral strength of each minority were recorded from the 1980 census reports regarding the percentage of a city's voting age population (VAP) that is Black or Hispanic.

Different electoral arrangements specify variables that affect, at least theoretically, the relationship between minority electoral strength and minority representation. In other words, electoral arrangements are not expected to have an unconditional influence on the election of minority candidates; rather, they are expected to specify the conditions under which minority voting strength is more or less translated into the election of minority candidates. Two aspects of this translation are examined. The first uses the percentage of city council seats to which Blacks or Hispanics have been elected in each city as the dependent variable. This variable is regressed onto the VAP percentage within each grouping of cities by electoral system type in order to assess how proportionately each minority group tends to be represented within each format. The second aspect of the analysis examines the dichotomous dependent variable of whether any Black or Hispanic person had been elected to the council. The probabilities that each group is totally excluded from membership on a council, across various percentages of VAP, are estimated through logit analyses for each electoral format.

Given that our interest concerns the impact of electoral systems on Black and Hispanic minorities, cities in which a majority of the VAP is Black (N = 0) or Hispanic (N = 5) have been excluded from the analyses for that particular group. In addition, VAP for Blacks and Hispanics has not been reported for 15 and 6 cities, respectively, and those cities have also been excluded. (In all of the cities without VAP figures, the minority group constitutes less than six-tenths of one percent of the city's total population and no minority person serves on the council.) The analyses focusing on the election of Blacks will therefore be based on 293 central cities, and those for Hispanics on 306.

PROPORTIONALITY OF BLACK AND HISPANIC REPRESENTATION

The relationship between the percentage of a city's voting age population that a minority group comprises and the percentage of councilmanic seats held by members of that group, ignoring differences in electoral systems, is for Blacks:

$$\text{Seat \%} = .41 + .70 \text{ VAP\%, with } R^2 = .51 \text{ and } s_e = 8.6;$$
$$(.76) \quad (.04)$$

and for Hispanics:

$$\text{Seat \%} = -.60 + .45 \text{ VAP\%, with } R^2 = .42 \text{ and } s_e = 3.8.$$
$$(.26) \quad (.03)$$

With the intercepts in both equations close to 0.0, the regression coefficients (b) are interpretable as measures of how proportionately each group's electoral strength converts into councilmanic seats. Thus, the .70 value of the regression coefficient for the equation on Black representation means that across the 293 cities, the percentage of council seats held by Blacks tends to be seven-tenths of the Black percentage of the VAP. For Hispanics, the corresponding figure across 306 cities is .45, considerably below that for Blacks.

Reported in Table 7.1 are the values of these coefficients when the relationships are examined for cities with particular types of electoral systems. The relationships for Blacks are similar to those reported in earlier studies

(Engstrom and McDonald 1981, 348). Across cities employing a district electoral scheme (N = 52), there is a tendency for Blacks to be elected to a percentage of seats that is almost proportional to their percentage of the VAP (b = 1.13). In mixed systems (some council members elected at-large, others by districts, N = 101), the relationship is less than proportional (b = .75). In cities electing the entire council at-large (N = 140), the percentage of seats tends to be less than half of the percentage of the VAP (b = .44).

The same ordering of systemic impact is reported for Hispanics. The relationship between the Hispanic percentage of VAP and the percentage of councilmanic seats to which Hispanics have been elected is greatest in district cities (N = 55, b = .69), weaker in cities with mixed systems (N = 109, b = .56), and weakest in the at-large context (N = 142, b = .31). The difference associated with electoral systems is not as great for Hispanics (b = .39 when elections are at-large versus .69 when by district) as for Blacks (.44 versus 1.13), but it is substantial nonetheless. The district versus at-large difference is less dramatic primarily because Hispanics do not benefit from district systems to the same extent as Blacks. Notice that while the Hispanic percentage of the VAP translates into Hispanic representation within *every* systemic type, this is especially true for the district cities (.69 versus 1.13). This is presumably due to the lower levels of residential segregation mentioned above, which result in proportionately fewer majority Hispanic districts (see Lyons and Jewell 1988; MacManus 1985, 489). These lower levels of segregation, however, do not eliminate completely a systemic impact, as previous studies relying only on correlation coefficients suggest (Taebel 1978; MacManus 1978; Karnig and Welch 1979). While Hispanics may not benefit from districts to the same degree as Blacks, district arrangements are still a more favorable systemic context than at-large arrangements in which to convert Hispanic votes into the election of Hispanic council members.

Additional evidence on the adverse effect of at-large elections on both groups comes from the separate analysis of the cities with mixed electoral systems. When the percentage of the district-based seats in those cities won by Blacks is regressed onto the Black percentage of the VAP, the resulting equation is:

$$\text{District Seat \%} = -.84 + 1.05 \text{ VAP\%}, \text{ with } R^2 = .69 \text{ and } s_e = 8.9.$$
$$(1.37) \quad (.07)$$

Blacks tend to win a proportional percentage of these district seats (b = 1.05) just as they do the seats in cities employing only districts (b = 1.13). The tendency for Blacks to be elected at a less than proportional rate overall in mixed cities (b = .75, from Table 7.1) must be due, therefore, to the at-large seats in those cities.

Table 7.1 Relationships between Minority Representation and Voting Age Population, by Type of Electoral System

	Blacks				Hispanics		
System	Intercept[a]	Slope (b)[a]	R^2	System	Intercept[a]	Slope (b)[a]	R^2
District (N=52)	-1.27 (1.00)	1.13 (.05)	.91	District (N=55)	-1.61 (.63)	.69 (.06)	.70
Mixed (N=101)	.08 (.98)	.75 (.05)	.70	Mixed (N=109)	-.42 (.36)	.56 (.05)	.49
At-Large (N=140)	2.06 (1.19)	.44 (.07)	.24	At-Large (N=142)	-.43 (.38)	.31 (.04)	.28

[a]The standard errors of the reported coefficients are provided in parentheses.

Similar results are found for Hispanics in the mixed context. When the percentage of the district-based seats within these cities won by Hispanics is regressed onto the Hispanic percentage of the VAP, the following equation results:

$$\text{District Seat } \% = -.68 + .82 \text{ VAP}\%, \text{ with } R^2 = .49 \text{ and } s_e = 4.5.$$
$$(.53) \quad (.08)$$

The regression coefficient in this equation, $b = .82$, actually exceeds that for this same relationship across city councils elected entirely by districts ($b = .69$, see Table 7.1). Once again, then, the greater underrepresentation in mixed cities compared to district cities is attributable to the at-large portion of the mixed systems. These results suggest that MacManus's claim that one of the most prominent features of mixed systems has been their "success at increasing and enhancing minority representation" (1985, 486-487) requires significant qualification. The enhancement is relative to at-large, not district, systems, and results from the district, not the at-large, portions of the mixed arrangements. Indeed, in many mixed cities the share of seats held by minorities would be greater if only districts were employed to elect the council.

One remaining concern, however, is the extent to which the underrepresentation in at-large systems is a function of that format per se or of other systemic features often appended to the at-large context, specifically features that preclude the use of single-shot voting to elect minority candidates. In what is often called a "pure" at-large system, voters are allowed, but not required, to cast votes for as many candidates as there are seats to be filled, and the winning candidates are determined by a plurality vote rule, that is, the top X vote recipients are elected to the X available seats. Under this at-large arrangement, minority voters may be able to elect a minority candidate despite polarized voting by engaging in single-shot (also called "bullet") voting. Minority voters simply cast fewer votes than they are entitled to cast, concentrating their votes upon one (maybe two) minority candidates and withholding votes from all of the competing candidates. If the votes cast by majority voters are sufficiently dispersed across the other candidates, a minority candidate (or candidates) may be elected under the plurality rule on the basis of minority votes alone.

Not all at-large systems permit single-shot voting. In 62 of the at-large cities included in our analysis, each at-large seat is contested separately. Candidates file for a particular place or post and voters are allowed to vote for only one of the candidates seeking that particular seat. Fifty-two of these place systems also require that a candidate receive a majority of the votes cast for the particular seat as a condition for election (runoffs being held between the top two candidates if necessary). The place system creates, in effect, a citywide single-member district, making it difficult for a citywide minority to elect a candidate from its group, especially if a majority of the votes is required.

Another systemic feature that prevents single-shot voting is a full-slate law (sometimes referred to as an anti-single-shot law). A full-slate provision requires voters to cast as many votes as there are seats to be filled; ballots on which fewer votes are cast are considered invalid and not counted (the same as if the voter had voted for more candidates than there were seats). Only three cities included in our analysis have this requirement.

The single-shot and anti-single-shot variation in at-large arrangements must be considered before it can be concluded that the at-large format itself is an impediment to the election of minorities (O'Rourke 1982, 96-97). Regression analyses of the relationship between the percentages of the VAP have been performed for each group of at-large cities, those that permit and those that preclude single-shot voting. The relationship for Blacks in those cities permitting single-shot voting (N = 78) is:

$$\text{Seat \%} = .05 + .60 \text{ VAP\%, with } R^2 = .40 \text{ and } s_e = 9.4,$$
$$(1.44)\ (.08)$$

and in those in which it is precluded (N = 62):

$$\text{Seat \%} = 5.5 + .24 \text{ VAP\%, with } R^2 = .09 \text{ and } s_e + 9.4.$$
$$(1.93)\ (.10)$$

The relationship is weaker in the cities that preclude the single-shot strategy (b = .24) than those that permit it (b = .60). Precluding single-shot voting would appear therefore to have a major depressing effect on the election of Blacks in the at-large context. It must also be noted, however, that regardless of the single-shot variation, the at-large format itself has an adverse impact. The relationship between seats and VAP within the pure at-large cities (b = .60) remains well below that for district cities (b = 1.13) and also below that for cities with a mixed system (b = .75). Permitting Black voters to single-shot for Black candidates in an at-large context does not generally produce electoral outcomes similar to those in district cities.

Precluding single-shot voting does not appear to have the same impact on Hispanics. The relationship between seats and VAP for Hispanics in those at-large cities permitting the single-shot strategy (N = 80) is:

$$\text{Seat \%} = -.28 + .22 \text{ VAP\%, with } R^2 = .18 \text{ and } s_e = 3.1;$$
$$(.42)\quad (.05)$$

while in those precluding it (N = 62):

$$\text{Seat \%} = -.44 + .37 \text{ VAP\%, with } R^2 = .35 \text{ and } s_e = 4.5.$$
$$(.68)\quad (.07)$$

The tendency to underrepresent Hispanics is more pronounced in those cities that permit the strategy (b = .22) than in those that preclude it (b = .37). Once again, however, that at-large format is associated with less minority representation. Compared to the district systems (b = .69) and also to the mixed systems (b = .56), both types of at-large systems have a depressing effect on Hispanic representation.

Figure 7.1 provides a graphic illustration of the relationships discussed above. The estimated seats/VAP relationships for blacks (1a) and Hispanics (1b) are displayed for five electoral system conditions; district arrangements (the solid lines), mixed systems overall (the large dash lines), the district portions of the mixed system (the small dash lines), at-large systems that permit single-shot voting (the dash and dotted lines), and at-large systems that preclude the single-shot strategy (the dotted lines). The major distinctions are readily apparent. The ability to convert minority electoral strength into a proportionate election of minority council members clearly varies with the degree to which elections are by districts or at-large.

EXCLUSION OF BLACK AND HISPANIC REPRESENTATIVES

As noted above, the underrepresentation of minorities on city councils not infrequently takes the form of complete exclusion from those decision-making bodies. Indeed, in almost half (47.8 percent) of the 293 cities in the black portion of our analysis, no black person had been elected to the council at the time of our survey. Among the 306 cities in the Hispanic portion, 88.9 percent were without a Hispanic representative. The absence of minority council members in many cases, of course, is attributable to Blacks and Hispanics constituting only a small portion of the city's population. But our analyses suggest that once a minority group constitutes about 10 percent, and even less, of the voting age population in a city, the type of electoral system does relate to whether a member of that group sits on the council.

Displayed in Figure 7.2 are the empirically estimated probabilities, derived through logit analyses, that a Black or Hispanic has been elected to a council given different VAP percentages and different electoral arrangements. The horizontal axes reflect the respective percentages of VAP and the vertical axes, the estimated probabilities that at least one Black or Hispanic person has won election to a council. The different curves illustrate the estimated probabilities, across VAP percentages, for the different electoral systems.

When either minority group constitutes less than 5 percent of the VAP, the type of election system employed has little impact on the probability that a member of that minority has been elected. When the percentage approaches 10, the probabilities associated with the different systems are distinctly different. The estimated probability that a Black has been elected to a council when, for example, the Black percentage of the VAP is 10.0 is about five in six (.834) under the district system. When all seats are elected at-large and Black VAP is 10 percent, the estimated probability is only .41, about half that for the district

Figure 7.1 Predicted Black (a) and Hispanic (b) Council Seat Percentages from Respective Black and Hispanic Voting Age Population Percentages

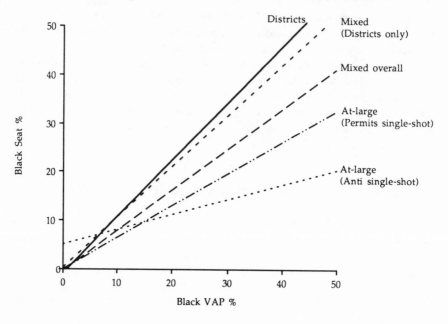

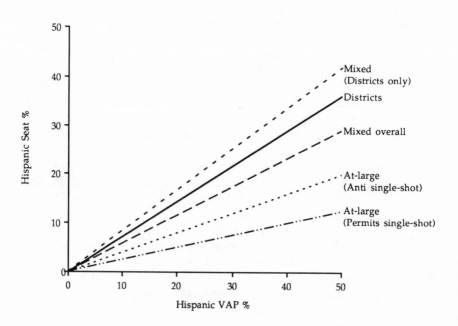

Figure 7.2 Predicted Probabilities of Election of at Least One Black (a) or Hispanic (b) across Levels of Black or Hispanic VAP Percentages

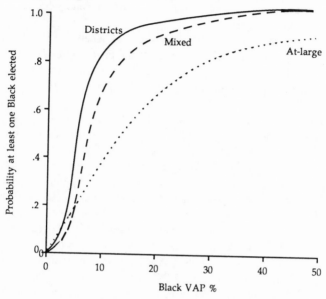

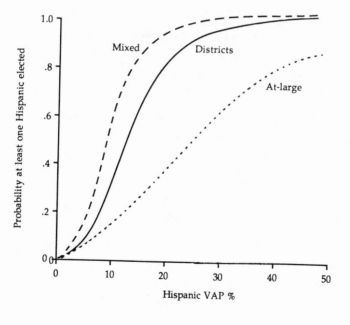

system. Indeed, the probability of electing at least one Black to a council in at-large cities does not approximate five in six until the Black VAP percentage is 40.0. At that 40 percent point the probability is .828. Blacks are, quite clearly, much more likely to be excluded from councils when elections are at-large rather than by district.

This generalization applies regardless of whether an at-large system permits single-shot voting. Table 7.2 reports the proportion of councils with at least one elected Black member among those cities with at least 10 percent Black VAP. Among the 31 at-large cities with at least 10 percent Black VAP and that permit single-shot voting, no Black was elected to the council in 25.0 percent (that is, 9 of 36). In the 34 comparable cities that prohibit single-shot voting, 41.2 percent (14 of 34) had no Blacks elected to the council. At least one Black had been elected in all 24 cities with at least 10 percent Black VAP that employed a district scheme. The probabilities for the mixed systems fall between the other two but are generally much closer to those for the district systems. This is due, not surprisingly, to Blacks being elected to district seats in those systems. Among the 57 mixed cities with at least 10 percent Black VAP, no Black had been elected to an at-large seat in 77.2 percent, while none had been elected to a district seat in only 17.5 percent.

The estimated probabilities that at least one Hispanic has been elected to a council, as shown in Figure 7.2, reflect a similar difference between at-large and district systems. When the Hispanic percentage of the VAP is at 10, the estimated probability that a Hispanic has been elected in a district city

Table 7.2 Percentage of Councils Elected by Different Systems with at Least One Elected Minority Member (Cities with at Least 10 Percent Minority Voting Age Population)

System	Blacks		Hispanics	
	Percent of Councils	(N)	Percent of Councils	(N)
District	100.0	(24)	66.7	(9)
Mixed	84.2	(57)	84.6	(13)
a. Districts	82.5	(57)	84.6	(13)
b. At-Large	22.8	(57)	0.0	(13)
At-Large	67.1	(70)	29.2	(24)
a. Single-Shot	75.0	(36)	18.2	(11)
b. No Single-Shot	58.8	(34)	38.5	(13)

(.347) is again more than twice that for the at-large context (.151). That probability exceeds .8 among the district cities when Hispanic VAP is at 22 percent (.805), but does not reach .8 for the at-large cities until Hispanic VAP is at 50 percent (.808). Hispanics, as are Blacks, are much more likely to be excluded from councils when elections are at-large rather than by districts.

   This generalization also applies regardless of whether or not single-shot voting is permitted in the at-large systems. In the right side of Table 7.2, one sees that among the at-large cities with at least 10 percent Hispanic VAP, no Hispanic had been elected to the council in 81.8 percent of those that permit single-shot voting (9 of 11), and in 61.5 percent of those that preclude it (8 of 13). In only 33.3 percent of the district cities with at least 10 percent Hispanic VAP (3 of 9) were Hispanics excluded completely from the council. The estimates in Figure 7.2 as well as the numbers in Table 7.2 reveal that the probabilities of a Hispanic being elected are greatest among the mixed cities. For example, when Hispanic VAP is at 10.0 percent, the probability of a Hispanic being elected in a mixed city is .610, considerably higher than in the district-only cities, in which it is only .347. This probability exceeds .8 in mixed cities when VAP is at 15 percent (.819), compared to a required 22 percent Hispanic VAP in district cities and a required 50 percent Hispanic VAP in at-large cities. A closer look at these mixed cities, however, demonstrates that it is the district seats that are responsible for this. In the 13 mixed cities with at least 10 percent Hispanic VAP, an Hispanic had been elected to a district seat in 11, and to an at-large seat in none.

CONCLUSION

   The debate in the United States concerning whether city council members should be elected by districts or at-large addresses a serious structural policy issue. The evidence reported here strongly supports the proposition that members of the two major minority groups in the United States, Blacks and Hispanics, are more likely to be elected if elections are held by districts rather than at-large. District electoral systems do not guarantee the election of minorities, of course, and may easily be gerrymandered to the disadvantage of minority voters (Engstrom and Wildgen 1977; and Lyons and Jewell 1988). But the tendency for minorities to be elected more frequently to district than at-large seats is empirically undeniable.

   This tendency, in the case of Blacks, has been well documented previously, and our results simply reinforce conclusions reported in other studies. In the case of Hispanics, however, our findings are contrary to previously reported conclusions. Hispanics tend to be less residentially segregated than Blacks (Massey 1979a; 1979b; Lopez 1981; Bohland 1982; Hwang and Murdock 1982), and therefore do not, as a general matter, benefit from districts to the same extent as Blacks. Hispanic integration is apparently not so great, however, that districts have no positive impact at all on their electoral opportunities. Hispanics are more likely to be elected when the district format rather than the at-large format is employed. Whether election is to be by districts or at-large, therefore, is a serious issue for the Hispanic minority as well as the Black.

APPENDIX

The tables below provide descriptive information on the two primary variables used in the analyses--(1) Black/Hispanic percentage of the voting age population and (2) elected Black/Hispanic council members as a percentage of all council members. The summary statistics are reported for all cities used in the analysis and are broken down by electoral system types.

City Type	N	Mean	Std. Dev.	Min.	Max.	Summary Statistics on Black VAP Percentage		
						Number of Cities with Black VAP %		
						< 10%	10-30%	> 30%
All Cities	293	14.2%	12.5%	.1%	48.9%	142	110	41
District	52	14.2	13.7	.1	45.9	28	14	10
Mixed	101	14.9	12.7	.3	48.9	44	43	14
At-Large	140	13.7	11.8	.2	48.6	70	53	17
Single-Shot	78	12.6	11.8	.2	43.9	42	26	10
Anti-Single Shot	62	15.0	11.8	.2	48.6	28	27	7

City Type	N	Mean	Std. Dev.	Min.	Max.	Summary Statistics on Black Percentage of Council Members		
						Number of Cities with Black % Members		
						=0	1-30%	>30%
All Cities	293	10.4%	12.3%	0.0%	57.1%	140	137	16
District	52	14.8	16.3	0	55.6	20	22	10
Mixed	101	11.3	11.5	0	42.9	41	56	4
At-Large	140	8.1	10.5	0	57.1	79	59	2
Single-Shot	78	7.6	11.2	0	57.1	47	29	2
Anti-Single	62	8.7	9.7	0	28.6	32	30	0

Summary Statistics on Hispanic VAP Percentage

City Type	N	Mean	Std. Dev.	Min.	Max.	Number of Cities with Hispanic VAP% <10%	10-30%	>30%
All Cities	306	4.6%	7.6%	.3%	48.0%	260	39	7
District	55	5.2	8.6	.4	48.0	46	7	2
Mixed	109	3.7	5.4	.3	30.7	96	12	1
At-Large	142	5.1	7.7	.3	41.4	118	20	4
Single-Shot	80	4.6	6.6	.3	38.7	69	9	2
Anti-Single Shot	62	5.8	8.8	.4	41.4	49	11	2

Summary Statistics on Hispanic Percentage of Council Members

City Type	N	Mean	Std. Dev.	Min.	Max.	Number of Cities with Hispanic % Members =0	1-30%	>30%
All Cities	306	1.5%	5.0%	0.0%	40.0%	272	32	2
District	55	2.0	7.2	0	40.0	47	6	2
Mixed	109	1.7	4.3	0	16.7	93	16	0
At-Large	142	1.1	4.4	0	28.6	132	10	0
Single-Shot	80	.7	3.4	0	20.0	76	4	0
Anti-Single	62	1.7	5.5	0	28.6	56	6	0

Note: Twenty-four of the possible 317 cities are not included in the analyses of Black representation either because the Black voting age population information is not reported by the Census or because the 1980 Black voting age population percentage is above 50. The cities excluded because of missing VAP information are: Dubuque (IA), Lewiston (ME), Bangor (ME), St. Cloud (MN), Billings (MT), Medford (OH), Fargo (ND), Sioux Falls (SD), Laredo (TX), Provo (UT), Bellingham (WA), Eau Claire (WI), La Crosse (WI), Wausau (WI), and Sheboyan (WI). The cities excluded because Blacks are a majority of the 1980 VAP are: Birmingham (AL), Atlanta (GA), Gary (IN), Baltimore (MD), Benton Harbor (MI), Detroit (MI), Newark (NJ), Petersburg (VA), and Washington D.C.

Eleven of the possible 317 cities are not included in the analyses of Hispanic representation because the Hispanic voting age population information is not reported by the Census or because the 1980 Hispanic voting age population percentage is above 50. The cities excluded because of missing VAP information are: Lewiston (ME), Bangor (ME), Bismarck (ND), Sharon (PA), La Crosse (WI), and Wausau (WI). The cities excluded because Hispanics are a majority of the population are: Miami (FL), Brownsville (TX), El Paso (TX), Laredo (TX), and McAllen (TX).

8

Voting for Minority Candidates in Local British and American Elections
Donley T. Studlar and Susan Welch

The quantity and quality of minority group political representation is one test of how well racially or ethnically integrated an advanced industrial society is.[1] Studies of minority group popular representation often focus on the central legislative body. In the United States, for instance, the growth of Black representatives in Congress has been carefully documented, as has the fact that almost all of them represent majority or near-majority Black districts (Karnig and Welch 1980, 4). In the United Kingdom, attention was directed to the 1987 election of the first four non-white Members of Parliament for half a century.[2]

Despite the importance of this representation, the more significant events for ethnic and racial integration may be at lower levels of government. Members of Congress and Parliament are few, but local government representatives are much more numerous and socially diverse. Furthermore, the ranks of lower-level representatives provide a base from which some attempt to move to higher-level office.[3] In short, if we truly want to understand the processes at work in popular elections of minority group members, we need to examine the base as well as the pinnacle. In this study, we examine the electoral fate of minority candidates for office. Our major data collection and analysis effort focuses on London, in Britain, but we will examine these findings in light of research on Black candidates for local office in the United States.

*The authors acknowledge the assistance of Zig Layton-Henry and Marian Fitzgerald, who provided some of the data used in the paper, and the University of Nebraska Research Council and the Centre College Faculty Development Committee, which supported other data collection. Suggestions offered by a seminar at Iowa State University, especially those of Jorgen Rasmussen and James Simmons, were also helpful.

BLACK ELECTED OFFICIALS IN BRITAIN

Descriptive data on Black elected officials in Britain are spotty. On the one hand, data collection is easier than in the United States, where local elections take place at diverse times in different cities and states, and where differences in election structures make comparisons difficult. By contrast, British local elections take place once a year, and the results of many of these elections are collected and published in a central location (Rawlings and Thrasher 1985; 1986; London Residuary Body, 1986). On the other hand, only in the 1980s has the number of non-white candidates and elected officials been sufficiently numerous for generalizations about them to be made with any confidence. This is particularly true since most of this growth in candidates and councilors has occurred in London, obviously a major part of the British polity, but not necessarily a representative part.

Few analyses have been done of the non-white candidates and officials in Britain. Anwar (1986) summarizes the position of non-white candidates in local elections. The most systematic, though highly descriptive, examination of non-white candidates in British local elections has been carried on by LeLohe (1975; 1979; 1984), focusing principally on Asian descendants in the city of Bradford. More recently, and with a broader focus, Fitzgerald (1986) has explored both the nature of the districts and attitudes of non-white local councilors in London. Other than these specific studies, there are only passing comments on local candidates and officials in more general works on the role of non-whites in British politics (Crewe 1983; Fitzgerald 1984; Layton-Henry 1984; Studlar 1985).

The descriptive data we do have indicate that, starting with only 4 minority councilors in London boroughs in 1974, the number grew to 35 in 1978, more than doubled by 1982, and increased again, to 132, in 1986. Outside the capital, both non-white candidates and knowledge about them drop precipitously. In 1982, there were estimated to be about 76 non-white councilors outside of London (LeLohe 1984; Anwar 1986).

Given the growth of non-white candidates and elected officials, it seems a propitious moment to analyze systematically the electability of non-white candidates to local government councils in Britain. It is also useful to put these findings in the context of what we know about non-white candidates in American local politics, though as we shall see, our knowledge there is not as rich as one might expect.

COMPARING MINORITIES ACROSS POLITIES

The comparison with the United States seems useful because of the tendency of political observers in Britain to point to the United States as an example of what might occur in race relations in the United Kingdom (Anwar 1986; Glazer and Young 1983). This perspective has been applied in studies of the immigrant experience (Katznelson 1973), the values and social structure underpinning racial disadvantage (Rose et al. 1969), urban riots (Benyon 1984), the general structure of decision making and policy implementation in urban areas (Jacobs 1986), and the mass political behavior of racial minorities (Welch and Studlar 1985).

As Richard Rose (1974) reminds us, however, one must be careful in making comparisons, especially those concerning the United States as the model that the United Kingdom is impelled (if not compelled) to follow. This advice holds true for race relations as well. There are as many, if not more, points of dissimilarity between the two countries as points of similarity.

In race relations, obvious major points of similarity include having a small minority (12 percent in the United States, 5 percent in the United Kingdom) of people socially designated by skin color, mainly living in urban areas, subject to discriminatory practices based on their racial identity in a society ostensibly devoted to equal rights. But the basic differences are also striking. Despite the fact that the first appearance of non-whites in Britain was in the Roman era (Ramdin 1987, 1), there is a much longer experience of significant minority group residence in the United States, the culture of Blacks in the United States is much more uniform than the culture of "Blacks" in the United Kingdom,[4] and the history of state-enforced discrimination, beginning with slavery, in the United States has not been matched in Britain, where non-whites entered under the legal guarantee of equal rights (Ramdin 1987).

For present purposes, we shall assume enough similarity between the two polities and the situation of racially defined minority groups in the two societies to enable a reasonable comparison to be done. There is, however, at least one important difference relevant to this analysis. While elections at the central level in both systems are now firmly based on the single-member district, simple plurality electoral system, at the local level there are significant variations that may affect racial minority group representations.[5] In both countries, some localities have multimember districts, not in the continental European pattern of party list proportional representation, but in what Lakeman (1970) calls the block vote. At the local level in the United States, such block votes usually have the whole city as a constituency, the so-called at-large electoral system which has been the subject of challenge by Black and Hispanic groups claiming that it inhibits their representation (Davidson 1984). In Britain, multimember election is usually based on the principle of two or three (or sometimes more) members per district and is never at-large.

Our study of non-white representation in London will examine the following questions: (1) In what kinds of local election districts do non-whites tend to receive party nominations? (2) How does race influence electability of candidates? (3) Do patterns of candidacy and electability vary by party?

DATA AND METHODS

The data for this chapter are from the London Borough Council elections of May 1986. Most of these elections were multimember, with two or three seats per ward, with the same boundaries as in the 1982 elections. Every other ward was sampled using a systematic sampling procedure with a random start and using as the sampling frame the list compiled by the Research and Intelligence Unit in the London Residuary Body (1986). Within each sampled ward, data were collected on all candidates. Through this procedure, 2,960 candidates were sampled, about half of the 5,992 candidates in the election.

Using the candidate as the unit of analysis, several candidate characteristics were coded, including first whether or not the candidate won, and second, the candidate's party. Party labels other than Labour, Conservative, Social Democratic party (SDP), and Liberal were coded in an eclectic "other" category (comprising only 6 percent of all candidates), while SDP and Liberal were joined together in an Alliance category. Using similar data from the 1982 London Borough Election results to determine if the candidate had won previously, we also coded whether each candidate was an incumbent.[6] The sex and ethnic identity of each candidate were also coded.

Since the race categorization is crucial to this analysis, further explanation about coding is imperative. Candidates with South Asian names were coded as Asian.[7] Names that were obviously African in origin were coded as Afro-Caribbean, but most Afro-Caribbean candidates' names are not different from other typically British names. We were greatly aided in identifying Afro-Caribbean candidates and verifying Asian ones by a publication called *New Life & Gujarat Samachar Election Special*, which published a lengthy article called "Meet Your Afro Asian Candidates." Complete with photos of many of the candidates, this publication identified by borough Afro-Caribbean and Asian candidates of all parties. We also cross-checked candidates' names against lists published in "The Asian Voice," *Shakti*, September 13, 1986; "Meet Your Councillors," *New Life*, May 18, 1986; and a list of Afro-Caribbean councilors in London as of 1982 compiled by Marian Fitzgerald (1986). While we make no claim to have correctly identified every Afro-Caribbean or Asian candidate in our sample, we are confident that we have come close, especially with Asian candidates.

Aside from the characteristics of the candidates, three characteristics of the contest itself were also coded: the total number of candidates, the number of incumbents running, and the number of seats contested. From these data, we created a variable measuring the ratio of candidates to seats and one assessing competition from incumbents, created by dividing the number of incumbents who were opponents by the number of seats available. In both cases, the higher the ratio, the more competitive the seat.

We also measured the party incumbency for the seat. Again using the 1982 election returns, we assessed which party had held the seats before the 1986 elections. For each candidate, we coded two dummy variables based on this assessment: one, whether or not his or her party held all the seats in the ward; two, whether or not the party held some but not all the seats.

Our primary mode of analysis is regression. A simple model of electoral success is used (for previous uses of the model see Welch and Studlar 1988; Studlar and Welch 1987; Welch et al. 1985). The model predicts that electoral success is a function of party and personal incumbency, the opponent's incumbency, competitiveness (candidates per seat), and party. We also controlled for the candidate's sex and the number of seats in the district. Thus, we regressed whether or not the candidate won on the characteristics we have just described and on the two non-white dummy variables. The unstandardized regression coefficients for our race variables indicate the extent to which the characteristic of being Afro-Caribbean or being Asian affects the outcome of the election, taking into account the other factors in our model.

FINDINGS

The Success of Non-White Candidates in London

Table 8.1 indicates that, not surprisingly, most candidates for London borough seats were white. Only 1.5 percent were Afro-Caribbean and only

Table 8.1 Ethnic Identity of Candidates by Proportion Non-White in Constituency

	Candidates	Percent Non-White			
		Less than 7	7 to 20	21 to 46	Total
Afro-Caribbean	(45)	.1	1.2	4.0	1.5
Asian	(126)	1.3	3.0	10.4	4.3
White	(2789)	98.6	95.9	85.5	94.2
Total	(2960)				

Note: Based on all candidates in a sample of half the ward elections in the London borough elections of 1986. Percent non-white in the constituency is a population, not an electorate, figure based on parliamentary constituencies which encompass several (often 6 to 10) wards (Waller 1983).

slightly more, 4.3 percent, were Asian. Thus, as candidates, the non-white population is underrepresented by about half relative to their population proportions in London.[8] Even so, these figures represent an increase from 1978, when non-whites were 2 percent of the candidates, and 1982, when they were 4 percent. We can assume the numbers will continue to rise (LeLohe 1984).

One aspect of discrimination against non-whites could, of course, be to select them only for contests in which they would have no chance of winning in anything but a freak election. However, Table 8.2 indicates that this does not appear to be the case in London. Afro-Caribbean candidates are considerably more likely than whites to be nominated for seats where their party is securely in control. Asian candidates are slightly less likely than whites to be nominated in secure seats, but the difference is fairly small and not significant.

However, there are clear party differences in the propensity to nominate non-whites for safe seats. Labour's non-white candidates are much more likely to be nominated for safe seats than their white candidates, while for the Conservatives the reverse is true (Anwar 1986). The Alliance has only a few wards they control, and only a few of their candidates, all white, have the luxury of running in such races.

In some senses, Labour's nomination of non-white candidates is not surprising, in that those wards with high proportions of non-whites are likely to

Table 8.2 Candidates by Ethnicity and Prior Party Control of Seat

	Afro-Caribbean	Asian	White
Percent of Candidates in Contests Where Party Controls All Seats	47[a]	25	30[c]
Percent of Candidates in Contest Where Party Controls Part but Not All Seats	7	5	4
Percent of Candidates in Contests Where Party Controls All Seats, by Party:			
Labour	57	58	33[c]
Conservative	20	11	56[c]
Alliance[b]	0	0	7

[a]This means that 47 percent of all Afro-Caribbean candidates ran in races where their party previously controlled all the seats.
[b]No other party controlled all seats in a ward.
[c]Ethnic differences significant at .05.

be Labour strongholds. Labour in part, then, is appealing to its own constituency by nominating non-whites in these wards (LeLohe 1984). But one should not overstate the point. Most of the wards of high non-white populations are still majority white, as best we can determine from the census data.[9] Thus, it is not a foregone conclusion that Labour must run non-white candidates.

In Table 8.3 we examine the probabilities that candidates of different races will win, categorized by the proportion of non-white population of the parliamentary constituency within which the ward lies (Waller 1983). Here we see that Afro-Caribbean candidates win twice as often as whites, overall, and that Asian candidates win an almost identical proportion of the time as whites. LeLohe found the same pattern in London borough elections of 1982, so these are not anomalous results. As might be expected, Afro-Caribbean and Asian candidates win most often when the non-white population is over 7 percent, but clearly many of these candidates are winning races in districts where non-whites are a rather small minority.

Reasons for greater Afro-Caribbean success are complex. One is that Afro-Caribbeans may not be as recognizable on the ballot as Asians, whose names are distinctive. Many white voters may not realize certain Afro-Caribbean candidates are in fact Afro-Caribbean, so that these candidates do not have a great disadvantage with white voters and may still have a special advantage with Afro-Caribbean voters. Most Asian candidates, on the other

Table 8.3 Proportion of Races Won, by Proportion Non-White in Constituency

Percent Non-White	Percent of Successful Candidates		
in Constituency	Afro-Caribbean	Asian	White
7 or Less	0[a]	25	33
	(1)	(12)	(925)
8 to 20	60	23	32
	(15)	(39)	(1249)
21 to 46	69	36	29
	(29)	(75)	(615)
All Constituencies	64	31	32
	(45)	(126)	(2789)

[a]Numbers in parentheses are number of candidates of each race running in the constituencies of specified proportion non-white. Thus, of 15 Afro-Caribbean candidates running in constituencies of 8 to 20 percent non-white, 60 percent won. Note that constituency data are from parliamentary constituencies which encompass several (most are 6 to 10) wards.

hand, are clearly recognizable by their names, and any white voter who wants to act in a prejudiced manner can do so easily. And, in fact, relative to their numbers, Afro-Caribbean candidates are somewhat more likely to finish first on their ticket than Asians.

Moreover, as we have already seen, most Afro-Caribbeans are Labour candidates, and it is among the Labour candidates that Afro-Caribbeans do better (not shown). Only 10 percent of Afro-Caribbean Conservatives and Alliance candidates won, but their numbers are so small that the differences between them and white candidates are not statistically significant. Greater Afro-Caribbean electoral success is also partially explained by the fact that most Afro-Caribbean candidates are nominated in districts of more than 21 percent non-white, safe Labour constituencies in which Labour candidates of all races win at rates around 80 percent. Only a small minority of white Labour candidates run in these districts, while over two-thirds of Afro-Caribbean candidates do. Then, too, for some reason, Afro-Caribbean Labour candidates are much more likely than Labour's Asian or white candidates to win election in constituencies that are 8 to 20 percent non-white.

Another factor worth noting when we examine different rates of success by party is that Asian candidates in the Labour party do somewhat better than white candidates at each level of non-white population. However, Conservative Asian candidates do worse than whites in districts that are over 8 percent non-white. Again, this appears to be because these are relatively safe Labour seats. Indeed there are many instances where white Labour candidates defeat Asian Conservatives in these areas of greatest Asian concentration.

Finally, we examine the other factors that predict election victory: party, incumbency, and competition. As demonstrated in Table 8.4, our eleven variables measuring these factors and candidate characteristics explain a rather substantial 54 percent of the variation in whether candidates win or lose. The most important predictor of victory is, not unexpectedly, party incumbency. Running in a ward where a candidate's own party controls all the seats enhances the prospect of victory by about 87 percent, and even running in a ward where one's party controls only some of the seats increases winning prospects by about 40 percent. Personal incumbency increases the chance of winning, but less so, as does running in London on the Labour ticket rather than on one of the others.

Not only is British local politics highly partisan, but local election outcomes are also heavily influenced by the current popular standing of the parliamentary parties (Peterson and Kantor 1977). With this double impact of partisanship, central and local, there is little room left for characteristics of individual candidates, even incumbency, to have an effect on the results. Yet even after controlling for party, personal and party incumbency, and competition, Asian candidates do just as well as whites and Afro-Caribbeans win about 15 percent more of the time.

Table 8.4 The Effect of Ethnicity and Other Factors on Election Success

		All	
	b	beta	t
Afro-Caribbean	.15[a]	.04	3.01
Asian	.02	.01	0.58
Sex	.00	.00	0.35
Party			
Conservative	-.22[a]	-.22	-14.65
Alliance	-.11[a]	-.11	-6.84
Other	-.15[a]	-.08	-5.39
Incumbency	.14[a]	.11	6.99
Party Incumbency = All	.67[a]	.65	37.00
Party Incumbency = Some	.40[a]	.17	12.75
Opponent Incumbent/			
Seat Ratio	-.04[a]	-.03	-2.33
Number of Seats	.00	.00	0.05
Candidates per Seat	-.01	-.01	-0.97
R^2	.54		
N	2952		

[a]Significant at .05

We have seen that being Afro-Caribbean or Asian does not seem to harm a candidate's chance of winning and may even help it. But are voters completely color-blind? To answer that question we look at the order in which candidates of the same party finish in their election. We compare whether non-white candidates finished first as often as their white counterparts of the same party, and whether white ones finished last as often as their non-white colleagues. Thus, our comparisons are candidates of the same party running for the same seats when at least one of the candidates is non-white. If three Labourites are running in a three-seat constituency and at least one is white, for example, we compare the fate of the non-white candidate(s) with that of the white one(s) in that race.

Non-white candidates do tend to run behind white candidates of the same party. For example, in two seat-races where one candidate of a particular party was non-white and the other white, the non-white finished ahead of the white only about one-quarter of the time, compared to the half one would expect by chance. In three-seat races, where by chance one would expect the non-white candidate to finish in third place only 33 percent of the time, in fact they finish in third place 58 percent of the time.[10]

Interestingly, however, the strength of voters' partisan loyalties is such that the vote spreads between the first and last candidate of a particular party are usually very small. Thus, in all of the instances where the non-white candidate finished behind the white, only eight times was the vote spread enough to cost the non-white candidates the election when their white counterparts won, and in two of those cases, another white candidate of the same party also lost. In a ninth case, the non-white candidate won and a white counterpart lost. In all other cases, either all candidates won or all lost.

Thus, in Britain, on average non-white candidates win as often as white candidates and sometimes more often. This is partially due to the tendency of Afro-Caribbean candidates, particularly, to run in safe seat races for the Labour party. However, there is a tendency for non-white candidates to finish somewhat behind their party cohorts in votes, but rarely is this difference large enough to cost the election. In sum, once non-white candidates are picked to run, they win as often or more often than whites.

Non-White Candidates in American Local Elections

How do these findings compare with the situation in the United States? First of all, there are many more Black elected officials in the United States, about 8,700 at all levels, about 2 percent of all officeholders. However, since tens of thousands of officeholders serve in rural areas where there are no Blacks, this figure is not especially meaningful. More meaningful is the fact that Blacks comprise about 6 percent of American state legislatures and about 5 percent in the U.S. House. Both of these represent somewhat less than half their population proportion.

There have been numerous studies that have tried to explain why Black representation fluctuates from city to city or state to state (Cole 1976; MacManus 1978; Engstrom and McDonald 1981; Taebel 1978; Robinson and Dye 1978; Karnig and Welch 1980; Davidson and Korbel 1981; Browning, Marshall, and Tabb, 1984; Grofman, Migalski, and Noviello, 1986). Two types of research on minority representation dominate the literature. The first compares the percent of Black elected officials serving on city councils with the percent of Blacks living in the community. This research, usually based on data from 100 or more cities of 25,000 or 50,000 and above, has fairly consistently found that in cities that elect council members in single-member districts, Blacks are represented at near parity with their population proportions (for reviews of this extensive literature see Karnig and Welch 1980; 1982; Engstrom and McDonald 1981; 1982; Davidson and Korbel 1981; Grofman 1982). In cities that elect council members at-large, Blacks are represented at less than 50 percent of their population proportion (Engstrom and McDonald 1981). These findings have led U.S. courts to order cities of substantial Black population and few Black representatives to adopt district based electoral systems.

Other research examines voting patterns for Black candidates in local elections. Though this research would seem somewhat comparable with that of the authors, it is only vaguely so. Few studies as broad-based as ours in London exist. Most of them are case studies, focusing on one or a few elections in one city (many of the studies have been done in only two cities, Los Angeles (Halley, Acock, and Green, 1976; Hahn and Almy 1971; Hahn, Klingman, and Pachon, 1976); and Atlanta (Bullock and Campbell 1984; Jennings and Zeigler 1984), while other studies have examined Charlotte, Chicago, Cincinnati, Cleveland, Dallas, Gary, Houston, Memphis, and New Orleans (Levine 1974; Nelson and Meranto 1977; Arrington 1978; Murray and Vedlitz 1978; Lieske and Howard 1984; Perry and Stokes 1987). Though a single-city study is not especially limiting when, as in London, we can examine elections for over 1,900 council seats, with dozens of minority candidates, no American city has councils approaching that size. Chicago, which has by far the largest council of any major American city, has 50 council members. Most cities have between 7 and 15 members. Thus, in the United States a one-city approach limits the kind of generalizations that can be made about the success of non-white candidates. The ability to generalize is limited even further by the tendency of these studies to focus on mayoral races.

Moreover, given the limitations of the data, these studies have not really been able to develop generalizations about the fate of Black and white candidates controlling for relevant party and incumbency variables. Indeed, because of the small number of candidates examined (often candidates for only one office in one election), most of the studies do not, or cannot, control for incumbency and competition, factors key to understanding legislative election outcomes, if not mayoral races.

What this research does tell us, however, is that voting for non-white candidates in U.S. municipal elections is largely based on the voter's race. Blacks tend to vote for Blacks and whites for whites. In Black versus white mayoral contests, from 10 to 20 percent of whites will vote for the Black candidate, and the proportion of Blacks voting for the white candidate is even less (Rich 1987; Henry 1987). Obviously, many voters cross racial lines, but the race-based pattern is clear.[11]

The influence of class, issues, and especially partisanship does mitigate the purity of racial voting (Lieske and Howard 1984; Jennings and Zeigler 1984; Murray and Vedlitz 1978). In partisan elections voters are more likely to cross racial lines in their voting.

While we cannot derive from these studies an understanding of the overall voter bias for or against Black candidates as we could with our London data, we can conclude that in the United States, race plays a major role in shaping individuals' voting behavior when candidates of different races compete.

DISCUSSION

The situation of non-white candidates in London appears to be one of continuing gradual integration into party politics and local government. Both the number of candidacies and the number elected have grown. Although these trends are more evident in the Labour party, all parties present non-white candidates to the electorate. The Labour party, however, makes more of an effort to nominate both Afro-Caribbean and Asian candidates in winnable seats. Since party nominations are in the hands of local ward selection committees, significant non-white Labour membership in heavily non-white wards undoubtedly influences the choice of candidates.

While non-whites are still underrepresented as candidates and local councilors in comparison to their share of the population, the disparity is not as great at the local level in London as at the parliamentary level. Nonetheless, some non-white London local councilors, principally Afro-Caribbeans, are vociferous proponents of Black sections within the Labour party. Briefly, their argument is that non-whites should constitute a separate, formally recognized part of the party in order to insure adequate non-white inclusion in all Labour party deliberations. While it is indeed true that non-whites are not proportionally represented in these elections, the data here indicate a dramatic rise in the numbers of non-whites running and great success for those nominated. Thus, unless progress is stalemated, this sort of formal separation of non-whites is not necessary in order to secure a greater share of candidacies and seats on the local level, an argument that Labour party leader Neil Kinnock has made in opposing Black sections.

The multivariate analysis shows that, far from being an electoral liability, compared to whites Afro-Caribbeans are more likely to be elected and Asians as likely, once the party and incumbency effects are controlled. The only evidence of any voter backlash is the tendency of non-whites to finish slightly behind their white counterparts in contests with both white and non-white candidates of the same party. The uniqueness of these findings is not just that the much-discussed white backlash against ethnic minority candidates is not much in evidence in these London elections (other studies have shown the white backlash to have been reduced or eliminated at the parliamentary level, Fitzgerald 1983), but that Afro-Caribbeans are actually advantaged in winning once nominated.

The electoral system in London and the party system in Britain both may contribute to the good showing of non-white candidates. The electoral system for the London boroughs, largely multimember districts, in combination with a strong party system, offers some advantage to minorities. Proponents of multimember systems, even those without proportional representation, often contend that minority representation is improved by the need to appeal to various sectors of society with a team of candidates, that is, by ticket balancing

(Bogdanor 1984; Lakeman 1970). Evidence supporting this hypothesis is not overwhelming, largely because a country usually has one dominant electoral system. Nevertheless, our London borough findings, as well as others (LeLohe 1984), suggest that the hypothesis deserves further investigation.[12] The opportunity for ticket balancing in a multimember electoral system may have helped dissipate the white backlash evident in the past, and perhaps still existing in attenuated form, for single-member plurality parliamentary elections.

However, this ticket balancing advantage would seem to work only in cases where there are strong parties that can select party nominees. In the United States, where the party system is weak and where the nominees are chosen in primaries, the multimember district system only intensifies whatever voter prejudice exists. Without party slates offering a representative group of candidates, in multimember systems voters find it easy to pick and choose among the candidates to vote for only those of their own skin color.

Since party nominations are locally controlled in Britain, party ward organizations can take action on their own as they feel it necessary to bring non-whites into the system. The London Labour party is known for trying to bring more minorities into the political process.

Furthermore, with a declining Labour party membership and voter allegiance, non-whites have become a larger share of the total. Thus, they are in a good position in London local elections to get a reasonable portion of nominations and seats. They are not as well situated in other parties and in other areas of the country, however.

The tenacity with which electors stick to their chosen party, irrespective of the personal characteristics of the candidates or voters, is remarkable. Party politics overwhelms racial and ethnic politics. Nominating non-white candidates for local office does not appear to harm the voters' otherwise strong party feelings. Though minority candidates do disproportionately run second or third on their party's ticket, it is usually only by a small margin, and only in a literal handful of cases did this cause one to lose an election. These findings support Fitzgerald's (1983) contention that party is more important than ethnic identity, even at the parliamentary level. The findings can be contrasted with those from the United States, where in largely nonpartisan elections, the voter's race becomes the most important determinant of whether he or she will vote for a Black candidate. The partisan glue binding together voters and candidates of different races is weak or nonexistent. In this situation, unless Black voters have their own majority Black districts, Black candidates fare relatively poorly.[13]

CONCLUSION

It is ironic that our examination of the role of non-white candidates in local elections in Britain and the United States should reach conclusions at such variance with much of the conventional comparative wisdom concerning race and politics in these two countries. An often-expressed goal is that British non-whites achieve the degree of representation that Blacks in the United States do. But in at least one important dimension, British non-whites are already better integrated than U.S. Blacks. While U.S. Blacks depend on large, often majority Black populations to elect them to public office, British non-whites can be elected without such a substantial block vote. Having a large non-white population in the ward is undoubtedly helpful in securing party nominations, an important feature to remember, but once nominated, party takes over as the main impetus for voter choice.

For some time a debate has been raging over whether non-whites in the United Kingdom are becoming more integrated into the society and polity or more alienated. The 1981 and 1985 urban riots, the Black sections furor, and the pronouncements of some Black intellectuals and group leaders indicate alienation (Husband 1982; Centre for Contemporary Cultural Studies 1982). On the other hand, surveys of non-white political opinion, studies of voting for non-white candidates in parliamentary elections, and the general political behavior of non-whites suggest increasing integration (Crewe 1983; Fitzgerald 1983; 1984; 1987). Some observers have preferred to emphasize the complex and open-ended nature of the process, with some behavior potentially more integrating, other tendencies reflecting alienation (Layton-Henry 1984).

Increasingly, comparisons have been made between the experience of Jews in the United Kingdom and that of New Commonwealth immigrants and their descendants (Alderman 1983; Crewe 1983; Fitzgerald 1984, 98-97). These comparisons stress that Jews have become integrated into British society by de-emphasizing their social and political distinctiveness; indeed, such political distinctiveness has nearly disappeared by a long-term partisan shift from Labour to the Conservatives. Some observers believe that a similar process is at work today, at least among Asians.

But contemporary minorities in Britain are a diverse group, socially, culturally, residentially, and politically (McAllister and Studlar 1984; Fitzgerald 1987; Carter 1987). What non-whites have in common is a recent history of immigration and the experience of racial discrimination. However, studies of non-white political behavior indicate that some of the responses of non-white groups are similar to those of white Britons, while others are distinctive (Layton-Henry and Studlar 1985; Welch and Studlar 1985; Studlar 1986). Much more influence on political behavior has been attributed to race than is empirically justified (McAllister and Studlar 1984), though this does not mean that non-white officeholders will be indistinguishable in their policy positions from whites. To the contrary, we might expect that Afro-Caribbeans and Asian office holders will represent the distinctive group interests of non-whites. Fitzgerald (1986) finds that Afro-Caribbeans, especially, consider the election of non-white representatives a crucial sign of acceptance in the British polity.

Regardless of the policy distinctiveness of non-white MPs (Members of Parliament) and councilors, the symbolic benefits of having non-whites in office may be considerable. Descriptive representation such as this may possibly decrease feelings of alienation and increase awareness of government. There is some evidence of this in the United States (Foster 1978), where a great majority of Blacks believe that Black elected officials have been helpful to the Black cause (Jackson and Gurin 1987). On the other hand, in the United States, some Blacks have unrealistic expectations of what Black office holders can reasonably accomplish given the setting in which they work (Nelson and Van Horne 1974). Unmet expectations may lead to considerable frustration in Britain as well (Fitzgerald 1987, 97-98).

Racial discrimination still exists in the United Kingdom, and there is still widespread prejudice and animosity toward non-whites in many social and political institutions, including political parties (Bochel and Denver 1983). The legal system is not as protective of minority rights as one with a more explicit bill of rights and interventionist judiciary might be. In many ways, British political leaders are insensitive to the demands of ethnic minorities and, indeed, to the whole question of racial and ethnic differences (Bulpitt 1986; Studlar 1985). It may be that in many aspects of race relations, the British do have a lot to learn, positively and negatively, from the United States.

But despite earlier qualms about the capacity of British local politics to incorporate newly emergent racial groups (Katznelson 1973; Kantor 1976; Peterson and Kantor 1977), the London experience indicates that the highly partisan nature of British urban areas can help integrate non-whites. In this sense, strong British parties may be playing a role similar to that of urban political machines integrating immigrant ethnic groups in the pre-New Deal United States. Institutions do make a difference. Our argument is that, at least in one respect, Britain is the leader and the United States is the laggard in race relations. In local elections in London, there is no need for an individual candidate to build a "rainbow coalition." The impact of party loyalties goes a long way toward making the electorate, if not completely color-blind, at least visually impaired.

Part III

Political Consciousness, Organization,
and Participation

Minority Consciousness and Political Action:
A Comparative Approach
Richard D. Shingles

Political consciousness, the perception that politics is integral to goal attainment, is a prerequisite for political action. When group identities are linked to politics they are part of the political consciousness. The relationship between identity, political consciousness, and political participation has been the source of some confusion. Two facts are often ignored. First, it is not a matter of a single relationship, but of many, depending on the type of the group consciousness and the mode of action. Second, the effects of group consciousness on action are indirect. They influence beliefs that immediately comprise the decision whether and how to participate. This chapter strives toward a comparative theory of minority politics that will account for varied relationships between types of group consciousness and modes of political action. It centers on four prominent, political minorities in the United States: Black, Mexican, Native, and female Americans.

    Political minorities are groups that are underrepresented in positions of authority and control in the major institutions of society. They are limited to ineffectual, low-prestige, poorly paid positions within major institutions or excluded from the institutions altogether. Political minorities need not be numerical minorities. This is evidenced by Blacks in South Africa, Muslims in prerevolutionary Lebanon and the West Bank, Black and Mexican Americans in numerous communities throughout the United States, Native Americans on their own reservations, and women in most societies. Even where these groups are in the majority they are typically less influential than white men of European ancestry. Women outnumber men in the United States. Married women share the socioeconomic status of their husbands. However, most do not share their power. They have been and remain grossly underrepresented in positions of authority and control. In the 1980s, most were confined to domestic, non-wage labor or to low-wage, low-prestige, impotent jobs in a finite number of occupations commonly labeled "women's work" (e.g., domestics, waitresses, secretaries, nurses, teachers of Kindergarden through grade 12, etc.). Combined with the increased incidence of female-headed households, this has contributed to the "feminization of poverty" in the United States. Women of color, who suffer from the double jeopardy of racism and sexism, are the most deprived.

The four groups considered here have several characteristics that make them worthy of special study. First, they are biologically distinct. Physically identifiable characteristics (sex and race) have made them particularly vulnerable to prejudice and discrimination. Unlike European male immigrants, most members of biopolitical minorities find it exceedingly difficult, if not impossible, to divorce themselves from their group identities and successfully blend with the majority (Robinson and Kelley 1979; Deckard 1983, 109, 119-141; Williams 1982). For them, assimilation is not the panacea suggested by the myth of the American "melting pot." This seriously frustrates the traditional route to success, individual mobility. Second, though unique in their histories, subcultures and resources, American political minorities share with the political majority a common culture and institutional context that define available modes of political action. Thus certain systemic factors that influence the relationship between minority consciousness and political action are controlled. Third, Black, Mexican, Native, and female Americans are the four most visible biopolitical minorities in the United States with the most incessant histories of subordination. All have been the victims of sustained, systematic legal and de facto discrimination that has traditionally excluded them from positions of individual wealth and influence and relegated them to inferior status. They have suffered the stigma of well-developed ideologies (sexism and racism) that rationalize their status. Although they have made significant gains since World War II and numerous individual members have obtained positions of considerable authority and control, the groups as a whole remain subordinate, suffering the effects of persistent prejudice and institutional discrimination. They are relatively powerless and deprived.[1]

The histories and statuses of prominent U. S. biopolitical minorities are well documented (Marable 1983; 1984; Deckard 1983; Wise 1971; Acuña 1981). The purpose of this chapter is to provide a theoretical framework for understanding the diverse ways members of these groups respond to minority status. Attention will be given to identifying prominent types of minority consciousness and their influence in the decision whether and how to participate politically. A detailed documentation of the generalization for each group awaits a larger work.[2]

UNDERSTANDING MINORITY RESPONSES

Minority political action takes place within the context of institutional and cultural forces that determine and rationalize the minority's subordinate status. Predominant cultural images and conceptual frameworks bolster the major institutions in society, legitimizing the status quo. A principal task of minority leaders is to provide alternative images and frameworks that will mobilize their followers to alter the status quo. These alternative views constitute a form of group consciousness, a variety of political ideologies collectively labeled *minority consciousness*. Prominent forms of minority consciousness are found among all four biopolitical minorities (Marable 1983; 1984; White 1985; Murguía 1975; Garcia 1974; Garcia and De la Garza 1977; Chávez 1984; Hammerback, Jensen, and Gutierrez, 1985; Padilla 1985; Steiner 1968; Josephy 1969; Churchill 1986; Jaggar 1983; Jaggar and Rothenberg 1984).

Explanations of Minority Status

Objective deprivation--the actual state of being deprived--rarely leads to political action. In the United States, most manifestly disadvantaged people do not think of themselves as deprived (Schlozman and Verba 1979). They do not experience subjective deprivation. Most of those who do seek private remedies. Few see politics as an appropriate or practical solution (Shingles 1987b). Whether subjective deprivation contributes to political action depends upon a finite number of factors. Chief among these is the type of explanation one accepts for his or her status. Some explanations politicize subjective deprivation, directing grievances into the political arena. Political explanations lie at the very heart of minority consciousness.

There are available in the United States a number of prominent explanations for minority status that politicize subjective deprivation. They have a decided impact on the nature of minority politics. The choice of explanations has a direct bearing on: the nature and level of competition within each political minority, the tenor of relationships between minorities and the majority, and relationships among minorities. It influences whether the response to perceived deprivation is political or not and the mode of political activity. Explanations influence goals, political strategies, leadership styles, the nature of political organizations, and levels and types of political involvement. Different mixes of explanations, goals, and strategies constitute competing political ideologies. Similar ideological debates are found within each minority community. This chapter describes these parallels.

Comparing Minority Responses

The chapter focuses on similarities among the groups, not their differences. The differences are inescapable. The similarities are often overlooked. I consciously try to avoid two somewhat contrary pitfalls familiar to the literature on minority politics. The first is the lack of generalizable results. There is a rich and growing body of research on each of the groups discussed (most prominently for Blacks and women; somewhat less for Mexican Americans; least of all for Native Americans). Unfortunately, much of this literature is akin to area studies. Many scholars specialize in a single minority. Comparative analyses are far less common. Yet it is only by making comparisons that we can differentiate what is unique to each group from what is general to all. My purpose is to distinguish between the group consciousness of specific minorities and minority consciousness generally.

The second pitfall is the problem of overgeneralization. Research that addresses attributes common to all political minorities strives for universal, lawlike generalizations--a principal goal of science. Unfortunately, such statements can be so simplistic they border on stereotypes. An example is previous work in this area (Gurin, Miller, and Gurin, 1980; Miller et al. 1981; Shingles 1981) that leaves the impression that there is a uniform ideological response to minority status loosely called group consciousness. As this chapter makes plain, there is no single response. There is no one set of beliefs that can be identified as group consciousness. There are, however, a number of political ideologies that collectively fall under the general rubric minority consciousness. The principal goal of the current research is to identify these beliefs and determine their consequence for minority politics.

Modes of Adaptation

The most salient explanations for minority status in the United States are provided by a common culture. The myths Americans have about themselves, their values, and their norms determine how people deal with subjective deprivation. Most responses are private and quiescent (Edelman 1977; Schlozman and Verba 1979). The dominant culture prescribes both goals and the legitimate means for acquiring them. Prominent goals are: individual material well-being, education, social acceptance, prestige and control over one's life. Wealth is considered to be a key to their obtainment. The American dream is to obtain sufficient income to ensure individual security and quality of life. The work ethic prescribes the appropriate method: self-advancement. Success is said to depend on individual initiative and personal responsibility. People are supposed to work hard, save and invest (James 1972, 21ff.). It is assumed that status is based on personal achievement, not ascription or group mobility; the game is fair, the system is open to individual upward mobility, and opportunities are equally distributed. In short, the principal explanation for subjective deprivation is personal failure; the conventional remedy is private: work harder within the existing rules.

The conventional wisdom is flawed. For many, culturally defined goals are not attainable through socially sanctioned avenues; the chances for advancement are highly skewed. Independent of native ability, the son or daughter of a business executive has far better odds of making it than the children of a single parent on welfare. Opportunities correlate with one's initial social status. The correlation is significantly conditioned by race and gender. Regardless of parents' social status or one's own individual merit, the possibilities of advancement in many avenues are frustrated or blocked by racism and sexism.

What is a person to do if she or he cannot obtain socially prescribed goals by sanctioned means? The logical possibilities are described by Merton (1938; 1968, 676).[3] As long as people internalize responsibility, there are a limited number of options. They can (1) try even harder within conventional avenues, (2) seek the same goals through socially unacceptable or illegal means, (3) conform to the rules but lower their expectations, or (4) totally drop out, rejecting both goals and means (by resorting to indolence, drug addiction, alcoholism, or suicide). All four are generally private modes of adaptation. They are summarized in Table 9.1 where the symbol ($+$) indicates acceptance of goals or methods and (-) signifies rejection.

Table 9.1 also indicates a fifth response: rejection and replacement of conventional goals and methods with new ones. This is represented by the symbol ($\pm$). Redefining the game is an attempt "to *change* the existing cultural and social structure rather than to accommodate efforts within the structure" (Merton 1968, 194). This is a political response. Any effort to modify or change the game fundamentally threatens the existing distribution of values in a society, spawns group conflict, requires extensive political power, and necessitates collective action. A political response to subjective deprivation is atypical in the United States, even though permitted within the framework of constitutional democracy. Purely private responses are the norm, especially among the poor (Piven and Cloward 1977; Schlozman and Verba 1979).

The conditions that determine whether the disadavantaged opt for political remedies, and the reasons so few do, are threefold: (1) available resources, (2) self-images, and (3) the explanation given for deprivation. Deprived groups are politically powerless (Lasswell and Kaplan 1950; Tilly 1978; Piven and Cloward 1977). They lack the very things that provide political clout: wealth, education, prestige, and social connections. Often political recourse is not a viable option. Only when the disadvantaged pool their limited resources or ally themselves with outside benefactors do they enter the political fray in significant numbers (Tilly, 1978).

A low sense of self-worth and feelings of personal incompetence further discourages political activity. Low self-images encourage people to lower their expectations or drop out all together (response types III and IV). Strong self-images inspire people to try even harder and to seek political solutions (response

Table 9.1 Possible Responses to Perceived Deprivation

Modes of Adaptation	Cultural Goals	Institutionalized Means	Type
I. Try Harder	+	+	private
II. Cheat	+	−	private
III. Lower Expectations	−	+	private
IV. Quit	−	−	private
V. Redefine the Game	±	±	political

types I and V). A political course requires considerable ego strength, which disadvantaged people often lack. Only those who overcome this handicap will sustain an active role in politics.

The type of explanation given for relative deprivation is critical to this end. Most significant is the answer to the question who or what is to blame. When responsibility is *internalized* it contributes to self-ridicule, guilt, diminished self-esteem, and lowered self-confidence. A focus on personal responsibility encourages private solutions. Explanations that *externalize* blame direct attention toward objects in one's environment (other individuals, groups or institutions). By doing so, they encourage the fifth, political mode of adaptation.

As we have seen, the dominant American culture places direct responsibility for material deprivation on the individual. Poverty carries a stigma of personal inadequacy: a lack of will (laziness, immorality) and incompetence (stupidity, irresponsibility). Sexism and racism carry their own, similar messages. People who are devalued by society because of their race, gender, or income are encouraged to blame only themselves. They may not fully accept the responsibility. For example, many people accredit their fate to luck or divine will. Yet, relatively few economically disadvantaged people explain their status in terms of *structural causes*--such as the motives and actions of the advantaged members of society, flaws in the dominant culture, or biased and ineffective institutions. Biopolitical minorities with a clear history of discrimination are more likely to consider these explanations, especially when informed by higher education, indigenous leaders, episodes of overt conflict with the majority, or examples set by other minorities. It is in the light of structural explanations that self-confidence can be restored and subjective relative deprivation is politicized.

Political Responses

Politicos are the people who pursue goals by political means. Objectively deprived politicos can be divided into two broad categories: accommodationists and reconstructionists. *Accommodationists* profess the legitimacy of the game, seeking prescribed goals by conventional means. Their involvement in politics is a pragmatic extension of private action repertories typically encompassed by the first response type, I ("try harder"). Their strategies are conventional, involving electoral politics, lobbying, and litigation. Their motives, which are similar to those of majority activists, include material advancement, moral issues, party loyalty, civic duty, and the desire for group affiliation (Verba and Nie 1972, ch. 5; Milbrath and Goel 1977, ch. 3). Some act to protect what they have, while others seek to improve their lot. Many accommodationists do not feel deprived. Those who do either internalize responsibility for their status or believe political protest to be counterproductive. Accommodationists do not use politics to challenge the system. They seek to play the game, not to change it.

Reconstructionists are identified by the fifth response type. They too have varied reasons for participating in politics. Where they differ from accommodationists is in their belief that the game is unfair and their intention to alter it. Reconstructionists attribute group deprivation to structural defects, not to the intrinsic characteristics of the group or personal failure. The nature of the explanations differ. So does what is rejected. It is very rarely total and usually quite selective. The criticisms sometimes focus on specific goals of the dominant culture. More typically, they address available means for obtaining culturally prescribed goals. The tone may be restrained or ardent. Proposed solutions can involve moderate reforms or radical transformations of society. Reconstructionists are a very diverse lot. The specific choice of goals, strategies, and tactics chosen depends upon the type of subjective deprivation and the specific aspects of the system that are critiqued. A useful theory of minority politics must provide criteria for identifying, classifying, and explaining different modes of political adaptation in terms of these criteria.

MINORITY CONSCIOUSNESS

Whether and how one seeks to restructure the game is influenced by his or her ideology. *Minority consciousness* is a type of ideology found among political minorities. It identifies one as a member of a political minority, explains the group's status in terms of structural causes, and indicates how the status can be changed.[4] Specifically, minority consciousness: (1) rejects explanations of the group's condition that put responsibility solely on its members, (2) offers alternative explanations externalizing the blame for the deprivation, (3) selectively identifies aspects of the status quo (specific groups, beliefs, or institutions) believed to have contributed to the group's deprivation, (4) provides visions of a better world (complete with myths and values) for which members of the minority can strive, and (5) indicates strategies for effecting change. Minority consciousness takes a variety of forms that differ considerably in their explanations, what they reject, and proposed alternatives. All have a clear bearing on collective political action: by politicizing subjective relative deprivation, they create political consciousness, directing efforts toward ameliorating the group into the political arena (Shingles 1987b). Different types of minority consciousness encourage different modes of political action.

Components of Minority Consciousness

Minority consciousness should not be confused with the group consciousness of specific political minorities (e.g., Black consciousness or women's consciousness) or a single viewpoint.[5] People may be conscious of their membership in a group without believing it is a political minority or espousing reconstructionist ideologies. Differences between group consciousness and minority consciousness and between types of minority consciousness can be identified in terms of four attitudes: (1) subjective group identification, (2) relative affect for the group, (3) the perceived status and power of the group and (4) explanations for the group's status (Schlozman and Verba 1979; Gurin, Gurin, and Beattie, 1969; Miller et al. 1981).

Subjective Group Identification. Objective members of a group may or may not think of themselves as members. People who are not objective members may nonetheless identify as such. Inconsistent objective and subjective memberships are not uncommon. However, they are far less likely for biologically defined groups, based on race or gender. Physical characteristics simplify labeling.

Because people are members of numerous social categories, they have multiple group identities. For example, a white women objectively belongs to a political majority, whites, and a political minority, women. She is also a member of a social strata, a country, possibly a church, and so on. Membership in diverse groups exposes people to conflicting beliefs which may lead to indecision and inaction. Alternatively, they may encourage innovation.

Subjective group identification is a component of group consciousness. Identification with a perceived political minority is a component of minority consciousness. Group consciousness need not be political. It depends on the perceived relevance of the group to contemporary political issues that are important to the individual. Minority consciousness is inherently political. It interprets the group's fate in terms of larger political struggles. Minority consciousness may refer to a specific demographic group of which one is an objective member or it may encompass a class of deprived groups with whom one identifies; for example, the proletariat, people of color, have-nots, or *all* political minorities. The latter serve as a basis for broad-based minority coalitions (e.g., worker coalitions, progressive coalitions, rainbow coalitions, etc.).

Relative Affect for the Group. Identification with a group influences feelings towards it and other groups. The groups with whom one identifies may serve as positive or negative references. Usually they are positive. People tend to identify with those with whom they feel they have something in common (Dawson, Prewitt, and Dawson, 1977, 173-182). The desire for a positive self-image encourages them to think well of their groups (Maslow 1954). Racial and gender conflict generally serve to enhance this process (Coser 1956). However, minorities may also provide a negative reference for their members. Disparaging group stereotypes lead some people to try to dissociate themselves from their own race or sex. Such ambivalence has been reported for all political minorities and is the subject of extensive psychological study (e.g., Kvaraceus et al. 1965; Kohlberg 1966; Martinez 1977, chs. 17-19).

Ethnocentrism (an attraction toward one's own group accompanied by contempt for members of other groups) is common to all societies (Segall 1976, 117ff). However, it should not be confused with positive affect toward one's own group. It is possible to be more attracted to some groups than to others without being hostile to any. This is most clearly the case with multiple subjective memberships. White women may be especially attracted toward other white women while feeling an affinity for all women or whites generally. Most also have a strong affinity toward the political majority, white men. Men of color may have an affinity toward all people of color or all men; they may or may not be hostile toward white men. It is not unusual for members of political minorities to tolerate, even like, members of the political majority, based on common religious principles, shared political beliefs, fellow citizenship, more general notions of shared humanity or a deferential acceptance of patron-client relationships.

It is useful to distinguish between two very different types of group pride (Shingles 1979). One is based on a sense of group superiority; the other involves feelings of equal worth. All reconstructionists reject stereotypes that denigrate their group. All seek to construct a shared sense of pride and confidence among the members of the political minority. However, they differ considerably in their attitude toward the dominant group. Some disparage the political majority, claiming superior minority values and life styles. Others emphasize similarities (e.g., based on common citizenship or religious preferences), claiming equal virtues. The first type of pride is a form of ethnocentrism and typically is characterized by out-group hostility. The second need not involve out-group hostility. These differences in relative affect for political majorities and minorities have dramatic implications for political behavior, including the choice of goals (e.g., integration and separatism) and a willingness to form cross-race or cross-gender political coalitions.

In short, neither positive feelings toward members of one's identified group nor hostility toward other groups is necessary for group consciousness. No presumption need be made about the relationship between subjective group identification and relative affect for groups. The association varies across groups and among members of the same group and helps to account for differences in individual behavior. Group consciousness is simply the sum of salient beliefs people have about groups with whom they identify. In contrast, minority consciousness entails positive feelings toward the minority. It involves a deliberate effort to replace negative stereotypes and self-debasement with group pride. It may or may not include antipathy for the majority.

Perceived Group Status and Power. Members of political minorities may not think of their group as deprived or powerless. The propensity to do so depends upon the group (e.g., women are less likely to think in this way than racial minorities), the individual's social status, personal experiences, and the pervasiveness of the majority culture. To the extent that the majority culture permeates society, creating a sense of equity and fairness, all citizens will believe they have similar opportunities, resources and influence; any perceived differences will be believed to be their own doing.

Minority consciousness is the belief that one's group is relatively powerless. The perceived exclusion of a group from positions of authority and control in major institutions can be, and frequently is, used to account for the group's overall condition. This politicizes other forms of deprivation, prompting the group to direct grievances on a potentially wide range of values into the political arena. The specific form this takes is influenced by the other types of deprivation. The values on which the group feels deprived determine political goals. Goals have a direct bearing on the choice of strategies. Thus, various forms of minority consciousness emphasizing different types of relative deprivation contribute to diverse modes of political action.

Explanations for the Group Status. Within the American context, there are readily available a finite number of salient structural explanations for minority status. They reflect specific institutional impediments to minority progress and the ideological traditions of the nation. The labels, rhetoric, and logic of classical ideologies are potentially available to all minority activists. Most prominent are capitalism, democracy, conservatism, and liberalism. Less salient are nationalism, communism, socialism, and fascism. Minority leaders generally choose from among existing explanations those that are most applicable to their personal experiences and those of their followers, weaving them to the peculiar needs of the group. The results can be highly original contributions to political thought and action. However, most forms of minority consciousness are adaptations (sometimes wholesale applications) of existing paradigms. Efforts to develop reconstructionist ideologies begin, and typically end, within the confines of existing conceptual frameworks.

All reconstructionist ideologies are similar in their externalization of the responsibility for deprivation. They differ in the specific objects blamed and the scope and intensity of the critiques. The typology below is based on attitudes toward three types of objects: (1) the political majority, (2) political institutions, and (3) economic institutions. The terms conservative, liberal and radical are used to refer to the extent and intensity of support or alienation. They indicate whether critiques are limited to specific practices or extend to the basic integrity of an object.

Conservatives vocalize contentment with the status quo. They do not openly complain about their group's condition, express criticisms of the system, or challenge the existing distribution of values. There are two types of conservatives. The first type is *apolitical*. People in this category specialize in private modes of adaptation. By their own political apathy they help to sustain the status quo. The second type are *accommodationists*. Accommodationists are politically involved, but they either (1) do not believe the minority has unique problems, (2) think the problems are not political, or (3) believe collective efforts to change the system would be futile. Those who meet all three conditions--who do not experience politicized relative deprivation--may be called *total accommodationists*. They see no reason to challenge the status quo. Those who meet the first two conditions but not the third (i.e., they believe protest is legitimate, but futile), are *strategic accommodationists*. They do not openly express their alienation, fearing reprisals from both the political majority and total accommodationists. Both types of accommodationists expressly eschew reconstructionist ideologies. However, while total accommodationists genuinely support, even defend, the game, strategic accommodationists play under duress, making the best of what they believe to be a bad situation.

Liberals are highly critical of the majority behavior and/or existing institutional practices. However, they retain faith in the basic integrity of the majority and the guiding principles upon which the political and economic systems rest. Consequently, the changes they propose are limited reforms. Liberals make a distinction between the basic integrity of an object and its actual behavior, between cardinal, overriding values and principles of the system, which they accept, and the flaws that exist in practices that they want changed. The expressed goal is to make practices conform to principle. Minority liberals prefer to reform the system from within, usually in alliance with liberals in the political majority and other minorities.

Radicals are more extreme in their rejection and, consequently, are willing to resort to extreme measures. They are more alienated than the liberals. Their critiques go far beyond prevailing practices and limited reforms. Radicals tend to look on liberals suspiciously, accusing them of being accommodationists or being simply naive. They trace the origins of racism and sexism to the intrinsic nature of the majority group and/or the underlying fundamental principles of political and economic systems. America's minority radicals disagree among themselves about what specifically is to be rejected and how it is to be replaced. Most reject the idea of cooperation with members of the majority; some rebuke capitalism; a relative few assail democracy.

The three objects of alienation and these three broad explanations of minority status are listed in Table 9.2, where (+) indicates support, (-) indicates moderate alienation, or rejection of specific practices of the political majority and/or specific aspects of political and economic institutions, and (-!) indicates extreme alienation, that is, rejection of the majority itself and/or entire political and economic systems. Minority consciousness entails some level of alienation.

Across-the-board alienation from all three types of objects rarely occurs. The possible mix of attitudes is much more interesting and complex. All combinations of rows and columns in Table 9.2 are logically possible. Most have precedent in the histories of African, Mexican, Native, and female Americans. For example, a person may entertain a liberal critique of the polity while being a total accommodationist on the economy. Another type of liberal is politically sensitized to individual racism and sexism but not to institutional racism and sexism. Radicalism is an equally expansive category, encompassing

Table 9.2 Attitudes toward Minority Status: Objects of Affect and Cognition by Type of Explanation

	Vocalized Explanations of Minority Status					
	Accommodationist		Reconstructionist			
	Conservative		*Liberal*		*Radical*	
Objects	Specific Practice	Basic Integrity	Specific Practice	Basic Integrity	Specific Practice	Basic Integrity
Affect:						
Majority Group	+	+	–	+	–!	-!
U.S. Polity	+	+	–	+	–!	-!
U.S. Economy	+	+	–	+	–!	-!
Cognitions:						
Majority Group	------------integrationist--------------				nationalist	
U.S. Polity	-------------democratic---------------				nondemocratic	
U.S. Economy	-------------capitalist------------------				marxist	

a wide range of views. This is evident from the concept of nationalism. Nationalism (i.e., separatism) is a form of ethnocentrism involving the rejection of the political majority. *Right nationalists* unreservedly endorse capitalist principles. *Left nationalists* may have organic liberal or marxist leanings. Among right nationalists we may distinguish between those who reject democracy, or *Fascists*, and those who value it, *Democratic-capitalistic nationalists*. Similarly, left nationalists may be divided into those who support democracy, *or democratic-socialistic nationalists*, and those who do not, *communists*.

I now turn to a more detailed examination of some of the more prominent forms of minority consciousness. An extensive discussion of minority conservatism (though significant in its own right and an important source of minority apathy) is not central to the topic of this chapter: the relationship between minority consciousness and political action. It is minority consciousness that makes the political behavior of political minorities unique. Therefore, the subsequent comments are limited to liberal and radical reconstructionist and various subgroups. The discussion describes ideal types (Weber 1947). Individual personalities and organizations are far too complex, idiosyncratic and variable, often cutting across or combining categories. The topology describes logically consistent patterns that are prominent among all biopolitical minorities in the United States.

PROMINENT FORMS OF MINORITY CONSCIOUSNESS

Minority Liberalism

Minority liberalism rests on several traditional, structural explanations of minority status. The first, the *moral dilemma view* (Myrdal 1944), addresses the political majority: the reasons for their prejudice and the likelihood that they will change. The second, *critical pluralism*, identifies strengths and weaknesses of the American polity. A third view, *organic liberalism*, advocates private property, a free market, and individual initiative while recognizing a social obligation to compensate disadvantaged individuals for imperfections in capitalist economies. The moral dilemma explanation provides a moral basis for political protest as well as a strategy for eliminating prejudice. Critical pluralism and organic liberalism legitimate the use of political power and government largess to aid disadvantaged groups.

The Moral Dilemma View. The first view focuses on the political majority. It explains minority status primarily in terms of individual sexism and racism. Prejudice is assumed to be correctable. Members of the dominant group are faulted for ethnocentrism, cruelty and intolerance, but they are believed to have the potential for good. The dominant culture is considered to be, at its core, just. The liberals point with pride to principles of democracy, Christian precepts of brotherly love and charity, capitalist prescriptions about freedom of competition, and general notions of fair play and support for the underdog. These precepts comprise the very fabric of the American culture and society. Because racism and sexism are inconsistent with such tenets, liberals assume prejudice is primarily due to ignorance.

The solution is enlightenment. Liberals believe that if inconsistencies between principle and practice are forcefully exposed, the majority will be made to understand its errors, repent, and right past wrongs. They debunk dominant myths and stereotypes that rationalize the status quo. They emphasize the equal worth and essential similarity of all peoples. Much effort is spent attacking biological or other deterministic theories that explain as inevitable and natural the dominance of one race or sex over another.

Those who accept the moral dilemma view have a reserved affinity for the dominant group. They vigorously protest their status and denounce the transgressions of the political majority while seeking reconciliation. The ultimate goals are the end to individual prejudice and, usually as a perceived by-product, institutional racism and sexism. They envision the minority's acceptance as equals in an integrated society. Their purpose is not to destroy or even greatly change existing political and economic institutions, only to modify them to more perfectly realize American principles. Sexist and racist institutional practices are challenged, not the principles underlying the institutions. In short, to use the analogy of a game, liberals do not wish to quit the game, nor to drastically alter it; they want equal access and fair play.

Minority liberals favor multiracial, cross-gender coalitions where they can participate in unison with like-minded members of the political majority. Coalitions implement the goal of integration. They are possible and appropriate among people who share the same principles and a mutual respect. The moral dilemma view emphasizes education as a central strategy. Education has a dual purpose: to uplift and inspire the minority and to reform the majority. The task is to point out the inconsistencies between moral principles and actual practice and repudiate dominant myths and stereotypes. Edification takes many forms: the introduction of minority subject matter into formal curricula of schools, the liberalization of the mass media, lobbying before legislative bodies, litigation to restore constitutional principles, moral leadership from those in top positions of power and authority (from presidents on down to clergy), equal-status contact through neighborhoods and school integration to familiarize the majority with minorities, and nonviolent civil disobedience.

Non-violent civil disobedience was taught by Thoreau, begun on a mass scale by Gandhi in India, and popularized in the United States by Black civil rights leaders, most notably Martin Luther King, the Southern Christian Leadership Conference, the Congresss for Racial Equality, and the early Student

Nonviolent Coordinating Committee. It has become a principal tool in the arsenal of grass-roots political organizations. The strategy is to refuse peacefully to obey unjust laws, to accept arrest without resistance, and thereby reveal to all the evils of racism and sexism. This is a viable tactic for fighting injustice in an otherwise moral society. It is typically the most effective and safest recourse for peoples who are locked out of the conventional political process. In taking the moral high road, it appeals to the conscience of the majority, dissuading a violent, military response.

Nonviolent civil disobedience was used effectively in the early 1960s by the Black civil rights movement to desegregate public facilities in the South. "Separate but equal laws" were challenged using a variety of direct-action techniques, including sit-ins of restaurants and bus terminals, integrated interstate bussing, and unauthorized marches. The tactics served as a model for the women's movement and other racial minorities. Non-violent civil disobedience restores dignity to the oppressed and forces the majority to confront its transgressions. If police use force to break up peaceful demonstrations it simply highlights the conflict between principle and practice. King spoke of the "creative tension" (Oates 1982) that confronts the evil of society, rather than people who do evil (without humiliating them), a tension that forces that evil out into the open where it can studied, repudiated and abandoned.

The Critical Pluralist View. The second liberal view of minority status is critical pluralism. Pluralism is the American version of democratic ideology. Its precepts of checks and balances were built into the United States constitution by the framers and are widely believed to characterize the whole of the American polity (Dahl 1956). Pluralism defines the distribution of power in an indirect democracy where government leaders are elected and controlled by majority coalitions. It presupposes multiple centers of power and an open system where organized interests can gain fair and equal access to officials. Officials are assumed to be capable of making and implementing effective public policy. The principal methods of political influence are sanctioned by law: voting, litigation, and lobbying. The typical strategy for liberal leaders is to organize and mobilize their constituencies to influence government through legally sanctioned channels.

Pluralism has proven to be a viable ideology for most Americans. However, it has no validity for groups that are legally barred from formal political participation, as historically was the case for female, Black, Mexican, and Native Americans and remains true for millions of undocumented Mexicans. It is an unrealistic ideology for the poor generally, who have few resources, are exceedingly difficult to organize, highly unlikely to act politically, and have little political clout (Piven and Cloward 1977). The traditional pluralist view overlooks the effects of race, sex, and class on American politics. Power is highly inequitably distributed in the United States. Political equality pertains only to certain legal rights, including the right to participate, and to the value of an individual vote. The major form of citizen involvement, voting, is relatively ineffective in influencing the day-to-day conduct of government. The resources necessary to maintain more continual vigilance are highly correlated with social and economic status (Verba and Nie 1972). Racial minorities and female heads of households, who are disproportionately poor, are at a clear disadvantage. More fundamental, it is the very nature of a pluralist society that many of the decisions that determine the distribution of values are made by institutions outside of formal government. By definition, political minorities are unlikely to exercise authority or control in these institutions.

Minority liberals are usually constructive critics of the pluralist view. They perceive its limits and its potential for self-reform. In this sense they are *critical pluralists*. Critical pluralists attempt to overcome handicaps of a pluralist society. They organize their constituents and apply pressure through all available conventional channels, challenging sexist and racist laws and customs. They also have made innovative use of less conventional strategies, including strikes, boycotts and non-violent civil disobedience. Civil rights activists recognize non-violent civil disobedience as more than the moral high road or a costly method of enlightenment. It is an application of organized power. Creative tension comes not only from revealed moral dilemmas but also from the refusal of hundreds or thousands of citizens to cooperate with unjust practices and the ever-present possibility that peaceful protest will turn to violence.

The third liberal view of minority status is essentially economic. American economic liberalism is a complex mix of sometimes contradictory public policies (Patterson 1986). Most Americans, conservatives and liberals alike, are influenced by a cultural heritage that puts the onus of poverty on the individual. These traditions include: classical liberalism, Calvinism, the myth of self-reliance fostered by the American frontier, and Malthusian and social Darwinian theories, which describe poverty unsympathetically as a natural and inevitable condition (Waxman 1983, 75-93; James 1972, 21-32). American liberals and conservatives value private property, materialism, and individualism. Both recognize the existence of deserving poor, those who are indigent through no fault of their own. Liberals differ in that they have a broader, more encompassing definition of "deserving" and in their conviction that assistance to the truly needy should go beyond private philanthropy to include government largess.

Contemporary liberals are influenced by *organic liberalism*. They recognize that poverty is often not a matter of the individual doings but the product of structural forces, including social and economic interdependencies, inequalities of birth, dislocations and malfunctions in the market, natural calamities, aging, and racial and sexual discrimination. They believe that government has a moral obligation to assist the victims of such forces. This includes the provision of equal opportunities and affirmative action for groups historically disadvantaged by legal and de facto discrimination.

The moral dilemma, critical pluralist, and organic liberal views are by far the most popular reconstructionist ideologies among politically conscious minorities in the United States. Prominent organizations based on liberal principles include the National Association for the Advancement of Colored People, the Southern Christian Leadership Conference, the League of United Latin American Citizens, the National Farm Workers Association, the National Congress of American Indians, and the National Organization of Women.

Experience has demonstrated serious limitations to the liberal approach. The ultimate consequence (if not the goal) of structural integration is cultural assimilation. This is an unattractive prospect to those who are proud of their group heritage, who fear absorption by the dominant culture and a loss of identity. Education, the debunking of dominant myths and stereotypes, and revelations about a moral dilemma may have little consequence for reducing prejudice. Education assumes members of the dominant culture are motivated by democratic and Christian principles more than by their aversion to the minority, their superior status, and vested economic interests. It presumes that ideals are more important than self-interest and power. Political solutions are often found wanting. The obtainment of the franchise and equality before the law provide the right to participate, but they do not guarantee equal political clout or success. Hard-won legal battles often have little consequence in rooting out prejudice and ending de facto discrimination. It is extremely difficult to mobilize materially deprived groups to demand policies ending poverty and discrimination. Many liberal-supported government policies are half-hearted, under-financed, punitive, and confusing. For these reasons, some minority group leaders and their followers opt for more cynical explanations of their status, explanations that require more extreme solutions.

MINORITY RADICALISM

Minority radicals totally reject as fundamentally wrong either the political majority, major institutions, or entire political and economic systems. Radicals may be identified in terms of what they oppose. Nationalists reject the political majority, Marxists repudiate capitalism, and authoritarians dismiss democracy. The latter course is not seen as an attractive option for most Americans. Democratic ideals are widely valued in the United States. They are the inspiration for minorities' demands for equality and liberty. They, more than any other ideas, provide the impetus for political protest. Thus, authoritarian ideologies are exceptionally rare among political minorities. Much more common are attacks on the integrity of the majority and the virtues of capitalism.

The Nationalist View

Minority nationalism is likely to be adopted after education, conventional political tactics, and more conventional public policies have been tried and found wanting. It is a form of ethnocentrism, similar to the racism and sexism of the majority, but typically defensive in nature. It is a natural response to hostility and repeated rejection. In the nationalist view, the dominant group is unalterably prejudiced, even evil. Other values (e.g., racial purity, wealth, or custom) are believed to be more important to the majority than those of democracy, freedom of competition and fair play. Nationalists turn inward, looking to their own kind for acceptance, group identity, pride, and culture. Like liberals, nationalists debunk the dominant myths and stereotypes with which the majority rationalize the status quo. Unlike liberals, they consider biological and historical theories that explain as superior the values and traditions of the minority. In this sense, they are similar to conservatives in the political majority: both may believe in biological determinism and prefer the separation of racial and gender groups. Examples include the Lost Nation of Islam, women-identified women (Bunch 1975), Aztlan (Murguía 1975, 93-94) and Pan Indianism (Steiner 1968).

Two strategies for redressing minority grievances are logically consistent with the view of uncorrectable majority prejudice.[6] The first is to combine the goals of *cultural pluralism* and *structural integration*. This entails some level of social interaction with the dominant group (involving equal access to positions of status and power in society) without requiring cultural assimilation. Cultural pluralists prefer the company of their own kind but recognize that the principal avenues to status and security lie within institutions currently controlled by the political majority. They seek the best of two worlds: equal access and cultural autonomy. Examples of cultural pluralism may be found among all biopolitical minorities as well as in the ethnic politics of first- and second-generation Americans of European and Asian extraction.

A second, more desperate, strategy is *total separation*, culturally and structurally. Nationalists choose this course. They believe that any level of contact with the dominant group is harmful. This leaves few alternatives: emigration, the violent overthrow of the political majority, and the more modest goal of community control within a democratic, capitalist context. Overt acts of rebellion have been tried without success in the American context. It is suicidal for numerically or militarily inferior political minorities to use organized violence against an overpowering majority. Emigration and community control generally have proven more viable, though how viable depends upon the minority. Mexican Americans can exercise the options of going south of the border or controlling the barrios. Native Americans can seek refuge on reservations. However, alienated women have no mother country to which they can return. Throughout American history, southern Blacks have migrated north to escape the poverty and repression of the Old South only to find them again. Back to Africa movements and efforts to establish a separate Black state (e.g., the Republic of New Africa) within the United States generally have had limited appeal. Principal exceptions are the Liberian movement in the 1820s and the Garvey movement a full century later (Bennett 1984). The politics of community control are more prevalent. Militant organizations that typify such policies are the Nation of Islam, the American Indian Movement, the Brown Berets, and the Stanton-Anthony Brigade.

Total separation is a salient option for most racial minorities. Not so for alienated women. Yet, separation of the sexes is presented as a well-organized and articulated alternative by radical feminists (Jaggar 1983, 270ff.; Bunch 1975). There are documented cases of short-lived, all-women communities (Shakeshaft 1984). Radical feminists see sexism as inherent in society, imbedded in the family, heterosexuality, and biological identities. Consequently, sexual oppression is seen as the inevitable consequence of men and women living together. A viable alternative for some is lesbianism, not necessarily nor solely as a sexual preference, but as an intellectual choice and political doctrine. Radical feminists, like all separatists, eschew political coalitions with liberals in the political majority. Men are seen as part of the problem, not the solution.

Right versus Left Nationalists

Historically, many separatists have been right nationalists. They accredit oppression primarily or solely to race or sex, not to intrinsic flaws in the American economy or constitution. Self-government is taken to mean democratic government. Self-help translates into minority capitalism. However, some minority leaders believe existing economic structures would limit the prospects of minorities even if all prejudice were eliminated, the right to participate in politics were guaranteed, and minorities acquired control over their localities. Left nationalists identify capitalism as a cause of minority status.

A class analysis of minority status need not be, and often is not, Marxist. It does not require a reading of Marxist-Leninist thought to realize that historically prejudice and discrimination have conveniently served economic interests, that the right to participate politically is meaningless without the resources to be effective, and that once elected to office, minority leaders are often powerless to doing anything constructive for their economically depressed communities. Organic liberals also make these observations. However, within every minority community, there are Marxists who find liberal analyses and solutions inadequate for addressing gross inequalities of wealth and power. Marxism provides a radical explanation for these maladies and strategies for remedying them. Straightforward, orthodox applications of Marxist-Leninist doctrine are relatively rare in the United States. More eclectic, socialist perspectives are more common. Left nationalists see problems of race and class, or sex and class, as inseparable. The end to minority status is believed to lie in class struggle. In the United States, the struggle is generally conceived of as non-violent and democratic. It typically takes the form of union politics and class-based voting coalitions. Among left-wing cultural pluralists, political coalitions cut across racial and gender lines.

There are active left-wing nationalists among all political minorities, though classical Marxism appears to have least appeal among Native Americans (Cruse 1987; Hartmann 1984; Churchill 1986; Acuña 1981). The principal problem with explaining minority status in class terms is the danger of being labeled "Marxist," "communist," or "socialist" and shunned by other members of the minority. The great majority of Americans, men and women of all races, fail to distinguish between degrees of "left." They lack the diverse ideological experiences of other peoples. Americans of all types are highly patriotic. Many associate left-wing labels with a world communist movement antithetical to American national interests. The recent period of renewed conservatism and patriotism in the United States and the failure of one brand of Marxism in Eastern Europe have further dampened the prospects for viable left-wing nationalist alternatives in the near future.

MINORITY CONSCIOUSNESS AND POLITICAL ACTION

Minority consciousness is a set of beliefs about one's own group: a positive identification with the group, its perceived status as a political minority, and the reasons given for the status. These beliefs stimulate and guide political action. However, their effect is indirect. They influence the more immediate beliefs, which directly comprise the decision whether and how to participate in politics. The typical participation calculus is described by the theory of *bounded rationality* (Simon 1985). It assumes that self-interested people choose from among salient alternatives those courses of action that they believe have the highest marginal utility (i.e., net benefit for the individual). Estimates of marginal utility are based on several types of beliefs. Formally, the marginal utility of any one act may be stated as the sum of its expected benefits minus its expected costs. That is, $U_a = \Sigma(B^e_a - C^e_a)$, where:

U_a = the estimated marginal utility of an act,
B_a = a perceived benefit of the act,
C_a = a perceived cost of the act,
e = the expectation (likelihood) of benefits and costs.

No matter how great the desired benefit, rational individuals will not act unless they think their efforts have some chance of success and the rewards will outweigh any losses. (Riker and Ordeshook 1973, ch. 3).

The participation calculus is directly influenced by a person's (1) value priorities, and (2) beliefs about salient, alternative courses of action. The benefits of an act are the values obtained by it. The costs are the values lost. Potential benefits of political action include the attainment of policy goals (e.g., economic, defense, environmental, or moral), expression of group loyalty (including partisanship, citizenship, and patriotism), social rewards (like prestige, companionship, and power), and various form of psychological gratification (e.g., self-esteem or group pride). Common costs are a loss of time and energy, disapproval by others, and threats to one's physical or economic security by social or government repression (Tilly 1978, 98ff).

Beliefs about the available courses of action play a critical role in the calculus. They determine *the salience of an act*, its *instrumental value,* and its *moral value.* The moral value of an act is its propriety. It influences both the B and C terms in the participation calculus: impropriety is a cost, propriety is a benefit. The instrumental value of an act is its perceived efficacy, the likelihood that it will effectively obtain benefits and avoid costs (the e term in the calculus). People are most motivated to participate when the act is thought to be both moral and effective (Barnes, et al. 1979, 69-84). The absence of either characteristic decreases the marginal utility of the act.

Sense of political efficacy is the belief that political action is effective. It is influenced by the perceived instrumental value of salient courses of action. It is useful to distinguish between different types of subjective political efficacy (Shingles 1981, 1987). A sense of *internal political efficacy* is the part of a person's political efficacy that one attributes to his or her personal attributes (e.g., skills, intelligence, will, physical assets, etc.). It is related to general feelings of self-confidence. A sense of *external political efficacy* is that portion which the individual attributes to objects in the environment (e.g., other groups and various institutions, most particularly government). We may further distinguish between two types of external subjective political efficacy: *incumbent-based efficacy* (the belief that incumbents are responsive) and *regime-based efficacy* (the belief that conventional political institutions are responsive).

Strong feelings of internal political efficacy are essential for most forms of high-initiative political behavior (Shingles 1981). Different combinations of the types of subjective external political efficacy contribute to unique modes of political action (Shingles 1987a). For example, people with high feelings of both incumbent-based efficacy and regime-based efficacy are apt to use conventional modes of access to petition public officials. Those who think the institutions are responsive but the incumbents are not are likely to use conventional modes of action to circumvent or replace officials. Low feelings of both incumbent-based and regime-based efficacy encourage total abstention from conventional politics. When such attitudes are accompanied by beliefs in the effectiveness of alternative courses of action, they contribute to unconventional political protest (Muller 1972).

The decision whether and how to participate politically may operate quite independently of minority consciousness. For example, minority consciousness is the belief that one's group is relatively politically powerless. However, political minorities are not completely powerless. Positions of control and authority in major institutions are an important, but not the sole, basis of external political efficacy. Other sources include organizations that are controlled by minorities (e.g., churches, businesses, labor unions, party factions, civil rights, and other voluntary organizations), spiritual and moral strength, a belief in divine intervention, political allies, and, for larger groups, strength through numbers. Internal political efficacy is influenced primarily by early socialization and personal relationships with family, friends, co-workers, and neighbors (Rosenberg 1981, 604-607). In short, despite evident power deprivation, members of political minorities may have sufficiently strong feelings of internal and external political efficacy to spur high-initiative political involvement. Similarly, the perceived costs and benefits of political action are a function of many values, only some of which are associated with minority status.

Still, minority consciousness plays a critical role in the political behavior of biopolitical minorities. It has influenced every component of the participation calculus. First, it provides a important motive for political action: politicized relative deprivation. A primary goal of minority political involvement is the end to the minority status. Second, minority consciousness provides a moral justification for collective action. Positively self-identified members of a group are more likely to believe in the propriety of group action. In a democracy, where popular values legitimize power sharing, minority status presents a strong moral catalyst for collective political action. It justifies restructuring the game. Third, minority consciousness often increases expectations that collective action will succeed. By transferring blame for minority status from individuals and their group to other groups and institutions, it permits a higher sense of internal political efficacy and heightens political cynicism (mistrust of government officials and institutions). This encourages high-initiative, policy-oriented behavior. Self-confident, cynical people, who do not trust government to act on its own but think they can make a difference have a relatively high rate of political participation (Shingles 1981, 1987a).

Fourth, minority consciousness helps to overcome a serious obstacle to collective political action: *the free rider problem*. This is the tendency of people in large groups to abstain from helping to obtain collective goods, gambling that other more motivated and influential members will do it for them (Olson 1965). *Collective goods* are values that, if provided by some members of the group, are available to all. Olson claims it is irrational for people in large groups to contribute to the obtainment of collective goods because: (1) they will receive the benefits achieved by others whether they help or not, and (2) they are likely to perceive their own efforts to be inconsequential. People are most likely to help in the obtainment of collective goods when there are selective incentives, goods that only can be acquired by the individual's own efforts. Olson's theory is highly relevant to political minorities because many of their goals are collective goods, for example, government programs intended to end discrimination, restore dignity, alleviate material deprivation, and guarantee political rights.

Minority consciousness works in several ways to discourage free riding. First, it fuses perceptions of the group's interests with those of the individual. To the extent that people identify with a common group, their interests become one. The distinction between private and collective goods is blurred. Collective goals can become essential private needs (Fireman and Gamson 1979, 35). For politically conscious minorities, group pride, fear of out-groups and the belief that their group is disadvantaged by an unjust system all contribute to strong group cohesion and feelings of solidarity (Coser 1956, 34-37, 87ff).

Second, individual contributions to collective ends can have immediate and very real, selective psychological payoffs. For example, in demanding group respect, individuals obtain self-respect; in seeking the group liberation, they discover their own personal autonomy. Third, solidarity creates a collective responsibility, referred to by Marvin Olsen (1970) as "participatory norms." These are moral prescriptions, often backed by group sanctions, to contribute to collective action. Finally, identification with a large, seemingly powerful group can heighten people's own sense of importance and political efficacy, raising expectations that they (in consort with others) can make a significant contribution to the collective good. Members of otherwise politically powerless minorities often exhibit feelings of shared strength. A primary task of leaders is to instill such beliefs (Frolich, Oppenheimer, and Young 1971, 105-108).

The final manner in which minority consciousness effects political action is by guiding it. Different explanations of minority status lead to unique estimates of the instrumental and moral value of alternative strategies. They differ in their assessments of the nature and causes of social injustice. They disagree on the relative benefits and costs of alternative courses of action. For example, critical pluralists have greater conviction in the efficacy and propriety of conventional political tactics than do radicals. Integrationists see cooperation with members of the political majority as proper and useful, whereas nationalists see it as odious and dangerous. All estimates in the participation calculus vary with whether the explanation for minority status focuses on the political majority, the polity, or the economy and the nature of the critiques. Which of the dominant cultural goals and socially sanctioned means should be modified or replaced, the extent of the proposed changes, and the choice of tactics vary from one ideology to another.

CONCLUSION

Minority consciousness stimulates and guides political action. The nature of the effect depends on the type of consciousness. Several prominent forms have been discussed in this essay. The topology is not inclusive. Within each minority community, there are unique modes of thought and action which have not been considered here. Some ideologies do not have clear parallels across groups. Many activists and ideologues hold eclectic, changing, even contradictory, ideas which do not fit neatly into any one classification scheme. Nevertheless, the broad categories of the topology identify principal divisions within prominent biopolitical minorities.

The purpose of this chapter has been to progress toward a theory of comparative political minorities. A systematic comparison of the similarities among minorities, while recognizing essential differences, will contribute to our understanding of political minorities generally, specific minority groups, and the varied relationships between group consciousness and political action. The comparative approach promises to develop parallels among groups that heretofore have been largely neglected. An explicit treatment of types of consciousness will move us away from broad generalizations that border on stereotypes while refining our ability to explain variations in minority behavior.

Most important is the intrinsic value of understanding minority thinking. Innovative and original thought is often associated with crises and change. Throughout American history, the unique experiences of political minorities have produced extensive reanalyses of American society. Many interesting and challenging ideas are expressed in the actions and writing of minority leaders and authors. Their legacy is a profound contribution to American social and political thought.

The Organizational and Strategic Consequences of Reaganomics among Latinos: Actual and Possible
Isidro D. Ortiz

Prognoses and analyses of the impact of the federal budgetary cutbacks that were an integral part of President Ronald Reagan's agenda have been offered by various analysts since the early eighties. Implicit in some of the prognoses and analyses, such as those by Stockman (1986), Piven and Cloward (1982), and Dolbeare (1984), are two notions about the impact of the cutbacks on Latino organizational life and the strategic responses of the organizations. One notion is that the cutbacks did not affect Latino organizational life inasmuch as the Reagan assault on the welfare state failed. A second notion is that in response to the cutbacks the organizations exclusively opted to pursue an anti-corporate coalition-building and electoral strategy conducive to a class-based electoral realignment in American politics.

That the cutbacks did not affect Latino organizations or that the organizations opted to pursue an anti-corporate strategy is far from the case. Indeed, the budgetary cutbacks substantially affected organizational operations. More importantly, in response to the cutbacks, the organizations, in particular the three largest national organizations, the Mexican-American Legal Defense and Education Fund (MALDEF), the League of United Latin American Citizens (LULAC), and the National Council of La Raza (NCLR), opted to pursue a strategy at odds with the anti-corporate coalition-building and electoral strategy. Specifically, they chose to pursue a new strategy, the corporate grantsmanship and partnership strategy, involving the submission of proposals by the organizations to corporations for funding for organizational activities and the creation of formal partnerships with corporations. As a result of the pursuit of the strategy, the organizations became participants in formal relationships with corporations. These relationships continue today. They also came to perform a function that is vital to the enhancement of the image of corporations among Latinos and that appears to have contributed to the erosion of Latino opposition to corporate advocates of capitalism and free market policies.

THE DISRUPTION OF ORGANIZATIONAL OPERATIONS
AND THE EMERGENCE OF PESSIMISM

As a result of the cutbacks from 1981 to 1983, Latino organizations across the country lost over 4,000 programmatic staff positions (Whisler 1983), an average of 20 percent. The impact of the cutbacks on the Mexican-American Legal Fund characterize the effects of the reductions on Latino organizations. In 1981, as a result of the cutbacks, MALDEF lost $600,000 in federal funds. This sum amounted to 20 percent of MALDEF's 1981-1982 budget. Because of the loss of the funds, MALDEF's leadership had to undertake a "painful staff reduction" that concluded in the elimination of about one-fourth of MALDEF's staff positions in 1982-1983 (Avila 1983, 1). The reductions disrupted MALDEF's programmatic activities in the areas of urban crime prevention, equal employment, and immigration (Martinez 1981; 1982; Avila 1983).

The budgetary cutbacks also evoked pessimism about the possibility of regaining federal funding and the federal government as a source of funding. Only 11 percent of the organizations that survived the budgetary reductions thought they would regain federal funding in the succeeding two years. Fifty-six percent concluded that the federal government was not a viable source of funding for their operations in the future (Whisler 1983, 54).

A NEW STRATEGY: CORPORATE GRANTSMANSHIP
AND PARTNERSHIP

After drawing the conclusion that the federal government would no longer be a source of funding for their programs, the organizations decided to attempt to secure funding from and to form partnerships with corporations. In 1981, over fifteen Latino organizations submitted grant proposals to 135 corporations, including 59 corporations among the Fortune 500 (*Nuestro* 1982a). Fifty-eight percent of the organizations experienced success in having one or more of the grant proposals funded (Whisler 1983). The Mexican-American Legal Defense and Education Fund, the National Council of La Raza, and the League of United Latin American Citizens were among the most successful of the organizations.

MALDEF obtained approximately $460,000 from a range of corporations. Large portions of the funding were unrestricted and made it possible for MALDEF to pay basic operating costs and launch new projects. MALDEF also obtained in-kind contributions. In 1981 MALDEF, for example, received data on the results of Levi-Strauss Company's minority recruitment and employment efforts. The data enhanced MALDEF's testimony on affirmative action before the U. S. Congress (MALDEF 1982c). MALDEF's pamphlets were printed by Chevron. MALDEF also received critiques on public relations matters from Anheuser-Busch, Inc. Moreover, corporate executives, such as Walter Haas, Jr., of Levi-Strauss, recruited "influential leaders" to appear at MALDEF's fund raising dinners. They also hosted peers, enabling MALDEF to recruit additional corporate support (MALDEF 1982c).

In 1982, the NCLR obtained support for its technical assistance project, Project *Raices,* from the Atlantic Richfield Foundation, Chevron USA, Levi-Strauss Foundation, Conoco, Inc., Standard Oil of Ohio, Aetna Life and Casualty Foundation, Coca-Cola Co., Citibank/Citicorp, Westinghouse, and Tenneco Oil. With the assistance provided by these corporations, the NCLR provided training and technical assistance to the staff of local Latino organizations (NCLR 1985c).

LULAC obtained grants of $5,000 each from Pabst Blue Ribbon and Digital Corporations. The latter's contribution was for the Follow-up Program of the LULAC National Educational Service Centers, which linked college graduates with corporate employers. The Pabst Blue Ribbon award was for the LULAC national office program operations (*LULAC* 1981a, 23). LULAC also garnered a $20,000 grant from the Adolph Coors Company. The grant was to provide administrative assistance for LULAC's national office.

In 1982 LULAC also garnered support for its scholarship fund. By March 1982, thirteen corporations had contributed $86,000. The corporate contributors included the American Gas Association; the Nabisco Company; American Broadcasting Companies, Inc.; Avon Products Foundation; CBS, Inc.; Cheseborough-Ponds, Inc.; Chevron USA, Inc.; Phillips Petroleum Foundation; Santa Fe Industries Foundation; Shell Companies Foundation; Stauffer Chemical Company; Tesoco Petroleum Corporation; United Services Automobile Association; Abott Corporation; and Kimbel Clark, Inc. The largest contributor was CBS, Inc. It contributed $15,000. In addition, forty-three other corporations contributed to the fund (*Latino and LULAC* 1982e, 28).

After seeking to obtain support from corporations, the organizations sought to establish sustained and formal relationships with corporations. LULAC took the first steps to elaborate a relationship with the corporate sector. LULAC's leadership invited corporations to sponsor events at LULAC's annual convention. Moreover, in an attempt to create a forum for the discussion of the desired partnerships at the 1981 convention, the officials of LULAC's National Educational Services organized a breakfast and luncheon with the theme, "Salute to Corporate America toward the Unrealized Hispanic Dream."

To enhance its ability to form the partnerships, LULAC's leadership emphasized the advantages to corporations of recognizing Hispanics and collaborating with LULAC. In an editorial after the 1982 Super Bowl, the editor of the organization's magazine declared that advertising firms were "fumbling the ball" when it came to the Hispanic market by failing to incorporate Hispanics into the commercials of clients, such as those who paid for television commercials during the Super Bowl. He declared:

> While Hispanics and other minorities are tired of being studied into the poor house, one major problem remains: Hispanics are almost non-existent in the fields of advertising, in the marketing departments of corporations, and in decision-making positions of corporate board rooms.... Both Hispanic America and Corporate America are losers for this shortcoming. . . . For Corporate America, the responsibility is to address the needs of the Hispanic, if for no other reason than to take advantage of the more than $50 billion buying power of the Hispanic community. (*Latino & LULAC* 1982g, 1)

The LULAC national president in 1982, Tony Bonilla, advocated Hispanic-corporate cooperation as one answer to the federal budgetary cutbacks in education. Speaking at the Higher Education Conference at Northern Illinois University, Bonilla declared that President Reagan's education policies would foster elitism in higher education at the expense of Hispanics and other minorities. Hispanic-corporate cooperation could mitigate such a development and would occur if corporations recognized that Hispanic buying power had surpassed $50 billion and was rising. He called upon corporations to develop intern programs to train Hispanics in areas traditionally closed to them (*Latino & LULAC* 1982b, 28).

In March 1982, LULAC formally linked itself to the corporate sector through its LULAC National Educational Service Center. Three corporate officials were appointed to the board of the service center. They were Sam Martinez, Manager of Special Projects for the Adolph Coors Company; Carolyn Hernandez, Manager for Affirmative Action Programs for Kraft, Inc.; and James D. Schwab, Manager of Employee Relations for General Electric Company's Manquila Management Operation. After they assumed office, the editor of LULAC's magazine announced the new working relationship, declaring, "We have now brought corporate America and Hispanic America to the decision-making table." (*Latino & LULAC* 1982a, 17).

During the first months of 1982, Tony Bonilla, the LULAC president, traveled across the country for the purpose of meeting with the presidents and executive officers of major corporations. His meetings with these officials involved "selling the growth of Hispanics as consumers and LULAC as an organization dedicated to advancing the causes of social justice of the underprivileged." The efforts concluded with the receipt of $96,500 in contributions from corporations at the LULAC national convention on July 2. Two days before the official opening of the convention, Bonilla again called for the establishment of a "full partnership" between LULAC and "Corporate America." In calling for the partnership he reminded corporations of the advantages of such a relationship. He declared that it was "in the best interest of Corporate America to fully note that the Hispanic buying power" was "more than just $60 million per year, that Hispanics" were "loyal brand buyers and many companies depended on the Hispanic dollars for their existence." He announced that LULAC sought a full partnership. He declared, "A paltry gift of $500 to $1,000 is no gift at all. We now seek a full partnership with Corporate America" (*Latino* 1982a, 19).

The envisioned partnership was realized at the convention during a luncheon sponsored by the Adolph Coors Company. Billed as Hispanics and Corporate America "Investing in the Future," the luncheon was the site for the receipt of the contributions from corporations. At the luncheon, Bonilla received contributions of $25,000 from Coca-Cola, $25,000 from Sears, $14,000 from El Paso Electric, $10,000 from Phillip Morris, $5,000 from Allstate Insurance Company, $5,000 from Alvarado Construction Company, and $5,000 from Kraeger Company. Constituting the largest contribution made on a single occasion from the private sector in the organization's fifty-three year history, the funding was to be utilized to help LULAC establish a national office in Washington, D.C. (*Latino* 1982b, 19).

LULAC's formation of a partnership with the corporate sector was succeeded several months later by the First Corporate/Hispanic Partnership Summit in San Francisco on October 23, 1982. At this day-long conference, the leadership of major national Latino organizations met with a wide array of corporate officials. Attended by approximately 125 persons, the meeting was sponsored by the Forum of National Hispanic Organizations and the Independent Sector. The former is an advocacy coalition of thirty-two Latino organizations with national programs and constituencies. Established in 1975, its objective is to increase Latino participation at all levels of the public and private sector through a unified approach. The Independent Sector is an umbrella organization of more than 400 voluntary organizations, corporations, and foundations with national interests and impact in philanthropy and volunteer action (Gallegos 1982).

Several months after the summit, the president of the NCLR, Raul Yzaguirre, promoted the creation of the "new partnerships" between Latinos and corporations at the fifth annual affiliates conference of the NCLR. The private sector, he noted in his annual speech to the affiliates, was "realizing the importance of Latinos." Private-sector executives believed that the private sector had an obligation to offset the federal cutbacks. Moreover, the corporate sector had demonstrated a willingness to provide support to Latino organizations. The participation of the corporate sector in the summit meeting in San Francisco was evidence of its willingness. The corporate sector and Latinos had a "lot to gain" if a "partnership" between them succeeded. Therefore, Latinos should work to make the partnership succeed, he concluded (*Caminos* 1983).

Shortly thereafter, the NCLR under Yzaguirre's direction took a formal step to create the partnerships. The NCLR formed a Corporate Advisory Council (CAC) composed of top-level officials of Gulf Oil Corporation; G. D. Searle & Company; The Equitable Life Assurance Society of the United States; Coca-Cola USA; Time, Inc.; Johnson & Johnson; Rockwell International Corporations; and General Motors Corporation. Its mission was to advise and assist NCLR in obtaining foundation and corporate funding and increased access to financing for NCLR-assisted projects. The CAC was also to serve as a source of technical consultation on the improvement of NCLR operations, projects and products, such as its publications.

In the wake of NCLR's action, LULAC took a step aimed at enhancing its ability to establish partnerships. This step was the formation of a coalition with organizations in the Black community with experience in negotiating with corporations. In March 1983, its president, Tony Bonilla, traveled to Atlanta, Georgia. There, in conjunction with the Reverend Joseph Lowery of the Southern Christian Leadership Conference and with Coretta Scott King, Bonilla announced the intent to build a Hispanic-Black coalition at a press conference. During the LULAC national executive board meeting in Atlanta, he and the Reverend Jesse Jackson, founder of the People United to Save Humanity (PUSH), announced the formation of a Hispanic-Black coalition. The coalition would seek to increase the political influence of the two minorities in the 1984 presidential elections and seek enforcement of the Voting Rights Act as well as monitor the nation's corporations to achieve equity with whites in the free enterprise system. In dealing with corporations, the coalition would seek to negotiate contracts and services for minority firms, franchises for minorities, better employment representation, especially in middle and higher management positions, and improved representation in the media (*Latino* 1983a, 6-7).

Shortly after the announcements, Bonilla and the Reverend Jackson initiated discussions with the Southland Corporation, the owners of the 7-Eleven chain of convenience stores, and Chief Auto Parts Stores. The discussions culminated in late July. On July 30, 1983, Bonilla, acting on behalf of LULAC and the National Hispanic Leadership Conference and in conjunction with the leaders of Operation PUSH, signed a five-year trade agreement with the Southland Corporation; the value was estimated at between $600 million and $700 million.

After the signing of the agreement, Bonilla announced the new partnership in an article praising Southland Corporation and declaring that the agreement was historically significant. Bonilla declared,

> The agreement covers all phases of the Southland operations.
> This is the first major initiative undertaken by the Hispanic
> community to become partners with corporate America....
> Corporate America has always been willing to give us

contributions that have the effect of neutralizing the Hispanic community. With the trade agreement, we at least will have a chance to get into business and expand our business development. We would rather have that kind of reciprocity than charity. That's the bottom line of this agreement (*Latino* 1983b, 18).

With this agreement in hand, LULAC, the National Hispanic Leadership Conference, and Operation PUSH began successful negotiations on a second accord. On June 1, 1984, they signed a pact with the Miller Brewing Company whose life span was open-ended and included few specific timetables. The agreement stipulated that the Miller Brewing Company would (1) strive to maintain a minimum minority placement rate of 26 percent among new employees hired, (2) attempt to maintain a minimum minority replacement rate of 26 percent among new employees hired, (3) reserve 26 percent of its purchases of goods and services for minority vendors, (4) ensure that 20 percent of its accounting and medical services were provided by minority-owned firms, (5) ensure that 15 percent of the company's group life insurance was ceded to a minority company, (6) ensure that 15 percent of the value of all of Miller's construction projects will be subcontracted to minority firms, (7) establish a "minority distributorship development fund" of about thirty million dollars, which could be used in joint ventures with prospective minority distributors who needed financing, and (8) ensure that 20 percent of its philanthropic gifts would be contributed to minority organizations (Beale 1986, 20-22).

As LULAC formalized its partnership, the NCLR acted to capitalize on and augment its corporate relationships. In 1984 the NCLR and its CAC jointly planned NCLR's Seventh Annual Conference. The theme of the conference was "Hispanic Leadership: Impact, Influence, and Involvement." As planned by the NCLR and the CAC, the conference was intended to provide a "showcase for the concerns and accomplishments of NCLR and its network of Hispanic community-based organizations and its corporate and public sponsors." NCLR's president promoted the conference as "a perfect opportunity to bring together and highlight Hispanic leaders, both for the Hispanic community and the nation, and to present them to corporate leaders. This stimulates the sharing of ideas and information, and more productive cooperation within the community and potential private-sector funding sources" (NCLR 1984c, 3).

As a result of the NCLR and CAC's efforts, over thirty-five companies agreed to participate through financial contributions, exhibit booths, and sponsorships of special events in the conference. Moreover, the NCLR obtained financial support for the conference from Sears, Roebuck and Company, the Nestle Company, Coca-Cola USA, and General Motors Corporation (NCLR 1984c).

On October 29, 1984, the leadership of NCLR and five other national Latino organizations built upon the steps taken in the preceding two years. The leadership of the organizations and the Adolph Coors Company signed a five-year agreement in Los Angeles. In developing the terms of the agreement, the leadership took into account and attempted to surpass the agreement reached by Coors and Black organizations, as one of the signators later noted. Under the terms of the agreement the Coors Company agreed to hire more Latinos and to donate a minimum of $2.5 million to Latinos and Latino organizations between 1985 and 1990, provided that sales of its products increased among Latinos. The immediate objective was to increase the percentage of Latinos in the Coors Company labor force from 8.5 percent to 12 percent. To achieve this objective, Coors would utilize Latino employment agencies.

Coors also agreed to pursue the appointment of a Latino to the vice presidential level of its administration, increase the number of Hispanic-owned distributorships, and donate at least $500,000 a year to Latino projects in the succeeding five years. One-third of the money was designated for educational programs. The agreement was signed by the leadership of NCLR, National Image, United States Hispanic Chamber of Commerce, American GI Forum, National Puerto Rican Coalition, and the Cuban National Planning Council. In accordance with the agreement, the leadership of the organizations and the Coors Company formed a committee to monitor the progress of Coors's commitment by meeting on a quarterly basis in 1985 and semi-annually every year thereafter (Diaz 1985; Coors 1984).

WORKING FOR CORPORATIONS: THE PERFORMANCE OF AMPLIFICATION

Piven and Cloward (1971, 22) have noted that "the occasion of giving vitally needed assistance can easily become the occasion of inculcating the work ethic ... of enforcing work itself, for those who resist risk the withdrawal of that assistance." In pursuing corporate support and partnerships, the organizations created an opportunity for corporations to expect and demand that Latino organizations engage in the performance of amplification. Amplification involves the articulation within the minority community of the good will and material achievements of the corporation (Orren 1976, 58). Amplification may occur in written form in organizational publications. It may also occur at organizational events, such as annual conferences, fund raisers, and banquets.

The expectation that the organizations perform amplification is evident in the statement of an official of one of the brewing companies. Shortly after the initiation of corporate relief giving, he declared:

> It's understood that if I'm making a major contribution at a banquet, you will ask me to say a few words. It's like routine now, that is, "It's my pleasure to present $5,000 for a scholar-

ship." Latino organizational leadership is becoming very professional. They know they have to stroke their sponsors.

It's nice when you get it. In fact, the wiser organizations will publish our contributions. When you see that sort of thank you note, I circulate it because it means that we are appreciated. I may not remember if I don't receive this kind of thank you. But I'll remember when the organization approaches again for contributions. If I can't remember any follow-up to our contributions, like a thank you note in our files or some sort of publicity, then it will probably influence me later on. (interview 22 March 1984)

The demand that the organizations perform amplification was spelled out in the agreement between Coors and the six organizations. In return for Coors's assistance, the organizations had to agree to the following provision: "Each member of the Coalition agrees to cooperate with Coors, including appointing an organization to address ongoing issues and potential political and social difficulties that may occur in the national scene regarding Coors and its products over the life of the agreement." In addition, the organizations were to hold press conferences announcing the signing of the agreement, the termination of the boycott.

From 1982 to 1985, the organizations fulfilled the expectation and demand. After garnering corporate support, MALDEF, for example, amplified corporate endeavors in its annual reports, newsletters, and events. In its 1981, 1982, 1983, and 1984 annual reports, MALDEF performed the amplification function through the listing of its corporate supporters for the preceding program year. In its newsletter, *MALDEF*, the organization amplified corporate endeavors as early as 1982 through articles specifying corporate deeds on behalf of MALDEF and Latinos and photos of one or more corporate officials involved in activities such as providing support to MALDEF or being honored for the corporation's assistance to MALDEF. In an article entitled "Some Corporate Friends," MALDEF declared,

Do corporations owe it to society to pursue anything other than the almighty dollar? Some companies say no. But a growing number believe it's not only good citizenship, but also good business to help minority communities. That turn of mind often means useful advice, lively printed work, cooperative allies, and dependable financial support for MALDEF's work." (MALDEF 1982c)

The article then proceeded to delineate the level of corporate support received by MALDEF, the nature of the support, and the corporations whose support had been exceptional. Lastly, it detailed the diversity of support and noted that each contribution was helpful and encouraging to MALDEF and facilitated MALDEF's efforts on behalf of Latinos.

Subsequently, in an article entitled "Anheuser-Busch Grant Spurs Leadership, Citizenship," MALDEF publicized the receipt of a grant from Anheuser-Busch for the operation of leadership development and citizenship programs. It proclaimed, "Advancement for Hispanics nationwide through three innovative programs will be the product of a major $200,000 grant to MALDEF from Anheuser-Busch, Inc." (MALDEF 1982a). MALDEF also reported the results and proceedings of a MALDEF fund-raising dinner and graphically documented MALDEF's acknowledgement and amplification of corporate support (MALDEF 1982b).

The NCLR also amplified corporate efforts in a similar manner; in 1984, at its National Conference Awards Banquet, the NCLR honored John McNulty, Vice President for Public Relations, General Motors Corporation. One of the original members of NCLR's Corporate Advisory Council (CAC), McNulty was awarded the NCLR's President Award for contributions to the philosophy, goals, and mission of the NCLR. According to NCLR's president, McNulty had "played a key role in improving NCLR visibility in the corporate sector." He was deserving of the award because "he had demonstrated an understanding concern and willingness to take action in support of Hispanics and Hispanic issues" (NCLR 1984c).

In addition, in a page of its convention program formally acknowledging its appreciation of corporate support, the NCLR listed its corporate supporters. It encouraged members of the NCLR to review the list and express their appreciation to the representatives of the corporations who were attending the conference. It also expressed its hope that when members of the NCLR were purchasing goods or services, they would "remember--and buy from--these friends of the Council" (NCLR 1984a, 23).

In its newsletter, *El Noticiario* (1984c) NCLR also publicized the donation of computer equipment and software by TRW, Inc., for the development of a job fair in its 1984 NCLR Affiliate Conference. The computerization, the NCLR noted, promised to enhance the employment prospects for Hispanics in cities throughout the country. In the article entitled "New Computerized Job Fair Offers Link with Success," the NCLR also noted that TRW, Inc., had promised to give NCLR the software developed for the job fair, thus making possible additional Job Fairs at future NCLR conferences and other Hispanic events.

LULAC preceded its amplification by underscoring the logic and legitimacy of profit-making activity and the necessity of Latino economic development. Its magazine, *LULAC*, published an article offering a rationale for entry into business. The article was entitled "There Is Only One Reason to go into Business: To Make a Profit." The article quoted Robert J. Gans, president of Gans Ink and Supply Company in Los Angeles, who declared, "Profits are patriotic" (*LULAC* 1981c, 21).

LULAC's national director for economic development, Linda Alvarado, declared that total economic development should be a major goal for Hispanics in the 1980s. She wrote,

> We must realize that while many have made the proclamation that this will be "our decade," to finally achieve influence and power, this will not be attained by our sheer numbers alone. Without a solid economic base, Hispanics will leave the 80s without any real change in per capita wealth. Hispanics must move to maximize the economic potential that will be available to us during this growth period. Critical to this goal will be the development of Hispanic enterprise. We must create an environment that will enhance the opportunity for the development and expanded utilization of Hispanic business. A solid economic foundation will be the backbone for achieving total economic development of our community.
>
> The bottom line that Hispanics have sought in the past is equal opportunity. The opportunity to obtain equal jobs and equal pay. But our agenda for the 1980s must also include equal opportunity to build a solid economic base in order that we may provide these very things to other Hispanics. We cannot relive or whimper about the past, but must take care not to make the same mistakes in the future. The challenge is ours. (*Latino & LULAC* 1982d, 8-9)

In her capacity as LULAC's national director of economic development, Alvarado, in conjunction with Dr. Alicia Cuaron, LULAC National Director of Leadership and Educational Development, organized and chaired a conference to promote Hispanic economic development and to enhance Hispanic participation in the free enterprise system. Entitled the "National Hispanic Economic Development Leadership Summit," the conference was held April 23-24, 1982. It brought together Hispanic leaders in business and economic development for the purpose of "identifying the needs of Hispanics in developing a solid economic base, and to explore the options and alternatives that need to be looked at to establish and expand that base." One of the principal goals of the conference was the development of a strategy for increasing Hispanic participation in the free enterprise system (*Latino & LULAC* 1982h, 16).

LULAC also highlighted the views of William Coors, Chairman of the Board of Adolph Coors Company, by reporting in an article in its magazine parts of his speech to a group of Hispanic businessmen. Coors believed, LULAC reported, that the United States had "lost sight of the fundamental law of productivity" on its way to success. As a result, Americans were heavily paying financially for the mistake. But the financial price was exceeded by the loss of freedom. If Americans wanted to continue to enjoy their freedom, they had to increase their productivity. Coors offered two suggestions, "getting the government off the backs of the American people" and balancing the federal budget. After delineating the specific details of these suggestions, LULAC also noted that Coors had acknowledged that the federal budget cuts had been felt by most Americans. However, the cuts were necessary because the United States could not afford it. Lastly, it noted that Coors realized that free enterprise capitalism was controversial in some circles and regarded by some as the worst economic system in the world. However, Coors regarded it as the best and had rhetorically asked what its critics would replace it with if it was "dumped" (*Latino & LULAC* 1982c, 18).

At the tenth-anniversary banquet of the LULAC National Education Service Center in February 1983, LULAC awarded Robert W. Brocksbank, Manager of College Relations and Recruitment with Mobil Oil Corporation, its first Annual Trustee of Education Award. The award recognized individuals who had made "outstanding contributions to the betterment of American education." Brocksbank was cited for his contributions in helping Hispanic students (*Latino* 1982a, 26).

In the September 1982 issue of its magazine, LULAC also amplified the contribution made by Sears, Roebuck, to the achievement of LULAC's goal of establishing a partnership. It published a photo of its president, Tony Bonilla, receiving a check from representatives of Sears during the LULAC annual convention. The caption read as follows: "True corporate-Hispanic partnership is shared between officials of Sears, who presented a check for $25,000 to Tony Bonilla, LULAC National President, during the league's annual convention. It was the second of three $25,000 contributions made by Sears" (*Latino* 1982b, 19).

In establishing amplification as a condition for the receipt of assistance, some of the corporations anticipated that the amplification would enhance their support among Latinos. The expectation was fulfilled for the Coors Company. Before the signing of the agreement between Coors and the six organizations, the company had lost a significant portion of the beer market. The loss was, in large part, due to a boycott against the brewery by Chicano organizations. The boycott was fueled by the Coors family's advocacy of cowboy capitalism and Reaganomics. In the aftermath of the amplification by the organizations, Coors's sales increased among Latinos. In 1984 Latinos accounted for 5 percent of Coors business. By the end of 1985, they accounted for 9 percent of the business. Latino sales increased from $56.6 million in 1984 to $115 million in 1985. This was an increase of more than $59 million (Simons 1986, 47; *Fortune* 1986).

THE STRATEGIC RESPONSE: AN EXPLANATION

Why did the organizations opt to pursue the corporate grantsmanship and articulation strategy? An answer to this question can be provided by focusing on the NCLR, MALDEF, and LULAC and relying upon the framework developed by Jo Freeman (1979) for the analysis of social movement organizational decision making. In this framework, strategic choice is a function of four factors: (1) mobilizable resources possessed by the organizations, (2) the constraints on the resources, (3) the structure and internal environment of the organizations, and (4) expectations about potential targets.

Resources

One reason that the strategy was selected is that the organizations possessed the experience and expertise necessary for the reliance on the strategy. The three organizations had been involved in grantsmanship activity for at least ten years before the advent of Reaganomics. Prior to the 1980s, their principal targets had been the federal bureaucracy and foundations. All had been successful in garnering grants from these sources. Their success rested in large part on their possession of staff with expertise in writing and submission of grants and negotiation of agreements.

At the beginning of the eighties, the organizations continued to possess such staffs. The expertise was lodged in the organizations' "development" units. MALDEF's "development and public relations" department was the most sophisticated and developed.   It was directed by a vice-president for development and was staffed by six professionals whose primary responsibility was the development and implementation of fund-raising strategies as well as public relations strategies conducive to the enhancement of MALDEF's image and visibility.

A second reason that the organizations developed and pursued the strategy was that they lacked the personal funding bases sufficient to sustain their operations.   For example, since 1973, MALDEF had unsuccessfully pursued the creation of such a base. Entering the eighties, however, it found itself having to continue to seek funding from external sources. As its former president and general counsel, Vilma Martinez, observed, "My big dream was that we'd have enough money just to live off the interest. But we've never been able to do that. So, basically, MALDEF has to go out there every year and raise money" (Martinez 1984).

The Structure of the Organization

Additionally, the organizations did not have a membership base from which to generate funding to compensate for the federal budgetary cutbacks. They lacked this base, in large part, because at least two of them, MALDEF and NCLR, were created as national professional social movement organizations (Sierra 1982). Such organizations do not rely on members for the performance of their tasks or for their support. They consist largely of professionals who carry out the organization's activities and rely upon contributions for the resources necessary to maintain the organization (McCarthy and Zald 1973).

Above and beyond the lack of resources sufficient to maintain themselves, the organizations were led and staffed primarily by Chicanos who can be described as pragmatists committed to the integration of Chicanos into American life. The pragmatic orientation of the organizations' leadership was echoed by the president of LULAC at the beginning of the 1980s. He declared, "We Hispanics have got to start practicing pragmatic politics" (Ericksen 1980, 26).

LULAC was created by the generation of Latino political activists now known as the Mexican American generation. As San Miguel (1984) has noted, this cadre of activists were individuals who subscribed to liberal pragmatism. The founders and initial leadership of MALDEF and NCLR came from the ranks of LULAC (Sierra 1982). The individuals, such as Pete Tijerina of San Antonio, Texas, created MALDEF with the assistance of one of the more prominent liberal institutions, the Ford Foundation. The individuals also provided the initial leadership for the organizations. Their successors have continued to subscribe to the founder's ideology.

Expectations about Potential Targets

Lastly, the organizational leadership was highly optimistic that corporations would respond to the utilization of the corporate grantsmanship and articulation strategy. The roots of this optimism lay in part in the findings of a survey by the Council of Foundations in the early 1980s. The study sought to determine the "giving attitudes" of the chief executive officers of major corporations. The results of the study were deemed to be "very promising" by the leadership of the organizations, in particular the president of NCLR (*Caminos* 1983, 43). The leadership recognized that there was no guarantee that Latinos would "receive a fair share" of corporate support. However, the organizational leadership was optimistic that the potential could become a reality through work and cooperation with the private sector (*Caminos* 1983).

The optimism was also rooted in a perception that the orientation of corporations toward Latinos was undergoing change in the 1980s. As a former high officer of MALDEF noted in 1984, "Corporations are changing themselves. They are also undergoing change. They are becoming more sensitive to the issues presented by the Hispanic community. They are trying to improve their standing within the community. They are making very positive efforts in their minority representation at all levels. Those kinds of corporations really are, in essence, investing in themselves--which is good. Part of that investment is to the benefit of the Hispanic community." (interview 22 March 1984)

CONCLUSION

The impact of the budgetary cutbacks on Latino organizations and the response of the largest organizations to the cutbacks offers some lessons for the future. One lesson is that some organizations among Latinos possess the capacity to cope with retrenchment. Thus, Latinos will continue to enjoy advocacy on behalf of their interests in the future. A second lesson is that given the option of pursuing a confrontation with corporate power or accommodating to corporate power, the major Latino organization will prefer the latter. Third, the responses suggest that the major Latino organizations are unlikely to spearhead the formation of class coalitions, which some analysts (Piven and Cloward 1982) have seen as vital to the emergence of a class-based electoral realignment in American politics. If such coalitions are to be formed, other sectors of the Latino population will have to serve as a vanguard for the development of the coalitions. Needless to say, in the absence of the emergence of such a vanguard, the current patterns of American politics are likely to remain largely unaltered.

Ethnicity as a Political Tool in Britain and the Netherlands
Jan Rath and Shamit Saggar

Throughout many parts of Western Europe today, the presence of immigrant ethnic minority populations has become an indelible feature of national and local political systems. A short glance at urban politics in many of these countries reveals the extent to which issues of race and ethnicity have become entrenched in political debate and public policy-making. Far-right, anti-immigrant movements have emerged to varying degrees, often with an abrupt and sharp impact on the political process. Meanwhile, mainstream political parties have taken action to recruit ethnic minority membership and support, as well as to tackle questions of racial inequality and discrimination. Finally, immigrant ethnic minorities have begun to organize themselves in order to play a role in the political processes that surround them.

An important aspect of the new multi-ethnic politics of these countries has been the rise of ethnicity amongst immigrant ethnic groups, as well as in their patterns of political participation. While significant, explanations based on either Black solidarity or class consciousness appear to be inadequate and simplistic (Castles and Kosack 1973). In particular, many of these immigrant groups have systematically organized themselves into well-bonded and sometimes traditional ethnic organizations. It is the purpose of this chapter to examine the comparative impact of these organizations on different aspects of British and Dutch politics and vice versa.[1] Additionally, we shall focus upon aspects of the role of the government in relation to these ethnic organizations.

The reader ought to be alerted to a number of crucial differences that shape the role of ethnic minorities in the political process in these two European cases and the U.S. case. To begin with, it is noticeable that not all immigrants are considered ethnic minorities in the United States. This particular label is reserved for a handful of categories whose ethnic attributes and/or recent history have served to separate them in some way from mainstream American society. Blacks and Hispanics are prime examples. In the British and Dutch cases, in contrast, ethnicity and ethnic minority status are closely intertwined with both countries' recent experiences of immigration.

Furthermore, the role of the state differs sharply an ocean apart. The development of ethnic organizations in the U.S. political process--particularly at the subnational level--has proceeded with only limited initiative from the center. The government has generally taken the lead in Britain and the Netherlands, inasmuch as it has set out a broad framework for the political participation of immigrant ethnic minorities. While such frameworks may have presented differing conceptualizations of ethnicity at different times and with different outcomes, the British and Dutch cases paint a picture of governmental activism. A more minimalist picture, in contrast, is observed in the United States.

Our choice of comparisons reflects a number of significant features of the niche occupied by ethnic minorities in British and Dutch society that are of interest to us. First, we cannot avoid the historical legacies of conflict in these countries. The politics of social class (Britain) and pillarization (the Netherlands) begs further questions regarding the different impact of immigrant ethnic minorities. Second, while both countries have experienced significant immigrant influxes during the past quarter century, the societal and political consequences have been markedly different. Country-specific variations in the experiences of ethnic minority political participation are of interest. Finally, despite the similarities involved in large-scale colonial immigration, certain sharp contrasts in the "integration" of ethnic minorities stand out between these countries. To be certain, the differential position of Afro-Caribbeans in British society and the Surinamese in Dutch society point to important clues about ethnicity as a political tool in these countries (Cross and Entzinger 1988).

We discuss the following questions--among others--in relation to the two cases. What has been the historical development of ethnic organizations in both countries? What have been the main ethnicity-related strategies of these organizations and how, if at all, have these strategies evolved? In considering this question, it is noticeable that there has been a gradual shift of emphasis away from homeland-oriented concerns and toward a maximization of political leverage in British and Dutch society. Nonetheless, attitudes and priorities differ, and many of these organizations retain a strong interest in issues that have little to do with British and Dutch politics. Equally, many of these organizations were originally established on the basis of shared ethnicity as defined by common ancestry, language, religion, belongingness, and self-identification, as well as a variety of situational factors (Koot and Rath 1987). Ethnicity is a complex phenomenon. Not surprisingly, therefore, immense difficulties of reshaping priorities and activities has dogged many of the ethnic elites who have attempted to reshape priorities and activities within ethnic minority communities. Lastly, how have these organizations deployed their shared ethnicity as a political tool to mobilize their membership; moreover, what has been the role of other political actors such as parties, local authorities, and voluntary bodies? Here we observe that considerable activity has taken place in both countries for many years, sharply accelerating in recent times. Both British and Dutch ethnic organizations are well versed in attempting to secure support and legitimacy on the basis of their ethnically bonded membership. This has yielded different spoils at different times, but certainly the impression is left that a number of groups are convinced of the viability of this route.

It may be, however, that this is more a sign of these groups' relative powerlessness in both political systems. The dividends in terms of access, funding, resources, insider status, legitimacy in their memberships' eyes, and so forth may appear to be important, but ethnic organizations have not been universally successful in obtaining all that they have sought. Indeed, many writers continue to characterize the position of British and Dutch immigrant ethnic minorities as one of political weakness, widespread discrimination and relative poverty. Public agencies--ranging from the central government to local voluntary advisory bodies--have been only partially successful in their attempts to deal with the problems facing immigrant communities and in their attempts to secure increased participation. One of the channels used to this end has included the encouragement of ethnically based organizations. In this context, perhaps, we are better able to understand the use of ethnicity as a political tool and the motivations that lie behind it: it has offered unique and occasionally promising resources in a political environment with few convincing alternatives.

This chapter is divided into four sections. We start by examining some historic and demographic features of immigrants in Britain and the Netherlands. Next, we discuss the British case and, subsequently, the Dutch case. Finally, we conclude with a discussion of similarities and differences between the two cases.

HISTORIC AND DEMOGRAPHIC CONTEXT

It is clear to even the most casual observer that race and ethnicity have become important and far-reaching features of the British and Dutch political maps. In both countries this development is strongly related to recent immigration. It is true that Britain has known previous waves of mass immigration of peoples of different "race" such as the Irish in the nineteenth century and the Jews in this century, and the Netherlands has in the past likewise experienced heavy immigration of peoples such as the Portuguese Jews, the French Huguenots, and the German Westphalians. However, practically all these categories of immigrants have virtually assimilated into the larger society so that, until recently, the British and Dutch societies were essentially mono-racial or mono-ethnic.[2] Non-white, ethnic minority settlement has thus been a relatively new phenomenon taking place during the postwar epoch. In Britain it took place over a short, concentrated spell dating from about the mid-1950s, accelerating sharply through the 1960s and early 1970s, and gradually tapering off thereafter. In the Netherlands a similar immigration process occurred about ten years behind.

The overwhelming bulk of Britain's ethnic minority population today is comprised of two broad ethnic groups: Asians and those with ethnic origins (however measured) in South Asian countries, and Afro-Caribbean originating from Black African and Caribbean counties. According to self-selection-based survey data from 1983, 1984, and 1985, the non-white ethnic minority population totals almost 2.3 million persons. Table 11.1 describes the sizes of the various ethnic minority populations in greater detail than do the descriptions "Asians" and "Afro-Caribbeans."

The debate on race has often been influenced by the debate over numbers. In all, however, something around 4 percent of the population are from an ethnic minority background of one form or another. Data sources tend to overlap and are commonly based on different conceptions of the ethnic minority population (Saggar 1987). In particular, New Commonwealth and Pakistani (NCWP) status has structured both measures and political debates because, for many, Britain's non-white communities are looked upon in terms of their ex-colonial background. As a consequence of this background, virtually all NCWP immigrants and their spouses have British citizenship.

An important feature has been geographical settlement patterns. Survey figures in 1985 suggest that more than two-thirds of non-white ethnic groups are to be found in metropolitan areas, compared with less than a third of whites (OPCS 1986, 5). Their age structure is also significantly different: 62 percent of non-whites compared to 42 percent of whites are below thirty years of age (OPCS 1986, 4). And so the list of distinctions goes on. Several important differences exist between the minority and majority populations, and indeed there are many contrasts within different ethnic minority groups. Furthermore, factors of religion and language all serve to further differentiate these communities, with the result that a number of aspects of British politics and policy-making are currently having to be revised to accommodate this new ethnic pluralism.

The situation in the Netherlands is relatively similar. Quite a few immigrants form more or less coherent groups manifesting themselves on the basis of their specific ethnicity, although there are many internal divisions creating subgroups. To be sure, more immigrants belonging to these categories identify themselves as members of groups that are different from the native white Dutch majority, and indeed that majority also identify and treat them as such. The overwhelming bulk of today's ethnic minority population have come

Table 11.1 Ethnic Population in Britain[a]

Ethnic Group	Thousands	Percentage[b]
White	50,971	94.2
Non-White	2,347	4.3
West Indian/Guyanese	526	1.0
Indian	763	1.4
Pakistani	378	0.7
Bangladeshi	91	0.2
Chinese	112	0.2
African	101	0.2
Arab	64	0.1
Mixed	211	0.4
Other	101	0.2
Not stated	782	1.5
Total	54,100	

Source: *OPCS 1986.*

[a]The results of the Labour Force Survey are averaged over three years, 1983-1985, in order to reduce the distortions of sampling fluctuations from one survey to another.

[b]Percentages are rounded to single decimal point and therefore column total does not equal 100.

from former colonial areas--Moluccans from the former Dutch East Indies, Antilleans and Arubans from the Caribbean, and Surinamese from the former South American colony of Surinam--or from Mediterranean countries, most of them initially as guest workers. The numbers of various ethnic minority groups are shown in detail in Table 11.2.

There are a few other categories of immigrants, for instance the Chinese and Pakistani, that anthropologically constitute non-white ethnic minority groups but have not been officially recognized as such for reasons that will be explained later. For now, it is important to understand that ethnic minority groups in the Netherlands, unlike similar groups in Britain, are subject to a selective definition process by the state. The British definition is principally based on racial aspects. This explains why the so-called Eurasians--people of mixed Dutch-Indonesian ancestry who came to the Netherlands in the 1950s, who are racially different from the majority but are practically fully absorbed into Dutch society--do not constitute a "racial" or ethnic minority group and are consequently not recognized as such (cf. Amersfoort 1982).

Table 11.2 Ethnic Population in the Netherlands

Ethnic group	Thousands	Percentage[a]
Dutch	13,769[b]	94.2
Mediterraneans	346	2.4
Turks	161	1.1
Moroccans	123	0.8
Spaniards	18	0.1
Italians	17	0.1
Yugoslavs	12	0.1
Portuguese	8	0.1
Greeks	4	0.0
Tunesians	3	0.0
Cape Verdians	2	0.0
Surinamese	195[c]	1.3
Antilleans and Arubans	55	0.4
Moluccans	40[d]	0.3
Other	210[e]	1.5
Total	14,615	

Source: Muus 1987.

[a]Percentages are rounded to single decimal point and therefore column total does
   not equal 100.
[b]Estimated number.
[c]Estimated number. This number includes 11,638 Surinamese passport holders.
[d]Estimated number. This number includes about 30 percent stateless Moluccans.
[e]This number includes among others about 40,000 Chinese and 9,000
   Indonesians.

     The officially recognized ethnic minorities constitute 5-6 percent of the present population of the Netherlands. Most of them live in the densely populated western part of the country, particularly in big cities like Amsterdam, Rotterdam, the Hague, and Utrecht. In these cities the average concentration of immigrant ethnic minorities may amount to 13-20 percent, and in the older inner-city areas up to 40-50 percent--this proportion usually refers to an ethnically mixed population.

     Practically every ex-colonial immigrant has Dutch nationality, except a tiny number of Surinamese citizens and a small number of Moluccans who have chosen to stay stateless for political reasons.[3] Most of the Mediterranean and other foreigners have kept their own nationality and are treated according to the Aliens Act. Neither the government nor the political agencies put them under pressure to naturalize. Rather, they remove the existing legal differences between Dutch and non-Dutch residents.

The ethnic minorities both in Britain and the Netherlands have a disadvantaged social position: their education is substandard, their unemployment is relatively high, their employment is concentrated in the lower sectors of the labor market, their housing is poor, they experience discrimination, and, moreover, they have limited political influence. In the Netherlands this is partly due to the fact that the non-Dutch citizens among the ethnic minorities have fewer political rights. In practice this means that they are not allowed to take part in elections for representative legislative bodies like the provincial councils and national parliament.

Let us now turn to consider aspects of ethnicity in the British and then the Dutch case. We will focus on the increasing importance of ethnic organizations in the policy process and on the role of the government.

THE BRITISH CASE

Ethnic organizations have occupied an awkward place in British race-related politics and public policy. During the 1960s their main role was as supporting appendages to the community relations movement. The prevailing philosophy of the period centered on local, ad hoc voluntarism, in which ethnic organizations were encouraged to assist in the process of reducing the impact of racial and ethnic issues in public policy debate. Ethnic organizations, in short, were all about the effective non-mobilization or selective mobilization of ethnicity. More recently, however, developments within local borough politics have served to give ethnic organizations a new and more dynamic role in local public policy making. Ethnic organizations have been elevated to an unprecedented position of importance, at least in part as a legitimation exercise for the pioneering race equality initiatives of certain local authorities. There has been a rediscovery of ethnicity and its mobilization.

Community Relations Councils and Ethnicity

The 1960s are often thought of as the liberal hour in British race relations. Banton (1985) notes the tremendous pace of activity during this period in which "laws were enacted, enforcement agencies created, and community relations councils established." During this short period a large part of the future framework for race relations and the role of ethnic organizations was established.

Emphasis was placed on two themes. First, discrimination was to be tackled in a piecemeal, non-compulsive manner; thus, legislation on this front was modest and dependent on conciliation to resolve conflicts. Second, racial harmony was nominated as a broad policy goal to which all responsible parties would subscribe. This was taken a step further through the backing given to local voluntary bodies to lead and coordinate the local promotion of race harmony. A number of these local bodies already existed at the time of the first Race Relations Act and the White Paper *Immigration from the Commonwealth* (1965). By the mid-1980s, the number of Community Relations Councils (CRCs) in operation was well over one hundred (Commission for Racial Equality 1980).

Early studies rightly attached great importance to the ill-defined remit given to CRCs. Hill and Issacharoff's now dated study (1971) rounded on CRCs for failing to address--often by steering clear of--many basic issues pertaining to race equality. Katznelson (1973) characterized CRCs as performing the role of "buffer institutions" designed to remove some of the venom of race conflict from public debate. They may have been catapulted into the front line of local race relations, but, it was argued, their role remained ambiguous. The result was that different CRCs in the name of racial harmony varied enormously (Barker 1975). The environment of local race relations policy-making could not even be firmly anticipated between neighboring London boroughs (Fitzgerald 1984).

More recently Messina (1987) has described the role of CRCs as central to the two-party agreement to try to remove race from party politics in Britain. Race and race conflicts were therefore seen as political hot potatoes for which the major parties were unwilling to assume any greater responsibility than was necessary.   Thus, a series of intermediary bodies were assigned this responsibility. Allied to this was the need to try to neuter strong independent Black political activity.   As stated by Ben-Tovim and Gabriel, "Local community relations councils . . . have been regarded as *buffer institutions* heading off a direct assault on the Establishment by the Black community" (1982, 155).

With the repoliticization of significant aspects of race relations in recent years, the resultant pressure placed on CRCs has escalated massively. In the present climate, CRCs work alongside radical left Labour local authorities as well as color-blind Conservative authorities (not to mention areas where CRCs and Labour authorities are in conflict with one another). The contrast in the conceptualization and salience of race and ethnicity is noticeably sharper today than it was a decade ago.

While race harmony and conciliation were set out as guiding themes in the liberal settlement, little was defined in the way of the work of CRCs or how they should carry out their duties. In other words, considerable room for local ad hoc strategies existed. It is here that the relationship between CRCs and ethnic minorities and ethnic organizations is of particular importance. What is the nature of this relationship, how have CRCs attempted to mobilize ethnic groups, and with what success?

First of all, it is important to mention that CRCs do not, of course, function in isolation from other policy actors. Foremost amongst these has been local authorities. A loosely defined relationship was envisaged between the two in the 1965 White Paper. At first CRCs' main reference point was the National Committee for Commonwealth Immigrants (NCCI), a government-sponsored liaison and umbrella body.[4] Throughout this period, CRCs were encouraged to develop closer links with their local authorities. A prime motivation behind this was to try to get local authorities to shoulder a greater part of the financial cost of CRCs. Not surprisingly, CRCs feared for their independence and autonomy in local politics.

The CRC-local authority nexus, therefore, has been central to the development of community relations in Britain. In the face of a combination of ambiguous policy goals, poorly defined political roles, and the encroachment of local authorities, how have CRCs responded? The answer has to do with CRCs' selective utilization of one of their main yet untapped resources; the indirect participation of ethnic minority organizations.

The CRC framework for local race relations offered ethnic minorities what has been described as a participatory margin, which would assist their longer-term participation in more mainstream politics and public policy. This was clearly a firm indication to ethnic minorities that the group organization to which they belonged was the most valued of their various identities in British society. Value was not placed on Black coalition groups, nor was it necessarily placed on other non-ethnically based groups. The ethnicity of immigrant groups--defined as a coherent bonding force--was singled out as the basis on which they should and would participate in community relations.

This is, however, something of dated view, since in recent years CRCs' ability to perform the ethnic consultant role has been questioned. Ethnic groups are given more attention today as proxy participation agencies. Renewed emphasis has been placed on creating a consultative dialogue with ethnic minority communities on the basis of their ethnicity and ethnic organizations. CRCs' claims of close and unparalleled links with ethnic organizations are suspect: "How does one consult with the ethnic minorities? I think there is no alternative to a series of dialogues with the communities as they present themselves, rather than expecting them to merge themselves under one umbrella and present a coherent view" (Young 1984).

Where does the community relations movement go from here? After more than two decades of trying to forge a racial peace in many parts of urban Britain, CRCs in recent years have shown signs of having lost a sense of direction. Their work continues to be superficially valued by the central government. However, their level of support and funding from local authorities on the ground tends to vary enormously. Quite simply, there is no obvious nor accessible niche into which community relations can be lodged in the picture of contemporary race initiatives in Britain. Having grown accustomed to such a role in which they were able to map out and deal with local race relations issues, many now find this role being overshadowed by the work of their local authorities. The major locomotive of change in grass-roots race relations has altered dramatically and, in all probability, irreversibly.

Local Government and the Rise of Ethnicity

Recent developments in British local government--ostensibly in the inner cities--have led to a renewed interest in ethnicity as a potential tool for mobilization of political support. As part of this wide-ranging process, certain local authorities have sought to involve the ethnic minority communities themselves. Sometimes this is at the level of ad hoc, informal consultation; elsewhere, more formal, direct representative input is sought from ethnic organizations; and, in a few cases, some groups have found themselves co-opted into key aspects of local policy-making. Arguably, many of these developments are of immense significance and are presently reshaping our understanding of ethnic minority participation in British politics and public policy-making.

Following the election to office of a number of Labour administrations in London and other major cities in the early 1980s--culminating in 1986 and 1987 polls--race policy initiatives in town halls have gathered considerable pace (Saggar 1987). It is probably too early to say whether these changes will undermine the role of CRCs altogether. However, a number of CRCs are only too conscious of such an outcome and some have already begun to resurrect their traditional liberal identity in response. Such an identity is largely centered on being seen to promote harmonious local race relations, especially in the eyes of potential critics. This serves as a reasonably sharp contrast to the bolder, more radical aims and activities of certain Labour-ruled local authorities.

Prashar and Nicholas's (1986) study of consultative processes in five London boroughs provides further evidence of the dislocation of CRCs. They pointed to the recent massive escalation in these administrations' use of consultative devices. However, it was noted that this was closely associated with other aspects of local authority policy development: their narrow race equality and broader community consultation initiatives often went hand in hand. This suggests that these local authorities are keen to formulate their own in-house strategies on race and that they see the consultative exercise as the other side of the same coin.

The role of central government in the growth and activities of ethnic organizations has been significant--in this case primarily because of its conspicuous absence. While central government has been active in other aspects of race relations--for example, anti-discrimination legislation, community relations machinery and funding, and so forth--it has largely avoided close involvement in the affairs of ethnic organizations. These have been seen as autonomous bodies, best left to their own devices and, depending on local circumstances, open to enter into specific arrangements with their local authorities. There has been little central coordination or encouragement. The government's main national race relations watchdog body--the Commission for Racial Equality (CRE)--is organized without the need for subnational ethnic organizations to affiliate to it. Therefore, it neither seeks nor claims any role in relation to the numerous local and handful of national ethnic organizations.

In recognition of the slow pace of change, a variety of local political actors (such as ethnic leaders, local political parties, and Black sectional groups) have moved to encompass ethnic organizations into local political and policy-making processes. How has this been done, for what purpose, and with what outcome?

The first thing to note is that the relationship between local government and ethnic organizations is an embryonic one. Moreover, it is patchy in nature and therefore not universal to all, or even most, local authority areas. In the main, we are examining an interaction between groups and subnational government in localities run by progressive-left Labour administrations. In these selected areas the Labour urban left has gained ascendancy since the late 1970s (Boddy and Fudge 1984).

The factors behind this are partly internal developments within the party and partly a polarization of competitive two-party politics (Jacobs 1986; Saggar 1987). As Young (1985) notes, there has been a "rediscovery of race" in local government in recent years. This has involved radicals on the left set on building urban coalitions of support amongst a variety of minority groups; ethnic minorities constitute one among many groups in this mobilization process (Ousely 1984).

However, issues of race equality are by no means on the policy agenda of all or even most labor local administrations. An inventory of developments in London boroughs, arguably a stronghold of the Labour left, in spring 1987 revealed that while most Labour authorities had adopted some form of committee and officer structure to tackle race issues, their achievements beyond that were very patchy indeed (Saggar 1987, 4-5). Among the remaining half of non-Labour-run boroughs, progress on "race issues" was more or less negligible (Saggar 1987, 6-7).

A major element of the race strategies adopted by this handful of authorities has been to make overtures toward their local ethnic organizations in order to involve them in the local policy process. This has ranged from informal consultation to formal co-option onto resource allocating committees. These authorities have slowly found that their local CRCs are not the only nor the obvious body with whom to consult on matters of race. This realization, not surprisingly, has been more readily accepted by certain authorities than by others. Moreover, the contrast has not always been explained by party labels, since many Labour authorities have turned to CRCs to off-load their own responsibilities just as readily as their Conservative counterparts (Prashar and Nicholas 1986; Saggar 1987).

Subtle, yet important, encouragement for local authorities to look upon their local ethnic minority communities as positive consultative resources has also occasionally come from other sources. In 1981 the House of Commons Home Affairs Committee's report, "Racial Disadvantage," stated: "We . . . encourage local authorities to make every effort to make as much direct contact as possible with [ethnic] minorities and to rid themselves of the notion that the local CRS is or should be their sole spokesman. . . . Each council will develop its own *modus vivendi*, but none can afford to neglect the interests and concerns of its ethnic minority citizens" (Home Affairs Committee 1981). In order to do this, authorities have been placed--indeed have placed themselves--in a position whereby they view non-white ethnic minority political participation as a leading function of ethnic organizations.

Inevitably, the problems with this rationale are immense. To begin with, a number of such organizations neither see themselves nor can easily be seen as performing such a function. Certainly, those concerned with the narrowly defined affairs of their own ethnic community--as based on religion and language--can only take up a wider participation role as a secondary function at the most. Furthermore, such an arrangement is likely to attract organizations which, although loosely based on some form of shared ethnicity, are in fact far more interested in performing a race pressure group role. Ethnicity and ethnic organizations, thus, come to mean different things, particularly in an environment that actively courts such organizations for consultative and other purposes.

Another drawback is that certain ethnic organizations can become easily and excessively labelled as proxy participatory bodies, thereby limiting the points of access available to ethnic minorities to the broader political process (Fitzgerald 1984; Prashar and Nicholas 1986). There is also an allied problem of raising expectations of ethnic organizations and their members, often by implying an exaggerated status in local authority policy-making. Such a problem was highlighted by research on the relationship fostered by the now-defunct Greater London Council (GLC) and the plethora of ethnic organizations it sought to champion and involve in its decision-making process between 1981 and 1986 (Fitzgerald 1984). Jacobs (1986) notes that the elaborate consultative mechanisms adopted by some authorities have given many ethnic organizations the impression that their presence has changed the nature of local authority policy-making. In fact, there is very little basis for such a collectively and widely held view. "Blacks in Britain have at times been able to modify public policy," he states, "but this has been . . . largely based upon adaptation of Black organizations to prevailing administrative and political practices" (Jacobs 1986, 72).

Related to this is another danger. As Prashar and Nicholas (1986) point out, grand overtures on the part of local authorities to involve ethnic organizations may lead to greater difficulties in the longer term if such groups continue to feel they have too little say in policy decisions affecting them. They warn, "The illusion of consultation without any change will only feed cynicism. Consultation and liaison with [ethnic] minorities is part of local authority practice, and what is clear is that having opened the door for consultation, there is no going back" (Prashar and Nicholas 1986, 50). In other words, a particular notion of ethnicity has been captured in the way in which local authorities consult ethnic organizations and seek to mobilize support from them. To relinquish such a notion of ethnicity--either in favor of another or altogether-- will be considerably harder to do. For this reason, a notion of ethnicity based on tapping the mobilization resources of ethnic organizations is likely to remain a crucial feature of British local politics and public policy.

Clearly, therefore, important alternative strategies for the management of local race relations are now being offered: the CRC approach and the Labour left approach. We can also add to this the approach taken by Conservative administrations based on non-race-specific, or color-blind, conceptualizations of race relations. The first two approaches are at least partially built on bringing ethnic minorities and ethnic organizations into a legitimate policy development role. The success of these respective strategies will therefore ultimately depend on which is more effective in mobilizing the support of ethnic organizations.

THE DUTCH CASE

As in Britain, the Netherlands has experienced the gradually increasing involvement of immigrant ethnic minorities in the political process. It took the Dutch a long time to get used to the idea that immigrants had become part of the society and the polity. However, once this fact was recognized, many efforts have been made at both stimulating their political participation and fostering their ethnicity.

The Dutch political ideology, which is still deeply rooted in the pillarization system of olden days, may have encouraged both the concern of the government and political agencies and use of ethnicity by minorities themselves. It is difficult to assess the true value of this ideology and the resulting political practices for ethnic minority participation, but these practices obviously do come into it and they tend to produce important differences with Britain (Rath 1988b). As Lijphart (1975) showed, Dutch society was divided up into social pillars based on religion. A pillar was the social and political organization of individuals belonging to the same religion or denomination. It thus united individuals of different socioeconomic classes against individuals of other religions. Most pillars were rather centrally organized. Since no pillar was strong enough to dominate every other group around it, every leadership sought consociation with the leadership of other pillars, and thus took account of the sensitivities, religious and cultural traits, and resulting political demands of the others. Consequently, a sociopolitical system developed based on the pragmatic principle of giving and taking both material and non-material resources. The system of consociationalism as such does not fully exist anymore, although there are many surviving features; for example, there is still a rather pillarized educational system and, what is more important, an ideology of consensus and of respecting the particularistic needs of minorities. To be sure, this is not to say that racism and discrimination against the present ethnic minorities is absent in the Netherlands. For now, we only want to highlight an important difference with Britain, where polarization rather than pillarization seems to be the hallmark of politics. In Britain, political organization is basically along socioeconomic lines rather than along religious lines. Having said this, let us now examine how ethnic minorities have become involved in Dutch politics and how ethnicity has been used in that process.

Dutch Welfare Foundations

In the 1960s and 1970s, many--including the government, political parties, and newcomers themselves--assumed that the immigrants were only temporarily resident in the country and that they would return to their home countries sooner or later. In consequence, nobody but a few self-proclaimed advocates and private organizations such as churches were concerned with the integration of immigrants into the Dutch society; few bothered about their participation in the political process. Government policy toward immigrants aimed mainly at alleviating their worst problems during their sojourn. A series of welfare agencies--the so-called *welzijnsstichtingen* (welfare foundations)--were founded for Moluccans, Surinamese, and Mediterranean workers; since the mid-1970s, they have been fully sponsored by the government. These welfare foundations and a variety of action committees, chiefly consisting of Dutch individuals, emerged as the main advocates of immigrants' interests.

In this period, particularly during the 1960s, immigrants themselves virtually abstained from participation in Dutch politics; political activities--if any--were principally homeland oriented. There was a tiny number of immigrant organizations that functioned as sort of outposts for some homeland political movements. Amersfoort, for instance, described Surinamese organizations in Amsterdam in 1970 as breeding grounds for politicians-to-be in Surinam. Insofar as Mediterranean guest workers took interest in Dutch politics, they mainly lobbied Dutch politicians about homeland affairs (Penninx 1979).

The Rise of Ethnic Organizations

During the 1970s, the number of immigrant organizations grew rapidly. This was partly due to the fact that the central and local governments started subsidizing immigrant organizations--sometimes through the welfare foundations--provided they did not maintain any tie of whatever kind with fascist political movements such as the Moroccan Amicales and the Turkish Grey Wolves or with religious movements. Initially, these organizations were not necessarily seen as advocates of immigrants' interests. Most only fulfilled sociocultural functions. Nevertheless, a few organizations or, rather, a few individual immigrants, often with help of native Dutch, slowly began taking more interest in Dutch politics.

Many immigrant organizations were dissatisfied with the advocacy of welfare foundations. These foundations were chiefly manned by native white Dutch; few immigrants--if any--were employed, while other immigrants put them down for being "Uncle Toms" or political extremists. The fact that immigrants played a minor role in the promotion of their own interests stirred up bad feelings and provoked political action. Some immigrants demanded ethnicization of the foundations and, sure enough, succeeded in getting positions in the staffs or committees of these foundations (Koot and Uniken Venema 1985). Others converted their dissatisfaction into founding ethnic counterinstitutions.

Meanwhile, various immigrants became aware of their inferior social position and become involved in the political process. Although housing and education were incidental on the political agenda, probably the most salient issue then concerned their position on the labor market. In the mid-1970s, the government introduced a plan to combat the presence and employment of undocumented workers and to protect the interests of native Dutch workers on the labor market against newly arrived immigrant workers (Groenendael 1986). Immigrant activists perceived the plan as a threat to their position, and they resisted them by, among other activities, lobbying politicians, trade unionists, and the media, and holding mass demonstrations. Through ethnic networks thousands of immigrants were mobilized. These manifestations of both political awareness and ethnic loyalty were unprecedented in the Netherlands and encouraged new political action.

There was another series of events that made quite an impression. Groups of Moluccan youth hijacked trains and occupied a number of buildings, thereby taking dozens of people hostage. Although these events had, above all, an international political dimension--the Moluccans had striven to found their own independent republic--the Moluccans' marginal position in Dutch society interfered with it (Bartels 1986). In particular, these violent actions opened the eyes of many Dutch political leaders. While condemning the violence and rejecting the political motives behind it, many felt that one, and probably the best, way of avoiding future violent actions would be to improve the treatment of ethnic minorities. In short, this laid the foundation of a dramatic change in policy on immigrants (Köbben 1979).

A New Policy

In 1980, the government adopted the basic assumption that the immigrants had come to stay and that an integration policy had to be outlined (Entzinger 1985; Penninx 1981). From then on, various categories of immigrants have been referred to as "ethnic minorities." A background to this change was obviously the fear that conflicts and violent disturbances of social peace would occur without such a policy. In 1983, the government presented its White Paper on Minorities (*Minderhedennota* 1983). The major aim of that policy was to further the chances of social mobility of the ethnic minorities. The policy aimed, inter alia, at strengthening the political influences of the immigrant ethnic minorities (Rath 1983, 1988b). Thus, the government financially supported ethnic organizations that were involved in the political decision-making process. It further set up a series of local and national advisory councils for the interests of ethnic minorities. And finally, it granted non-Netherlands citizens the right to vote and to run for office at the local level. Incidentally, this suggests that the Dutch definition of ethnic minorities and the subsequent minorities policy partially reflects social policy.

As said earlier, the Dutch had a characteristic way of incorporating religious minorities into the political process, namely through consociationalism. Aspects of this can be observed with the ethnic minorities as well. The government clearly attempted to avoid the situation in which it would no longer communicate with certain categories, *casu quo,* would lose control. From 1980, the government deliberately sought the cooperation of immigrants when outlining and implementing the minorities policy.

Thus, a draft version of the White Paper on Minorities and also summaries in different languages were sent to ethnic organizations, welfare foundations, and other agencies working for the interests of immigrants and ethnic minorities, explicitly inviting comment. Special mass meetings were organized to involve rank-and-file immigrants in the policy process. Interestingly, a great many of the comments by the ethnic minority leadership concerned their ethnic identity and the proposed policy on that topic. They suggested that strengthening their ethnicity was not only a right of ethnic minorities but also a prerequisite for their emancipation process. They rejected any government interference with their cultures but, paradoxically, at the same time demanded government support for cultural activity. In fact, the ethnic minority leadership agreed with the policy to further the social mobility of immigrant ethnic minorities and showed every willingness to co-operate with the government in that respect, but they laid down an important condition: no cooperation without facilities to maintain or strengthen their ethnicity.

The ethnic leadership further demanded a special position in the political process. They argued that a more pluralistic political system would enable them to be politically active in their own, ethnically related ways and would consequently enhance their political role and influence. Sure enough, the government concentrated its sponsoring of those ethnic organizations that, apart from fostering ethnicity, also advocated ethnic minority interests and contributed to participation of ethnic minorities in Dutch society. In practice, however, things turned out differently. Graaf, Penninx, and Stoové (1988) contend that most rank-and-file members considered the organizations as mere meeting places of compatriots and as agencies that gave shelter rather than as advocacy groups. A few organizations, or rather a couple of individual leaders, nevertheless penetrated the Dutch political arena by, for instance, playing a role in advisory bodies, in political parties, or sometimes in both.

Advisory Bodies

In the late 1970s, a few municipalities founded advisory bodies for immigrants, usually on the initiative of native Dutch. These special institutions were to advise the mayor and the local council on all affairs concerning immigrants. Immigrants living in these municipalities were entitled to elect their own representatives onto these bodies. For various reasons, the advisory bodies failed. The main reasons for this included the dominance of native Dutch officials, the lack of support by rank-and-file immigrants, inter- and intraethnic quarrels and, last but not least, the lack of real power.

In spite of this, the government continued to favor the founding of more advisory bodies. It felt obligated to meet ethnic minority demands for a more pluralistic model of participation and, moreover, considered such bodies as an appropriate means of consociating with the ethnic minority leadership. While showing its democratic credentials, the government hoped to win the support and cooperation of the ethnic minority leadership for the minorities policy. That leadership, on their side, often considered their involvement in such bodies as a recognition of the legitimacy of their ethnic-specific demands. The central government made some arrangements in the minorities policy to ensure that every municipality would create such a provision. As a result, in virtually every municipality with ethnic minorities some form of participation was set up. In many cases the largest or (politically) most important ethnic organizations had delegates in the advisory bodies.

Although the local advisory bodies were still at the fringes of the power centers, many ethnic leaders dedicated themselves to the founding of a series of national advisory councils. In 1983, the central government proposed the founding of one national advisory council, the so-called *minderhedenraad* (Minorities Council). The major ethnic organizations would be represented in this multi-ethnic council. Though anxious for it to take place, they opposed the proposal and demanded separate institutions for each ethnic minority group. Contrary to the conventional viewpoint that divide and rule should be avoided and that intergroup solidarity and close cooperation are means to increase power, the ethnic minority leadership claimed that one council for all ethnic minority groups would considerably diminish their power. The government might seize the opportunity to manipulate interethnic differences and the minorities themselves might need to compromise. Remarkably, the leadership argued that their ethnic identity would be suppressed when under the obligation to cooperate in one council. Eventually, the political parties endorsed the counterproposal. The parties clearly did not want to get into the ethnic leaders' bad books, especially not during this period when the racist *Centrumpartii* (Center Party) had one seat in parliament (1982-1986). More than ever, most parties felt the need to demonstrate their opposition to racism and their respect for the needs of ethnic minorities. Besides, the parties took the opportunity to compensate for a little of their own failure to integrate ethnic minorities in their own ranks.

Electoral Politics

It was not until recently that both immigrant ethnic minorities and political parties took serious notice of each other. As for the minorities, or rather the activists among them, they spent most of their time and efforts in other institutions like ethnic organizations and advisory bodies. Their integration in the Dutch electoral system had been particularly accelerated by the enfranchisement of non-Netherlands residents in 1985. Not that immigrants campaigned for voting rights; quite the contrary. But the first immigrant elections in 1986 gave many ethnic minority activists cause to put pressure on the political parties to be more considerate of ethnic minorities. This resulted in a considerable increase in ethnic minority party membership. Furthermore, the 1986 local elections gave political parties cause to pay more attention than ever to the ethnic minorities both in their programs and in their campaigns.

The ethnic voters turned out en masse, except for Moroccans who followed the summons of the Moroccan King Hassan II to abstain from voting; he considered the elections as an undesirable step towards assimilation (Buijs and

Rath 1986). The overwhelming majority of the ethnic minorities voted for the social-democratic *PvdA* (Labour party). Many ethnic voters considered the Labour party as the party for the working man--which most of them actually were--and above all as the party with most concern for ethnic minorities. The support for Labour was also related to the relatively high number of social-democratic ethnic candidates.

The nomination of ethnic candidates was at least partly due to their ethnic background. Quite a few succeeded in getting nominated by implicitly or explicitly referring to their ethnic background (Rath 1988a). Some ethnic party members claimed that minorities should be given a fair deal, by which they meant preferential treatment, and that any other treatment would be an expression of Dutch supremacy. Others, if not most, did not need to articulate such a position, because many Dutch party members already supported them of their own accord. The Dutch considered their support a means to show their solidarity with ethnic minorities and their anti-racist credentials. Of course, they also hoped that the ethnic candidates would yield many ethnic votes.

The Dutch electoral system is based on the principle of proportional representation and opens up the possibility of preference vote-centered campaigns. Although such a campaign is unusual, many ethnic candidates conducted one either on their own initiative or on the initiative of Dutch fellow party members (Buijs and Rath 1986; Rath 1988a). In doing so they manipulated formal and informal ethnic networks and used the ethnic organizations of which they were commonly the leaders, too. In other words, they mobilized ethnicity and took advantage of the solidarity among the members of their ethnic communities. The resulting large number of preference votes helped their election and the party winning votes, and also served to strengthen their position within the party. This is another indication that ethnicity has become a salient feature of Dutch politics.

CONCLUSION

Through the developments reviewed above, it is apparent that immigrant ethnic minorities have become aware of the need to participate in the British and Dutch political systems. Although some ethnic minorities have unhesitatingly adopted the route of party-centered involvement, for many, local ethnic community organizations remain the first--and in some cases sole--vehicle of participation. This has not always been the case. For some time, the newcomers were only marginally involved in host country politics. If politically active, most attention was paid to home country politics. In the course of time, though, things have changed and immigrants have become involved in the political process of the country in which they were living. Historically, in Britain this change took place beginning in the 1960s, and in Holland, a decade or so later. This difference is probably due to the fact that mass immigration to Britain reached its height earlier than in the Netherlands, but probably also to the fact that the British central government has set up various institutions for the interests of immigrant ethnic minorities at a rather early stage. The Dutch central government needed more time for that. Presently we witness ethnic minorities' political activity in both countries at all levels. In this chapter we sought to describe a few aspects of these activities, in particular the role of ethnic organizations and their use of ethnicity.

Of course, this is not an exhaustive description, not least because this subject is an understudied aspect both in the British and Dutch cases. Evidently, there are many differences, since we are dealing with two different countries with different histories, different political systems, and different immigration patterns. The response of the government, political parties, and other political actors are not always similar. In Britain, for instance, the government definition of ethnic minorities is predominantly based on racial features. In the Netherlands the definition is not as racialized as in Britain. It is selective and based on ethnic rather than on racial features and it reflects social policy. Furthermore, it does seem to make a difference in Britain when dealing with left-wing authorities or with right-wing authorities, in particular at the local level. The former have recently adopted a more cooperative and supportive attitude toward ethnic minorities. Although there are differences in the Netherlands between left-wing and right-wing authorities, virtually all pursue a similar policy. This may be explained by the fact that local authorities follow the central governments' minorities policy, which is, moreover, endorsed by all major political parties. This may also be explained by the prevailing political ideology. Historically, Dutch politicians have been concerned about minorities and there has been a tendency toward consensus on this issue. It is thus relatively natural to give religious or ethnic minorities their own niche in the political system, even when this implies the use of ethnicity. The British class-ridden political system seems to lack such casualness over the use of ethnicity in mainstream political discourse.

Another difference is the relation between ethnic organizations and local participation bodies such as the British CRCs or the Dutch advisory councils. The CRCs exist next to the ethnic organizations; initially the government exclusively focused on these CRCs and it took the government some time to focus on the organizations as well. In the Netherlands, the first few advisory bodies were founded apart from ethnic organizations, but the organizations have quickly become involved in the bodies. The organizations are considered an important vehicle for ethnic minority political action, which should not be excluded from the policy process. The same assumption underlies the enfranchisement of non-Dutch residents.

Interestingly enough, there are also many parallels. The growing importance of ethnic organizations in the political process is related in both countries to threats to the position of immigrant ethnic minorities. The rise of far-right political parties like the National Front or the Center party are the most visible ones, but the restriction of immigration and the failure of governments to considerably improve the disadvantaged position of ethnic minorities have been perceived as other threats. Ethnic organizations have gained momentum by these factors. Their demands for a better position is strengthened by mobilizing members of their ethnic group using ethnic loyalties. This is not to say that *all* ethnic organizations are anxious to be involved in the policy process. Many serve mainly as a sort of shelter for the members of the ethnic minority groups.

It is remarkable that most attempts to form umbrella organizations, in which all ethnic minorities take part, have failed so far. It is equally remarkable that there are no large radical Black power movements in Britain or in Holland as there have been in the United States. Some authors argue that this failure results from the ethos of the two governments to somehow involve immigrant ethnic minorities in the policy process. There is certainly some truth in this argument, particularly in the Dutch case. Certainly, it is the case that the governments' attempts to involve minorities in the policy process are consequences of unrest or fear for unrest in the society. Both governments strive for racial harmony--however defined--and want to exclude every violent dissonance. At the same time, they need the cooperation of ethnic minorities themselves for legitimating and implementing their policy. Ethnic organizations have thus come to occupy a key position in central and local government policy initiatives. This much may be true, but what of the consequences for ethnic minorities in the political process? If we are to accept that ethnic organizations are to play this unique role, how is this likely to shape their future involvement in British and Dutch politics and policy-making? It is not entirely certain that current approaches will yield the long-term dividends for which many politicians, policy-makers, and ethnic minorities hope.

Part IV

Conflict Resolution
and Public Policy

Territorial Devolution as a Strategy to Resolve Ethnic Conflict: Basque Self-Governance in Spain's Autonomous Community System
Robert P. Clark

In the 1960s, somewhat unexpectedly, ethnic conflict became a regular feature of politics in advanced industrial democracies, and as we move through the 1990s, many of these struggles still seem far from being resolved. In many countries, political elites and scholars have been searching for policies that will mitigate, if not actually resolve, these conflicts. One such strategy, *territorial devolution*, involves the granting of certain specified powers and resources by the central government to territorially defined entities with the intention of giving a greater degree of self-rule to ethnic groups in their homelands. The jurisdictions to which these powers and resources are devolved may be already existing civil divisions, such as provinces or departments, or they may be regions especially created just for the purpose of implementing the policy, as is the case discussed here. The granting of powers may be undertaken on an ad hoc basis by means of ordinary legislation, or it may be done pursuant to some constitutional provision that either mandates devolution or simply makes it possible. Thus, states organized around the principle of territorial devolution belong to the general category political geographers have labeled "compound unitary." While they clearly are unitary, they also have some quasi-federal characteristics that move them somewhat toward the more decentralized end of the organizational spectrum (Paddison 1983, 31).

Territorial devolution may be a useful policy for some purposes, such as achieving greater administrative decentralization to manage a complex advanced industrial society. However, as a policy to resolve ethnic conflict, territorial devolution has definite limits, as we shall see when we examine Spain's Autonomous Community system and specifically how the problem of Basque self-governance is treated within that framework.

The transformation of the Spanish state that spanned the decade from 1976 to 1986 rested on the twin pillars of parliamentary democracy and regional autonomy. The successful transformation of Spain from a dictatorship to a democracy is well known and admired, and properly so. However, the second dimension--the transformation of the unitary Spanish state into one based on seventeen regional governments--has been much less successful. One of the central features of post-Franco reforms was the devolution of increased power to Spain's historic regions (those whose autonomous status antedated the Spanish Civil War) as well as other regions that gained autonomous status after 1978. Many would argue that the gains for the autonomous regions during the late 1970s were of monumental importance for Spanish politics. After the abortive coup attempt in 1981, however, relations steadily deteriorated between Madrid and the autonomous governments serving the Basque and Catalan peoples. As the decade of the 1980s closed, many salient issues in this area still had not been resolved. With the political transformation of Spain consolidated, then, one can question how much genuine ethnic autonomy has been achieved and how much more Spanish elites will be inclined to accommodate the demands of ethnic nationalist leaders.

From many different perspectives, the Spanish democratic transition is viewed as fundamentally positive and basically completed. Virtually all major political groups accept the legitimacy of what has taken place since 1976 (Clark and Haltzel 1987). Following their bloody civil war and forty years of Franco's dictatorship, most Spaniards appear to have mastered *convivencia*, or what de Tocqueville called the art of associated together. It is noteworthy, then, that the one place where the democratic transition does not enjoy legitimacy is in Spain's ethnic homelands. Spaniards may accept as legitimate what has transpired in their country since 1976; but many (perhaps most) Basques and Catalans still regard the democratization process as a long way from being completed.

What is it that has caused this challenging experiment to stall so far from a successful conclusion? In existence partially since 1979 and fully covering the country since 1981, Spain's autonomous communities could be viewed not only as a solution to the problems created by the demands of that country's ethnic minorities for self-rule, but also as a model that other industrial democracies could learn from to resolve similar challenges and conflicts. With the passage of time, however, it has become clear that there are several inherent flaws in the territorial devolution model itself, flaws that doom any policy based on its concepts that attempts to resolve ethnic disputes. In coming to understand better the shortcomings in the Spanish model, we will also appreciate the inherent limits of territorial devolution as a strategy to resolve ethnic conflicts in advanced industrial democracies.

The central thesis of this chapter is that the Autonomous Community system, as embodied in Title VIII of the 1978 Constitution and as subsequently implemented, contains two fundamental contradictions that virtually assure that it cannot succeed in resolving ethnic conflict. Put somewhat simplistically, the autonomous communities are neither communities (that is, ethnically homogeneous) nor *autonomous* (that is, independent of central government control). These contradictions were inherent in the strategy chosen to meet Basque and Catalan demands for self-rule in the late 1970s. As a result of pressures for consensus as Spanish and ethnonationalist elites worked to fashion a democratic constitution and to dismantle the remaining vestiges of the Franco regime, these contradictions were covered over by ambiguous interpretations that allowed people with fundamentally different visions of the future to cooperate with one another, or at least to tolerate one another's point of view. As constitutional provisions have been transformed into legislative, administrative, and political realities, however, these contradictions have surfaced; and what was originally thought to be some minimal consensus about ethnic autonomy has been revealed instead to be fundamental disagreement. The period since 1981 has seen, then, not the smooth development of a successful policy innovation, but the splintering of support for the territorial devolution model, not only between Madrid and the ethnic homelands but among the ethnic elites themselves as well.

SPAIN'S AUTONOMOUS COMMUNITY SYSTEM

Since 1833, the territory of Spain has been organized into 50 provinces, of which 47 are on the Iberian Peninsula, where 94 percent of the people live on 97 percent of the land area. In 1978, however, the new Spanish Constitution provided for autonomous communities as a new level of government between Madrid and the provinces, or what Victor Pérez Díaz and others refer to as meso-governments (Díaz 1984). There are two ways for an autonomous community to come into existence. The easier of the two, via the Constitution's Article 151, was established for those regions that had enjoyed autonomous status under Spain's Second Republic: the Basque country, Cataluña, and Galicia. The more arduous route, via Article 143, was reserved for other provinces or groups of provinces that wished to have a regional government. During the constitutional drafting and approval process, most Spanish leaders expressed the view that only the three historical regions would want, and would qualify for, autonomous status. Nevertheless, by May 1983, within five years after the constitution entered into force, all Spanish territory had been reorganized into 17 autonomous communities by one route or another.

The Autonomous Community system hinges on the evolution of authority and resources from the center to the regions on a negotiated basis. Whether through Article 151 or 143, the processes by which the regions acquired self-rule status had these features in common:

1. Submission of a proposed draft autonomy statute by the region to the Spanish government and the Congress of Deputies for approval. The draft statute contains a proposed parliamentary structure as well as a list of powers to be transferred to the region by Madrid.

2. Approval of the statute in Madrid through a process involving the president of the government, the ruling party in Parliament, the constitutional committees of the two chambers of Parliament, the Parliament in plenary session, and relevant cabinet ministries.

3. Approval by the citizens of the region voting in a referendum, either before or after approval of the draft statute, depending on the route followed to autonomy.

4. Promulgation of the appropriate decree by the king.

5. Election of the parliament of the autonomous community, which then selects the president of the autonomous government, who in turn selects his or her cabinet.

6. Negotiation on a case-by-case basis of the transfer of specific powers, responsibilities, and resources (primarily money, fixed and movable property, and personnel) to the autonomous community. Negotiations involve the autonomous government, a joint commission made up of representatives of both Madrid and the autonomous government, the Spanish Ministry of Territorial Administration, other affected Spanish government ministries, the Spanish Council of Ministers, and the president of the Spanish government, who must ratify each transfer of power. These negotiations, especially in the Basque and Catalan cases, were protracted and frequently contentious, at least in part because the affected Spanish ministry or ministries were extremely reluctant to lose important powers and resources.[1]

From General Franco's death in November 1975 until late 1977, ethnic or regional autonomy enjoyed a relatively low priority on Spain's political agenda. In these early days of the transformation of the country from a dictatorship to a parliamentary democracy, there were simply too many other problems clamoring for attention, including legalizing political parties and labor unions, freeing the press from censorship, and organizing the first democratic parliamentary elections in June 1977. These elections produced the constituent assembly that began, in late July, to draft the country's new constitution. At this point, autonomy for the ethnic homelands became a major issue and was to remain so throughout the constitutional drafting and ratifying process (Bonime-Blanc 1987).

A decade and a half removed from this turbulent era in Spanish history, there is considerable disagreement about what motivated the drafters of the Constitution to incorporate a plan for regional autonomy. Rightly or wrongly, many Basque nationalists came to believe that Spanish political leaders supported the idea not out of a profound conviction that power had to be disaggregated if democracy were to succeed, but for short-term instrumental objectives that had to do with serious problems in the Basque region. Instead of abandoning armed struggle after Franco's death, the Basque insurgent organization Euzkadi ta Askatasuna (ETA) reaffirmed its commitment to continue violent confrontation until the Basque people had been given their independence. In the spring of

1976, amnesty for members of ETA became a major political issue in the region. Committees were formed to coordinate a pro-amnesty campaign of public demonstrations to force Madrid to release these and other Basques from prison. The pro-amnesty campaign, whose high point was the March for Freedom across the region in August 1977, produced street riots, police suppression, and the image of massive public disorder. Finally, the historical standard bearer of Basque nationalism, the Basque Nationalist Party (PNV), emerged from forty years in exile in the spring of 1977 with surprising vigor, an ideology that advocated an independent Basque state integrated into a confederated Europe of the Peoples, organizational strength, especially at the grass-roots level, and strong, charismatic leadership. These factors were to lead the party, in coalition with several other groupings known as the Frente Autonomico, to a strong electoral showing in the 1977 elections, which made it a force to be reckoned with in Madrid.

All these disturbances would have been unsettling to a firmly established democracy, but in Spain in the midst of undoing forty years of dictatorship, they were perceived by leaders such as Prime Minister Adolfo Suárez as grave threats to the very success of the democratic experiment. As events were to show in early 1981, when the country barely survived a military coup attempt, elements within the armed forces and the Guardia Civil flatly opposed the transition to democracy. Neo-Francoist forces remained in control of most of the state's administrative apparatus, and politically the rightists seemed to hold the high ground. On the left, Spain had one of Europe's strongest Communist parties, a well-entrenched Socialist party that still advocated Marxist-Leninist-inspired policies, and a hardened labor movement that was well organized throughout the country's heavy industry. Add to this mixture the absence of any legitimate political institutions (except the monarchy, which turned out to be key to the success of the transition), a political culture that did not encourage bargaining and compromise, and economic instability brought on by mistaken policies as well as the oil crisis of the mid-1970s, and one can see easily how Spain's leadership could be so troubled by tremors rippling out from the restive ethnic homelands.

Events conspired, then, to push regional autonomy to the top of Spain's political agenda through the last half of 1977. Understanding Suárez's desire to placate Basque and Catalan sentiments, however, we may still wonder why a policy of territorial devolution was chosen in preference to some other option.

To begin, we should note that there was a shortage of appropriate models in other countries from which the Spaniards could draw for illumination and inspiration. During the drafting process, much was made of the significance of foreign models, but this argument seems to be overdrawn. The federal model was unacceptable because of pressures from powerful conservative elements, especially in the armed forces, who regarded federalism as the beginning of the end for Spanish unity. The Belgian constitutional reforms of the 1970s and the

Swiss canton system both went far beyond what Madrid was willing to grant in the way of local home rule. The Italian model, which resembles what the Spanish finally devised, does not seem to have been consulted at all. Another possible foreign model might have been that offered by the United Kingdom and its special territorial governance mechanisms established for Scotland, Wales, and Northern Ireland. In fact, however, the special arrangements for Scotland and Wales would never have satisfied the ethnic elites in Spain, and the evolutionary regime for Northern Ireland--which did indeed resemble to some extent the Spanish autonomous communities--had been withdrawn by London in 1972.

If foreign models failed to offer much in the way of raw material from which a constitutional provision could be crafted, the history of Spain itself was not so barren. In fact, there was an ample historical precedent, drawn from the experience of the 1931 Republican Constitution, that was based on territorial devolution for the Basque provinces (minus Navarra) and for Cataluña. Indeed, when ethnic leaders presented their demands for self-rule, they usually did so by calling for a restoration of the 1931 constitutional arrangements. In late September 1977, fully six weeks before the Constitution drafters would approve the wording that recognized Spain as a state composed of many "nationalities," Madrid reestablished the Catalan Generalitat, and in late October Catalan President Tarradellas returned from exile to assume his post in the new government. In mid-November, Madrid announced the formation of pre-autonomy regimes in the three historical regions that had enjoyed some kind of autonomy under the Second Republic: Cataluña, Galicia, and the Basque country (excluding Navarra). These three interim regimes went into effect in early 1978, and paved the way for the establishment of similar autonomous communities within the next two years.

It is noteworthy that Spain's leaders felt a need to establish a new set of institutions midway between the provinces and Madrid. After all, Spain already had a well-developed set of provinces with a strong sense of identity and, especially in the Basque case, some historical tradition of self-governance. Apparently, however, Spanish leaders wanted to create an entirely new kind of territorial-political entity to symbolize the break with past traditions, especially those involving the *fueros*. The *fueros*, or foral laws, had been the underpinning of the Spanish state in the Middle Ages. They had specified the local privileges enjoyed by provinces and even by small towns and cities, and they stipulated certain ways in which the provinces were shielded from royal power and prerogatives, especially in sensitive areas such as taxation, collection of customs duties, maintenance of law and order, and providing troops to serve in the Spanish armed forces. The last of the foral privileges for the Basque provinces of Alava, Guipúzcoa, and Vizcaya were formally abolished in 1876 at the end of the Second Carlist War. To have vested in the provinces any kind of autonomy would have recalled memories of the fueros, and this the centralist Spanish elites would not have supported.

From December 1978 to February 1981, the regional autonomy movement experienced its Golden age, when Basque and Catalan autonomous communities registered most of their advances. Both regions approved their draft autonomy statutes in October 1979, and both elected their regional parliaments in March 1980, with ethnic nationalist parties scoring impressive triumphs in both elections. By December 1980, the Basque government had negotiated with Madrid solutions to the two principal remaining problems--taxation and law enforcement. And in late December, the voters of Galicia, the last of the three historic regions, approved their draft autonomy statute. Thus, by the close of 1980, the vexing issue of ethnic autonomy appeared to be on the verge of resolution.

The hopes of the late 1970s, unfortunately, were not to be realized. As a consequence of a number of dramatic challenges to the stability of the Spanish state from both left and right, Spain's political elites decided to halt the progress being made toward decentralization of the country's political structure. There were, of course, some significant steps taken toward devolution in the rest of Spain during 1981 and 1982, but apart from Galicia, most of these involved the mainly symbolic approval and implementation of regional autonomy statutes in the rest of the country.

It was suggested earlier that the inventors of the autonomous community concept originally envisioned that there would be only three such communities, the three historic regions, with the rest of the country still governed directly from Madrid. Whatever these original views might have been, they were quickly rendered irrelevant by the granting of autonomy to Andalucía, despite the fact that Andalucía was not one of the original historic regions. After much delay, the statute received final approval in Madrid in January 1982, and Andalucía's first parliament was chosen in May. Once that step had been taken, all the other regions clamored for their statutes, as if to suggest that anything less would denote second-class status. *Café para todos*, as the popular saying put it. In any case, other regions pressed ahead with the approval of their autonomy statutes, and by early 1983, statutes had been approved that covered the entire country. On May 8, 1983, when Spanish voters went to the polls to elect municipal councils and provincial assemblies, they also selected members of thirteen of the new regional parliaments, excepting only the four original assemblies elected earlier in the Basque country, Cataluña, Galicia and Andalucía. As of that moment, then, one could say that the formal or constitutional decentralization of Spain's political system was complete.

At another level, however, where politics and ordinary legislation prevail over constitutional provisions and symbolism, the regional autonomy process was reversed in 1981 and 1982. At the time, the cause of this reversal seemed clear: the dramatic and violent assaults on the stability and legitimacy of the Spanish state. In February 1981, the regime narrowly averted being overthrown by a coup mounted by rightist elements within the army and the Guardia Civil. In March, violent attacks attributed to ETA rose to such a level that Madrid deployed regular Spanish army and navy units to the Basque provinces, the first time that regular military forces had been used in a counterinsurgency role. In May, a small group of Spanish rightists seized a major bank in Barcelona and held its customers hostage in an unsuccessful attempt to force the government to release a number of officers arrested for their role in the coup attempt the preceding February. In sum, the period of late winter to spring of 1981 saw a series of blows to the Spanish body politic that weakened the resolve of the country's democratic elite to carry through on the more ambitious aspects of the decentralization effort. Since regional autonomy, especially for the ethnic minorities, was considered by rightists to be the first step leading to the dismemberment of Spain, the leadership in Madrid concluded that brakes would have to be applied to the regional autonomy movement to avoid further attacks on the state itself.

In April 1981, the two major Spanish political parties, the center-right governing party, Union of the Democratic Center (UCD), and the left-wing opposition party, the Socialist party (PSOE), initiated a series of meetings and studies aimed at harmonizing the autonomy process. These steps led to a summit meeting of Spain's political leaders to discuss regional autonomy, to which Basque and Catalán leaders were not invited. The outcome of this meeting was a Pacto Autonómico, or Autonomy Pact, between the two parties, whose purpose was to stop further devolution of power to the regions. In July, UCD and PSOE leaders unveiled the Organic Law on the Harmonization of the Autonomy Process, referred to by its Spanish acronym, LOAPA. Spanish leaders insisted that they were still committed to regional autonomy and that the LOAPA was nothing more than an effort to restore order and system to what had become a disorderly, even chaotic, process. Basque and Catalan leaders responded with bristling criticism of the draft law, calling it a betrayal of Madrid's commitment to devolving real power to the ethnic minorities.

Basque and Catalán leaders did what they could to block the implementation of the LOAPA. In private meetings with Spanish political leaders, they urged the withdrawal of the draft law. When that failed, they took to the streets in massive demonstrations against the LOAPA: in Bilbao in October 1981, in Barcelona in March 1982, and across the Basque and Catalán provinces in September 1982. During the campaign prior to Spain's parliamentary elections in October 1982, Basque and Catalán leaders formed an Anti-LOAPA Front to mobilize the voters against any candidate who had voted for the LOAPA in the parliament. During the parliamentary debate over the LOAPA, the ethnic minorities' deputies did succeed in inserting a provision to delay implementation of the LOAPA until Spain's Constitutional Tribunal could decide its constitutionality. After much delay, in August 1983, the court held that certain provisions of the LOAPA violated the Constitution and that it therefore could not be implemented.

Notwithstanding the court's findings regarding the LOAPA, the PSOE government, elected in October 1982, continued to insist on the homogenization of the Autonomous Community system. Since most of the regions are uninterested in acquiring, and incapable of using, as much autonomous power as are the Basques and Catalans, the result was to limit those two regions to some lesser degree of autonomy.

The position of the socialist government of Felipe González on the autonomy question can be seen in a number of different areas. For one thing, between October 1982, and March 1985, there were no new powers transferred to the Basque Autonomous Community, even though the Joint Basque-Spanish Committee on the Transfer of Powers had agreed to more than a dozen such transfers during this period. Second, even in those areas where powers had been transferred earlier, the PSOE-controlled Congress of Deputies passed legislation that took precedence over, and essentially negated, laws passed by the autonomous parliaments. One such area was education, where, despite a clear understanding that the jurisdiction of the autonomous communities would be paramount, the Spanish Congress intruded by approving the Organic Law for the Development of Education (LODE). Third, the Gonzáles government resisted attempts to place on the agenda the discussion of new transfers of authority, such as the administration of courts and prisons, an issue of special importance in the violence-wracked Basque region.

Relations between the Basque government and the PSOE seemed to improve in early 1985 following the *pacto de legislatura* between the new Basque president, José Antonio Ardanza, and the Basque Socialist party's members in the Basque parliament, led by Txiki Benegas. This pact has several important consequences, including the unblocking of the transfer of the fourteen pending powers or authorities, and the passage of the 1985 budget of the Basque government, which had been stalled in the deadlocked parliament. Nevertheless, in order to get socialist cooperation in governing the Basque Autonomous Community, the PNV had to retreat from a number of its demands regarding home rule.

Many Basque voters seemed to feel that the PNV had betrayed the cause of autonomy, and in the 1986 Spanish parliamentary elections, the PNV lost two seats, from eight (in 1982) to six, while more radical ethnic nationalist parties increased their seats from three to seven. Moreover, the vote total for the PNV declined sharply from 450,000 in the 1984 Basque Parliament elections to 300,000 in 1986. Many reasons could be advanced to explain the decline of the more moderate PNV and the rise of the more intransigent parties, but a close scrutiny of the electoral data suggests that about 30 percent of the lost PNV votes shifted to more radical Basque nationalist parties because of voter restiveness over what appeared to be an excessively conciliatory attitude toward the socialists by the Ardanza government (Clark 1987). Thus, the faction within the PNV that favored cooperation with Madrid was weakened, and the more hard-line faction strengthened, by the election outcome.

Less than three months after the PNV debacle in the 1986 elections, the factional split resulted in the expulsion from the party of former Basque President Carlos Garaikoetxea and a number of his followers, who responded by forming their own party. There were a number of significant factors leading to the split, including differences over relations with Madrid. Regardless of the causes, the effects were disastrous for Basque home rule. With the PNV's membership in the Basque Parliament split in half by the schism, Ardanza realized he could not continue to govern, so he dissolved parliament and convoked new elections for November 30. Despite the fact that 69 percent of the voters voted for one of four Basque nationalist options, the parties were so split between themselves that they were unable to form a Basque governing majority. The result was that for the first time a Spanish party--the PSOE--joined in a governing coalition in one of the ethnic homelands. This development obviously ushered in a new phase in the history of the Spanish regional autonomy movement.

Two years of euphoric gains in 1979 and 1980, followed by seven years of disappointment and failures, produced in the Basque people feelings of betrayal and frustration. Vote data illustrate the depth of anti-Madrid sentiment in the Basque country. Excluding referenda, between 1977 and 1987 Basque voters went to the polls ten times. On eight of those occasions, a clear majority of them chose a rejectionist or anti-Madrid, option. The rejectionist choice won exactly half the vote on a ninth occasion. The rejectionist option was the preferred choice of a majority of voters in the Basque provinces in each of the seven elections held since the Basque Autonomy Statute entered into force. When one considers that about 35-40 percent of the population of the Autonomous Community of the Pais Vasco (CAPV) are not ethnic Basque and therefore can be presumed to vote most of the time for a Spanish party, it is easy to conclude that the rejectionist option is favored by an overwhelming majority of ethnic Basques. Most significant, the share of the vote given to the rejectionist position has risen fairly markedly since the autonomy statute went into effect, despite the general perception outside the Basque country (and especially abroad) that the Autonomous Community system in general, and the Basque Autonomy Statute in particular, was a generous policy that recognized legitimate Basque aspirations for home rule and that reasonable Basque nationalists should have welcomed and supported.

THE BASQUE AUTONOMOUS COMMUNITY
IS NOT A "COMMUNITY"

For our purposes, community is defined as a society of people having common rights and privileges or common interests--civil, political, or ecclesiastical--or a society living under the same laws or regulations. A central feature of this definition is the common character, similarity, and likeness of the people who make up the community. In other words, community equates with homogeneity, at least insofar as the organizing principles of the particular population in question (e.g., race, language, class, and so forth) are concerned (Suttles 1972, ch. 3).

What is central here is the set of cultural and other markers used by people to determine their collective identity (Ross and Cottrell 1980). For a population to be a community, it must be reasonably homogeneous at least according to the criteria its members have chosen to define their collective identity, and substantially all the members of the group so defined must live under a common regime. (For a threshold definition of "reasonably homogeneous" and "substantially all" I would suggest 90 percent.) These definitional criteria need not, by the way, be the usual list of primordial markers like language or race, but may also include more modern characteristics such as citizenship. We should also recognize the likelihood that the members of any given population may possess multiple collective identities whose boundaries and labels are in a constant state of flux, depending on both internal and external conditions of stress. Obviously this definition becomes difficult to make operational when the members of the population in question differ markedly among themselves as to what these criteria should be, as we shall see shortly in the case of the Basques.

It is clear that the population governed by the Autonomous Community of the País Vasco (CAPV)--officially 2,141,809 in 1981--is not a community because of its cultural fragmentation and diversity.[2] There are two dimensions of this cultural fragmentation: first, not all Basques live in the CAPV, and second, the population of the CAPV is not made up solely of Basques. Since there is no single consensus definition--official or otherwise--of what a Basque is, I shall have to defer that question for a moment. The following discussion includes as Basque anyone who could consider him or herself to be Basque on the basis of any reasonable criterion.

For centuries, the Basque country has been a large-scale exporter of people to other lands, principally to the Western hemisphere (Douglass and Bilbao 1975, 5-6). While there are to my knowledge no official counts of Basques outside Spain, Basque linguist Pedro de Yrizar, in a study done in the early 1970s, estimated the number of Basque-language speakers living outside the Basque region at 80,000 (Yrizar 1973, 76-77). If accurate, this figure could translate into a diaspora population of about a quarter of a million. Without even counting the diaspora, however, there are still two major and politically significant Basque populations residing outside the CAPV. The first is in Navarra, which in 1981 numbered slightly more than 507,000 persons, and the second is in France, which contained about 237,000 persons in the same year (*Euskadi* 1983, 129).

For reasons that are historical, ethnic, linguistic, political, and economic, the status of Navarra in any Basque autonomous arrangement has been a divisive issue since the turn of the century (Collins 1986; Payne 1985). Although many Basques consider Navarra to be the cradle of their ethnonation, and the important role of the kingdom of Navarra in Basque political history stretches back to the tenth century, there are a number of factors that prevent the integration of Navarra into the CAPV. Of crucial importance is the question of collective identity. Several surveys conducted in the past decade show that slightly more than half the residents of the province identify themselves solely as Navarrese, about one-third as a mixture of Navarrese and Basque, between one-tenth and one-quarter as Spanish, and only 7 to 15 percent as solely Basque (Clark 1985, 226-230). Both before and after the Spanish Civil War, Navarra enjoyed special privileges not bestowed on any other province, and many Navarrese fear that their integration into some broader Basque community would mean the loss, or at least the dilution, of their privileged status. The 1978 Spanish Constitution excluded Navarra from the procedures by which the other Basque provinces were to obtain their autonomy, and the integration of Navarra into the CAPV (or, perhaps, the merger of the CAPV with the Navarrese Autonomous Community) must await approval by the people of Navarra in a referendum that lies years away, if indeed it is ever held.

The separation of the three Basque provinces of Labourd, Basse Navarre, and Sould (or Zuberoa) from the rest of the Basque region by the French-Spanish treaty of 1512 seems even more durable than the split between Navarra and the other three Spanish provinces. Nevertheless, Basque nationalists have never given up hope that some day the three provinces under French sovereignty will be freed to join an independent Basque nation-state.

Data on the collective identity of the French Basque population suggest that those who see themselves as Basque rather than French are in the minority. A 1979 survey found that 11.7 percent of the respondents define themselves as "Basque" or "more Basque then French"; 28.5 percent as "equally Basque and French"; and 55.4 percent as "French" or "more French than Basque" (Linz 1985, 214). We also know that slightly more than a third (81,000, or about 34 percent) of Basques living in France still speak the Basque language, a proportion about the same as for the ethnic Basque population residing in the CAPV. Nevertheless, despite anecdotal evidence about the strength of anti-Paris sentiment in the population, the fact remains that Basque nationalist candidates poll insignificant shares of the vote in French elections; and the idea that France (an even more centralized state than Spain) would ever release its grip on these three provinces lies in the realm of fantasy.

Of much greater significance is the second dimension of Basque cultural fragmentation: the fact that the population of the CAPV is not uniformly ethnic Basque.

If Basque society has sent many of its sons and daughters abroad, the Basque economy has also attracted thousands of non-Basque Spaniards who have migrated there in search of jobs and a better way of life. Between 1900 and 1980, the number of people moving into the Basque region exceeded those who left by nearly 450,000, or an amount equal to nearly one-fourth of the 1981 population (*Euskadi* 1977-1982; 1983, 172). This massive wave of migration has not been spread evenly across time. Before World War I, there was a net outflow of population from the four provinces. Between 1911 and 1951, the population remained roughly in balance, with modest losses from Navarra and Alava being balanced by modest gains in Vizcaya and Guipuzcoa. In the 1950s, however, the region received 130,000 more people than it lost; and in the 1960s, this balance soared to nearly 275,000 (more than half of the total net in-migration for the century). In the 1970s, the flow began to reverse itself once again, and between 1971 and 1980 the net inflow was only 45,000. Since the onset of the Basque economic crisis in 1976, the outflow has increased, although it may have peaked in 1979 and 1980. Between 1977 and 1984, the net population loss was nearly 51,000 persons (*Deia* 1986).

What these changes have produced is a population that is only marginally ethnic Basque, and in many areas distinctly non-Basque in both language and in identity. On the basis of extensive surveys, Basque sociologist José Garmendia and his associates have conclude that only about 52 percent of the population were born in the region of parents also born there, 11 percent were born in the region of parents born outside it, and 35.5 percent were themselves born outside the Basque provinces. Thus 46 percent of the Basque population is composed of immigrants who have come in two waves (11 and 35 percent, respectively) (Garmendia, Luna, and Agote 1982, 49). Moreover, the ethnic Basque portion of the population is distributed unevenly across the several provinces. Census data from 1975 reveal that of the 2.1 million people then living in one of the three provinces of the CAPV, almost exactly 33 percent had moved there from outside the Basque region. In Alava, outsiders were 34.8 percent of the total (82,344 immigrants in a total population of 236,897); in Vizcaya, 35.7 percent (409,721; 1,148,825); and in Guipúzcoa, 27.8 percent (187,072; 673,749) (*Euskadi* 1977-1982; 1983, 171).

For that portion of the population that is ethnic Basque, there is an absence of consensus as to their fundamental interests, and even as to their notions of Basque collective identity.[3] About 80 percent would define Basque identity by territory (i.e., living and working in Euskadi), but more than 40 percent would, in addition, insist on family descent, and nearly 30 percent would require being able to speak Euskera. Of those born in the Basque provinces and able to speak Euskera, more than 70 percent identify themselves as "Basque only." But among those native-born who do not speak Basque, the percentage drops to about one-third, with 14 percent identifying themselves as "more Basque than Spanish," 37 percent as "equally Basque and Spanish," and 17 percent as "more Spanish than Basque." Such cultural fragmentation is reflected in a lack of consensus about important public policy issues, of which the most significant would be the form of political organization preferred by Basques. In a number of surveys conducted since 1975, Basque respondents have been asked about their preferred political organization: centralized unitary state, regional autonomy, independence, and so forth. No single option has ever received a majority approval, although "full autonomy" (by which Basques usually mean the 1979 autonomy statute developed to its fullest possible extent) usually receives most support, at about the 40 percent level.

Voting behavior demonstrates this cultural and political fragmentation most vividly. In the ten elections held in the Basque region since 1977, no party has ever won a majority of the vote or a majority of the seats in any of the major representative assemblies. Until the party's two factions split in 1986, the leading political force was the Basque Nationalist party, or PNV (Partido Nacionalista Vasco). At the height of its popularity, in the 1984 Basque parliament election, the PNV captured about 450,000 votes out of about 1,085,000 votes cast. Since the 1986 split of the PNV, no party is capable of winning more than 250,000 to 275,000 votes out of an electorate that customarily includes about 1.1 million persons. Thus, despite the fact that the rejectionist political option has won an average of 58 percent of the vote since 1977 and polled close to 70 percent in 1986 and 1987, Basque nationalist parties are so badly divided internally and among themselves that they have been incapable of translating this electoral strength into coherent policies (Clark 1987).

Thus not even Basques feel themselves to be Basque completely and all the time. Clearly the great majority of the population have mixed or multiple identities. The salience of each person's Basqueness depends on a number of factors including symbols, environmental conditions, events, and so forth. This multiplicity of identities should not really surprise us since it is a characteristic of all structurally and functionally differentiated societies created by industrialization. In fact, one of the most important characteristics of industrial societies is the multiplicity of the collective identities of their people. Nevertheless, this complexity of identities does make it much harder to meet ethnic demands by means of policies intended for territorially compact, homogeneous populations with a single dominant community identity. Nevertheless, by basing its ethnic policies on a mistaken principle--that of cultural homogeneity in the ethnic homelands--the 1978 Spanish Constitution aggravated still further this most worrisome feature of Basque politics.

THE BASQUE AUTONOMOUS COMMUNITY IS NOT "AUTONOMOUS"

To assert that there is no consensus about a definition of "autonomy" would be putting it mildly. One recent survey of the subject cites the late jurist John Chipman Gray, who wrote at the beginning of this century that "on no subject of international law has there been so much loose writing and nebulous speculation as on autonomy" (Hannum and Lillich 1981, 215). This same study goes on to define autonomous areas as regions of a state, usually possessing some ethnic or cultural distinctiveness, that have been granted separate powers of internal administration, to whatever degree, without being detached from the state of which they are a part. This definition would apply the label of autonomy to any entity having any separate powers of internal administration, which would seem to extend the list of such entities almost endlessly, but elsewhere in the article the authors seem to restrict sharply their definition, equating autonomy with federalism by listing the 1979 Basque Autonomy Statute as an example of the federal model, which it clearly is not. Autonomy has little utility as a concept unless we can distinguish it from other concepts, such as administrative decentralization or devolution at one end of the spectrum or federal arrangements at the other.

Autonomy is defined here as the condition of being independent in government, of having the right of self-government. Implicit here is the notion that an autonomous entity functions independently of other units, is not subject to the control, influence or determination of others, and is not subordinate to others in its functioning. I would also restrict the word autonomy to those instances in which the state may not modify, rescind, or otherwise interfere with the powers enjoyed by the autonomous entity, and where the charter of that entity--in deriving from a source of authority that transcends the organic law of the state--cannot be unilaterally amended either by the state or by the autonomous entity, but only by mutual consent of both (Boehm 1948).

In sum, autonomous associations are a constituent part of a sovereign state, subject to the constraints of that sovereignty in certain clearly demarcated areas but also possessing certain powers or competencies not exercised by the state within the association's jurisdiction. Autonomous territories differ, then, from those that have received devolved powers by the constitutionally assured nature of the powers of the former; they differ from the more politically disaggregated federal or confederal models in that the charter of autonomous jurisdictions is amendable only by mutual consent, whereas federal units can amend their own constitutions as they wish, within certain limits.

Using this definition of the term, I contend that the Basque Autonomous Community is not autonomous. It should be pointed out here that Basque nationalist and Spanish elites differ over the meaning of autonomy, a term not defined precisely in the Spanish constitution. Article 2 of the constitution reads simply: "The Constitution is based on the indissoluble unity of the Spanish Nation, the common and indivisible fatherland of all Spaniards, and it recognizes and guarantees the autonomy of the nationalities and regions that comprise it [the Spanish Nation], and the solidarity among them." Basque nationalists see autonomy as synonymous with federalism, an irreversible grant of power, and eventually as sovereignty. As recently as April 1985, the Basque Nationalist party's governing national council issued a proclamation on the occasion of the Basque national holiday, Aberri Eguna, in which it pledged the party to continue to struggle "for the freedom *and sovereignty* of Euskadi" (*Deia* 1985). The various regimes in Madrid, on the other hand, have interpreted autonomy as mainly decentralization for administrative reasons, with no fundamental cession of sovereign authority.

This dispute over the true meaning of autonomy has been joined over three sets of issues: the origins of Basque rights, the process for devolving powers and resources to the autonomous community, and the question of residual sovereignty.

Many ethnonationalist groups contend that their rights to autonomy stem from some grant of political authority that may predate the existence of the modern nation-state and may even be primordial in its origins, but which in any case does not depend on any contemporary document such as a constitution or fundamental law. In this, Basque nationalists are no different, arguing that their rights derive from their historic status vis-à-vis the Spanish state before the Carlist Wars, and thus do not depend on any specific grant found in the 1978 Spanish Constitution (Monreal 1985; Ayestaran et al. 1979). As the Basques see it, in the Middle Ages, between 1200 and 1512, the several Basque provinces (voluntarily or under compulsion) entered into a special relationship with the Kingdom of Castile that was governed by the foral laws of that era. Changes in that relationship during the nineteenth century were imposed by force and did not invalidate the earlier status of the Basque provinces.

This version of history and of rights that predate the Spanish Constitution is, from the Basque viewpoint, validated by two statutory provisions. The first is the Primera Disposición Adicional of the 1978 constitution: "The Constitution maintains and respects the historic rights of the foral territories. Said foral regime will be made current within the framework of the Constitution and the Autonomy Statutes." The second is the Disposición Adicional of the Basque Autonomy Statute: "Acceptance of the autonomy regime established in this Statute does not imply renunciation by the Basque People of the rights that might have corresponded to them as such by virtue of their history, which can be made current in accord with the provisions of the juridical framework." For the Basques, if Madrid had had some doubt about the so-called *derechos históricos*, then the Spanish government should not have approved the Constitution and the statute containing such wording.

Spanish elites, on the other hand, contend that the Basque autonomous community is not entitled to anything not specifically addressed by the Constitution and by their autonomy statute. This position is supported by the conventional legal interpretation of the constitutional rights of minority nations in modern nation-states, where the organic law of the state is the origin of all rights of all citizens, and none predate that document or are derived from any higher source of authority. Modern constitution-based nation-state elites cannot accept the premise that there exist within their jurisdiction certain groups whose rights and privileges derive from some supra-constitutional origin. Such a premise would erode severely the very nature of nation-state sovereignty.

The Spanish government's position on the two statutory provisions is that the operative wording in both has to do with the paramount authority of the 1978 Constitution. In other words, while the *derechos históricos* of the Basques are guaranteed by the Constitution, they can only be given form and reality within the framework that the Constitution establishes, and then only if all parties recognize the ultimate supremacy of the Constitution. This the Basques have been unwilling to do.

The refusal of the Basques to accept the legitimacy of the Spanish Constitution has been demonstrated on several occasions. In the 1978 referendum on the Constitution, for example, after the Basque Nationalist party urged its members to abstain as a show of Basque discontent, abstentions reached 51 percent in the four provinces as a whole and 57 percent in Guipúzcoa and Vizcaya. In 1984, following his election as president by the Basque Parliament, Carlos Garaikoetxea had himself sworn into office before King Juan Carlos had officially proclaimed him elected, as the Spanish Constitution requires, on the grounds that Garaikoetxea owed his status to the popularly elected Basque representatives and not to the provisions of the Spanish Constitution. Finally, the most radical of the Basque nationalist parties, Herri Batasuna, has refused to occupy the seats its members have won in the Basque and Spanish parliaments on the grounds that neither body is legitimate because of the fundamental illegitimacy of the Spanish Constitution.

There is also fundamental disagreement between Basques and Spaniards over whether the autonomy process should be, or was intended to be, automatic or negotiated. The Basques believed that once the autonomy statute was approved and the government established, all the powers envisioned in the statute would be transferred more or less automatically, along with the resources (people and money) and authority necessary to implement them. In Madrid, the view was that the mere approval of a statute and election of a regional assembly did not in itself transfer any power to the regions. Instead, each transfer had to be carefully and painstakingly negotiated between the autonomous government that was to receive the authority and the Spanish government ministry that was to lose it. The intermediary in all cases was to be the Spanish Ministry of Territorial Administration, and in each instance, a Joint Commission on the

Transfer of Powers was established to negotiate on a case-by-case basis the transfer of each specific power or authority.

In the Basque case, this joint commission has been a major obstacle to regional autonomy. Following the reversal of Spanish policy on regional autonomy in 1981, the commission met only twice in all 1982, and agreement was reached on the transfer of only one set of powers. In January 1983, the Basque representative on the Commission charged that the process of transfer of powers had been "paralyzed for quite some time." Even when the joint commission has agreed on the transfer of powers, however, its decisions must still be ratified at the political level of the Spanish government and implemented by means of decree. From the socialist electoral victory in October 1982 to the spring of 1985, no new powers were transferred. Following the *pacto de legislatura* in January 1985, another fourteen powers were transferred, but very few have been transferred since that time.

An equally difficult issue has to do with *residual sovereignty*. The Basques contend that once a specific question was debated and included in the devolved powers in the autonomy statute, the Spanish Parliament and government in effect yielded, relinquished their control over the issue, and cannot presume to legislate further in the area. Madrid's leaders respond that such an interpretation would negate Spanish sovereignty over its territory, which they would find intolerable. These differences have been sharpest in the issue-areas of language policy, especially television and education, and law enforcement.

The CAPV is one of five autonomous communities in Spain that gives special status to a regional language. The Basque language, Euskera, is a co-official language of the Basque Autonomous Community, along with Castilian. No citizen will be discriminated against because of an inability to speak either language. Eventually, all public sector agencies, including courts and schools, will be required to conduct their business in both languages. The Basque government is to have the requisite political authority and economic resources to make the Basque country bilingual (Clark 1988).

On May 20, 1982, the Basque Parliament approved the law creating a public agency to manage the region's first television station, Euskal Telebista. The station began to transmit its programs in early 1983 on a channel assigned to the Basque Autonomous Community by the Spanish government. In the beginning programming was almost entirely in Euskera, but eventually a Castilian-language channel was added. From the beginning, the Spanish government, through the Spanish national television service, has intruded repeatedly into the operations of the station. Euskal Telebista has been denied the right, for example, to transmit live broadcasts of soccer games involving Basque teams. Madrid has also denied Basque television the authority to receive and retransmit television signals from nearby French stations or from international broadcasts transmitted by satellite. If Euskal Telebista wishes to rebroadcast a satellite transmission of an event like the U.S. Open tennis matches, it must tape the transmission from the Spanish national television broadcast in Bilbao and carry the tape to the Basque station in Durango, from where the rebroadcast can occur.

Education is another area of considerable controversy. While many Basque nationalists believed that the autonomy statute granted to their government the right to manage the region's educational affairs as they wished, developments in local school districts have cast doubt on this. On several occasions in 1982, non-Basque-speaking parents who did not want their children to learn Euskera protested local school policies that were aimed at making Euskera instruction compulsory. The Spanish Ministry of Education intervened on these occasions to protect the rights of these parents, and in so doing left in question exactly how much latitude Basques have to manage their local school affairs. There were also problems at the university level. After the creation of the Basque government in 1980, the University of the Basque Country opened its three campuses (in Lejona, Vitoria, and San Sebastián) to an enrollment of some 35,000 students. This university was governed by the Education Ministry in Madrid until mid-1985, when the *pacto de legislatura* unblocked the transfer of authority for university-level education to the Basque government. Finally, the Spanish Organic Law for the Development of Education (LODE) clearly stakes out Madrid's continuing authority to oversee education at all levels, provisions to the contrary in the autonomy statutes notwithstanding.

Another area where there is dispute over the extent of residual sovereignty retained in Madrid is the autonomous Basque police force. Although the Basque Autonomy Statute foresees the eventual withdrawal of all Spanish law enforcement authorities and their replacement with forces under the control of the Basque government, authority is shared by the two governments in such matters as the protection of Spanish citizens in the region and the maintenance of public order. Through a joint Spanish-Basque security committee, Madrid ensures constant monitoring of the status of public order in the Basque provinces, as well as the ultimate right to reinstate direct control over the provinces from Madrid if a deterioration of public security threatens to undermine the interests of the Spanish state in the region.

In October 1982, the first elements of the Basque autonomous police, called the Ertzainza, went into service, the first time in history that the maintenance of law and order had been the responsibility of a Basque law enforcement agency. However, the relatively small size of both the force and its budget; its restricted powers, limited primarily to traffic control and building security; and the continued exercise of authority over the maintenance of public order from Madrid have meant that this force is still some distance away from taking over responsibility for all law enforcement in the Autonomous Community. The Spanish minister of interior, through the Spanish representative on the Joint Security Board, exercises authority over the budget of the Ertzainza, the kinds of weapons its members may carry, the zones where they may operate, the extent to which they can become involved in criminal investigations or in immediate crises such as hostage and barricade situations, and so forth. Thus, despite the creation of a Basque police force, the Basque government is not yet ready to assume sole responsibility for the maintenance of public order, so the Spanish units--the national police and the Guardia Civil-- have not yet been withdrawn, nor are they likely to be any time soon.

CONCLUSION

From this review of Spain's Autonomous Community system, what can we conclude about the limits of territorial devolution as a policy to resolve ethnic conflict? In considering the future of this conflict, we ought to keep in mind these observations of Robert A. Friedlander:

> Autonomy relationships during the twentieth century were mainly designed as placebos to frustrate independence movements and offset secessionist pressures. Whether created for colonial dependents by controlling Mother Countries and mandatory powers, for victor combatants over vanquished enemies partially dismembered via peace settlements, or for majority regimes confronted by an unassimilable minority, autonomy has always been a stopgap measure. In almost every instance, grants of autonomy were reluctantly given and ungratefully received. (1981, 136)

Ironically, given the subject of this chapter, Friedlander uses the continuation of violence in the Basque country after 1979 as proof that autonomy usually doesn't work to relieve secessionist pressures. Implicitly, then, he accepts the conventional wisdom that what the 1978 Spanish Constitution enshrines is really autonomy, when, as I have tried to argue, the status of the autonomous communities is far from autonomous. In any case, autonomy-- however defined--seems to be a very hard policy to implement successfully.

This case study suggests that the policy of territorial devolution may succeed in resolving ethnic strife only if the ethnic minority in question is fairly homogeneous in its homeland and there exists sufficient accord between the central government and the ethnic group that the latter is willing to accept the arrangement as de facto autonomy even though de jure it may not be. In other words, the ethnic group must be willing to accept the arrangement as permanent and not susceptible of being withdrawn or cancelled by the central government, even though that government may continue to enjoy the right to withdraw what it has granted. (It should also be made clear that success under these two conditions is only possible, not guaranteed. Ethnic conflicts are apt to be difficult to resolve even under the best of circumstances.)

If only one of these characteristics is present--either ethnic homogeneity in the homeland or a level of mutual trust that turns devolution into de facto autonomy--then the prospects for a successful resolution by means of territorial devolution will be small, if not near zero. Such a situation tends to be unstable in and of itself, apart from the policy solutions selected. This instability stems from the mutual contradiction between the two characteristics. If the ethnic group is homogeneous and desires to remain so, the central government will fear eventual attempts at separation, and so will resist any moves toward true autonomy (de facto or de jure). The elites of the center may even encourage migration of non-ethnics to the homeland to dilute the ethnic homogeneity that they define as a threat. If the ethnic group is not homogeneous in its territory, then the center's elites will resist true autonomy even more, out of fear that local policies will be enacted that will harm the rights and interest of the non-ethnic citizens of the region, who are, after all, still citizens of the more inclusive state. Thus, while in theory there may be a situation in which one or the other feature of our formula may apply, in practice such an arrangement would be unstable and would not last long.

An analysis by Yoram Dinstein bears out the truth of this insight. "Whether an arrangement of autonomy is to be crowned with success or doomed to failure depends, in the final analysis, on the state of mind of the parties. The legal or procedural intricacies of the arrangement cannot guarantee the outcome. Success is contingent on the goodwill of the parties and their desire to live jointly under one legal-political roof. The indispensable condition for a viable autonomy is the existence of a spirit of togetherness which unites two groups despite their differences" (1981, 295).

To this I can only add two observations. First, if these conditions do apply, then some form of consensus democracy or perhaps even federalism may work, eventually making experiments in autonomy unnecessary.   Second, attempts to resolve ethnic crises through autonomy carry within them the seed of their own destruction, since the two sides see the desirable outcome in opposite terms. The ethnic minority sees autonomy as the first step toward eventual separation; the state sees the policy as precisely the element that will block such a change. To cite Dinstein again, "When two parties are negotiating a certain move, thinking that it will produce mutually contradictory results, one of them (at least) is bound to be grievously disappointed" (1981, 302).

Finally, if neither of these features is present, as is the case with the Basques in Spain in the 1980s, then territorial devolution will fail to resolve ethnic conflict. If the ethnic group is not homogeneous in its homeland, then the requirements for community are lacking; if there is little mutual trust between the ethnic minority and the central state elite, then the requirements for autonomy are lacking. The policy may still succeed from the perspective of the central government if it meets some other need, such as the maintenance of order or administrative decentralization, but from the vantage point of the ethnic minority, the essential problems remain unaffected and may even be aggravated by the mistaken application of an inappropriate policy.

To propose a solution to this dilemma would take us far beyond the confines of this chapter. One possibility would be to design institutions for ethnic self-governance that are based on culture and not territory. Such a solution will not come easily, since, as numerous scholars have observed, territory is thought to be an absolutely essential feature of durable communities in general, and of ethnostates in particular.[4] Indeed, as one political geographer put it, "We live out our lives within a hierarchy of territorial organizations" (Knight 1983, 115). More important from a practical standpoint is the finding by Juan Linz that it is the more radical Basque nationalists who define their identity in terms of territory and who would stoutly oppose any effort to meet Basque demands by means of policies divorced from territorial bases (1985, 206-208, 226-231).

However, I would also point out that the disengaging of ethnic self-rule from territory would coincide with three other powerful trends now visible in advanced industrial societies: privatization (the removal of an increasing number of issue-areas from the public or state arena), demassification (the search for smaller-scale institutions and the disaggregation of large ones), and segmentation (the fragmentation of large, broadly heterogeneous culture groups into their smaller, more narrowly defined and more homogeneous component parts). What these four trends working together will yield over the next generation or so in the way of institutions for small community self-rule can only dimly be perceived; but I would guess there are some surprises in store for us in the next century.

13

Language Policy and the Pursuit of Equality: Canada and the United States
Ronald J. Schmidt

> In running over the pages of our history for seven hundred
> years, we shall scarcely find a single great event which has
> not promoted equality of condition. . . .   The gradual
> development of the principle of equality is, therefore, a
> Providential fact. It has all the chief characteristics of such a
> fact: it is universal, it is durable, it constantly eludes all
> human interference, and all events as well as all men
> contribute to its progress. (Tocqueville, *Democracy in
> America*)

Whether or not a gradual movement toward "equality of condition" is a
"Providential fact" in the West (and it was Tocqueville who also wrote that there
is nothing so difficult to apprehend as a fact), there can be little doubt that
equality continues to be one of the central public values of our time.   So
widespread is the support for equality within the political culture of the modern
world that its opponents nearly always find it more fruitful to attempt a
reinterpretation of the word than to try a frontal assault.   Partly as a
consequence of that fact, and partly also because of the term's inherent
ambiguity (Rae 1981), lack of consensus on the meaning of the word *equality*
itself is virtually endemic in the modern polity.

Nowhere is this lack of consensus more evident than in the effort to
achieve equality for linguistic and cultural minorities in the modern,
industrialized nations of the Western world. During the past several decades,

---

*The author wishes to thank F. Chris Garcia and Frank Baumgartner for
helpful comments on earlier drafts of this essay.

racial and ethnic minority groups in these nations have become increasingly
mobilized in a struggle for equality, and nearly all states involved have accepted
the legitimacy (in some sense) of that goal. But while political authorities and
minority advocates have agreed on the name of the goal being sought, rarely has
consensus been reached on the operational meaning of the goal. It is difficult
enough to reach consensus on the meaning of equality for social classes, but this
difficulty pales by comparison with the complexity introduced by the inclusion
of racial, cultural, religious and linguistic differences between groups. Yet the
inclusion of these complexities is increasingly necessary because the Western
world is experiencing one of the largest waves of immigration from non-Western
regions in its history (Glazer and Young 1983, 1). Adding to this complexity,
moreover, the birthrates of non-Western origin groups continue to be
significantly higher than that of the general population throughout Europe and
North America. The combination of differential immigration and birthrates
virtually guarantees increasing ethnic diversity in these regions for the
foreseeable future.

In view of these developments, the primary assumption of this chapter
is that one of the most important unresolved issues facing those interested in the
fate of linguistic and ethnic minority groups in the modern world is the question
of what we mean when we aim for equality for those groups. By explicating
and comparing the conflicts over language policies in Canada and the United
States in recent years, this chapter aims to make a contribution toward the
clarification of this issue.

The chapter begins with a discussion of the controversy over language
policy in the public schools in the United States, with particular reference to
conflicts about the meaning of equality for language minorities. A similar
discussion of the conflicts over language policy in Canada provides a basis for
comparison and some degree of generalization. The chapter concludes with the
assertion that at least three understandings of equality as a policy goal for
linguistic minority groups may be discerned in recent U.S. and Canadian
controversies over language policy, but that none of these interpretations is
presently capable of resolving the political and philosophical conflicts underlying
these controversies.

LANGUAGE POLICY AND EQUALITY IN THE UNITED STATES

Unlike many other nation-states in the modern world, the United States
does not have an official language or languages (Wagner 1981). Nor does it
have a coherently formulated language policy. Nevertheless, as a largely
immigrant nation it does have a long history of public controversy and policy
related to language. As Wagner notes, "English was never the only language

spoken by the American people" (Wagner 1981, 30), and this fact has occasioned social and political conflict from the colonial period to the present.

Controversy over language policy has heated up in recent years as the number of non-English-speaking residents has dramatically increased. For example, debates have raged in various parts of the country for about a decade over the issue of declaring English to be the official language of the nation--a movement spearheaded by a group known as U.S. English. While the movement has been unsuccessful in its drive to amend the U.S. Constitution to that effect, it has succeeded against stiff opposition from language minority activists and political elites in campaigns to so amend a number of state constitutions (including California's in 1986) and local government charters. While such constitutional amendments may yet have far-reaching consequences, at this point in time they are primarily of symbolic significance. At a more substantive level of policy, much of the recent controversy has centered on the education of minority-language children in the public schools. And here it is possible to see quite clearly the underlying ambiguity of and conflict over the meaning of equality that divides protagonists over language policy in the United States.

Controversy over the education of language-minority children in the public schools has centered in recent years on bilingual education--a phrase that, like equality, masks a wide variety of interpretations. In the 1970s, the political conflict over bilingual education was largely over two versions of that pedagogical method: transitional bilingual education and maintenance bilingual education. In the former approach, *bilingual* refers to a teaching method and not to the goal to be reached. That is, language-minority students are taught bilingually (in their home language and in English) only until they have sufficiently mastered English to be transferred into a mainstream classroom. The theory is that unless instruction (in subjects such as math and social studies) is in the student's home language until English is mastered, the student will fall hopelessly behind native English speakers. In this version of bilingual education, the student's home language has no intrinsic value; it is to be dropped from the instructional process as soon as the student is mainstreamed. The goal of transitional bilingual education, then, is a student who will prosper in a monolingual English-speaking classroom. Whether or not the student becomes a bilingual person is not the concern of the public schools.

The maintenance version of bilingual education, on the other hand, has the goal of creating bilingual students. Language-minority students are to master the English language in this approach as well, but where their numbers are sufficient to make this practicable, classroom instruction is designed to enable them to develop and maintain their home languages and cultures. Clearly, the transitional approach is *assimilative* in intent, while the maintenance approach is guided by the values of *cultural pluralism* (Kallen 1924). While the maintenance approach gained the support of a variety of educators, ethnic activists, and language-minority parents (Hernandez-Chavez 1978), successive legislative refinements at both the state and national levels made it increasingly clear that most U.S. policymakers were interested in supporting bilingual education only for the purpose of mastering English and not to maintain minority languages and cultures with public funds.

By the early 1980s the center of the bilingual education controversy had shifted away from transitional vs. maintenance approaches and to an attack on the efficacy of bilingual education as a pedagogical method. Citing hotly disputed evaluation studies (see Hakuta 1986, Chapter 8, for an overview), a growing number of voices argued that bilingual education did no better at aiding language-minority students in mastering English than did traditional classroom instruction in an English-only environment. As an alternative, many critics began promoting English immersion for U.S. language-minority children--a teaching method to be modeled on the highly successful French immersion programs for anglophones in Quebec (see California State Department of Education, 1984). At the very least, critics argued, local school districts should have the option to experiment with various pedagogical methods of teaching language-minority children rather than be forced to use the bilingual method. In short, the debate began to focus on how best (i.e., most efficiently and economically) to aid language-minority students in mastering English. The values which had guided the promotion of maintenance bilingual education became increasingly ignored in this discussion, although supporters of that approach figured prominently in the ranks of bilingual education's continuing defenders.

At the level of policy, then, by the late 1980s there was little public debate on the goal of education for language-minority children. All sides in the controversy agreed that the goal was improved educational achievement and even mastery of English for language-minority children, and debate concentrated on the means to that end. The apparent consensus on the goal of language minority education, however, was only on the surface; underneath that surface considerable conflict continued over the place of students' home languages and cultures in the public school curriculum. The critics of bilingual education as the mandated approach to language-minority education tended to be quite hostile to the idea that minority languages and cultures should be perpetuated in any way by public policy. Defenders of the bilingual education mandate, on the other hand, tended to be much more tolerant, and often supportive, of that aim. In some respects, in short, the conflict of the 1970s over transitional versus maintenance bilingual education merely shifted ground in the 1980s, and is now being replayed as a conflict over the continuation of a mandate for bilingual education per se.

LANGUAGE POLICY AND EQUALITY OF OPPORTUNITY

What is the relationship of this debate over bilingual education in the United States to the question of equality for minority groups? The understanding of equality that has the broadest popular support in the United States is surely equality of opportunity, and it is that formula which is most helpful in understanding the conflict over bilingual education. Equality of opportunity promises to each individual that he or she will be judged and rewarded on the basis of ability and performance, not on the basis of "irrelevant" characteristics such as birth, nationality, color, religion, sex, and so forth (Friedman and Friedman 1981, 123). Putting bilingual education policy into historical perspective, it seems clear that the policy was enacted by Congress with the intent to work toward equality of opportunity for language-minority children.

As national policy, bilingual education was adopted in 1968 as a supplementary amendment to a keystone of Lyndon Johnson's Great Society Program: the Elementary and Secondary Education Act of 1965. The ESEA itself (especially Title I) was legitimated primarily on the grounds that children from poor and minority homes needed the assistance of the federal government to be able to have an equal opportunity to compete with those living in more favorable circumstances (Sundquist 1968). Thus, when Senator Ralph Yarborough (D-Tex), the principal congressional architect of the 1968 Bilingual Education Act, took up the cudgel to amend the ESEA, he did so because language-minority students (especially Latinos in his own state) were falling behind majority students on standardized tests and dropping out of school at alarming rates (Schneider 1976). A similar rationale lay behind the U.S. Supreme Court's ruling in Lau v. Nichols (1974) that language-minority students placed in classrooms where they could not understand the language of instruction (i.e., English) were denied their equal right to an education in violation of the Civil Rights Act of 1965.

If bilingual education policy is thus justified to provide an equal opportunity for language-minority students, however, from this formulation it is still not clear equal opportunity *to do what?* It is in response to this question that conflict over bilingual education has developed, and this conflict reveals interesting (and incompatible) assumptions underlying the equal opportunity interpretation of equality.

Supporters of an early and complete transition to English-only education for language-minority children are very clear in their response to this question. They begin from the assumption that the United States is a monolingual English-speaking society, and that to the extent that language-minority children need extra assistance to have an equal opportunity it certainly must be the aim of policy to assimilate them into the dominant language and culture as quickly as possible. To do otherwise would not only be divisive for the nation as a whole, it would also doom language-minority children to permanent inequality in this society. The *New York Times* summarized the point well in a 1976 editorial: "A misguided linguistic separatism [represented by maintenance bilingual education] . . . can only have the effect of condemning to permanent economic and social disadvantage those who cut themselves off from the majority culture" (1976). From this point of view, the current debate over bilingual education versus the English immersion approach is simply a question of which pedagogical method is most efficient and economical at reaching its assimilative goal. While few would prevent language-minority parents from seeking to teach their children to preserve their home language and culture privately, most would counsel against it because it would hold these children back from full participation in the public culture of the nation (Rodriguez 1982). From this perspective, in sum, the goal of public policy--and of public education--must be to ensure that no child suffers from the arbitrary obstacle to equal opportunity created by the inability to communicate in English (Epstein 1977). In recent years most U.S. policymakers have left little doubt that this is the aim that should guide language policy in the public schools.

AN ALTERNATIVE INTERPRETATION OF EQUALITY

While the understanding of equality underlying the argument of the English-only advocates is quite clear, the same may not be said of their opponents--a fact which may put the latter group at some political disadvantage in the United States. By digging beneath the surface of the positions advocated by those favoring a multilingual policy, however, it is possible to uncover the outlines of an alternative interpretation of the meaning of equality for language minority groups.

Before turning to an articulation of that alternative, it must be stated unambiguously that few (if any) proponents of a multilingual policy resist the goal of mastery of English for non-English-speaking groups in the United States. As indicated earlier, virtually everyone with a stake in this policy issue agrees that in the United States opportunity for social, economic, and political advancement requires facility in the dominant language (see Tienda and Neidert 1985 for a discussion of evidence that inability to communicate in English hinders the economic advancement of Latino males in the United States). Those favoring a more pluralistic language policy are solidly behind efforts to assist language-minority members in learning English so that they may pursue opportunities in the sectors requiring facility in the dominant language.

That having been said, however, opponents of an English-only language policy are quick to challenge other assumptions underlying the above interpretation of the equal opportunity formula. The first challenge is to the contextual assumptions made by the English-only advocates. That is, while equal opportunity seems an individualistic doctrine (i.e., it makes promises to each person), in fact it requires that assumptions be made about the social context in which it operates as a value. As political theorist John Schaar has pointed out,

> Out of the great variety of human resources available to it, a given society will admire and reward some abilities more than others. . . . Hence, to be accurate, the equality of opportunity formula must be revised to read: equality of opportunity for all to develop those talents which are highly valued by a given people at a given time. . . . Before one subscribes to the equality of opportunity formula, then, one should be certain that the dominant values, institutions, and goals of the society are the ones he really wants. (Schaar 1981, 194-195)

In this context, our earlier question--equality of opportunity *to do what?*--takes on added political importance.

And here proponents of a multilingual policy challenge the assumption of English-only advocates that the United States is a monolingual, monocultural society. They argue that the United States has always had and continues to have multiple languages and cultures among its population and citizenry. Further, they point out that this linguistic and cultural diversity is the result of the conquest of non-English-speaking territories (e.g., the conquest of Native American tribes and the acquisition of Mexican territory under the Treaty of Guadalupe Hidalgo) as well as a result of immigration from throughout the non-English-speaking world. From their perspective, the United States is a pluralistic society with a pluralistic history. Thus, minority languages and cultures are conceived to be integral parts of the larger American culture, and the English-only position is a future policy goal of some citizens, not the status quo of the society. As one participant in the debate has put it, "My ethnic culture is a part of this American culture" (Cardenas 1977, 77).

Beginning from this contextual position, many proponents of a multilingual educational policy have argued that asking people to give up their native language and culture as the price of full participation in the American society and polity is a prima facie denial of equality. That is, if it is conquest and/or political oppression that have formed the historical bases for state policies discouraging non-Anglo peoples from retaining their languages and cultures, then these policies virtually exemplify state inequality toward those peoples. It follows from this reasoning that policies aiming toward greater equality for language-minority groups would seek to preserve their native languages and cultures (assuming that this is desired by group members), even while incorporating them into full membership economically, socially, and politically. Thus, many Latinos and Native Americans, as C. B. Paulston has written, "want to maintain their cultural pluralism with structural incorporation, that is, access to goods and services and to social institutions like education and justice. In short, they want to retain their values and ways of being without being denied their fair share" (Paulston 1980, 65).

Looking toward the future rather than the past, another alternative equal opportunity interpretation emphasizes the necessity for a multilingual society in a shrinking world. Thus, some activists and public officials have urged that the political and economic well-being of the United States requires a citizenry with multilingual skills and multicultural understanding. Consequently, if the opportunity structure in the United States increasingly promises to reward those with these skills and understanding, it makes little sense to follow an English-only policy toward language-minority children. Indeed, following this reasoning, genuine equality of opportunity would seem to require not only that the United States attempt to maintain and develop the non-English skills of language-minority children in bilingual education programs, but that policy should aim at opening up such programs to all other students as well. In other words, a broader contextual understanding of the developing U.S. economy and polity leads to a new understanding of the concept of cultural deprivation that underpinned the original equal opportunity rationale for bilingual education: henceforth all students who are monolingual--whether in English or some other language--must be seen as culturally deprived and in need of remedial policy to give them an equal opportunity to compete in the evolving world polity and economy (Fishman 1978, 46; President's Commission 1979, 1-6).

Still a third line of argument supporting a multilingual educational policy avoids the assimilation vs. cultural pluralism argument, yet is also linked with the equality of opportunity doctrine. Some have argued (most notably Cummins 1981; 1984) that providing language-minority students with an opportunity to achieve academic success in any language may require that they be helped to master their home language along with the majority language of the society. That is, Cummins suggests that if students have not reached a certain "threshold" of competence in their first languages (L1), empirical studies indicate that efforts to teach them in a second language (L2) will be less successful than if they had reached that threshold (Cummins 1981). Thus, maintenance and even development of home language skills may be a necessary component of efforts to enable language minority students to have an equal opportunity for academic success generally in the public schools, quite apart from the value-loaded question of assimilation versus cultural pluralism. In a more recent article (1984), Cummins cites evidence that this conclusion is especially true for students who come from minority groups with a caste-like subordinate status in the society (e.g., Native Americans, Latinos, etc.).

Each of the three lines of argument summarized above, then, makes a case for the proposition that equality, and especially equality of opportunity, for language-minority students in the United States requires that public education seek to maintain and develop the home languages of those students, though none of these arguments challenges the dominance of English in the United States. Having reviewed rationales for both English-only and bilingual language education policies, however, we are left without clarity or consensus on just what equality means for linguistic minorities in the United States. Perhaps a review of the Canadian situation will clarify the meaning of the conflict raging amongst its neighbors to the South.

LANGUAGE POLICY AND EQUALITY IN CANADA

Canada offers an instructive contrast to the situation of linguistic minorities in the United States. Like the United States, Canada is a nation-state that has evolved from a colonial territory settled by more than one European power; unlike the United States, however, Canada's linguistic-cultural majority never overwhelmed the legitimacy of the minority's continued existence as a distinct cultural and linguistic group. From its earliest beginnings as a territory united under one flag (i.e., following the ceding of French territories to England under terms of the Treaty of Paris in 1763), "Canada's rulers have given equal recognition to English and French" (Yalden 1981, 72). In each constitutional act following that beginning (i.e., The Act of Union of 1840 and the British North America Act [B.N.A.] of 1867), both French and English were recognized as legitimate political languages for Canada.

In 1969, moreover, Canada's national Parliament adopted the Official Languages Act, which made both English and French official languages of Canada and sought to provide some definition and institutional form to the language rights thereby established. In some ways a response by the federal government to Quebec's Quiet Revolution, the law culminated a six-year study and effort at national consensus building by the Royal Commission on Bilingualism and Biculturalism. Essentially, the act attempted to resolve the growing national polarization between anglophones and francophones by establishing the right of both groups *not* to assimilate linguistically or culturally, that is, to retain their distinctive characters--and it sought to use the federal government as a model for bilingualism. For example, a number of federal government administrative positions were declared to be bilingual, thereby seeking to institutionalize the right of Canadian citizens of both language groups to interact with "their" government in either language (Brazeau and Cloutier 1977, 205). Additional provisions of the act also attempted to establish and institutionalize the principle that Canada is a bilingual nation-state. The Constitution Act of 1982 contains similar provisions, and as late as June 1987, the Mulroney government put forth a bill "intended to strengthen, by court action if necessary, the right of people to work for or be served by the government in the official language of their choice" (Lemco 1987, 9).

Despite this seemingly constant record of national support for bilingualism, however, open conflict between the largest language groups has erupted periodically, leading to subsequent searches for both political consensus and equality for members of the two communities. Canada, as is well known, has a federal system that retains more independent power at the provincial level than is true of the states in the U.S. federal system. Much of the most important domestic legislation is enacted at the provincial level, and Canada's provinces have had what amounts to a veto power over some important areas of national policy. In order to understand Canadian language policy, then, it is necessary to sketch out the actions of the provincial governments on this subject. And at the provincial level there has been far less support for bilingualism than one might suppose from reading the official pronouncements of the national government. For years, French Canadians pointed to a long history of discrimination against francophones and French-language education in those provinces in which they were a minority. As one source has summarized the situation until the recent past,

> The Confederation arrangement [i.e., the 1867 B.N.A.] allowed Quebec to legislate in the field of education and gave constitutional protection to the French language community in that province. English was also a legal language in the Quebec legislature and courts. In the other provinces, however, the practice until the 1940s was for English-speaking Canadians, wherever they were in the majority, to deprive French-speaking minorities of public school facilities in their native language, and to refuse them the use of their language in government institutions. (Jackson, Jackson, and Baxter-Moore 1986, 240)

In part because of this historical experience, francophones outside of Quebec found it increasingly difficult to maintain their language and culture. This record of discrimination by anglophone Canada toward francophones is also important because it helps to put into perspective the position of many francophones in Quebec toward recent federal government efforts supporting a bilingual-bicultural Canada.

That is, just as the national government began to take stronger steps in support of a bilingual-bicultural nation-state at the end of the 1960s, Quebec's increasingly nationalistic francophone majority seemed to move toward a monolingual French policy for that province. Reacting to serious concern about the survival of French in predominantly anglophone North America, Quebec's National Assembly adopted a series of three policies from 1971 to 1977 that chronicle the shift away from a bilingual policy and toward provincial monolingualism: Bill 63 in 1971 (which proclaimed Quebec to be bilingual), Bill 22 in 1974 (which sought to make French the official language in Quebec and to place English in a subordinate position), and Bill 101 in 1977 (aimed at making Quebec virtually monolingual in French).

Concern for the survival of French derived from the decreasing birthrate among French Canadians, the small number of French-language immigrants to Quebec, and the assimilation of nearly all other immigrants into the English-speaking population of the province, the combined effect of which had been to reduce francophones significantly below their historical proportion of the Canadian population. In addition and very importantly, the increasingly restrictive legislation was motivated by the continued economic subordination of francophones in Quebec (Brazeau and Cloutier 1977, 206; Lemco 1987, 15-17; for a more theoretical background analysis, see Morris and Lanphier 1977). Bill 101, the last comprehensive language policy adopted in Quebec, restricts the rights of parents to have their children educated in languages other than French and imposes a number of sanctions designed to advantage francophones in economic and commercial activities (e.g., employment obstacles for anglophones in the public sector, "Francization" programs required for businesses to ensure that francophones are not deprived of employment because they are not fluent in a language other than French, etc.). Thus, the national government's campaign to promote bilingualism across the nation (having received a skeptical hearing in anglophone areas) was ultimately opposed in Quebec in part because it failed to address francophone concerns about economic equality and cultural survival. To date, neither the federal government nor the provinces have resolved the political conflicts underlying language policy.

EQUALITY AND LANGUAGE IN CANADA

What are the implications of the political conflict over language policy in Canada for an understanding of equality for language-minority groups? The Canadian dilemma with language policy is particularly instructive because it demonstrates with greater clarity (than does the U.S. conflict) the difficulties of reconciling linguistic diversity and equality within the boundaries of liberal assumptions about the polity. That is, the federal government, operating within the assumptions of a liberal democratic tradition, has attempted in recent years to resolve its controversy on this issue by establishing equal language rights for individuals who are nevertheless viewed as members of legitimately distinct linguistic and cultural groups.

Thus, in its 1969 report, the Royal Commission on Bilingualism and Biculturalism set out as its goal an "equal partnership not only of the two peoples which founded Confederation but also of each of their respective languages and cultures" (Canada, Royal Commission 1973, 4-5). After acknowledging the concept of an equality "of the group itself considered collectively," however, the commission defined *individual equality* as follows (in

language very similar to that used by U.S. advocates of bilingualism), and
proceeded to focus almost exclusively on the latter concept. Cultural and
linguistic equality, according to the commission,

> means essentially that everybody has the same access to the
> various benefits of a society without being hindered by his
> cultural identity. Thus, it is not enough for members of a
> minority group to have access to the same activities,
> institutions, and benefits as the members of the majority
> group; that simply requires an absence of discrimination
> against individuals as such. The equality to which we refer
> requires that a person who engages in some activity or
> associates with some institution need not renounce his own
> culture, but can offer his services, act, show his presence,
> develop, and be accepted with all his cultural traits. (Canada,
> Royal Commission 1973, 5)

Attempting to recommend policies that would give effect to this pluralistic yet
individualistic concept of equality, the commission put forth a variety of
measures that focused on three types of essentially liberal remedies: (1)
ensuring equal treatment under the law in their native language for members of
each language group by institutions of the federal government (and by provincial
governments in certain bilingual districts), (2) ensuring that parents in each
language group enjoyed the right to have their children educated in their own
language, and (3) equalizing the employment, consumption and social
opportunities of individuals within the existing social and economic order (both
public and private) through a series of affirmative action-type programs. The
latter two categories of these measures, however, were to be constrained by the
"territorial principle" requiring that sufficient numbers of each language group
were available to make them practicable. A number of these measures were
ultimately adopted by the federal government, and the 1982 Canadian Charter
of Rights and Freedoms attempted to give constitutional status to at least the first
two types of remedy.

     The response of Quebec to these measures provides the clearest
demonstration of their limitations from a collective or cultural, as opposed to an
individualistic or liberal, perspective. As sketched above, Quebec has moved
away from these seemingly humane and generous policies of equality and toward
monolingualism in French, thereby discriminating against anglophones and other
minority language groups in that province. On what grounds is this policy
justified? On the grounds of "equality," of course.

     The rationale proceeds in the following manner. First, note is taken
that throughout Canada, and even within Quebec itself, francophones have
tended to have lower levels of education, wealth, and social status for many
years. That is, the relationship between the two language groups is unequal in

wealth, power, and status. Moreover, anglophones have typically had a superior position economically and socially even within Quebec, where they have been vastly outnumbered. If the goal is to attain greater equality between the two groups as groups or as cultures, there are reasons for believing that policies based on individualistic premises will not be effective. That is, if the language-minority group begins from a position of social, economic, and political subordination, it is likely that the social context will work against an individualistic policy of pluralism. Thus, if the most favored opportunities (employment, status, power) in a society are in the hands of one language group, policies designed to enable individual members of a subordinate group to achieve equal access will elicit responses shaped by that very social context toward conformity with the dominant language and culture. Concluding a similar analysis with respect to Quebec, Brazeau and Cloutier write:

> Even when prevailing modes are alleged to involve a merit system [i.e., equality of opportunity], it is evident that some types of knowledge and skill are considered more pertinent than others. It thus appears that rendering a different set of people more competitive consists of inculcating them with the culture-bound, socially pertinent qualities that they lack. In other words, the liberal solution to group inequalities rests on the gradual assimilation of the members of the minority groups into the existing system. Basically, the end result is the disappearance of the group as such, because assimilation involves not only a sizable proportion of the individuals in the group but also the ever-expanding number of group activities of the social minority. (Brazeau and Cloutier 1977, 222-223)

In short, it is only inequality itself that makes possible the continuation of group differences within the assumptions of liberal individualism. Movement toward greater equality in this context literally means movement toward assimilation.

It is precisely for reasons such as this that recent immigrants to Quebec from non-founding countries have opted for English-language, rather than French-language schools, and that the francophone majority in that province has sought more collective means to greater equality. Quebec's policies of restriction on parental educational rights and on the mobility rights of anglophones and its seemingly heavy-handed Francization programs for business and commerce have all been efforts to equalize the partnership between French Canada and English Canada. As such, however, they have contradicted the individualistic liberal understandings of equality embedded in Canada's Constitution and Anglo political tradition. Thus, as in the United States, the search for agreement on a policy to achieve greater equality for language-minority groups has foundered on the shoals of conflicting understandings of equality itself.

CONCLUSION

What conclusions may be drawn from a comparison of the above explications of language policy politics in the United States and Canada? From the point of view of the relationship between language policy and the quest for equality for language-minority groups in these two nation-states, three relatively coherent positions may be articulated from the above. The first is what I will term the *liberal assimilationist* position, most strongly argued in the United States by opponents of bilingualism generally and bilingual education in particular. Though strongest in the United States, there are many anglophone Canadians (particularly in the western provinces) who articulate the same position. The essential assumption of this position is that it is possible for only one culture and related language to exist harmoniously and productively in a nation-state, and within this assumption the liberal tradition dominant in both countries understands *equality* to mean equality of opportunity to compete against others for the highest values within that society. These values, of course, are assumed to be those of the Anglo cultural tradition and language. The obvious path to equality for language-minority persons, then, is to assimilate into the dominant culture and language; any other path is sure to perpetuate inequality, since it is argued that it is impossible for two distinct cultural and linguistic groups to be equal in the same polity. If public policy has any role in this process, it is to assist those who are disadvantaged (by virtue of being in the linguistic or cultural minority) to acquire the traits necessary for equal opportunity. In this context, U.S. readers are regularly reminded that Canada's travails with language policy are proof of the folly of trying to legislate equality between two language groups within the same polity (e.g., Brimelow 1987).

From the point of view of language-minority persons, the principal defect of the assimilationist position is that it requires them to shed key aspects of their personalities (e.g., language, certain cultural values) as a condition of equality or even membership in the polity. This seems an obvious violation of other central values of the liberal tradition (e.g., the belief that individual rights are grounded in personhood or nature and not in the state, one example of such a right being the equal freedom to be different, etc.). The typical assimilationist response (at least in the United States) to these criticisms is that in joining the polity one voluntarily enters a going concern with a dominant language and culture, and that assimilating is a fair price for the benefits accruing from this voluntary membership. The difficulty with this position, of course, is that it assumes what is at issue: that the "going concern" is legitimately and exclusively conducted only in the nation's dominant language. It was noted above that in the United States there are some grounds for questioning this assumption, particularly for Latinos and Native Americans. And in Canada, of course, the predominant national self-understanding is that both the French and the English are legitimate founders of the polity--or at least it has become politically unacceptable in recent years to question this understanding in public discourse. (The positions of immigrants from non-founding lands and of the aboriginal peoples, on the other hand, are less recognized and more comparable to that of similar groups in the United States.)

At the other end of the spectrum is the position of the *group or "corporate" egalitarians.* Represented most vigorously by the Québécois, this position holds that not only are both the francophone and anglophone language groups legitimate in Canada, but public policy should aim at making the two groups equal in their respective capacities for self-determination. The central difference in this position from that of assimilationists is that here it is not individual opportunity that should be equal, but group self-determination. The assumption of this position is that group survival and self-determination are of highest priority. While it may be desirable (or simply a fact of historical life) for the two groups to hold membership in the same polity, joint membership is acceptable only if it is possible under conditions of equal membership. From this perspective, requiring francophones to accept a subordinate position within the polity (notwithstanding their being numerically out-voted by the anglophone majority) would be an unacceptable violation of the principle of equality. And it is the political strength of this perspective that has led Canada to adopt some (though only some) of the features of consociational democracy (Smiley 1977).

In the United States, on the other hand, this position has received little support from language-minority group members, though it has received a good deal of attention as a "danger" by advocates of the liberal assimilationist position (*New York Times* 1976; Brimelow 1987). While some minority group political advocates in the United States have periodically articulated a group egalitarian stance toward self-determination and equality (e.g., Castro 1976), this approach has never been a strong political force within any American ethnic community or within the nation as a whole. The fact that no U.S. language or cultural minority group is sufficiently concentrated geographically to constitute a statewide majority voting bloc, as contrasted with the situation of francophones in Quebec, may go a long way in explaining this difference between the two countries.

The normative difficulty with this second position is that it runs afoul of the individualistic assumptions inherent in the liberal political traditions dominant in both Canada and the United States. That is, in attempting to shape public policies that will make possible equal self-determination for two or more groups, it is seemingly necessary to establish legal group rights and powers; that is, the group itself must be given legal standing and be incorporated in some manner into the state as a group.

As Michael Walzer has pointed out, however, there is "a major difficulty here: groups cannot be assigned rights unless they are first assigned members" (Walzer 1982, 20). And assigning individuals to group membership, especially by the state, not only is in conflict with the liberal individualistic ideology that has been dominant in the United States, but also would revive painful memories of past practices that operated to deny equality to members of American minority groups (e.g., Black slavery, Japanese American internment in World War II, etc.). For better or worse, as Walzer has further noted, membership in American ethnic groups usually has been thought to be something akin to membership in a voluntary association.

Aside from some form of geographic and political separatism that would minimize relationships between members of the different language and cultural groups, it is difficult to see how these problems with the group egalitarian position could be overcome without abandoning the liberal values that have heretofore been dominant in both countries. In any case, such a position of separatism is seemingly impractical in the United States and was once rejected by the voters in Quebec (though see Laponce's chapter in this volume for a more optimistic view by way of Canada's federal system).

The third position that emerges from the above review of language policy politics in the United States and Canada may be termed *liberal pluralism*. It is liberal because it rests upon voluntaristic and individualistic assumptions about social and political relationships. It is pluralistic because it assumes that the society may support and contain a variety of ethnic, racial, language, and cultural groups without destroying the unity of the polity. Within these assumptions, *equality* means that each individual has an equal right to be different (in the sense of maintaining diverse languages and cultures) without being deprived of equal membership in the polity. And the role of public policy is to enable such individuals to maintain their linguistic and cultural diversity through educational and other related programs *if they so choose*. This articulation has the virtue of avoiding both the coercive monolingualism of the assimilationist position and the coercive membership assignment of the group egalitarian position. It is the position articulated by U.S. supporters of maintenance bilingual education as well as by bilingual federalists in Canada such as former Prime Minister Trudeau.

Like the other two positions, however, the liberal pluralistic view has difficulties as well as strengths. From the perspective of liberal assimilationists, as noted above, the pluralistic position risks the development and exacerbation of dangerous and unnecessary ethnic conflict. Moreover, for those who choose to maintain their minority language and culture, this approach risks permanent inequality, since in any society the rewards of social activity are inevitably allocated according to the skills and understandings of the dominant cultural group. Public policies that attempt to interfere with these "natural" social processes are doomed to be both wasteful and unsuccessful. Within the voluntaristic assumptions of liberalism, that is, most people will naturally choose to participate in those ways of life that provide them with the most personal and material satisfaction. In both Canada and the United States (with Quebec being a partial and problematic exception), this process has meant adopting the Anglo ways of life.

The group egalitarian critique of the pluralist position is based upon a similar analysis. From this perspective, the weakness of the pluralist position is that it fails to articulate and establish a public domain in which the minority language and culture may seek to attain equal status, or even in which it may operate. That is, where will non-English speakers (outside of Quebec) use their native languages? Presumably in their homes and with other voluntary members of the same groups, but in this conception there is no public domain for the minority-language group that may sustain it over the long run or give it status in the larger society. Canada's Official Languages Act was an attempt to overcome this problem, but it was precisely because many people in Quebec seemed to be naturally adopting the language of political and economic power that the francophone leaders of that province adopted the "illiberal" language policies outlined above. And in the United States, even some of the strongest advocates of a maintenance approach to bilingual education are not optimistic about the possibility of maintaining a viable Spanish-speaking community over the long run (see Fishman 1985, for an example). Thus, while the liberal pluralist position may give to individuals an equal right to be different, it does not seem to provide the social, economic, and political foundations under which those differences can be sustained over time, much less be made equal.

It may be possible to develop policies that would satisfy the individualistic and voluntaristic criteria of liberalism and yet support the maintenance (and equality?) of linguistic and cultural diversity, but the intellectual work necessary to conceptualize such policies remains to be done. However that may be, this chapter has demonstrated the complexity that must be taken into account in any effort to advance toward equality for language-minority groups in Canada and the United States through public policy. Further, it is hoped that the chapter has clarified the understandings of that protean value which underlie much of the political conflict over language policy in those two countries.

14

What Kind of Bilingualism for Canada: Personal or Territorial? The Demographic Factor

J. A. Laponce

This chapter presents evidence supporting the thesis that linguistic minorities are best protected by group rights and territorial unilingualism.

It would be possible to reason the case in very general terms, since ethnolinguistic groups have, compared to other ethnic groups--religious or racial for example--very special needs, the need for territorial compactness in particular (Laponce 1986, ch. 6). But arguing a specific case has the advantage of greater vividness and also, more important, the advantage of focusing on a society whose particularities can be taken into consideration.

Let the French Canadians be the ethnic group considered, or more precisely, let the French language in Canada be the object of our attention.

THE BACKGROUND

Let us consider the case of French in Canada against the backdrop of the worldwide competition among languages--a competition akin to that among animal species, since we can ask about languages the very questions that help map the evolution of living organisms: Is the relationship between two languages conflictual or symbiotic? Is a language expanding, contracting, or vanishing? What is a language's life span? Do languages have, taken as a whole, a positive or a negative birthrate?

In an article published in 1953 in the *Société préhistorique française*, Cailleux estimated that, on the average, languages live for approximately 2,000 years and that two languages are born for every one that dies. These were, of course, impressionistic measures based on partial data; but measures that summarized well the basic trend if not the exact magnitude of the evolution of languages from the most distant past to very recent times.

In the last few decades, a major revolution appears to have taken place; a change of direction appears to have occurred in a trend that dated back, probably, to the origins of our species. By all counts at our disposal, the birthrate of languages has become negative. More languages die than are born. Within a few hundred kilometers from my university there are ten or so languages that are down to a few speakers. And that experience is not limited to the Canadian West Coast; it is repeated many times in the Americas, in Asia, and in Africa.

What explains this global change? Most likely and very simply: what Paul Valery called *l'ère du monde fini*, the era of the completed world. The world has become a closed entity, or it has at least moved from being a set of sets toward being a single system. And in a closed system, languages in contact do typically become languages in conflict. In rare cases they establish a kind of division of labor that stabilizes one language in the performance of certain roles while another language is used for other functions (one language may be assigned religious roles while another is assigned secular functions, or, as in some primitive tribes, one language may be reserved for males and the other for females). More commonly, in a closed system, languages in contact fight a conflict of extinction; the system tends to reject redundancy and, consequently, moves toward unilingualism. Typically the move from linguistic heterogeneity to unilingualism has two phases. In a first phase, the dominant group (provided it has strength in numbers as well as in political power) shifts the cost of bilingualism onto the dominated group. In a second phase, it is the dominated group itself that rejects the extra cost of language learning by concentrating its resources on the language of the dominant group, the language with greater social power.

In the era of intense linguistic competition--an intensity that is related to the very density of communication within and across the societies concerned-- what is the strategy best adapted to stopping or at least retarding the process of assimilation of ethnolinguistic minorities? What solution should we recommend to the Prince: the Canadian and Finnish systems of flexible linguistic boundaries or the Belgian and Swiss systems of fixed and rigid intrastate language separations? An examination of the dynamics of language contact in Canada will lead us to recommend the Swiss and Belgian solutions.

A PRELIMINARY QUESTION

Why should the hypothetical Prince to whom we address our remarks be advised to protect a minority language? Why not advise him to do the very reverse? Why preserve a language other than that of the dominant group? There is more than one answer for wanting to proceed from our stated assumption. We may say, first of all, that since our Prince is hypothetical, so is the Prince's preferred outcome. Choosing one side of a particular policy for the sake of separating the functional from the dysfunctional does not mean that we exclude the other. That other policy has indeed been proposed to the British Crown. In the nineteenth century, Lord Durham, in a famous report, advised his Prince, the British Queen, to let the French Canadians be assimilated by the English. There is, however, a reason other than convenience for our wanting to proceed from an assumption of protection rather than one of assimilation. That reason rests in the fact that Lord Durham's preference has not materialized. French Canadians have remained a sufficiently large segment of the Canadian population to be reckoned with electorally, and they have remained sufficiently determined to protect their language to make the English dominant group fear that secession might be used as a means of obtaining that protection. That fear has contributed to the dominant group wanting to protect now the language that they had been advised to assimilate. Additionally, Canada finds in its bilingualism a means of distinguishing itself from its southern neighbor. English-Canadian nationalists, in their quest for a specific Canadian identity, frequently point to Canada's Frenchness, even when they themselves remain unfamiliar with Quebec's culture.

For these various reasons, we shall assume that our Prince takes to the letter Canada's official policy of equality between French and English and that he or she wants to guarantee the survival of the French language in North America.

THE CANADIAN CASE

Two sets of related factors need be considered when planning a language policy intended to protect the French language in Canada: geographical and demographic.

The Geography of French/English Contacts

The percentage of people who, in the census of 1981, indicated that French was the language they spoke habitually at home gives us a first measure of territorial concentration of Canada's second official language. See Table 14.1. In no province outside Quebec and New Brunswick is French the language of the home of more than 5 percent of the population. The territorial concentration of French in Quebec appears even more clearly from the percentage distribution by province of the total francophone population of Canada. As shown in Table 14.1 nearly 90 percent of Canadian francophones live in one province. A policy intended to protect French will thus, of necessity, be one that is primarily intended for that province.

Table 14.1 'French' in Canada

	Percentage 'French' of Each Province's Population		Percentage of the Total 'French' Population in Each Province	
	French Mother Tongue	French Home Language	French Mother Tongue	French Home Language
British Columbia	1.6	0.5	0.6	0.2
Alberta	2.7	1.3	0.8	0.4
Saskatchewan	2.6	1.0	0.5	0.3
Manitoba	5.1	3.0	1.0	0.7
Ontario	5.4	3.9	8.3	6.3
Quebec	82.4	82.5	84.0	87.8
New Brunswick	33.6	31.4	3.7	3.6
Nova Scotia	4.2	2.9	0.6	0.5
Prince Edward Island	4.8	3.0	0.5	0.0
Newfoundland	0.4	0.3	0.0	0.0

Source: Canadian Census 1981.

The statistics presented thus far might give the impression that Quebec is the equivalent of a French-Swiss canton. This is what the Parti Québecois would have liked Quebec to become, at least as a second choice to the independence project that failed in the referendum of 1980.[1] But a French canton Quebec is not. It is more like a bilingual canton, with major differences that will be considered later.

A thematic rendition of the relationship between internal political and linguistic boundaries--see Figure 14.1--shows the French unilingual zone to straddle the Quebec-New Brunswick border while a bilingual zone (where English dominates) straddles the Ontario-Quebec border. As in a Dufy painting, the color (language) is somewhat dissociated from the structure (the political boundaries).   The tensions generated by this dissociation have not been particularly severe along the New Brunswick border.   The francophone populations of northwestern New Brunswick have their own culture, their own history; they do not wish to join Quebec, and Quebec has no claim on them. The linguistic tensions have been concentrated in the western, particularly in the southwestern, part of Quebec, in the area that extends roughly from the middle of Montreal to the Ontario border. The attempt to push the French unilingual

Figure 14.1 Thematic Rendition of the Relationship between Language and Provincial Boundaries in Canada

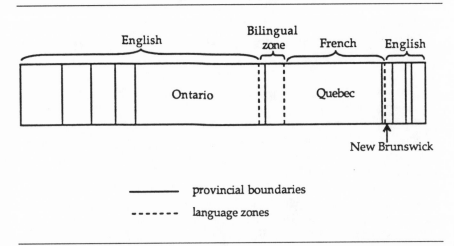

Note: The provinces are drawn roughly according to population size.

zone toward that border--either by intraprovincial migrations or by constraining provincial legislation regarding the language of schools, road signs, billboards, labor contracts, and so forth--and the strong resistance met by this attempt seriously destabilized the Canadian political system throughout the 1970s and early 1980s and led to major constitutional reforms (McRoberts 1977; McWhinney 1979; Laponce 1984a).

Socio-Demographic Factors

French Canadians number roughly six million--the count varies depending upon whether one uses as a criterion mother tongue, official language, or language used at home; they represent roughly 25 percent of the total Canadian population and less than 3 percent of that of anglophone North America. Until the 1950s French Canadians managed, thanks to a very high birthrate, not only to survive as a distinct culture with a language of universal use--the language of jokes and prayers as well as of business transactions and university--but to expand their population base and regain some of the Quebec territory that had been lost to English settlers following the conquest in the eighteenth century. That reconquest has however been slow and partial, the high French Canadian birthrate being counterbalanced by high levels of immigrations that were not favorable to the French language, either because the immigrants came from English-speaking countries, or, increasingly so in the twentieth century, because the new immigrants that spoke neither French nor English preferred learning English, a more powerful language than French for insertion in the North American economy and society.

THE EFFECT OF TERRITORIAL DISPERSION ON A MINORITY LANGUAGE

At the geographical peripheries of Canada, in British Columbia as in Newfoundland, the proportion of the provincial population with French as a mother tongue is under 2 percent. Obviously, in such environments one will not be able, except in the most abnormal cases, to live in French. One might find a primary school or even a secondary school program using French as a language of instruction, but not a French university, and even in French immersion programs, one would have to speak English to one's schoolmates outside the classroom. Typically, in these two provinces one has to work, shop, and be entertained in English. The language of the social environment exerts such pressure that French has difficulty surviving even as a home language. Table 14.2 shows that outside Quebec and to a lesser extent New Brunswick, in other words outside the French unilingual area, French is seriously eroded; even in Ontario, where only 65 percent of those reporting French as their mother tongue use it as their home language. English maintains itself much better in

Table 14.2 Percentage of Individuals Using Their Mother Tongue Habitually as Their Home Language

Province	English	French
Newfoundland	99.9	30.4
Nova Scotia	99.7	64.8
New Brunswick	98.1	90.1
Quebec	86.3	97.7
Ontario	98.8	65.6
Manitoba	99.1	55.0
Saskatchewan	99.5	34.2
Alberta	99.1	44.6
British Columbia	99.3	26.9

Source: Canadian Census 1981 (2 percent sample) interrogated by computer.

Note: Prince Edward Island is not included because of the small number of cases.

Quebec (86.3 percent) than French in Ontario. The two factors--being dispersed, and being a minority language--reinforce each other in their negative impact on language survival. In Canadian cities of more than 25,000 inhabitants where over 90 percent of the population speaks French at home, the level of English retention as a home language stands at 60 percent. By contrast, in cities where over 90 percent of the population speaks English, the level of retention of French is only 35 percent (Laponce 1984). Clearly, the francophone who leaves the French unilingual zone enters a powerful assimilation system that grinds minority languages away, if not in the first, at least in succeeding generations. This phenomenon is not limited to French. A survey conducted by O'Bryan in the 1970s, among respondents of non-French and non-English origins, indicates that in urban centers only 70 percent describe themselves as fluent in their ethnic language in the first generation, that the proportion drops to 11 percent in the second generation, and 1 percent in the third (Laponce 1984b, 57). The normal defensive strategy is thus for francophones to remain within what is sometimes called the "Quebec fortress," and by and large they do. The francophones are more likely to stay in Quebec than the anglophones are likely to stay in Ontario. The Census of 1981 indicates that 96 percent of francophone Québecois born in Quebec still resided in that province at the time of the census, while the percentage of anglophones of Ontario still residing in their province was only 86 percent. Furthermore, the percentage of anglophones born outside Ontario who have migrated to that province is lower than the percentage of francophones born outside Quebec who have come, one is tempted to say "come back" to reside in Quebec (see Table 14.3). But notwithstanding

Table 14.3 Province of Residence and Birth for the Francophone and Anglophone Residents of Quebec and Ontario

Province of Birth	Percent Francophones in Quebec	Percent Anglophones in Ontario
Newfoundland	55	19
Nova Scotia	20	20
New Brunswick	27	20
Quebec	96	21
Ontario	32	86
Manitoba	15	11
Saskatchewan	10	6
Alberta	25	5
British Columbia	37	5

Source: Census of 1981 (2 percent sample) interrogated on line.

a strong power of attraction for the francophones born in other provinces and notwithstanding a remarkable rate of retention of its own French-speaking population, Quebec loses more francophones to the rest of Canada than it gains from it. The very strong pull back to Quebec described by the percentages of Table 14.3 applies to a small population pool, while the relatively low rate of migration of Quebec francophones refers to a large population base. The overall in/out migration ratio of francophones is thus negative for Quebec: 10 leave the province for 9 that come from the rest of Canada. It should be noted, however, that the migration deficit is higher for anglophones: 10 leave Quebec for 8 coming in.

In short, other things being equal--notably birthrate and foreign immigration--the internal migrations recorded by the 1981 census would lead one to predict a slow decline of the percentage of francophones in Canada and a slow decline of the percentage of anglophones in Quebec. But the other things are not equal. A traditionally very positive factor--the birthrate--has ceased to be favorable to the Québecois, and foreign migrations continue to have a negative effect on the relative weight of the French language.

THE QUEBEC BIRTHRATE

For the past hundred years, the proportion of French Canadians has remained stable nationwide, in the neighborhood of 25 percent--a remarkable achievement considering that the Canadian population has increased fivefold. As already mentioned, this survival was largely due to an extremely high birthrate. But a demographic revolution occurred in Quebec after the Second World War. The birthrate became negative and is now below that of English Canada. One measures this dramatic reversal by separating (see Table 14.4)

Table 14.4 Average Number of Children Born to Canadian Women by Age, Mother Tongue, and Province

	French	English	Other Language
Women Aged 50 or Over			
Quebec	4.06	2.72	2.85
Ontario	4.19	2.78	2.97
Women Aged 15 to 49			
Quebec	1.89	1.85	2.35
Ontario	2.16	1.88	1.96

Source: Canadian Census 1981 (2 percent sample) interrogated by computer.

the number of children of francophone, anglophone, and other Canadians for the present and for the previous generation of women of child-bearing age. If the Quebec English reproduction rate is taken to be 100, the French Quebec reproduction rate shows a drop from 150 among women over 50 to 102 for women under 50. Compared to the other language groups, the decline is even more considerable: from 142 to 80. The Franco-Ontarians have, better than the Québecois, maintained the tradition of large families, but the size of the Franco-Ontarian community and its relatively high level of assimilation to English (see Table 14.1) result in the overall picture being unchanged by their partial adherence to tradition. Quebec is losing the "revenge of the cradles," and outside Quebec, French Canadians are also losing the "battle of the wedding bands." The only large community of francophones outside Quebec, that of Ontario, has a very high rate of exogamy. Outside Quebec, and to a lesser extent New Brunswick, the French enter monolinguistic marriages less frequently than do Chinese or Italian speakers (see Table 14.5). Marrying across languages, even when the marriages do not involve anglophones, facilitates the rapid spread of English, the dominant lingua franca. Note that in Quebec itself, notwithstanding the significantly different proportions of francophones to anglophones (80 percent to 20 percent) the Chinese are as likely to marry an English speaker as they are to marry a French speaker, and the Italians are not as likely to marry French speakers as they are to marry English speakers (3.1 compared to 4.4 percent).

In short, our survey of the major geographical and demographic factors internal to Canada--geographical concentration, assimilation rates, endogamy rates, and birthrates--lead us to note that outside Quebec and northern New Brunswick, French is losing to a more powerful language. The much advertised gains that it may have made outside Quebec in recent years (bilingual labeling on products sold in stores, translation of Manitoba laws in French, control of some school boards in Ontario, bilingual government forms and documents) are rear-guard symbolic victories incapable of reversing unfavorable social trends. Outside Quebec and northern New Brunswick, French may well gain as a second language, but as a first language, its future is bleak, even in eastern Ontario where numbers give it the possibility of surviving for a longer period of time as a home language but not as an all-purpose system of communication. In Quebec, concentration works to the advantage of French, as do both the high rate of intralinguistic French marriages and the low rate of out-of-province migrations of francophones, but the birthrate has ceased to be in its favor.

EXTERNAL FACTORS: IMMIGRATION

Can Quebec find abroad enough francophones to counter the growth of the anglophone Canadian community through migration and assimilation?

Table 14.5 Percentage of Women, by Mother Tongue and Region, Whose Husbands Have the Same Mother Tongue

Mother Tongue of Husband	Mother Tongue of Wife					
	English	French	Chinese	German	Italian	Ukrainian
Maritimes						
English	97.6	41.6	100.0	60.0	8.3	33.3
French	1.5	55.5	-	4.0	25.0	11.1
Chinese	-	-	-	-	-	-
German	-	-	-	16.0	-	-
Italian	-	-	-	4.0	58.3	-
Ukranian	-	-	-	-	8.3	44.4
New Brunswick						
English	91.6	12.8	25.0	62.5	50.0	100.0
French	7.0	86.7	-	12.5	25.0	-
Chinese	-	-	75.0	-	-	-
German	-	-	-	25.0	-	-
Italian	-	-	-	-	25.0	-
Ukranian	-	-	-	-	-	-
Quebec						
English	68.7	3.6	5.3	19.1	3.1	12.1
French	23.8	95.0	5.3	13.7	4.4	11.2
Chinese	-	-	88.5	-	-	-
German	1.0	-	-	50.5	-	1.7
Italian	1.4	-	-	1.3	89.9	-
Ukranian	-	-	-	-	-	62.9
Ontario						
English	91.1	34.5	6.4	24.8	7.3	27.7
French	2.7	59.8	-	1.5	-	2.1
Chinese	-	-	92.2	-	-	-
German	1.2	-	-	60.8	-	1.7
Italian	1.2	1.3	-	1.5	89.6	1.6
Ukranian	-	-	-	1.8	-	56.0
West						
English	89.4	43.5	7.5	24.9	15.0	27.6
French	1.9	45.3	-	1.1	-	1.7
Chinese	-	-	90.5	-	-	-
German	2.7	4.0	-	65.6	1.3	3.6
Italian	-	-	-	-	78.5	-
Ukranian	1.8	2.5	-	2.8	-	61.2

Source: Canadian Census 1981 (2 percent sample) interrogated by computer.

Barring massive immigration from France--this would require catastrophic events--or large migrations of French-educated African elites, which would also require dramatic events, Quebec cannot get from abroad the francophones that would compensate for its low birthrate.

Judging by its dimensions, its agricultural, mineral, and educational resources, Canada is empty of population. In a few decades Mexico City will have as many inhabitants as the whole of Canada. In 1871, Canada had 3.5 million inhabitants. It had 25 million in 1981. Will it grow to 100 million in the next century? Let us suppose that it doubles and that the native birthrate stabilizes at the no-growth balance point. Where would the 25 million needed for doubling the present population come from?

Immigration from France has, since the conquest, remained negligible. In the best of years only 2 percent to 4 percent of migrants come from France and only 70 percent of them settle in Quebec. In 1984 only 36 percent of migrants coming to Quebec knew French, while 24 percent spoke English, the remaining 40 percent speaking neither of the two official languages (Lachapelle 1987).

POLICY OPTIONS

Under the adverse circumstances just described, what are the policy options available to the hypothetical Prince desirous of insuring the survival of French in North America?

A first option would consist of limiting drastically the numbers of migrants allowed in the country. In recent years, during an economic crisis the number has been limited to a little over 100,000 per year. This would add roughly ten million in one century. Assuming that nine out of ten become anglicized, the proportion of French Canadians would drop from 27 percent to roughly 22 percent, a major but not a catastrophic drop. The proportion of Québecois in Canada would then be comparable to that of French Swiss in Switzerland. But are migrations likely to be so limited? The Third World is banging at the doors of industrialized nations. Will Canada wish or be able to keep these doors shut or barely open? That is not likely. In multi-ethnic democratic systems with expanding economies, the recent immigrants act as poles of attraction to their ethnic kin and have enough political leverage to prevent the freezing of the ethnic balance at the point where it is still to the advantage of the old settlers. It is revealing that in 1981 more migrants came to Canada from Asia than from Europe. Restricting immigration--especially if economic prosperity returns--is unlikely to be a workable alternative.

A second option would consist of giving to Quebec the power of selecting the immigrants that settle on its territory. The provincial governments having the power to legislate in matters of immigration provided their laws do not violate federal laws, Quebec created a ministry of immigration in 1968 and negotiated with the federal government migration agreements (1971, 1975, 1978) giving it some limited rights over the choice of newcomers. The federally proposed constitutional reform of September 1991 would constitutionalize the Quebec/Ottawa agreements. These agreements could help Quebec, provided it is assured the means of assimilating and keeping the newcomers, but they could not prevent adverse internal migrations. Once in Canada, the new settler is free to move where he wishes.

A third option rests in policies favoring large families. I mention it for the sake of completeness, only to dismiss it as most unlikely to succeed. Quebec's electorate would be unlikely to accept that major financial rewards be given to families with more than two children, and even if the latter were given such rewards, it is unlikely that the society would respond positively.[2] In a liberal, urban, industrial, and comfortable society, the government has very limited power over the birthrate.

The fourth option, the one that I would recommend to the Prince, has the advantage of clarity, simplicity, and effectiveness. It is the Swiss solution, a solution that consists of distinguishing bilingualism by superposition from bilingualism by juxtaposition, reserving the first to the central government and using the second to separate the regional governments linguistically. Switzerland is administered by a bilingual civil service and a trilingual parliament, but the typical canton is administered in only one language (the few remaining bilingual cantons replicate the national picture by running a linguistic frontier through their territory). The linguistic border decides the language of schools, street signs, legal contracts, and public services. The rigid linguistic frontiers of Switzerland have the advantage that, being permanent, they cease to be the object of political partisan battles. It is known to all that Geneva is French and that Bales is German. The internal migrants know before changing residence that they will have to change language. A German Swiss moving to Geneva is thus, from the language point of view, very much like a German Swiss moving to France.

Such a solution to language conflict is, of course, restrictive of rights, and may be difficult to accept in a democracy where these rights are typically given to people. Rights, says the classical liberal, should be given to individuals against groups, not to groups against individuals. But some of these individual rights--the right to speak a language is one of those--require the existence of a supporting community. The right to speak implies the right to be understood. Hence, runs the counterargument, to protect the individual one must, first of all, protect a community. That is precisely the position taken by the Swiss Supreme Court, which justified as follows the restrictions on individual rights resulting from the cantonal policies of unilingualism, "The linguistic internal borders of our country, once fixed, must be considered as unchangeable; the certainty for each original founding group (*souche*) of the population, of the integrity of the territory throughout which its language is spoken and over which its own culture extends constitutes the guarantee of the harmonious relationships of the various parts of the country; and the right of each of these to forestall any encroachment must be recognized" (translated from Héraud 1974, 24).

In another judgment, a 1965 judgment denying an association of Swiss francophone parents the right for children to be educated in their mother tongue, the same tribunal argued "the risks [the linguistic risks] implicit in foreign immigrations, can only be modified through the linguistic assimilation of immigrants," an assimilation that applies to foreigners and citizens alike (Héraud 1974; Woehrling 1985, 67).

The Quebec Law 101, the major linguistic law passed by the Parti Québecois Government in 1977, ought in the long term to have turned Quebec into the equivalent of a French-speaking Swiss canton, since Quebec residents using government-funded schools had to send their children to French rather than English schools unless they themselves, or a brother or sister of these children, had been educated in English in Quebec. Newcomers were thus forced into the French educational stream. Not all abided by the law, but most did. In 1986, 62 percent of children from non-French non-English parents went to French public schools, compared to 15 percent in 1969-70.

However, this move toward making Quebec a unilingual province has been countered by the loss of the independence referendum of 1980 and by the Canadian Constitution of 1982. Language is recognized by the latter as an individual right. And the 1991 federal new constitutional proposals, while recognizing Quebec as a distinct society, do not change the language provisions of the Constitution of 1982, thus leaving it eventually to the federal judiciary to decide whether, in matters of language, Quebec can justify its restrictive language legislation by its distinct status. Quebec may well have lost its chance of establishing the whole of the province as a secure unilingual area for the francophones of North America, it may even have lost the possibility of imitating the practice of the few Swiss bilingual cantons and dividing its territory into unilingual zones.

The practical obstacles to transplanting the Swiss solution to Canada are considerable. What a Prince could do, a minority may not. The Quebec anglophones have considerable electoral influence in the province of Quebec and considerable political influence in the two major parties that have alternated in Ottawa. While the Quebeckers who give English as their mother tongue account for only about 10 percent of the total provincial population, regarding the language question they can normally count on the support of the largest segment of the non-French, non-English population, another 10 percent of the electorate. Furthermore, the anglophone community of Quebec is not isolated in its successful attempt to retain its traditional English-speaking institutions (schools, hospitals, universities, churches, and municipalities located in the bilingual zone of the province). It has, in this attempt, the full support of public opinion in the rest of Canada, and also, paradoxically, sizable support from Quebec francophones who prefer individual over group rights.

But relating linguistic desirability to political feasibility would lead us to another subject. Our purpose was simply to show that the more a linguistic minority departs from being a concentrated homogeneous community with unilingual institutions, the more it weakens its chances of survival, particularly when it has a very low birthrate.

Conclusion
Laurie A. Rhodebeck

A theme running throughout the foregoing chapters has been the persistence of ethnic and racial conflict and minority disadvantage within the advanced industrial democracies. Although they are not uniformly pessimistic, most of the essays agree that ethnic minorities currently participate in economic and/or political markets as disadvantaged actors, that the intervention of the state and government in ethnic conflict is not always productive or benign, and that such conflict will not significantly abate in the foreseeable future. In regard to this last point, it is important to note that traditional ethnic conflicts, such as those involving majority and minority groups in Canada and Western Europe, continue while tensions arising from the postwar settlement of foreign workers in the advanced industrial democracies have more recently become salient. As a result of the superimposition of one set of conflicts over another, issues of ethnicity now structure political discourse and influence political decision making in the industrial democracies to a degree unprecedented since World War II. At the very least, these conflicts make the advanced industrial democracies more difficult to govern. In the extreme, they threaten the very integrity of the nation-state as it has been traditionally defined (M. Heisler 1986; Nairn 1981).

In the introduction to this volume we surveyed a number of hypotheses about the persistence of group conflict in the industrial democracies. These hypotheses feature the following explanations: the intensification of group interactions, the emergence and persistence of economic inequalities, the expansion of state intervention, the declining salience of non-ethnic conflicts, the increasing political mobilization of groups, the growth of postbourgeois or postmaterialist values, the renewal of appeals for self-determination, the demonstration effect of ethnic demands, the entrepreneurial abilities of ethnic leaders, and the vagaries of the international political economy. To these we add the market orientation of contemporary politics in the advanced industrial democracies.

The ideal analysis would examine these hypotheses, if not simultaneously, then at least systematically, using diachronic data for all the advanced industrial democracies with significant minority populations. Falling short of that ideal, we have offered fourteen analyses that collectively provide evidence as to the validity of these explanations. Each explanation finds some support, although the evidence is stronger or more direct for some than for others. In this final chapter we review the preceding discussions of ethnic and racial conflict, draw general conclusions about the conditions that foster conflict in the advanced industrial democracies, evaluate the hypotheses presented in our introduction, and suggest some directions for future research.

IMMIGRATION POLICY AND ETHNIC TOLERANCE

One hypothesized threat to the peaceful coexistence of majority and minority groups is the intensification of group interactions. Interactions between majority and minority groups may intensify when patterns of settlement among long-established groups shift, as happened with the urban-suburban and North-South migrations among Blacks and whites in the United States. More recently, group interactions have intensified in the industrial democracies as immigrants arrived in their host countries. With the arrival of immigrants have come many problems that fuel group conflict. These include the inability or unwillingness of the new ethnic and racial minorities to embrace the dominant culture of their host society, intolerance within the majority population toward the attempts of recent immigrants to preserve their cultural heritage, socioeconomic inequalities among ethnic groups, heightened anxiety among members of the majority population about the potential threat immigrants pose to the majority's economic security, the inability of minorities to gain adequate political representation and access to important arenas of decision making, and inadequate or clumsy efforts by host governments to develop policies that address the problems accompanying immigration.

The chapters in the first section of this volume focus on the experience of immigration, but rather than directly examine the intensification hypotheses, they analyze some of the problems that immigration engenders. Many of these problems stem from the fact that in their pursuit of a better life in new surroundings, immigrants not only suffer socioeconomic disadvantages similar to those of non-immigrant minorities but also face a unique set of cultural and political experiences arising from the conditions of their arrival in host countries and the subsequent process of mutual adjustment that confronts both immigrants and hosts. These disadvantages and experiences are major sources of group conflict. Based on observations of immigrants' experience in four countries--the United States, Great Britain, West Germany before unification, and France--the chapters suggest that the following factors affect the domestic situation of immigrants: the historical experiences of the host country with non-native groups, the immigration policies of the host country, public reaction to immigrants among members of the dominant culture in the host country, the conditions of immigrants' arrival and length of experience as immigrant groups, labor market conditions, the delivery of social welfare services, and the permeability of the host culture.

Both Britain and West Germany, for example, had early and mostly negative experiences with immigration--Britain with European Jews, West Germany with Poles--that precipitated restrictive immigration policies (in Britain) or forced assimilation (in West Germany). Following a long period with no significant immigration, after World War II both countries initiated labor recruitment programs that attracted foreign workers that neither country was prepared to integrate fully into its society. As a consequence, the response of government to immigrants' problems has been piecemeal and, in the case of Britain, alarmist. Hoskin and Fitzgerald find that these similar historical experiences with immigrants have been accompanied by negative public attitudes toward foreigners in both countries. Until the mid-1980s these attitudes were more negative in Britain than in West Germany, perhaps in part because of the alarmism of British leaders, but in both countries they tend to cut across partisan boundaries. The evidence suggests that policy initiatives on immigration issues, which the major political parties in each country have generally avoided, are shaped as much by the anticipated (negative) response of the non-immigrant population as by the perceived needs of the immigrants.

Freeman provides the most detailed analysis of the connection between immigration policies and the conditions immigrants face once they arrive in the host country. First, there is a strong association between laissez-faire immigration policies and the neglect or even the exploitation of immigrants. Governments that fail to manage the entry of immigrants usually fail to intervene positively into the lives of these new settlers. In addition, the failure to institute controls on immigration seems to generate fear among members of the host majority population, which in turn fosters hostility toward immigrants. As Hoskin and Fitzgerald and Freeman note, this hostility only prolongs the process of mutual adjustment between hosts and immigrants.

Second, the relationship between the degree of selectivity in immigration policy and the extent of egalitarianism in domestic immigrant policy is unclear. There is some evidence that ethnically restrictive control policies are incompatible with egalitarian domestic policies, but the causal relationship is ambiguous. Third, while an economically oriented immigration policy seems incompatible with the goals of improving the domestic living conditions of immigrants, most European countries have not pursued the sort of extremely exploitative policies that they might have. Hence, immigrants' rights have rarely been trampled by economically motivated immigration policies. Fourth, arriving in a host country with citizenship rights seems to be no more advantageous than arriving without them. Immigrants with citizenship rights are slow to employ this resource in politically effective ways, and immigrants without citizenship have been more effective in claiming rights than many observers had expected. Finally, to have permanent immigrant status rather than a temporary work permit has an indeterminant impact on the economic status of immigrants in the host country.

But not all groups currently labeled "immigrant" actually began as such; thus, some of their members' experiences have not been shaped by immigration policies. The first generation of Latinos in the United States, for example, became subjects of the United States government when portions of Mexico were conquered. Safran argues that this history contributes to a sense of grievance among present-day Latinos who, relative to such "voluntary" immigrant groups as the Maghrebis in France, are otherwise generally well adjusted to life in their host country. The experience of Latinos in America suggests that although conquest may provide an undesirable entree into a foreign country, its distastefulness may be offset by its timing. Descendants of vanquished Latinos have had time to gain acceptance as Americans while defining a role in American culture and politics that preserves much of their unique ethnic identity. The Maghrebis, in contrast, do not yet enjoy the degree of acceptance that would allow them to play a role in French life comparable to that of Latinos in the United States.

Once immigrants have arrived in a host country, their experiences are further shaped by a variety of economic factors. Freeman, Heisler, and Safran all argue that the level of affluence in a host country will affect both the ease with which immigrants enter the economy and the degree to which the natives manifest hostile attitudes toward immigrants. They hypothesize that economic contraction puts immigrants at a disadvantage in competing for jobs and puts natives on the defensive with respect to protecting the share of the economic pie they expect to receive. Evidence of native hostility toward immigrants during hard times, however, is slim, at least in the British and West German examples. After examining public opinion survey data from the 1970s and 1980s, Hoskin and Fitzgerald conclude that neither economic hardship nor occupational threat is strongly linked to negative sentiment toward immigrants.

Labor market conditions, though, are influential. Although the majority of employed immigrants tend to occupy semiskilled and unskilled positions in the advanced industrial democracies, their distribution across occupational sectors varies. As Heisler points out, this variance can affect immigrants' susceptibility to unemployment. It can also have implications for the socioeconomic integration of the offspring of immigrants, should they remain in the host country. Furthermore, to the extent that union structure and employee representation in the workplace differ by sector, immigrants will find that their economic well-being and security vary accordingly.

Another important economic variable is the delivery of social services. In general, the host countries of Western Europe have been more generous than the United States in attending to immigrants' needs in the areas of housing, education, and health care. The difference is not so much a matter of relative neglect but rather of comprehensiveness in policy formulation. As Klass points out in the second section of this volume, the United States has failed to grant welfare benefits as part of universal citizenship rights and consequently the impoverished, many of whom are members of minority groups, have been stigmatized and isolated.

One other key influence on immigrant experience is the permeability of the host culture. If the evidence offered by Safran can be generalized beyond France and the United States, we can conclude that when host cultures are more permeable, immigrants will find it easier both to maintain their own culture and to secure acceptance in the dominant culture. Cultural permeability manifests itself in a variety of ways in the United States but not in France, primarily because of the unique traditions of American institutional pluralism. Consequently, Latinos, in comparison to Maghrebis, have enjoyed greater access to politics, less majority group hostility, and more support for the preservation of their specific ethnic identity, including language.

In summary, these four chapters suggest that the experiences of immigrants are more positive when host governments impose general rather than group-specific regulations on immigration, the host country is experiencing economic prosperity, immigrant groups have two or more generations of ancestors residing in the host country, and immigrants encounter a permeable host culture, find employment in secure sectors of the labor market, have adequate labor representation, and receive social welfare benefits as part of universal citizenship rights. Negative experiences are more likely when the host country has had previous problems with immigration, immigrants trace their "arrival" in a country to conquest by the host or enter a country under laissez-faire immigration policies, the host country fails to develop comprehensive social welfare policies that address immigrants' needs, or natives are hostile to immigrants. Finally, the experiences of immigrants seem not to be affected by the restrictiveness or motivation of the host country's immigration policies or by the immediate receipt of citizenship rights or permanent immigrant status.

All four chapters offer evidence that group interactions have intensified, often in conflictual ways, with the arrival of immigrants. Immigration generates many problems that contribute to ethnic and racial conflict in the advanced industrial democracies, not the least among them the severe disadvantages that immigrant groups experience as they settle in their host countries. The failure of any one political party in these countries wholeheartedly to champion the cause of immigrants has prevented ethnic conflict from being polarized along the traditional left-right political dichotomy. If Lijphart is correct about the diminished salience of ideological conflict in the advanced industrial democracies, the non-traditional splits over immigration issues may define new sources of political conflict. In addition, evidence that governments in these four countries have responded to the problems of immigration in sluggish and contradictory ways supports Richmond's view that the state is not always a benign arbiter of ethnic conflict and sometimes, perhaps inadvertently, perpetuates the disadvantages immigrant groups suffer. And, finally, these chapters offer considerable evidence on the prominent role of political and economic as well as national and international markets in sustaining, if not precipitating, conflict between immigrant and majority populations.

MINORITIES, POLITICS, AND THE STATE

The four chapters in the second section of this volume offer evidence that disadvantage is not unique to immigrant groups; many minority groups in the advanced industrial democracies share the disadvantages of an inferior socioeconomic position and inadequate political representation. In comparison to members of the majority group in a country, ethnic minorities generally complete fewer years of education, are disproportionately represented in unskilled or semiskilled occupations, and earn lower median incomes. Because reducing socioeconomic inequality between majority and minority groups and increasing the political representation of minorities may ease some of the intergroup friction in the advanced industrial societies, it is appropriate to ask what circumstances foster such improvements. Several chapters in this volume collectively suggest that some circumstances pertain to individual characteristics and others pertain to systemic characteristics.

Grove, for example, offers evidence that educational and occupational differentials between majority and minority groups in Canada, Israel, and the United States have declined over time; and that the reduction in occupational differentials is associated with improved levels of education among minorities. Groups that have experienced relatively slow occupational mobility--New Zealand Maoris and Mexican Americans--are characterized by relatively slow rates of educational advancement. Improved levels of education also fostered upward mobility in income levels, after a ten-year time lag.

Although the income gap between groups in each of the four countries in Grove's study has declined, the beneficiaries of the decline are not always representative members of the groups. Progress over the period from 1950 to 1980 tended to be due to the upward movement of middle- and upper-middle income segments of minority groups, evidence that suggests minorities fare better when they are already doing relatively well. Changes among the Maoris are the main exception to this pattern: lower- and middle-income Maoris made progress while the upper-income Maoris actually lost ground. For all minorities in these four countries, however, income gains were most pronounced during the period from 1950 to 1970. During the following decade, in the wake of contracting social reform, minority groups experienced limited improvements in income levels.

Of course, the ability of a group to move up the occupational hierarchy or to enjoy a higher level of income depends upon having access to the opportunities for education and employment that can facilitate socioeconomic advancement. This matter of access is at the heart of the equality of opportunity issue and suggests that individual endeavors to improve socioeconomic status may be limited by social, economic, or political barriers. What sorts of systemic arrangements allow the members of minority groups to avail themselves of educational or occupational opportunities or, once having taken advantage of such opportunities, to assure themselves the means of avoiding a life of economic hardship?

Klass argues that the optimal means of achieving racial equality is through the promotion of universal citizenship rights that include not only property rights and political rights but also social welfare rights. A universalist policy agenda has integrative effects that transcend class, ethnic, and religious cleavages, eliminate the stigma of welfare, and reduce the social isolation of the impoverished. The industrialized democracies of Western Europe have already evolved into mature welfare states that provide some degree of economic security as an entitlement of citizenship. Although the United States government has also assumed the burden of insuring minimum levels of economic security for its citizens, it does so by targeting clientele groups rather than by enhancing citizenship rights. For example, the affirmative action policies developed in the United States over the last quarter century have contributed to equality by redistributing the opportunities for education and employment that ethnic minorities and females had found scarce. Nevertheless, by focusing on protected groups rather than universal rights, affirmative action policies have perpetuated minority-group stereotypes and fostered some of the majority-group backlash that fuels group conflict.

Another way to improve the welfare of minority groups is to elect politicians who will defend the interests of those groups. Although representatives from the majority group can act favorably on minority group members' interests, electing minorities to public office serves a powerful symbolic function in addition to the (assumed) practical function of promoting policies that advance ethnic and racial minority causes. As Studlar and Welch note, "The quantity and quality of minority group political representation is one test of how well racially or ethnically integrated an advanced industrial society is" (p. 143). Rather than ask if electing minorities to office effectively serves their groups' interests, research in this area typically focuses on the conditions that facilitate the election of minority representatives.

For example, in their study of city council elections in approximately 300 Standard Metropolitan Statistical Area (SMSA) central cities in the United

States, McDonald and Engstrom found that both Black and Hispanic candidates were more likely to be excluded from council seats in at-large electoral systems. Because of racially polarized voting and residential segregation, district electoral systems provide better representation for minorities in the United States.

In a rather different context, Studlar and Welch argue that the electoral system for the London Borough Council, a multimember system that allows for intraparty ticket balancing, enhances the electoral prospects of non-white candidates. Their data show that non-white candidates win as often as white candidates and sometimes more often. Unlike their American counterparts, the non-white candidates in Britain are helped by their partisan ties as well as by the electoral system. Running under the Labour party banner, in particular, confers an important advantage on non-white candidates. The Labour party runs well in non-white districts and actively brings non-white candidates into the electoral arena, but even more impressive is the "tenacity with which electors stick to their chosen party, irrespective of the personal characteristics of the candidates or voters" (p. 155). The partisan loyalty of British voters contrasts sharply with the tendency of white Americans to abandon their party when it nominates Black candidates to run under its banner. The only evidence that personal racial characteristics matter in London borough elections is that Asian candidates, whose names are distinguishable from whites' names in ways that Afro-Caribbeans' names generally are not, were somewhat less successful than Black candidates at the polls.

To summarize, these four chapters suggest that a combination of systemic and personal changes help alleviate the social, political, and economic disadvantages that minority groups face. District electoral systems and multimember electoral systems that allow for intraparty ticket balancing have facilitated the election of minority candidates in Britain and the United States. Electing minority candidates to office not only serves the symbolic function of visibly improving the representation of disadvantaged groups, which may decrease their feeling of political alienation and increase their awareness of government; it also enhances the likelihood that governments will enact policies that advance the interests of minorities. Some of these policies, such as those that provide food or medical assistance programs, aim directly at improving the welfare of disadvantaged groups; others aim at creating conditions that will make it easier for minorities to help themselves. Public education programs, affirmative action mandates, and vocational training, for example, provide members of disadvantaged groups with means to improve the skills that could help them secure better jobs, higher incomes, and overall improvements in socioeconomic status.

These chapters do not explicitly consider the connection between the disadvantages minorities face and the conflicts between majority and minority groups, but their analyses of disadvantage are all based on data from countries that have experienced enduring group conflict, and all support several of the hypotheses raised in the introduction to this volume. Grove's evidence for the persistence of socioeconomic inequality in Canada, Israel, New Zealand, and the United States is consistent with Lijphart's horizontalization hypothesis. His data also support our argument that disadvantages may intensify or reappear when efforts to alleviate them are not sustained, especially under conditions of economic uncertainty. Klass's analysis of American social welfare policy documents some of the negative effects that have accompanied government intervention in minority problems--for example, the generation of unrealistic expectations about what government can accomplish for minorities and the growth of resentment among majority group members who believe they are victims of reverse discrimination. These reactions often fuel group conflict, which is consistent with the hypotheses offered by both Lijphart and Richmond. Klass also provides evidence that targeting clientele groups for the receipt of welfare benefits, as American policy has tended to do, encourages these same groups to mobilize and participate in the policy process on behalf of their own specific, and often narrow, interests, thus perpetuating the clientelistic orientation of American social welfare policy. This phenomenon supports Lijphart's hypothesis about the role of the new wave of democratization in fostering group conflict and is consistent with Rothschild's argument that ethnic entrepreneurs perpetuate ethnic competition and conflict via the pressure-group activities they use to make claims on the state. Finally, one of the implications of the evidence presented by McDonald and Engstrom and Studlar and Welch is that in altering electoral systems to enhance the probability that ethnic minority candidates win public office, governments may inadvertently encourage the political involvement of previously non-participating minorities. Of course, we would not advocate their exclusion from the political process, but increased group mobilization is a characteristic of the new wave of democratization that Lijphart hypothesizes is a source of group conflict.

POLITICAL CONSCIOUSNESS, ORGANIZATION, AND PARTICIPATION

The first two sections of this volume describe the disadvantages that minorities face in various advanced industrial democracies and examine a number of the conditions that alleviate or exacerbate them. On the whole, the chapters in these sections assume that the state, through its capacity to formulate and enforce policies that serve groups' interests, has primary responsibility for improving the well being of minorities and, hence, muting group competition and conflict. The chapters in the third section refocus the analysis to consider how minority groups have attempted to overcome their disadvantages.

Minorities have a variety of options for furthering the interests of their groups. Shingles categorizes minorities' possible responses to their perceptions of group disadvantage as private (trying harder, cheating, lowering expectations, quitting) or political (changing the social, political, or economic structure). He argues that although the private options are the usual choice, the political options are more likely to be effective in improving the status of minority groups. Whether groups politicize their efforts to advance their interests depends on a variety of psychological, economic, and political factors.

In the realm of psychological factors, Shingles hypothesizes that the development of minority consciousness is an essential precondition to political action. Minority consciousness provides the psychological motivation for groups to politicize their discontent. No matter what specific form minority consciousness takes, the different varieties share a common set of psychological components. These include subjective identification with the minority group, positive affect toward the group, a belief that the group is systematically excluded from positions of power, and an explanation for the group's status that externalizes the blame for perceived deprivation. Minority consciousness provides a means for dissatisfied individuals to identify others like themselves, who might collectively provide the support and strength necessary for redressing the group's grievances. In addition, it absolves group members of individual responsibility for their less than satisfactory status and identifies aspects of the dominant culture that may have contributed to the group's deprivation. Finally, minority consciousness makes group members aware of the better life they could expect and indicates how they might achieve it.

Of course, motivation alone cannot improve the status of disadvantaged groups. Economic and political resources are necessary to combat the barriers to advancement and actualize the vision of a better life. Shingles acknowledges the necessity of resources for politicizing minority groups' responses to deprivation, but Ortiz and Rath and Saggar examine specific cases that document the role of economic and political resources in facilitating the progress of minority groups.

Federal budgetary cutbacks during the Reagan administrations, for example, seriously threatened the operations of major Latino organizations. Lacking internal funding sources or a membership base that could generate financial resources, organizations such as the League of United Latin American Citizens and the Mexican-American Legal Defense and Education Fund sought economic support from major corporations. These Latino organizations were quite successful. In exchange for advertising the philanthropy and good will of their corporate "partners," they received monetary contributions, increased employment opportunities for Latinos in both labor and management positions, and special consideration for contracts and services for minority firms.

Whether other minority groups could rely on a similar strategy for securing the economic resources necessary to support their organizational activity depends on two circumstances. One is that the groups have some experience and expertise in grant-getting activity. The other is that the groups be willing to tap into mainstream sources of support, a circumstance that will inevitably constrain the pursuit of anti-establishment goals and the use of confrontational tactics and reduce minority groups' capacity to promote radical change in the status quo. Working within the system, of course, raises questions about whether ethnic and racial minorities can best achieve equality by assimilating into the majority or holding out for success on their own terms.

Finally, minority groups require favorable political conditions. Access to the political arena is an important end in itself, but it also provides a means by which minorities can secure their social and economic goals. In their discussion of ethnicity in Britain and the Netherlands Rath and Saggar describe the importance of the government in fostering the political participation of ethnic groups. Despite historical and demographic differences, ethnic organization in both countries has been facilitated by government support--primarily local government in Britain, and both local and central governments in Holland. Linkage to other organizations has also played a role in fostering ethnic organizations. In particular, the Community Relations Councils in Britain and various advisory councils in the Netherlands have served as government-initiated means to mobilize ethnic groups. These arrangements were not created for solely altruistic reasons on the part of the respective governments; nor have they operated without friction. Initially, mobilizing ethnic groups in both countries was a means to depoliticize the role of ethnicity and race in politics and defuse potentially threatening forms of minority group participation. Often natives played a larger role in promoting the welfare of immigrants than did the immigrants themselves. More recently, however, minorities have moved, if not to center stage, at least to the wings of power and have not only gained control of the political fate of their organizations but also managed to use their organizations to gain political office. This recent, more prominent, political role of ethnic organizations has been fostered by left-of-center political parties in Britain and Holland.

The three case studies described by Ortiz and Rath and Saggar collectively suggest that considerable gains can be achieved if minority groups are willing to work through established public and private channels. One consequence, of course, is that minority groups lose the ability unilaterally to define and pursue their agenda, but on the other hand, economic and political partnerships may allow these groups to obtain substantial benefits for their members, benefits that would otherwise remain beyond their grasp.

In short, minorities can take initiatives to further the interests of their groups. Whether they actually do so depends on the presence of psychological, economic, and political conditions that facilitate such activity. According to Shingles, the psychological motivation for politicizing the grievances of minorities derives from minority consciousness, a constellation of empowering attitudes about what a group is entitled to and can hope to accomplish. Economic resources might come from government funds, as Rath and Saggar describe in their survey of ethnic organizations in Britain and the Netherlands, from the group members themselves, or from private sources, such as the corporations that provided grants and non-monetary support to American Latino organizations. Finally, minority groups need an entree to the political arena. Governments may provide routinized access before groups ever need to clamor for it, but having access and motivating group members to use it are two different matters. Rank-and-file minorities may need to be "socialized" into mainstream politics--a task that is probably best handled by the politically savvy members of the groups.

These three discussions of conditions that facilitate group initiative provide support for several hypotheses about ethnic conflict in the advanced industrial democracies. In particular, they are consistent with Rothschild's argument about the crucial role of ethnic entrepreneurs and with Lijphart's hypotheses about the new wave of democratization and the demonstration effect of ethnic demands. Ethnic entrepreneurs lead groups into the political arena to make group-specific demands on the state. A positive response from the state reinforces the solidarity of a minority group and encourages further use of group pressure tactics to advance the group's interests. The successful example of one group may motivate others to make their own demands, with the eventual result being the expansion of competition and conflict among ethnic groups.

CONFLICT RESOLUTION AND PUBLIC POLICY

Solutions to ethnic conflict inevitably raise questions about equality, rights, and the relationships among individuals, groups, and the state. The chapters in the final section of this volume consider these questions as they pertain to three different groups--Basques in Spain, francophones in Canada, and Hispanics in the United States. The critical problem these minorities face is achieving equality without sacrificing group identity. Efforts to do so have fueled some of the more virulent contemporary political disputes in the advanced industrial democracies.

Among the examples considered in this volume, territorial devolution stands as the most far-reaching attempt to resolve ethnic disputes. By granting specific powers and resources to territorially defined entities, central governments can provide ethnic groups with a measure of self-rule in their homeland. There are, however, inherent limitations to the policy that undermine its utility as an instrument of conflict resolution. Clark argues that territorial devolution might be an appropriate strategy if, at a minimum, two conditions prevail: the ethnic minority is homogeneous in its homeland, and mutual trust unites the ethnic minority and the central state elite. When only one of these conditions is present, the probability that the strategy will successfully resolve ethnic conflict is quite slim. The catch, however, is that these conditions may be mutually contradictory. A truly homogeneous ethnic community may appear threatening to a central state that fears eventual attempts at separation, while a marginally homogeneous ethnic community may, by enacting discriminatory policies, pose a threat to the rights and interests of the region's non-ethnic population. Either situation is likely to cause the central state to resist conferring true autonomy.

Even the "right" degree of homogeneity seems not to guarantee the trust necessary for an autonomous arrangement to succeed. In situations where autonomy has been granted, there has been an almost inevitable tendency for the two parties to the arrangement to view it in opposite terms. For the minority, autonomy is the first step toward separation; for the state, autonomy is a means to delay that outcome. At best, territorial devolution seems an unstable compromise. At worst, in a situation such as that of the Basques, where neither homogeneity nor trust prevails, territorial devolution will simply fail as a policy to resolve ethnic conflict.

One of the several issues at the foundation of the disputes over Basque autonomy is the matter of residual sovereignty as it pertains to language policy. Although part of a larger package of political problems unique to Spain, attempts to develop a language policy for the Basque region parallel efforts to achieve equality for linguistic minorities in Canada and the United States. Laponce and Schmidt present two different perspectives on this issue.

For Laponce the question is how to protect a linguistic minority, and the solution is to confer group rights and impose territorial unilingualism. These measures would retard the assimilation process through which minority languages tend to disappear. In light of the geographic and demographic characteristics of the Canadian francophone population, Laponce concludes that the Swiss solution of a multilingual central government and unilingual regional governments would be the simplest and most effective means of insuring the survival of the French language. The virtue of rigid linguistic frontiers is their permanence, a feature that removes them from periodic partisan dispute; but, of course, establishing such borders is itself so controversial as to render the Swiss solution politically infeasible in Canada.

Of the two North American cases, the Canadian example is more amenable to the sort of solution Laponce proposes. Where the United States has no official language or language policy, the Canadian government has constitutionally recognized both English and French as legitimate political languages. The linguistic geography of Canada is such that francophones are territorially concentrated. And during the 1970s, the Quebec National Assembly enacted a series of policies that pushed Quebec toward unilingualism. Subsequent constitutional developments halted the move to make French the dominant language of Quebec, but the political barriers to territorial unilingualism are perhaps more significant than the legal ones. First, Quebec anglophones wield considerable electoral influence both provincially and nationally. Second, Quebec francophones, along with the remainder of the

Canadian population, are willing to support the retention of English-speaking institutions in Quebec. When the very group for whom protection is sought takes a position that could threaten the survival of its language, the political folly of the Swiss solution is indisputable.

The crux of the problem is that the Swiss solution restricts individual rights, and classical liberalism advocates the rights of the individual against groups, not the rights of groups against individuals. Giving individuals the right to speak a language, however, implies the right to be understood, and this right assumes a community in which to speak. Hence, the Swiss solution protects a community in order to protect an individual.

Schmidt further elaborates on the problem of using classical liberalism to evaluate linguistic privileges. In brief, his argument is that policies based on individualistic premises will be ineffective in promoting equality between two groups qua groups. Language-minority groups in subordinate positions are prevented by the social context from benefitting from individualistic policies, no matter how well intended they may be.

In the United States, protection of a language minority invokes debate about the merits of bilingualism, not the possibility of preserving a minority language; yet the fundamental issue is the same as in the Canadian and Spanish examples: how to achieve equality for linguistic and cultural minorities. Schmidt suggests three possible solutions to the problem. The liberal assimilationist answer is that only one culture and language can exist effectively in a nation-state; hence, language policy should assist linguistic minorities in acquiring the cultural traits that will allow them to take full advantage of opportunities to compete in the dominant culture. Equality in the liberal assimilationist view is equality of opportunity and leads to integration into the dominant culture. The corporate egalitarian answer is to make the majority and the minority language groups equal in their capacities for self-determination. This solution requires that groups be given legal standing vis-a-vis the state, which cannot be accomplished without assigning individuals to group membership--an act that directly conflicts with liberalism. The liberal pluralist answer is that a society may tolerate a variety of ethnic and cultural groups without destroying the unity of the polity. Equality in the liberal pluralist view is the individual's equal right to maintain his or her ethnic or cultural distinctiveness--and participate in the sort of state-supported programs that foster such diversity--without being deprived of equal membership in the polity.

Thus, one source of ethnic conflict is disagreement over how best to achieve equality between minorities and majorities. The chapters in the final section of this volume forward several possible solutions: assimilation, pluralism, and self-determination represent three distinct approaches, with territorial devolution and territorial unilingualism providing two different means of self-determination. The failure of any of the three countries--Canada, Spain, or the United States--to adopt an acceptable solution arises as much from the lack of consensus within each minority and majority group as from the incompatible goals that minorities and majorities pursue. In most instances minority group members prefer to be treated as the equal of majority group members without becoming just like them, but how to achieve legal equality and maintain cultural diversity is not obvious, especially when cultural differences have provided the basis for the majority's discriminatory behavior.

That conflicts arise when the state tries to insure that different groups receive the same rights is consistent with Lijphart's hypotheses about the politicization of ethnic and racial identities. In particular, initial success in gaining the state's recognition of some group rights, even if they are not defined as such, tends to reinforce group solidarity and encourage mobilization within the political arena. The principle of self-determination provides a legal rationale for making further group-specific claims, including ones that may challenge--or be perceived as challenging--the authority of the state and the dominant position of the majority.

FURTHER ISSUES

As the chapters in this volume clearly demonstrate, multiple factors explain the persistence of group conflict in the advanced industrial democracies. The volatility of the international political economy, the continuation of socioeconomic disparities between minorities and majorities, ineffective attempts by governments to alleviate the inequalities minority groups suffer, minorities' own efforts to secure improvements in their status, and resistance of majority populations to the advancement of minorities all contribute to ethnic and racial friction.

Although no single study comparatively examines minority populations in every advanced industrial democracy, collectively these studies suggest that the commonalities of experience transcend the unique. Until very recently policymakers and analysts stressed the differences between long-established ethnoregional or ethnoterritorial minorities and new immigrant minorities. Apart from the timing of their appearance in various advanced industrial societies, the chief distinction between old and new minorities was political: immigrants lacked full citizenship and permanent residence status. The eradication of this distinction for many immigrant workers and their families undermines the rationale for making analytic distinctions between minority groups on the basis of their origins. Furthermore, the chapters by Safran, Grove, Klass, Shingles, and Clark indicate that minority groups with long-standing claims to residency and citizenship suffer from many of the same socioeconomic disadvantages that face more recent minorities. In like manner, the new and old minorities face the prejudice of various majority groups. These similar adverse circumstances indicate that future research on ethnic and racial conflict in the advanced industrial democracies should focus on the common difficulties of the minority experience and their implications for exacerbating group conflict.

Toward that end we offer several proposals for future research on the politics of conflict in the advanced industrial societies. One set of suggestions converges on the idea that ethnic and racial conflict is dynamic. As minorities settle into their respective societies, their needs and demands change. In order to understand how states and majorities respond to these changes, future studies should avoid the static analysis of policies aimed at alleviating the problems of minorities and instead examine the evolution of policy and its effectiveness under changing circumstances. Comparative analysis should reveal the extent to which the advanced industrial democracies experience similar patterns of demands and responses at specific stages in the evolution of majority-minority relations. Minorities, majorities, and states adjust to each other over time. They may do so intentionally or inadvertently, voluntarily or reluctantly; but in any case these adjustments never seem to be definitive. To expect ultimate resolutions to group conflict and to use this expectation as the standard for evaluating actual group behaviors and state policies obscures the perpetually adaptive nature of these political interactions.

Another line of research could examine the implications of the reality that the advanced industrial societies are organized by and oriented toward markets--markets that are political as well as economic, and international as well as domestic. These markets not only determine the allocation of political and socioeconomic outcomes but also mediate the conflicts of interest that arise among groups seeking to improve or maintain their socioeconomic or political status. Such market processes have contradictory outcomes: groups may achieve gains or suffer losses, and groups in competition may be rewarded or punished. Prosperity has not guaranteed reductions in relative socioeconomic disadvantage and group conflict, but the persistence or reappearance of disadvantage and conflict during periods of economic decline or uncertainty is all too well known. In trying to understand the failure of markets to eradicate group conflict, we suggest that scholars consider the following issues.

One matter to consider is the potential link between the group-specific demands of various minorities and the more general concerns with which polities must deal. Ethnic and racial groups have become increasingly sophisticated in developing appeals designed to prompt a response from the state that will satisfy their particularistic interests. Modern states, in turn, have found that these groups provide serviceable units for allocating benefits and managing the tensions that spring from misallocations. We think such appeals and responses raise important questions about more general goals that democratic polities typically pursue, among them the development of norms of justice and equality and the removal of barriers to full participation in social, political, and economic life. Do recent group appeals and state responses suggest that the nature of representation is narrowly defined in terms of singular groups' interests? Are particular minority groups seeking parity for their members alone? Can one group promote just, equitable outcomes for others? Does responding to particular groups help a polity reconsider the issues and goals inherent in its original claims to democratic government? Collectively, these questions should compel us to think about the positive and negative effects of politicized ethnicity on the realization of the broad objectives that advanced industrial democracies typically articulate.

A related, though somewhat narrower, issue is the politics of coalitions. One group might be able to achieve more of its goals if it were to join forces with another group seeking the same ends. When is it propitious for groups to work together in pursuing their interests? Which conditions support, and which ones constrain, the development of coalitions? Under what circumstances are intergroup relations likely to be cooperative rather than conflictual? One important variable may be groups' perceptions about the availability of desired "goods." If one group's benefits appear to come at another group's expense, cooperation to secure the benefits is unlikely. A competitive situation of this sort may have emerged as a consequence of the migration of ethnic and racial minorities to industrial democracies during the postwar period. Future research could address the question: Were long-standing issues and/or demands pertaining to traditional minorities pushed off the political agenda or assigned a lower priority as new ethnic and racial issues became salient? Answers would shed light on the issue of whether traditional and new minority groups are indirectly or directly competing for the same public goods or for access to the decision-making agencies of the state.

Two other variables central to the politics of coalitions are the number of politically relevant groups and the relative size of these groups. When competition for socioeconomic or political goods occurs between the dominant majority group and two or more subordinate minority groups, coalitions among minorities may develop as a means to increase the minorities' share of benefits relative to the benefits the majority enjoys. But if a minority group becomes a population majority, or even a plurality, in a particular political jurisdiction, it may begin to function as a majority group vis-a-vis the smaller minorities. In this situation the dominant (larger) minority would probably be less willing to cooperate with the smaller minorities. The subordinate minorities, in turn, would be more likely to cooperate not only with each other but also with the dominant majority group. Finally, coalition building is no doubt affected by responses from the state. How states reconcile multiple group interests may provide cues to groups about the potential rewards or penalties for coordinated petitions and the likelihood that such actions will succeed.

Questions about the effects of market processes on the allocation of socioeconomic and political benefits will also need to take into account contemporary developments that have put new wrinkles on some of the enduring issues addressed by the chapters in this volume. These developments reinforce our suggestion that analyses of group conflict should be more dynamically oriented.

First, demographic trends are rapidly altering the relative sizes of the groups that compose some of the advanced industrial democracies, at least in subnational political jurisdictions. In the United States, for example, differential birthrates, age distributions, and migration patterns for African American, Hispanic, and Asian minorities and the white Anglo majority are contributing to shifts in the majority-minority population balance. Ethnic minorities have become population majorities in some urban areas of the country, and current demographic projections indicate that within two or three generations such states as California, New York, and Texas will experience shifts in the balance of their populations that will transform some population minorities into pluralities. These demographic changes have important implications. The ability of various minority groups to coordinate their demands on the state will acquire increasing significance as the collective numeric strength of minorities grows, and differential increases in the sizes of minority groups will, as suggested above, affect the likelihood of coalition formation among these groups. In addition, policy issues relevant to minority groups' interests are likely to acquire increasing significance when minority populations expand in the very jurisdictions that legislate on such issues. Bilingual education in the United States is one such example.

Second, recent events in Eastern Europe and the former Soviet Union have created sociopolitical "laboratories" where fresh approaches to the resolution of group conflicts may be tried. As countries formerly ruled by communist regimes struggle to define democratic forms of governance, they are faced with the need to reconcile multiple group interests and conflicts. These problems could prove overwhelming for nascent democracies, but on a more optimistic note, they also provide opportunities for addressing the fundamental issues of democracy in creative and comprehensive ways. Two questions arise: Do the "mature" advanced industrial democracies whose experiences we have considered in this volume have viable models of group politics to offer to the republics of the former Soviet Union and the countries of Eastern Europe? Can these older democracies learn lessons from the newer ones? These recent developments seem to offer unique opportunities for new cross-cultural research on the dynamics of group conflict in the advanced industrial democracies.

Notes

CHAPTER 1

1. My use of the term departs from the meaning normally given it by those writing about international regimes, where more emphasis is given to norms that may underpin an emerging institutional arrangement. Here, I give institutional arrangements precedence.

2. Still, Cross concludes that the state achieved most of its objectives in this period: "State intervention . . . comprised a critical factor in the formation of a foreign labor system . . . It served and mediated conflicting French interests. It provided a step toward a corporatist or consensus solution to an outstanding social problem" (1983).

3. New race relations legislation was adopted in 1976 as well. See Layton-Henry (1984, 137-138).

4. One has to admit that the most intense campaigns of anti-immigrant agitation occurred after 1965. But the larger point is, I submit, that Enoch Powell's career as a nativist politician was short-lived and his loud complaints about the unending hordes invading the island rang less and less credible as time passed and the government squeezed entries more and more. Whether this was a craven collapse of the government in the face of a demagogue or a prudent response to a crisis I leave to the reader. See Schoen (1977); Messina (1985; 1989b); Studlar (1980); and Freeman (1979).

CHAPTER 2

1. Among European countries France has periodically encouraged immigration for demographic reasons. See, for example, Spengler (1938) and Dignan (1981).

2. These distinctions are never clear cut and are often subject to considerable political interpretation.

3. Although the so-called brain drain involves relatively few immigrants, the migration of highly skilled and professional workers has had significant consequences for the less developed countries in particular. See Portes (1976).

4. While structural theories have noted the "temporary but permanent" aspect of European migration, they have generally seen it in terms of host society policies and interpreted it as an additional indicator of exploitation and low labor market position.

5. For more detailed discussions of the West German case, see Rist (1978); Heckmann (1981); Castles and Kosack (1973); Castles (1984).

6. For a discussion of the methodology, see Merhländer et al. (1981), pp.8-21.

7. There was a slight decline in the total from 4,453,300 in 1980 to 4,365,900 in 1985.

8. Although the West German government also concluded recruitment agreements with Morocco and Tunisia, the number of Moroccans and Tunisians was too small to be socially significant.

9. Migrants arriving after 1973 came only under the auspices of "family reunion."

10. Excepting perhaps Italians who, as members of the European Community, faced no restrictions on their freedom of movement.

11. These figures reflect some changes since the previous survey in 1972, when 82 percent were in manufacturing and 2 percent in extraction.

12. These figures also indicate an overall improvement in the distribution of skills between 1980 and the previous survey in 1972.

13. As might be expected, segregation varied with length of stay. Those arriving after 1969 were more likely to live in segregated housing.

14. Yugoslavs presented a particularly interesting case. First, the Yugoslav government was particularly insistent that emigration was a strictly temporary phenomenon and set up large and effective networks of organizations in Germany. Second, Yugoslav immigrants were ethnically diverse. This diversity may account for some of the contradictions, as some ethnic groups (e.g., Slovenians) may be more inclined to adapt. Unfortunately, the 1980 data are not broken down by ethnicity and origin.

15. Turks not only expressed the lowest intent to return, they were also the nationality least likely to do so. See OECD (1986).

CHAPTER 3

1. The German study was conducted by Professors M. Reiner Lepsius of the University at Heidelberg, Walter Muller of the University at Mannheim,

Franz Urban Pappi of the University at Kiel, Erwin K. Scheuch of the University at Cologne, and Rolf Ziegler of the University at Munich. Cooperating institutions were the Zentrum für Methoden und Analysen and the Zentralarchiv. The combined dataset was made available through the Inter-University Consortium for Political and Social Research.

2. The British study was conducted through the Surrey Centre for Political Research, and also distributed through the ICPSR.

CHAPTER 4

1. In France, the problems of native-born and immigrant Maghrebis are usually discussed together. On the situation in the United States, see Browning and De la Garza (1986).

2. For example, Tahar Ben-Jalloun, a Tunisian-born writer whose books, written in French, deal primarily with the Maghrebi experience and one of whose novels won for him the *Prix Goncourt*.

3. See, for example, such sociological studies as Annie Krieger-Krynicki (1985); the writings of Bruno Étienne, Rémy Leveau, and Catherine Wihtol de Wenden; and the best-selling novel by Mehdi Charef (1983).

4. These figures are taken from a *Figaro* poll of November 22-28, 1985 and reported in *SOFRES* (1987).

5. For example, Bernard Stasi (1984) and Didier Bariani (1985). On the attitudes of different parties, see William Safran (1989a).

6. See the reviews of Allan Bloom's *The Closing of the American Mind* (1987) (in French translation) in *Figaro*, March 24, 1987.

7. On the *folklorisation and infériorisation* of ethnic minority cultures, see Henry-Lorcerie (1983), pp. 267ff. and 287.

CHAPTER 5

1. There are relevant studies in the United States where there is a vigorous debate between Farley (1984), Reich (1981), and others concerning the Marxist and neoclassical predictions about racial inequalities and who gains from them.

2. Variants on this theory show that dominant groups rationally discriminate against disfavored groups in order to maximize their own economic interests, and therefore, both dominant-group employers and workers would suffer from a reduction in ethnic inequalities (Glenn 1966).

3. The formula for the Grove-Hannum measure (Grove and Hannum 1986) is as follows:

$$\text{Intergroup Inequality (I)} = \Sigma\{(P_i - Q_i) \times M_i\}$$

Crossover (c) = $1/2\ \{\Sigma|P_i\text{-}Q_i|xM_i\text{-}|\Sigma(P_i\text{-}Q_i)xMi|\}/\Sigma|P_i\text{-}Q_i|xM_i$

Where

i = Category of a ranked income distribution

P_i = Cumulative proportion through category of the first group

Q_i = Cumulative proportion through category of the second group

M_i = Midpoint of category

Note that crossover (c) is composed of two pieces, the first of which, $D=\Sigma|P_i\text{-}Q_i|xM_i$ is a distance-type measure (it detects any discrepancies between two distributions) and the second of which, $I=\Sigma(P_i\text{-}Q_i)xM_i$, is a ratio of mean incomes measure. If the two distributional functions do not crossover (overlap) then either $P \le Q$ for all or $Q \le P$ for all i and so $D = 1$ and $C = 0$. Thus when the two distribution functions do not crossover the scores of distance and inequality are equivalent. The C can be interpreted as a descriptive statistic that locates the crossover and determines what portion of the overall difference between two income distribution functions is due to crossover.

4. I will use the change in I scores to measure the magnitude and direction of gain/loss by a particular group, and this can be expressed in the following way: $\Delta I_t = I_t - I_{t\text{-}1}$.

5. Lieberson's net difference (ND) is defined by the following formula:
$$ND = (\Sigma D_i CN_i - \Sigma N_i CD_i)$$

Where

D_i = the proportion of the dominant group in educational level i,

N_i = the proportion of the non-dominant groups in educational level i,

CD_i = the cumulated proportion of the dominant group in education ranked below educational level i,

CN_i = the cumulated proportion of the non-dominant group in education ranked below educational level i.

6. Gibbs's absolute standardized measure of differentiation (ASMD) is defined by the following formula:
$$ASMD = \frac{|Xc - Yc|}{2}\ (100)$$

Where

Xc is the standardized proportion of all members of the dominant group in the occupation,

Yc is the standardized proportion of all members of the non-dominant group in the occupation.

7. In order to make the percentage of people in the percentiles the same, we will divide the change in I scores by the percentile: average $\Delta I = \Delta I_t$ for each income category/percentile.

8. The census income data only allow us to go up to 1980. In the United States and Canada there are yearly surveys taken on family and household incomes, which will give us some idea about 1980 trends. Unfortunately, in Canada the data are only collected on French- and English-speaking Canadians,

and in the United States they are only collected on Black, white and Hispanic groups. The Israeli data are the same as in the previous analysis, only extended to 1982. The Canadian data are taken from Statistics Canada, Income Distribution by Size in Canada, 1969, 1977-84, Ottawa. The American data are taken from Department of Commerce, Money Income of Households, Families and Persons in the U.S., 1984, Consumer Income, P-60-151, p. 9.

CHAPTER 6

1. For a summary of the anti-pluralist minority faction literature see McFarland (1983). A recent addition to the "integration" social welfare literature is Schorr (1986).

2. The pension program provided an effective counterargument to populist and agrarian-socialist complaints about the high tariffs and the budget surplus that the tariffs created. When the commander of the Grand Army was appointed pension commissioner in 1890, he exclaimed, "God help the surplus" (Schlesinger 1983, 369). The pensioners were disproportionately farmers. Dearing (1952) offers an excellent account of the politics of the pension program.

3. See Piven and Cloward (1982, 86-96), Friedland, Piven, and Alford (1977, 447-471), Katznelson (1981), and Klass (1985).

4. Tufte (1978) notes that the increased Social Security benefits went into effect just before the 1972 election; to pay for the increased benefits the Social Security payroll tax was increased in January.

5. Among them are Moynihan's *The Politics of a Guaranteed Income* (1973), Burke and Burke's *Nixon's Good Deed* (1974), Lynn and Whitman's *The President as Policymaker* (1981), Aaron's *Why Is Welfare So Hard to Reform?* (1973), and Rochefort's *American Social Welfare Policy* (1986, 99-130).

6. Rainwater and Yancey (1967) provide an excellent account of the events and debate surrounding the Moynihan report. Their book also contains a reprint of the report and reprints of many of the contemporary commentaries on the report.

7. Robert Staples (1978) summarizes the four stages of evolutionary development in the field of Black family research: (a) the early "poverty-acculturation" period, including research by DuBois and E. Franklin Frazier, (b) the "pathological type of research generated by Moynihan's view of the Black family," (c) the reactive period (1966-1971) where "Blacks and whites" refuted Moynihan, and (d) the "Black nationalist family research" period that "not only considered Black families as non-pathological but began to delineate their strengths as well." Other examples of the new perspective on the Black family include Billingsley (1968), Scanzoni (1971), and English (1974).

8. The most bitter attacks on the Nixon reforms focused on the work registration requirements and work training proposals (e.g., Levi 1970). Moynihan (1973) and Burke and Burke (1974) devote a substantial portion of their books to sorting out the rhetoric and reality of this debate.   Changing attitudes toward work-fare programs and, since the Moyer's CBS documentary on the Black family, changing attitudes about single-parent families were largely responsible for the most recent Moynihan-sponsored welfare reform.

CHAPTER 8

1. We shall use the terms "race," "ethnicity," and "minority" in the manner followed by Stone (1985). Thus, even if we speak of British "race relations" as interactions based on the social relevance of skin color, we recognize that "ethnicity" (self-defined groups based on common culture) is an important part of the situation too.   Hence we separate Asians and Afro-Caribbeans in the analysis.   "Minority" refers to group power, not necessarily size.

2. In recognition of the fact that South Asian origin and descended people are not termed Blacks in the United States, we shall use the term "non-whites" to designate both Asians and Afro-Caribbeans in the United Kingdom. Even the U.S. edition of *Time* had a feature on the non-white candidates for the House of Commons in 1987. See "Our Time Has Come" (*Time* 1987).

3. At least three of the four non-white MPs in Britain served as local councillors.

4. See McAllister and Studlar (1984) and Fitzgerald (1987), for empirical examinations of the political distinctions of different ethnic groups usually lumped together under the general category of "Blacks" or "non-whites" in Britain.

5. The effect upon another "minority" (in social representation terms), women, is somewhat different. See Darcy, Welch, and Clark 1987, ch. 8.

6. Some small error creeps in here because a candidate could have won a by-election between 1982 and 1986 and thus would be an incumbent, but not coded as such in our data.

7. Assistance was rendered by Sreemoti Mukerjee-Roy, a graduate student at the University of Nebraska, in identifying the gender of Asian names.

8. There has never been a serious attempt to identify ethnicity or race in the British census. In fact, it has been the subject of much debate whether such a question should be asked, and if so, in what form. The closest question in the 1981 census identified the birthplace of individuals born outside the United Kingdom. Such a question obviously undercounts non-whites to the extent that it fails to identify the ever-growing adult second-generation non-white population in Britain. On the other hand, the survey overcounts non-whites to the extent

it counts whites born in the New Commonwealth as non-whites. Overall, however, the total number of non-whites is greater than the census reveals. We assume that a more precise ethnic count of non-whites and non-white voters by constituency would be highly correlated with the pattern based on New Commonwealth households, but the overall numbers of non-whites would be larger. How much larger is an open question. The data used here are the best that are available at present. For an estimate of the total 1987 non-white population in the London area see Anwar (1986, 164-167).

Although census data on persons born in the New Commonwealth can be categorized by the individual's place of birth, utilizing such a categorization would result in very small numbers for groups in many constituencies because of the incomplete information on British-born non-whites. Moreover, disaggregating the data introduces even more imprecision. For example, if we categorized those born in East Africa as Black, we would be overcounting Blacks and undercounting Asians, since many Asians came from East African nations such as Uganda and Kenya (McAllister and Studlar 1984). In this, as in so many other aspects of ethnic population measurement in Britain, there is much work to be done.

9. The lack of ward-level data inhibits our generalizations. However, relatively few constituencies have over 25 percent nonwhite population as the census measures it. Even taking into account second- and third-generation non-whites not counted in the census, it seems that most of these parliamentary constituencies contain majorities of whites. However, given ethnic segregation within the constituencies, a few of the wards might contain non-white majorities.

10. Both of these differences are statistically significant using a X^2 test. The number of such two-seat races was 72, the number of three-seat races 123.

11. The Jackson campaigns in 1984 and 1988 illustrate this, too. In 1988, for example, Jackson apparently received over 90 percent of the Black vote and about 15-20 percent of the white.

12. The now defunct Greater London Council, the higher-level unit, had only one non-white among 92 members elected in 1981. LeLohe (1984) reports that Leiceister in the East Midlands has about the same percentage of non-white councillors as the population percentage (20 percent), almost all Asian descended refugees from East Africa (Kenya and Uganda).

13. Of course, some Black mayors have been elected in majority white cities, several Blacks have been elected to minor statewide offices (and one to the U.S. Senate), and many Black members of city councils are elected in at-large elections by a majority white electorate. Nonetheless, the pattern is evident overall. For example, almost all Black members of Congress are elected from majority Black districts.

CHAPTER 9

1. Political minorities are objectively deprived across a broad range of values. Most prominent is their political powerlessness: their relative absence from positions of authority and control in major institutions. The biopolitical minorities discussed here have also been deprived of related values that collectively define social status (Robinson and Kelley 1979). These include education, wealth, social acceptance, and prestige. Groups deprived of one set of values are often deprived of others. The possession of any one is instrumental to the obtainment of others (Lasswell and Kaplan 1950). In this sense, all forms of value obtainment are sources of power. Therefore, political powerlessness cannot be understood separately from other forms of deprivation. Despite vast individual variations in native ability, members of biopolitical minorities traditionally have lacked equal opportunities to develop individual competencies and exercise them in responsible positions. Having little influence over the distribution of values in society has been the paramount cause of the scope of their deprivation.

2. This chapter is based on a book-length comparison of female, Black, Mexican and Native Americans, entitled *The Politics of Race and Gender: Parallels in the Political Thought and Action of Female, African, Mexican, and Native-Americans*. The specific forms of group consciousness and the political tactics found within each group are described in the larger work. The purpose here is to provide the theoretical framework.

3. Because Merton's labels for the five categories are somewhat misleading, I have provided my own. Our approaches also differ. First, he does not indicate why subjectively deprived persons might choose one mode of adaptation over another. Second, his primary concern is to explain "aberrant behavior" (1968, 188). He treats the last four modes of adaptation as forms of social deviancy. I have no argument with this portrayal of responses II, III and IV. However, it is a gross characterization of response V. Merton recognizes only the most extreme type of political behavior, "rebellion," which he defines as the potentially violent, total rejection of all conventional goals and means.

4. Members of the majority also may manifest group consciousness. *Majority group consciousness* is the perception of one's group as the legitimate political majority. It rationalizes and defends the status quo.

5. *Group consciousness* is the totality of salient beliefs an individual has about a group with which he or she identifies. I prefer this definition to the more conventional approach based on Marx's conception of working-class consciousness. Marx defines class consciousness as the recognition of an inevitable conflict between social classes that is rooted in the institution of private property. Working-class consciousness is the perception of a common fate for those who do not own the means of production: their subordination and exploitation by the capitalist, property-owning class. It is an ideology that

explains to the proletariat why they are subordinate, urges them to act to alleviate their condition, and instructs them in how to proceed: by the violent overthrow of existing institutions and cultural order.

The working class conception of group consciousness is appealing to students of minority politics because it can be generalized to all materially deprived groups in capitalist societies and it describes a potent set of beliefs that can politicize and mobilize people for collective action. Yet it is too restrictive for a general theory minority consciousness. It has two limitations, one empirical, the other normative. First, a purely Marxist approach provides an unnecessarily narrow definition of a complex subject by focusing on only one type of group consciousness. In particular, it fails to recognize the full logical range and historical incidence of alternative forms of political consciousness within the subordinate strata. Second, it has a valuational component that renders impossible objective accounts of minority politics. In prescribing one ideology as the "correct" view, it designates all others as "false consciousness."

6. A third strategy, *passing*, is repugnant to separatists. Believing that group mobility is impossible, too risky, or too exacting, some members of the biopolitical minority try to present themselves as members of the majority. Those with African, South American, or Native American ancestry who have European features can pass themselves off as white. Some women dress and act like men to deemphasize their own femininity. Historically, it was not uncommon for female authors to use male pen names. Passing is a private, individual strategy available to relatively few members of a political minority. Those who pass are likely to be marginal people, finding themselves unaccepted and uncomfortable in the worlds of both the majority and the minority.

CHAPTER 11

1. The research was supported in part by the Netherlands Organization for the Advancement of Research (N.W.O.).

2. As may be clear, we leave the question of the Scots, Welsh, and other nations in Britain aside.

3. During the decolonization process of Indonesia in 1951, the Moluccans were practically forced to come to the Netherlands as members of the dissolved colonial army. They have strived for an independent Moluccan republic in the Moluccan archipelago. Many do not want to betray this ideal by taking up Netherlands citizenship. See Bartels (1986).

4. The NCCI, the national parent body of CRCs, was superceded first by the Community Relations Commission (CRC) in 1968 and then again by the Commission for Racial Equality (CRE) in 1977.

CHAPTER 12

1. For the complete text of each autonomy statute, see Galvan and Rovira (1985). For a lengthy discussion of the development of the autonomy system, with a detailed chronology, see Elorriaga (1983). See also, Añoveros (1984) for a three-part article appearing in *El Pais*.

2. Population figures are from a Basque government publication, *1984 Panoramica* (Bilbao: Basque Government, Department of Statistics, 1984), chapter 3.

3. The following discussion is based on data found in Clark (1985b) and Linz (1985).

4. See Horowitz (1988, 86-89), for a discussion of the comparative merits of kinship and territory as state organizing principles. Also, see Knight (1982, 514-531) and Rokkan and Urwin (1982). Suttles (1972) devotes considerable space to demonstrating the many ways in which territorially based group attributes reinforce and aid in the definition of community sentiments.

CHAPTER 14

1. The Parti Québécois, elected to office in Quebec in 1976, devised a two-step referendum strategy to achieve its stated goal of independence. In a first referendum the government asked its electorate for the authority to negotiate with the central government a fundamental revision of the links between Quebec and Canada, the objective being political sovereignty and economic association; in a second referendum the Quebec government would have sought approval of the negotiated settlement. The second referendum was not held, the first having been defeated in 1980 by a vote of 60 to 40 by the Quebec electorate. According to the polls taken at the time the Quebec francophones voted 48 percent in favor, 52 percent against (Pinard and Hamilton 1984).

2. In May 1988 the Quebec government announced it would give families a bonus of $500 for each of their first two children and a bonus of $3000 for each of their subsequent children.

References

Aaron, Henry. 1980. *On Social Welfare*. Cambridge, MA: Abt.

Abramson, Paul, and Ronald Inglehart. 1987. "Generational Replacement and the Future of Postmaterialist Values." *Journal of Politics* 49: 231-241.

Acuña, Rodolfo. 1981. *Occupied America*. New York: Harper & Row.

Aissou, Abdel. 1987. *Les Beurs, l'école, et la France*. Paris: Editions L'Harmattan et C.I.E.M.I.

Albrecht, William P. 1982. "Welfare Reform: An Idea Whose Time Has Come and Gone." In *Welfare Reform in America*, ed. Paul M. Sommers. Boston: Kluwer-Nijhoff.

Alderman, Geoffrey. 1983. *The Jewish Community in British Politics*. Oxford, England: Oxford University Press.

Almond, Gabriel, and Sydney Verba. 1963. *The Civic Culture*. Princeton: Princeton University Press.

Amersfoort, H. van. 1982. *Immigration and the Formation of Minority Groups: The Dutch Experience 1945-1975*. Cambridge, England: Cambridge University Press.

Amersfoort, J. M. M. van. 1970. "Hindostaanse Surinamers in Amsterdam." *Nieuwe West-Indische Gids* 47: 109-138.

Andereggen, Anton. 1986. "The Turkish Lumpenproletariat: West Germany's Industrial Reserve Army." *German Life and Letters* 39: 314-321.

Anderson, Alan B., and George W. Pickering. 1986. *Confronting the Color Line: The Broken Promise of the Civil Rights Movement in Chicago*. Athens: University of Georgia Press.

Añoveros, Jaime Garcia. 1984. "Autonomías, un proceso abierto." *El País*, May 29-31.

Anwar, Muhammad. 1986. *Race and Politics*. New York: Tavistock.

Apps, R. 1985. "Minority Language Education Rights." *University of Toronto Law Review* 43: 45-71.

Arès, R. 1975. "Les minorités franco-canadiennes. Etude statistique." *Royal Society Transactions* 13: 123-132.

Arrington, Theodore. 1978. "Partisan Campaigns, Ballots, and Voting Patterns: The Case of Charlotte." *Urban Affairs Quarterly* 14: 253-261.

Ashford, Douglas. 1981. *Policy and Politics in Britain: The Limits of Consensus*. Philadelphia: Temple University Press.

Avila, Joaquin. 1983. *Report to the MALDEF Board of Directors*. San Francisco: Mexican-American Legal Defense and Education Fund.

Ayestaran, J. A., et al. 1979. *Euskadi y el Estatuto de Autonomía*. San Sebastián, Spain: Erein.

Bachrach, Peter, and Morton S. Baratz. 1970. *Power and Poverty*. New York: Oxford University Press.

Banton, M. 1985. *Promoting Racial Harmony*. Cambridge, England: Cambridge University Press.

Bariani, Didier. 1985. *Les immigrés: Pour ou contre la France?* Paris: France-Empire.

Barker, A. 1975. *Strategy and Style in Local Community Relations*. London: The Runnymede Trust.

Barnes, Samuel H., et al. 1979. *Political Action*. Beverly Hills: Sage.

Bartels, D. 1986. "Can the Train Ever Be Stopped Again? Developments in the Moluccan Community in the Netherlands Before and After the Hijackings." *Indonesia* 41: 23-45.

Başgöz, Ilhan, and Norman Furness, eds. 1985. *Turkish Workers in Europe*. Bloomington: Indiana University Press.

Beale, Stephen. 1986. "Friendly Persuasion: Pacts and Covenants." *Hispanic Business* 9: 20-24.

Becker, Gary. 1957. *The Economics of Discrimination*. Chicago: University of Chicago Press.

Bendix, John. 1987. "Foreign Worker Policies: Interest Group and Bureaucratic Interaction in Germany and the United States." Ph.D. dissertation, Indiana University.

Benenson, Bob. 1986. "After Years on the Sidelines, Cubans Finally Enter Politics." *Congressional Quarterly* 44: 1537-1540.

Bennett, Lerone, Jr. 1984. *Before the Mayflower: A History of Black America*. New York: Penguin.

Ben-Tovim, G., and J. Gabriel. 1982. "The Politics of Race in Britain, 1962-79: A Review of the Major Trends and of Recent Debates." In *Race in Britain: Continuity and Change*, ed. C. Husband. London: Hutchinson.

Benyon, John. 1984. *Scarman and After*. Oxford, England: Pergamon Press.

Berger, Suzanne, and Michael J. Piore. 1980. *Dualism and Discontinuity in Advanced Industrial Societies*. New York: Cambridge University Press.

Bernstein, R. B. 1971. *Class, Codes and Control, Vol. 1.* London: Routledge & Kegan Paul.

Berque, Jacques. 1985. *L'Immigration à l'école de la République.* Paris: Documentation Française.

Billingsley, Andrew. 1968. *Black Families in White America.* Englewood Cliffs, NJ: Prentice Hall.

Blau, Peter M., and Otis Duncan. 1967. *The American Occupational Structure.* New York: Wiley.

Bloom, Allan. 1987. *The Closing of the American Mind.* New York: Simon and Schuster. In *Figaro*, March 24, and *L'âme désarmée: Essai sur le déclin de la culture générale.* Paris: Julliard.

Bochel, John, and David Denver. 1983. "Candidate Selection in the Labour Party: What the Selectors Seek." *British Journal of Political Science* 13: 45-69.

Boddy, M., and C. Fudge, eds. 1984. *Local Socialism? Labor Councils and New Left Alternatives.* London: Macmillan.

Boehm, Max. 1948. "Autonomy." In *Encyclopedia of the Social Sciences*, ed. Edwin R. A. Seligman. New York: Macmillan.

Bogdanor, Vernon. 1984. *What Is Proportional Representation?* Oxford, England: Martin Robertson.

Bohland, James R. 1982. "Indian Residential Segregation in the Urban Southwest: 1970 and 1980." *Social Science Quarterly* 63: 749-761.

Boissevain, Jeremy, and Hanneke Grotenberg. 1986. "Culture, Structure and Ethnic Enterprise: The Surinamese of Amsterdam." *Ethnic and Racial Studies* 9: 1-23.

Bonacich, Edna. 1972. "A Theory of Ethnic Antagonism: The Split Labor Market." *American Sociological Review* 37: 535-559.

Bonacich, Edna. 1973. "A Theory of Middleman Minorities." *American Sociological Review* 38: 83-94.

Bonacich, Edna. 1978. "Korean Immigrant Small Business in Los Angeles." In *Sourcebook on the New Immigration*, ed. Roy S. Byrce-Laporte. New Brunswick, NJ: Transaction.

Bonacich, Edna, and J. Modell. 1980. *The Economic Basis of Ethnic Solidarity: Small Business in the Japanese American Community.* Berkeley: University of California Press.

Bonime-Blanc, Andrea. 1987. *Spain's Transition to Democracy: The Politics of Constitution-Making.* Boulder, CO: Westview.

Bonnet, Jean-Charles. 1976. *Les pouvoirs public français et l'immigration dans l'entre deux guerres.* Lyon, France: Centre d'histoire économique et sociale de las region Lyonnaise.

Bornschier, Volker, Christopher Chase-Dunn, and Richard Rubinson. 1978. "Cross-national Evidence of the Effects of Foreign Investment and Aid on Economic Growth and Inequality: A Survey of Findings and a Reanalysis." *American Journal of Sociology* 84: 651-84.

Boulet, J-A. 1980. *Language and Earnings in Montreal.* Ottawa: Economic Council of Canada.

Boulet, J-A., and Laval Lavallee. 1983. "L'évolution des disparities linguistiques des revenue du travail au Canada de 1970 à 1980." Economic Council of Canada, discussion paper no. 245.

Bourdieu, Pierre. 1977. "Cultural Reproduction and Social Reproduction." In *Power and Ideology in Education*, ed. J. Karable and A. H. Halsey. New York: Oxford University Press.

Bourdieu, Pierre, and Jean-Claude Passeron. 1977. *Reproduction in Education, Society and Culture.* London: Sage.

Bourdieu, Pierre, and Luc Boltanski. 1978. "Changes in Social Structure and Changes in the Demand for Education." In *Contemporary Europe: Structural Changes and Cultural Patterns*, ed. Salvador Giner and Margaret S. Archer. London: Routledge & Kegan Paul.

Bouvier, Leon F., and Robert W. Gardner. 1986. "Immigration to the U.S.: The Unfinished Story." *Population Bulletin* 41: 3-50.

Brass, Paul, ed. 1985. *Ethnic Groups and the State.* London: Croom Helm.

Braybrooke, David. 1985. "Contemporary Marxism on the Autonomy, Efficacy, and Legitimacy of the Capitalist State." In *The Democratic State*, ed. Roger Benjamin and Stephen L. Elkin. Lawrence: University Press of Kansas.

Brazeau, Jacques, and Edouard Cloutier. 1977. "Interethnic Relations and the Language Issue in Contemporary Canada: A General Appraisal." In *Ethnic Conflict in the Western World*, ed. Milton J. Esman. Ithaca: Cornell University Press.

Brimelow, Peter. 1987. "A Cautionary Case of Bilingualism." *Commentary* 84: 63-65.

Brischetto, Robert, Charles L. Cotrell, and R. Michael Stevens. 1983. "Conflict and Change in the Political Culture of San Antonio in the 1970s." In *The Politics of San Antonio: Community, Progress, and Power*, ed. David R. Johnson, John A. Booth, and Richard J. Harris. Lincoln: University of Nebraska Press.

Brosnan, Peter. 1982. "Ethnic Origin and Income in New Zealand." *New Zealand Population Review* 8: 358-368.

Brosnan, Peter, and Craig Hill. 1983. "Income, Occupation and Ethnic Origin in New Zealand." *New Zealand Economic Papers* 17: 51-57.

Browning, H. L., and Rodolfo O. de la Garza, eds. 1986. *Mexican Immigrants and Mexican-Americans: An Evolving Relation.* Austin, TX: CMAS Publications of the University of Texas.

Browning, Rufus P., Dale Rogers Marshall, and David Tabb. 1984. *Protest Is Not Enough.* Berkeley: University of California Press.

Brubaker, William Rogers. 1989. *Immigration and the Politics of Citizenship in Europe and North America*. Lanham, MD: University Press of America.

Bryce-LaPorte, Roy, ed. 1980. *Sourcebook on the New Immigration*. New Brunswick, NJ: Transaction.

Buijs, F., and J. Rath. 1986. *DeStem van Migranten en Werklozen. De Gemeenteraadsverkiezingen van 19 Maart 1986 te Rotterdam*. Leiden, Germany: University of Leiden.

Bullock, Charles, and Bruce Campbell. 1984. "Racist or Racial Voting in the 1981 Atlanta Municipal Elections." *Urban Affairs Quarterly* 20: 149-164.

Bulpitt, Jim. 1986. "Continuity, Autonomy and Peripheralisation: The Anatomy of the Centre's Race Statecraft." In *Race, Government and Politics in Britain*, ed. Zig Layton-Henry and Paul Rich. London: Macmillan.

Bunch, Charlotte. 1975. *Lesbianism and the Women's Movement*. Oakland, CA: Diana.

Burke, Vincent J., and Vee Burke. 1974. *Nixon's Good Deed*. New York: Columbia University Press.

Business Week. 1984. "A Shrinking Market Has Beer Makers Brawling." *Business Week*, August 20: 59-63.

Butler, David, and Dennis Kavanagh. 1984. *The British General Election of 1983*. London: Macmillan.

Butler, David, and Donald Stokes. 1983. *Political Change in Britain*. Second edition. London: MacMillan.

Cailleux, A. 1953. "L'évolution quantitative du language." *Société préhistorique française*: 505-514.

Cain, Bruce E., and D. Roderick Kiewiet. 1984. "Ethnicity and Electoral Choice: Mexican Voting Behavior in the California 30th Congressional District." *Social Science Quarterly* 65: 315-327.

California State Department of Education. 1984. *Studies on Immersion Education: A Collection for United States Educators*. Sacramento: California State Department of Education.

Calvez, Corentin. 1969. *Le problème des travailleurs étrangers*. Avis et rapports du Conseil économique et sociale. Paris: Journal Officiel.

Caminos. 1983. "Hispanics and the Private Sector: New Partnerships." *Caminos*, April, 42-43.

Canada, Royal Commission on Bilingualism and Biculturalism. 1973. *Bilingualism and Biculturalism: An Abridged Version of the Royal Commission Report*. Canada: McClelland and Stewart Limited, in cooperation with the Secretary of State Department and Information Canada.

Cardenas, Jose. 1977. "Response I." In *Language, Ethnicity, and the Schools: Policy Alternatives for Bilingual-Bicultural Education*, ed. Noel

Epstein. Washington: Institute for Educational Leadership, George Washington University.

Carlinger, G. 1981. "Wage Differences of Language Group and the Market for Language Skills in Canada." *The Journal of Human Resources* 16: 384-399.

Carter, Mark Bonham. 1987. "A Tale of Grievances Unheard." *Times Literary Supplement*, April 24.

Castles, Stephen. 1984. *Here for Good: Western Europe's New Ethnic Minorities*. London: Pluto Press.

Castles, Stephen, and Godula Kosack. 1973. *Immigrant Workers and Class Structure in Western Europe*. New York: Oxford University Press.

Castonguay, C. 1979. "Exogamie et anglicisation chez less minorités canadiennes françaises." *Canadian Review of Sociology and Anthropology* 16: 21-31.

Castro, Ray. 1976. "Shifting the Burden of Bilingualism: The Case for Monolingual Communities." *The Bilingual Review* 3: 3-30.

Cataldo, Everett, and John Holm. 1983. "Voting on School Finances." *Western Political Quarterly* 36: 619-631.

Cazemajou, Jean, and Jean-Pierre Martin. 1983. *La crise du melting-pot: Ethnicité et identité aux États-Unis de Kennedy à Reagan*. Paris: Aubier Montagne.

Centre for Contemporary Cultural Studies. 1982. *The Empire Strikes Back*. London: Hutchinson.

Charef, Mehdi. 1983. *Le thé au harem d'Archi Ahmed*. Paris: Mercure de France.

Chávez, John R. 1984. *The Lost Land: The Chicano Image of the Southwest*. Albuquerque: University of New Mexico.

Cheetham, Juliet. 1972. "Immigration." In *Trends in British Society since 1900*, ed. A. H. Halsey. London: Macmillan.

Churchill, Ward, ed. 1986. *Marxism and Native Americans*. Boston: South End.

Clark, Robert. 1985a. "Dimensions of Basque Political Culture in Post-Franco Spain." In *Basque Politics: A Case Study in Ethnic Nationalism*, ed. William Douglass. Reno: Basque Studies Program Occasional Papers Series, no. 2.

Clark, Robert. 1985b. "Spain's Autonomous Communities: A Case Study in Ethnic Power Sharing." *The European Studies Journal* 2: 1-16.

Clark, Robert. 1987. "'Rejectionist' Voting as an Indicator of Ethnic Nationalism: The Case of Spain's Basque Provinces, 1976-1986." *Ethnic and Racial Studies* 10: 427-447.

Clark, Robert. 1988. "Public Policies to Protect a Minority Language: The Basque Case." Paper presented at the XIV World Congress, International Political Science Association. Washington, D.C.

Clark, Robert, and Michael Haltzel, eds. 1987. *Spain in the 1980s: The Democratic Transition and a New International Role.* Cambridge, MA: Ballinger.

Club de l'Horloge. 1985. *L'Identité de la France.* Paris: Albin Michel.

Cole, Leonard. 1976. *Blacks in Power.* Princeton: Princeton University Press.

Colin, Jean-Pierre. 1984. "Les cultures minoritaires face à l'état." *Change International* 2: 106-112.

Colin, Jean-Pierre. 1986. *La beauté du manchot.* Paris: Publisud.

Collette, J., and P. O'Malley. 1974. "Urban Migration and Selective Acculturation: The Case of Maori." *Human Organization* 33: 146-158.

Collins, Roger. 1986. *The Basques.* Oxford, England: Basil Blackwell.

Commission for Racial Equality. 1980. *The Nature and Funding of Local Race Relations Work. Community Relations Councils.* London: CRE.

Committee on Labor and Education, U.S. House of Representatives. 1979. *Black Lung Benefits Reform Act and Black Lung Benefits Revenue Act of 1977.* Committee print, Government Printing Office, February.

Committee on Labor and Human Resources, U.S. Senate. 1985. *Barriers to Adoption.* Hearings held June 25 and July 10, 1985. Washington: Government Printing Office.

Conradt, David. 1982. *The German Polity.* Second edition. New York: Longman.

Conyers, James E., and Walter Wallace. 1976. *Black Elected Officials.* New York: Russell Sage Foundation.

Coors, Adolph, Company. 1984. "A Partnership of Trust: National Agreement between Adolph Coors Company and Coalition of Hispanic Organizations."

Coser, Lewis. 1956. *The Functions of Social Conflict.* New York: Macmillian.

Crewe, Ivor. 1983. "Representation and the Ethnic Minorities in Britain." In *Ethnic Pluralism and Public Policy,* ed. Nathan Glazer and Ken Young. London: Heinemann.

Crosby, Fay. 1976. "A Model of Egoistical Relative Deprivation." *Psychological Review* 83: 85-113.

Crosby, Fay. 1979. "Relative Deprivation Revisited: A Response to Miller, Bolce and Halligan." *American Political Science Review* 73: 103-112.

Cross, Gary S. 1983. *Immigrant Workers in Industrial France: The Making of a New Laboring Class.* Philadelphia: Temple University Press.

Cross, M., and H. B. Entzinger. eds. 1988. *Lost Illusions: Caribbean Minorities in Britain and the Netherlands.* London: Routledge.

Cruse, Harold. 1987. *Plural but Equal: Blacks and Minorities in American Plural Society.* New York: Morrow.

Cummins, James. 1981. "The Role of Primary Language Development in Promoting Educational Success for Language Minority Students." In *Schooling and Language Minority Students: A Theoretical Framework.*

Los Angeles: California State University Evaluation, Dissemination, and Assessment Center.

Cummins, James. 1984. "The Language Minority Child." In *Bilingual and Multicultural Education: Canadian Perspectives*, ed. Stan Shapson and Vincent D'Oyley. Clevedon, England: Multilingual Matters.

Dahl, Robert A. 1956. *A Preface to Democratic Theory*. Chicago: University of Chicago Press.

Dahl, Robert A. 1971. *Polyarchy: Participation and Opposition*. New Haven: Yale University Press.

Dahrendorf, Ralf. 1967. *Society and Democracy in Germany*. New York: Doubleday.

Darcy, R., Susan Welch, and Janet Clark. 1987. *Women: Elections and Representation*. New York: Longman.

Darity, William, and Samuel Myers. 1980. "Changes in Black-White Income Inequality, 1968-78: Illusions of Progress." *Review of Black Political Economy* 10: 354-379.

Davidson, Chandler, and George Korbel. 1981. "At-Large Elections and Minority Group Representation: A Re-Examination of Historical and Contemporary Evidence." *Journal of Politics* 43: 982-1005.

Davidson, Chandler, ed. 1984. *Minority Vote Dilution*. Washington: Howard University Press.

Davies, James C. 1962. "Toward a Theory of Revolution." *American Sociological Review* 27: 5-19.

Davis, J. A. 1959. "A Formal Interpretation of the Theory of Relative Deprivation." *Sociometry* 22: 280-296.

Dawson, Richard E., Kenneth Prewitt, and Karen S. Dawson. 1977. *Political Socialization*. Boston: Little, Brown and Co.

Dearing, Mary R. 1952. *Veterans in Politics: The Story of the G.A.R.* Baton Rouge: Louisiana State University Press.

De la Garza, Rodolfo O. 1985. "As American as Tamale Pie: Mexican-American Political Mobilization and the Loyalty Question." In *Mexican-Americans in Comparative Perspective*, ed. Walker Connor. Washington: The Urban Institute Press.

De la Garza, Rodolfo O., and David Vaughan. 1984. "The Political Socialization of the Chicano Elite: A Generational Approach." *Social Science Quarterly* 65: 290-307.

Deckard, Barbara Sinclair. 1983. *The Women's Movement: Political, Sociological and Psychological Issues*. New York: Harper & Row.

Deia. 1985. Bilbao, April 5.

Deia. 1986. Bilbao, June 22.

De Ridder, Martine, and Luis Ricardo Fraga. 1986. "The Brussels Issue in Belgian Politics." *West European Politics* 9: 376-392.

Deutsch, Karl. 1969. *Nationalism and Its Alternatives*. New York: Knopf.

Díaz, Tomas. 1985. "Coors and Hispanics: A New Business Partnership." *Hispanic Business Review*, January/February, 16-21.

Díaz, Victor Pérez. 1984. "Gobernabilidad y Mesogobiernos: Autonomías regionales y neocorporatismo en España." *Papeles de Economía Española* 21: 40-76.

Dignan, Don. 1981. "Europe's Melting Pot: A Century of Large-Scale Immigration into France." *Ethnic and Racial Studies*, 4: 137-152.

DiNardo, John. 1985. "Undocumented Migration from Mexico: Analysis and Policy Considerations." *Arizona Review* 33: 20-27.

Dinnerstein, Leonard, and David Reimers. 1975. *Ethnic Americans: A History of Immigration and Assimilation*. New York: Dodd, Mead.

Dinstein, Yoram, ed. 1981. *Models of Autonomy*. New Brunswick, NJ: Transaction.

Dolbeare, Kenneth. 1984. *Democracy at Risk*. Chatham, NJ: Chatham House.

Douglass, William, and Jon Bilbao. 1975. *Basques in the New World*. Reno: University of Nevada Press.

Dowty, Alan. 1987. *Closed Borders: The Contemporary Assault on Freedom of Movement*. New Haven: Yale University Press.

Dumas, Jean. 1987. *Rapport sur l'état de la population du Canada 1986*. Ottawa: Ministère des Approvisionnements et Services.

Duncan, O. D. 1967. "Discrimination against Negroes." *Annals of the American Academy of Political and Social Science* 371: 85-103.

Dunleavy, Patrick, and Christopher Husbands. 1985. *British Democracy at the Crossroads*. London: George Allen and Unwin.

Easton, David. 1957. *A Systems Analysis of Political Life*. New York: Wiley.

Edelman, Murray. 1977. *Political Language: Words that Succeed and Policies that Fail*. New York: Academic.

Edwards, Richard C. 1979. *Contested Terrain*. New York: Basic Books.

Elorriaga, Gabriel. 1983. *La Batalla de las Autonomías*. Madrid: Editorial Azara.

English, Richard. 1974. "Beyond Pathology: Research and Theoretical Perspectives on Black Families." In *Social Research and the Black Community: Selected Issues and Priorities*, ed. Lawrence E. Gary. Washington: Institute for Urban Affairs and Research, Howard University.

Engstrom, Richard L. 1985a. "Racial Vote Dilution: The Concept and the Court." In *The Voting Rights Act: Consequences and Implications*, ed. Lorn Foster. New York: Praeger.

Engstrom, Richard L. 1985b. "The Reincarnation of the Intent Standard: Federal Judges and At-Large Election Cases." *Howard Law Journal* 28: 495-513.

Engstrom, Richard L., and Michael D. McDonald. 1981. "The Election of Blacks to City Councils: Clarifying the Impact of Electoral

Arrangements on the Seats/Population Relationship." *American Political Science Review* 75: 344-354.

Engstrom, Richard L., and Michael D. McDonald. 1982. "The Underrepresentation of Blacks on City Councils: Comparing the Structural and Socioeconomic Explanations for South/non-South Differences." *Journal of Politics* 44: 1088-1099.

Engstrom, Richard L., and Michael D. McDonald. 1986. "The Effect of At-Large Versus District Elections on Racial Representation in U.S. Municipalities." In *Electoral Laws and Their Political Consequences*, ed. Bernard Grofman and Arend Lijphart. New York: Agathon.

Engstrom, Richard L., and Michael D. McDonald. 1987. "The Election of Blacks to Southern City Councils: The Dominant Impact of Electoral Arrangements." In *Blacks in Southern Politics*, ed. Laurence W. Moreland, Robert P. Steed, and Tod A. Baker. New York: Praeger.

Engstrom, Richard L., and John K. Wildgen. 1977. "Pruning Thorns from the Thicket: An Empirical Test of the Existence of Racial Gerrymandering." *Legislative Studies Quarterly* 2: 465-479.

Entzinger, H. B. 1985. "The Netherlands." In *European Immigration Policy: A Comparative Study*, ed. T. Hammar. Cambridge, England: Cambridge University Press.

Epstein, Noel. 1977. *Language, Ethnicity, and the Schools: Policy Alternatives for Bilingual-Bicultural Education*. Washington: Institute for Educational Leadership, George Washington University.

Ericksen, Charlie. 1980. "Hispanics Have to Practice Pragmatic Politics in the 80s." *LULAC* 51: 26.

Erikson, Robert, John H. Goldthorpe, and Lucienne Portocarero. 1982. "Social Fluidity in Industrial Nations: England, France and Sweden." *British Journal of Sociology* 33: 1-36.

Erikson, Robert S., Norman R. Luttbeg, and Kent L. Tedin. 1988. *American Public Opinion*. New York: Macmillan.

Esman, Milton, ed. 1977. *Ethnic Conflict in the Western World*. Ithaca: Cornell University Press.

Esser, Hartmut, and Hermann Korte. 1985. "Federal Republic of Germany." In *European Immigration Policy: A Comparative Study*, ed. Tomas Hammar. Cambridge, England: Cambridge University Press.

Etienne, Bruno. 1977. *Culture et Révolution*. Paris: Seuil.

Etienne, Bruno. 1987. *L'Islamisme radical*. Paris: Hachette.

Euskadi 1977-1982. San Sebastián, Spain: EGIN.

Euskadi 1983. San Sebastián, Spain: EGIN.

Farley, Reynolds. 1984. *Blacks and Whites: Narrowing the Gap*. Cambridge, MA: Harvard University Press.

Featherman, David L., and R. M. Hauser. 1976. "Changes in the Socioeconomic Stratification of the Races, 1962-73." *American Journal of Sociology* 82: 621-651.

Featherman, Sandra. 1988. "Voting Rights: The Fight Moves North." *Focus* 16: 6-7.

Fireman, Bruce, and William A. Gamson. 1979. "Utilitarian Logic in the Resource Mobilization Prospective." In *Dynamics of Social Movements*, ed. Mayer N. Zald and John D. McCarthy. Cambridge, MA: Winthrop.

Fishman, Joshua. 1978. "Positive Bilingualism: Some Overlooked Rationales and Forefathers." In *GURT 1978: International Dimensions of Bilingual Education*, ed. James. E. Alatis. Washington: Georgetown University Press.

Fishman, Joshua. 1985. "The Ethnic Revival in the United States: Implications for the Mexican-American Community." In *Mexican-Americans in Comparative Perspective*, ed. Walker Connor. Washington: Urban Institute Press.

Fitzgerald, Marian. 1983. "Are Blacks an Electoral Liability?" *New Society*, December 8.

Fitzgerald, Marian. 1984. *Political Parties and Black People*. London: The Runnymede Trust.

Fitzgerald, Marian. 1987. *Black People and Party Politics in Britain*. London: The Runnymede Trust.

Fitzgerald, Marian. 1988. "Study of Black Councillors in London." Mimeo.

Flexner, Elanor. 1959. *Century of Struggle*. Cambridge, MA: Harvard University Press.

Foot, Paul. 1965. *Immigration and Race in British Politics*. Harmondsworth, England: Penguin.

Fortune. 1986. "Coors Comes Bubbling Back." *Fortune* 113: 51-52.

Foster, Lorn. 1978. "Black Perceptions of the Mayor." *Urban Affairs Quarterly* 14: 245-252.

Fraga, Luis Ricardo. 1988. "Domination through Democratic Means: Nonpartisan Slating Groups in City Electoral Politics." *Urban Affairs Quarterly* 23: 528-555.

Fraga, Luis Ricardo, Kenneth J. Meier, and Robert J. England. 1986. "Hispanic Americans and Educational Policy: Limits to Equal Access." *The Journal of Politics* 48: 850-876.

Freeman, Gary. 1979. *Immigrant Labor and Racial Conflict in Industrial Societies: The French and British Experience, 1945-1975*. Princeton: Princeton University Press.

Freeman, Gary. 1986. "Migration and the Political Economy of the Welfare State." *The Annals of the American Academy of Political and Social Science* 485: 51-63.

Freeman, Jo. 1975. *The Politics of Women's Liberation*. New York: Longman.
Freeman, Jo. 1979. "Resource Mobilization and Strategy: A Model for Analyzing Social Movement Organization Actions." In *The Dynamics of Social Movements*, ed. J. D. Zald and M. N. McCarthy. Cambridge, MA: Winthrop.
Freeman, R. B. 1973. "Decline of Labor Market Discrimination and Economic Analysis." *American Economics Review* 63: 280-286.
Fried, C., ed. 1983. *Minorities: Community and Identity*. Berlin, Germany: Springer-Verlag.
Friedland, Roger, Frances Fox Piven, and Robert R. Alford. 1977. "Political Conflict, Urban Structure, and the Fiscal Crisis." *Inter-National Journal of Urban and Regional Research* 1: 447-471.
Friedlander, Robert A. 1981. "Autonomy and the Thirteen Colonies: Was the American Revolution Really Necessary?" In *Models of Autonomy*, ed. Yoram Dinstein. New Brunswick, NJ: Transaction.
Friedman, Milton, and Rose Friedman. 1981. *Free to Choose*. New York: Avon.
Frolich, Norman, Joe A. Oppenheimer, and Oran R. Young. 1971. *Political Leadership and Collective Goods*. Princeton: Princeton University Press.
Gallegos, Herman. 1982. "Making a Dent in the Corporate Sector." *Nuestro* 6: 49-51.
Gallissot, René. 1986. "Nationalité et citoyenneté." *Après-Demain* 286: 8-15.
Galvan, Enrique Tierno, and Antoni Rovira. 1985. *La España Autonómica*. Barcelona: Bruguera.
Gamble, Andrew. 1974. *The Conservative Nation*. London: Routledge and Kegan Paul.
Gamble, Andrew. 1988. *The Free Economy and the Strong State*. London: Macmillan.
Garcia, Chris F. 1974. *La Causa Política*. Notre Dame: University of Notre Dame Press.
Garcia, Chris F., and Rodolfo O. De la Garza. 1977. *The Chicano Political Experience*. North Scituate, MA: Duxbury.
Garfinkel, Irwin, and Sara S. McLanahan. 1986. *Single Mothers and Their Children: A New American Dilemma*. Washington: Urban Institute Press.
Garmendia, José A., Francisco Parra Luna, and Alfonso Pérez Agote. 1982. *Abertzales y vascos*. Madrid: Akal.
Garrard, John. 1971. *The English and Immigration, 1880-1910*. London: Oxford University Press.
Gaugler, Ernst, et al. 1978. *Ausländer in Deutschen Industriebetrieben*. Cologne, Germany: Happ Verlag.

Gibbs, Jack. 1965. "Occupational Differentiation of Negroes and Whites in the United States." *Social Forces* 44: 159-165.

Gilligan, Carol. 1982. *In a Different Voice*. Cambridge, MA: Harvard University Press.

Giordan, Henri. 1982. *Démocratie culturelle et droit à la différence: Rapport au ministre de la culture*. Paris: Documentation Française.

Glazer, Nathan. 1986. "Education and Training Programs and Poverty." In *Fighting Poverty*, ed. Sheldon H. Danziger and Daniel H. Weinberg. Cambridge, MA: Harvard University Press.

Glazer, Nathan. 1987. *Affirmative Discrimination: Ethnic Inequality and Public Policy*. Cambridge, MA: Harvard University Press.

Glazer, Nathan, and Ken Young, eds. 1983. *Ethnic Pluralism and Public Policy: Achieving Equality in the United States and Great Britain*. Lexington, MA: D. C. Heath.

Glenn, Norval. 1966. "Occupational Differentiation of Negroes and Whites in the United States." *Social Forces* 44: 159-165.

Gordon, Milton M. 1964. *Assimilation in American Life: The Role of Race, Religion, and National Origins*. New York: Oxford University Press.

Graaf, H. de, R. Penninx, and E. F. Stoové. 1988. "Minorities Policies, Social Services, and Ethnic Organizations." In *Ethnic Associations and the Welfare State*, ed. S. Jenkins. New York: Columbia University Press.

Grand Army of the Republic. 1890. *Journal of the 24th National Encampment*.

Granovetter, Mark. 1974. *Getting a Job: A Study of Contracts and Careers*. Cambridge, MA: Harvard University Press.

Greater London Council. 1982. *London Borough Council Elections, 8 May 1982*. London: Greater London Council.

Greenberg, Stanley B. 1980. *Race and State in Capitalist Development: Comparative Perspectives*. New Haven: Yale University Press.

Grillo, R. D. 1985. *Ideologies and Institutions in Urban France: The Representation of Immigrants*. Cambridge, England: Cambridge University Press.

Groenendael, T. van. 1986. *Dilemma's van Regelgeving. De Regularisatie van Illegale Buitenlandse Werknemers 1975-1983. Een Case Studie naar het Functioneren van Regels als Instrucment van Overheidsbeleid*. Alphen aan den Rijn/Utrecht, The Netherlands: Samsom H. D. Tjeenk Willink/NCB.

Grofman, Bernard. 1982. "Alternatives to Single Member Plurality Districts." In *Representation and Redistricting Issues*, ed. Bernard Grofman, Arend Lijphart, Robert McKay, and Howard Scarrow. Lexington, MA: D. C. Heath.

Grofman, Bernard, Michael Migalski, and Nicholas Noviello. 1986. "Effects of Multimember Districts on Black Representation in State Legislatures." *The Review of Black Political Economy* 14: 65-78.

Grove, D. John. 1985. "Cultural Participation and Educational Achievements: A Cross-cultural Analysis." *International Journal of Comparative Sociology* 26: 232-239.

Grove, D. John. 1986. "Restructuring the Cultural Division of Labor in Malaysia and Sri Lanka." *Comparative Political Studies* 19: 179-200.

Grove, D. John. 1989. "Ethnic Mobility or Ethnic Reproduction?" Mimeo. University of Denver.

Grove, D. John, and Robert Hannum. 1986. "On Measuring Intergroup Inequality." *Sociological Methods and Research* 15: 142-60.

Grove, D. John, and Eiichi Hoshino. 1989. "Who Benefits from Ethnic Income Distribution: A Cross-cultural Analysis." *Social Science Research* 18: 70-87.

Guillaume, P. 1985. *Individus, familles, nations*. Paris: Société d'édition de l'enseignement supérieur.

Gurin, Patricia, Gerald Gurin, and Leo M. Beattie. 1969. "Internal-External Control in the Motivational Dynamics of Negroes." *Journal of Social Issues* 25: 29-53.

Gurin, Patricia, H. Miller, and Gerald Gurin. 1980. "Stratum Identification and Consciousness." *Social Psychology Quarterly* 43: 30-47.

Gurr, Ted Robert. 1970. *Why Men Rebel*. Princeton: Princeton University Press.

Haex, J., A. Martens, and S. Wolf. 1976. *Labor Market Discrimination, Immigrant Labor*. Leuven, Belgium: S. O. I.

Hahn, Harlan, and Timothy Almy. 1971. "Ethnic Politics and Racial Voting in Los Angeles." *Western Political Quarterly* 24: 719-730.

Hahn, Harlan, David Klingman, and Harry Pachon. 1976. "Cleavages, Coalitions, and the Black Candidate: The Los Angeles Mayoralty Elections of 1969 and 1973." *Western Political Quarterly* 29: 507-520.

Hakuta, Kenji. 1986. *Mirror of Language: The Debate on Bilingualism*. New York: Basic.

Haley, Alex. 1964. *The Autobiography of Malcolm X*. New York: Grove.

Halley, Robert, Alan Acock, and Thomas Green. 1976. "Ethnicity and Social Class: Voting in the 1973 Los Angeles Municipal Elections." *Western Political Quarterly* 29: 521-530.

Hamilton, Charles V., and Donna C. Hamilton. 1986. "Social Policies, Civil Rights and Poverty." In *Fighting Poverty*, ed. Sheldon H. Danziger and Daniel H. Weinberg. Cambridge, MA: Harvard University Press.

Hammar, Tomas, ed. 1985. *European Immigration Policy: A Comparative Study*. Cambridge, England: Cambridge University Press.

Hammerback, John C., Richard J. Jensen, and Jose Angel Gutierrez. 1985. *A War of Words*. Westport, CT: Greenwood Press.

Hammet, France, and Michèle Proux. 1984. "L'enfant maghrébin en milieu scholaire." In *Les Nord-Africains en France*, ed. Magali Morsy. Paris: CHEAM.

Hannoun, Michel. 1985. *Français et immigrés au quotidien*. Paris: Albatross.

Hannoun, Michel. 1986. *L'autre cohabitation*. Paris: L'Harmattan.

Hannum, Hurst, and Richard B. Lillich. 1981. "The Concept of Autonomy in International Law." In *Models of Autonomy*, ed. Yoram Dinstein. New Brunswick, NJ: Transaction.

Hannum, Michael, and Alice Young. 1977. "Estimation in Panel Models: Results on Pooling Cross-sections and Time Series." In *Sociological Methodology*, ed. David Heisse. San Francisco: Jossey-Bass.

Hartmann, Heidi I. 1984. "The Unhappy Marriage of Marxism and Feminism: Towards a More Progressive Union." In *Feminists Frameworks*, ed. Allison Jaggar and Paula S. Rothenberg. New York: McGraw-Hill.

Harvard Law Review. 1987. "Official English: Federal Limits of Efforts to Curtail Bilingual Services in the States." *Harvard Law Review* 100: 1345-1362.

Harwood, Edwin. 1983. "Alienation: American Attitudes toward Immigration." *Public Opinion Quarterly* 6: 49-51.

Heckmann, Friedrich. 1981. *Die Bundesrepublik Deutschland: Ein Einwanderungsland? Zur Soziologie der Gastarbeiterbevoelkerung als Einwandererminoritaet*. Stuttgart, Germany: Klett-Cotta Verlag.

Heckman, F. 1983. "Towards the Development of a Typology of Minorities." In *Minorities: Community and Identity*, ed. C. Fried. Berlin, Germany: Springer-Verlag.

Heilig, Peggy, and Robert J. Mundt. 1983. "Changes in Representational Equity: The Effect of Adopting Districts." *Social Science Quarterly* 64: 393-397.

Heisler, Barbara Schmitter. 1985. "Sending Countries and the Politics of Emigration and Destination." *International Migration Review* 19: 469-484.

Heisler, Barbara Schmitter. 1986. "Immigrant Settlement and the Structure of Emergent Immigrant Communities in Western Europe." *The Annals of the American Academy of Political and Social Science* 485: 76-86.

Heisler, Martin O. 1986. "Transnational Migration as a Small Window on the Diminished Autonomy of the Modern Democratic State." *The Annals of the American Academy of Political and Social Science* 485: 152-166.

Henry, Charles. 1987. "Racial Factors in the 1982 California Gubernatorial Campaign: Why Bradley Lost." In *The New Black Politics*, ed. Michael Preston, Lenneal Henderson, and Paul Puryear. Second edition. New York: Longman.

Henry-Lorcerie, F. 1983. *Enfants d'immigrés*. Paris: CNRS.

Héraud, E. 1974. *L'Europe des ethnies*. Paris: Presses d'Europe.

Hernandez-Chavez, Eduardo. 1978. "Language Maintenance, Bilingual Education and Philosophies of Bilingualism in the United States." In *GURT 1978: International Dimensions of Bilingual Education*, ed. James E. Alatis. Washington: Georgetown University Press.

Hill, M., and R. Issacharoff. 1971. *Community Action and Race Relations*. London: Oxford University Press/Institute of Race Relations.

Hirschman, Charles, and Morrison G. Wong. 1981. "Trends in Socioeconomic Achievement among Immigrant and Native-Born Asian Americans, 1960-1976." *Sociological Quarterly* 22: 495-513.

Hirschman, Charles and Morrison G. Wong. 1984. "Socioeconomic Gains of Asian Americans, Blacks, and Hispanics." *American Journal of Sociology* 90: 584-607.

Hoffman, Saul. 1979. "Black-White Life Cycle Earning Differences and the Vintage Hypothesis: A Longitudinal Analysis." *American Economic Review* 70: 855-867.

Hollingsworth, T. H. 1969. *Historical Demography*. London: Hodder & Stoughton.

Holmes, Malcolm. 1984. "Ethnicity and Justice in the Southwest: The Sentencing of Anglo, Black, and Mexican Origin Defendants." *Social Science Quarterly* 65: 265-267.

Home Affairs Committee. 1981. *Racial Disadvantage*. Fifth Report HC424. London: Her Majesty's Stationery Office.

Horowitz, Donald. 1988. *Ethnic Groups in Conflict*. Berkeley: University of California Press.

Hoskin, Marilyn. 1984. "Integration or Nonintegration of Foreign Workers: Four Theories." *Political Psychology* 5: 661-685.

Hoskin, Marilyn. 1985. "Public Opinion and the Foreign Worker: Traditional and Nontraditional Bases in West Germany." *Comparative Politics* 17: 193-210.

Hoskin, Marilyn, and William Mishler. 1983. "Public Opinion Toward Foreign Workers: A Comparative Analysis." *International Migration* 21: 440-461.

Hoskin, Marilyn, and Roy Fitzgerald. 1987. "The Politics of Immigration: The German Case." Presented at the annual meeting of the Midwest Political Science Association, Chicago.

Hrychute, M., ed. 1986. *1986 Corpus Almanach and Canadian Sourcebook*. Don Mills: Corpus Info Services.

Huntington, Samuel. 1981. *American Politics: The Promise of Disharmony*. Cambridge, MA: Belknap Press of Harvard University.

Husband, Charles, ed. 1982. *Race in Britain*. London: Hutchinson.

Hwang, Sean-Shong, and Steve H. Murdock. 1982. "Residential Segregation in Texas in 1980." *Social Science Quarterly* 63: 737-748.

Ikenberry, G. John and Theda Skocpol. 1987. "Expanding Social Benefits: The Role of Social Security." *Political Science Quarterly* 1023: 389-416.

Immigration from the Commonwealth. 1965. Cmd. 2739. London: Her Majesty's Stationery Office.

Inglehart, Ronald. 1977. *The Silent Revolution.* Princeton: Princeton University Press.

Inglehart, Ronald. 1981. "Postmaterialism in an Environment of Insecurity." *American Political Science Review* 75: 880-900.

Jackson, James, and Gerald Gurin. 1987. *National Survey of Black Americans, 1979-1980.* Ann Arbor, MI: Inter-University Consortium of Political and Social Research.

Jackson, Robert J., Doreen Jackson, and Nicolas Baxter-Moore. 1986. *Politics in Canada: Culture, Institutions, Behavior and Public Policy.* Scarborough, Canada: Prentice Hall Canada.

Jacobs, Brian. 1986. *Black Politics and Urban Crisis in Britain.* New York: Cambridge University Press.

Jaggar, Alison M. 1983. *Feminist Politics and Human Nature.* Totowa, NJ: Rowman and Allanheld.

Jaggar, Alison M., and Paula S. Rothenberg, eds. 1984. *Feminists Frameworks.* New York: McGraw-Hill.

James, Dorothy B. 1972. *Poverty, Politics and Change.* Englewood Cliffs, NJ: Prentice-Hall.

Jennings, M. Kent, and Harmon Zeigler. 1984. "Class, Party and Race in Four Types of Elections: The Case of Atlanta." *Journal of Politics* 28: 381-407.

Johnson, Leanor B. 1978. "The Search for Values in Black Family Research." In *The Black Family*, ed. Robert Staples. Belmont, CA: Wadsworth.

Jones, Catherine. 1977. *Immigration and Social Policy in Britain.* London: Tavistock.

Josephy, Alvin M., Jr. 1969. *The Patriot Chiefs.* New York: Penguin Books.

Joy, R. 1978. *Canada's Official Language Minorities.* Montreal: C. D. Howe Institute.

Judd, Dennis R. 1988. *The Politics of American Cities: Private Power and Public Policy.* Third edition. Glenview, IL: Scott, Foresman.

Kallen, Horace M. 1924. *Culture and Democracy in the United States.* New York: Boni and Liveright.

Kantor, Paul. 1976. "Elites, Pluralists and Policy Arenas in London: Toward a Comparative Theory of City Policy Formation." *British Journal of Political Science* 8: 311-314.

Karnig, Albert K., and Susan Welch. 1979. "Sex and Ethnic Differences in Municipal Representation." *Social Science Quarterly* 60: 465-481.

Karnig, Albert, and Susan Welch. 1980. *Black Representation and Urban Policy.* Chicago: University of Chicago Press.

Karnig, Albert, and Susan Welch. 1982. "Electoral Structure and Black Representation on City Councils." *Social Science Quarterly* 63: 99-114.
Katznelson, Ira. 1973. *Black Men, White Cities*. New York: Oxford University Press.
Katznelson, Ira. 1981. *City Trenches: Urban Politics and the Patterning of Class in the United States*. New York: Pantheon.
Kettane, Nacer. 1986. *Droit de réponse à la démocratie française*. Paris: Editions de la Découverte.
Key, Victor O. 1963. *Public Opinion and American Democracy*. New York: Knopf.
Klasen, C. H., and P. Drew. 1973. *Migration Policy in Europe*. Lexington, MA: Lexington Books.
Klass, Gary M. 1985. "Explaining America and the Welfare State: An Alternative Theory." *British Journal of Political Science* 15: 427-450.
Knight, David. 1982. "Identity and Territory: Geographical Perspectives on Nationalism and Regionalism." *Annals of the Association of American Geographers* 72: 514-531.
Knight, David. 1983. "The Dilemma of Nations in a Rigid State-Structured World." In *Pluralism and Political Geography: People, Territory and State*, ed. Nurit Kliof and Stanley Waterman. New York: St. Martin's.
Köbben, A. J. F. 1979. "De gijzelingsakties van Zuidmolukkers en hun effekten op de samenleving." *Transaktie* 8: 147-154.
Kohlberg, Lawerence. 1966. "A Cognitive-Developmental Analysis of Children's Sex-Role Concepts and Attitudes." In *The Development of Sex Differences*, ed. Eleanor Maccoby. Stanford: Stanford University Press.
Koot, W., and P. Uniken Venema. 1985. "Etnisering en etnische belangenbehartiging bij Surinamers: een nieuw stijgingskanaal." *Migrantenstudies* 1: 4-16.
Koot, W., and J. Rath. 1987. "Ethnicity and Emancipation." *International Migration* 25: 427-440.
Krasner, Stephen. 1988. *International Regimes*. Ithaca: Cornell University Press.
Krieger-Krynicki, Annie. 1985. *Les musulmans en France*. Paris: Maisonneuve et Larose.
Kubat, Daniel. 1979. "Introduction." In *The Politics of Migration Policies*, ed. Daniel Kubat. New York: Center for Migration Studies.
Kvaraceus, William C., et al., eds. 1965. *The Negro Self-Concept*. New York: McGraw-Hill.
Lachapelle, R. 1987. "Immigration et politique d'immigration au Québec." In *Les communautés culturelles du Québec*, ed. Y. Oryschuk. Quebec: Fides.

Lachapelle, R., and J. Henripin. 1980. *La situation démolinguistique au Canada*. Montréal: Institut de recherches politiques.

Lacroix, Robert, and Francis Vaillaincourt. 1981. *Les revenues et la langue au Quebec, 1970-78*. Dossier N. 18. Quebec: Conseil de la langue Français.

Lagorce, Guy. 1982. "Non à la tribalisation." *Figaro*, March 11.

Lakeman, Enid. 1970. *How Democracies Vote*. London: Faber and Faber.

Laponce, J. A. 1981. "La distribution géographique des groupes linguistiques et les solutions personnelles et territoriales aux problèmes de l'État bilinque." In *L'Etat et la planification linguistique*, 2 vol., ed. A. Martin. Québec: Office de la Langue Française.

Laponce, J. A. 1984a. "The French Language in Canada: Tensions Between Geography and Politics." *Political Geography Quarterly* 3: 91-104.

Laponce, J. A. 1984b, 1987. *Langue et territoire*. Québec: Presses de l'Université Laval. Second edition, *Languages and their Territories*. Toronto: Toronto University Press.

Laponce, J. A. 1986. "L'ethnie comme consommatrice d'espace: exemples canadiens." In *Minorités et État*, ed. P. Guillaume et al. Bordeaux, France: Presses universitaires de Bordeaux.

Lasswell, Harold, and Abraham Kaplan. 1950. *Power and Society: A Framework for Political Analysis*. New Haven: Yale University Press.

Latino & LULAC. 1982a. "Corporate-Education Team." 53: 14-15.

Latino & LULAC. 1982b. "Is It Only for the Elitist?" 53: 27-28.

Latino & LULAC. 1982c. "Law of Productivity." 53: 18.

Latino & LULAC. 1982d. "A New Day for Hispanic Business." 53: 8-9.

Latino & LULAC. 1982e. "1982 Scholarship Fund Past Half-way Mark." 53: 28.

Latino & LULAC. 1982f. "Office Manager Hired Under Coors Grant." 53: 6.

Latino & LULAC. 1982g. "Superbowl Losers?" 53: 1.

Latino & LULAC. 1982h. "Workers or Owners?" 53: 16.

Latino. 1982a. "Brocksbank, Bonilla Are Winners of LNESC Award." 53: 26.

Latino. 1982b. "Hispanic-Corporate Partnership." 53: 19.

Latino. 1983a. "Hands of Unity." 54: 6.

Latino. 1983b. "7-Eleven Does It Right." 54: 18-19.

Latouche, D. 1987. "Immigration, politique et societé: Le cas du Québec." Unpublished manuscript.

Layton-Henry, Zig. 1984. *The Politics of Race in Britain*. Boston: Allen and Unwin.

Layton-Henry, Zig, and Donley T. Studlar. 1985. "The Electoral Participation of Black and Asian Britons: Integration or Alienation?" *Parliamentary Affairs* 38: 307-318.

Lazear, Edward. 1979. "The Narrowing of the Black-White Differential Is Illusory." *American Economic Review* 69: 553-564.

Leach, F. H., ed. 1983. *Historical Atlas of Canada*. Ottawa: Statistics Canada.

L'Express. 1983. "Immigrés: Le dossier explosif." *L'Express*, February 4, 46-66.

LeGallou, Jean-Yves, and le Club de l'Horloge. 1985. *La Préférence Nationale*. Paris: Albin Michel.

Leichter, Howard, and Harrell Rodgers. 1984. *American Public Policy in a Comparative Context*. New York: McGraw-Hill.

LeLohe, Michel J. 1975. "Participation in Elections by Asians in Bradford." In *The Politics of Race*, ed. Ivor Crewe. London: Croom Helm.

LeLohe, Michel J. 1979. "The Effect of the Presence of Immigrants upon the Local Political System in Bradford." In *Racism and Political Action*, ed. Robert Miles and Anne Phizacklea. London: Routledge and Kegan Paul.

LeLohe, Michel J. 1984. "Ethnic Minority Participation in Local Elections." Unpublished paper, University of Bradford, Bradford, England.

Lemco, Jonathan. 1987. "The Implications of an 'Official' Language: The Cases of Quebec's Bill 101 and California's Proposition 63." Presented at the Annual Meeting of the American Political Science Association, Chicago.

Lenski, Gerhard. 1966. *Power and Privilege*. New York: McGraw-Hill.

Le Point. 1983. "Les Français et les immigrés." *Le Point*, October 10.

Le Point. 1988. "Mobilisation à la carte." *Le Point*, January 18.

Leveau, Rémy. 1985. *Le Fellah marocain, défenseur du trône*. Revised edition. Paris: Presses de la Fondation National des Sciences Politiques.

Leveau, Rémy, and Gilles Kepel, eds. 1986. *Les Musulmans dans la société française*. Paris: Presses de la FNSP.

Levi, Edith. 1970. "Mr. Nixon's Speenhamland." *Social Work* 15: 7-11.

Levine, Charles. 1974. *Racial Conflict and the American Mayor*. Lexington, MA: Lexington Books.

Lieberson, Stanley. 1976. "Rank-Sum Comparisons between Groups." In *Sociological Methodology*, ed. David Heiss. San Francisco: Jossey-Bass.

Lieberson, Stanley. 1980. *A Piece of the Pie*. Berkeley: University of California Press.

Lieske, Joel, and Jan William Howard. 1984. "The Racial Factor in Urban Elections." *Western Political Quarterly* 37: 545-583.

Light, Ivan. 1984. "Immigrant and Ethnic Enterprise in North America." *Ethnic and Racial Studies* 7: 195-216.

Light, Ivan. 1986. "Ethnicity and Business Enterprise." In *Making it in America*, ed. Mark Stolarik and Murray Friedman. London and Toronto: Associated University Press.

Lijphart, A. 1975. *The Politics of Accommodation: Pluralism and Democracy in the Netherlands*. Berkeley: University of California Press.

Lijphart, Arend. 1977a. *Democracy in Plural Societies: A Comparative Exploration.* New Haven: Yale University Press.

Lijphart, Arend. 1977b. "Political Theories and the Explanation of Ethnic Conflict in the Western World." In *Ethnic Conflict in the Western World,* ed. Milton Esman. Ithaca: Cornell University Press.

Linz, Juan. 1985. "From Primordialism to Nationalism." In *New Nationalisms of the Developed West,* ed. Edward Tiryakian and Ronald Rogowski. Boston: Allen & Unwin.

Lipset, Seymour Martin. 1964. "The Changing Class Structure and Contemporary European Politics." In *A New Europe?* ed. Stephen R. Graubard. Boston: Houghton Mifflin.

London Residuary Body. 1986. *London Borough Council Elections, 8 May 1986.* London: London Residuary Body.

Lopez, Manuel M. 1981. "Patterns of Interethnic Residential Segregation in the Urban Southwest, 1960 and 1970." *Social Science Quarterly* 62: 50-63.

Lopez, Steven. 1977. "Clinical Stereotypes of the Mexican-American." In *Chicano Psychology,* ed. Joe L. Martinez, Jr. New York: Academic.

Lowi, Theodore J. 1974. "American Business, Public Policy, Case Studies, and Political Theory." *World Politics* 16: 677-715.

Lowi, Theodore J. 1979. *The End of Liberalism.* Second edition. New York: W. W. Norton.

LULAC. 1981a. "Digital, Pabst Blue Ribbon Make League Donations." *LULAC* 52: 23.

LULAC. 1981b. "A Salute to Corporate America." *LULAC* 53: 18.

LULAC. 1981c. "There Is Only One Reason to go into Business: To Make A Profit." *LULAC* 52: 23.

Lynn, Laurence E., Jr., and David de F. Whitman. 1981. *The President as Policymaker: Jimmy Carter and Welfare Reform.* Philadelphia: Temple University Press.

Lyons, W. E., and Malcolm E. Jewell. 1986. "Redrawing Council Districts in American Cities." *State and Local Government Review* 18: 71-81.

Lyons, W. E., and Malcolm E. Jewell. 1988. "Minority Representation and the Drawing of Council Districts." *Urban Affairs Quarterly.* 23: 432-447.

MacDonald, Ian. 1972. *The New Immigration Law.* London: Butterworths.

MacManus, Susan A. 1978. "City Council Election Procedures and Minority Representation: Are They Related?" *Social Science Quarterly* 59: 153-161.

MacManus, Susan A. 1985. "Mixed Electoral Systems: The Newest Reform Structure." *National Civic Review* 74: 484-492.

Macrae, Verena. 1980. *Gastarbeiter: Daten, Fakten, Probleme.* Munich: Verlag Beck.

MALDEF (see Mexican American Legal Defense and Education fund).

Malet, Emile. 1987. *Adresse sur l'immigration aux bonnes âmes de droite et aux belles consciences de gauche.* Paris: Joseph Clims Editions.

Marable, Manning. 1983. *How Capitalism Underdeveloped Black America.* Boston: South End.

Marable, Manning. 1984. *Race, Reform and Rebellion: The Second Reconstruction in Black America, 1945-1982.* Jackson: University of Mississippi Press.

Marangé, James, and André Lebon. 1982. *L'insertion des jeunes d'origine étrangère dans la société française.* Paris: Documentation Française.

Marshall, T. H. 1963. *Sociology at the Crossroads.* London: Heinemann Ltd.

Marshall, T. H. 1964. *Class, Citizenship and Social Development.* Garden City, NY: Doubleday.

Martinez, Joe, Jr. 1977. *Chicano Psychology.* New York: Academic Press.

Martinez, Vilma. 1981. *Report to the MALDEF Board of Directors.* San Francisco: Mexican American Legal Defense and Education Fund.

Martinez, Vilma. 1982. *Report to the MALDEF Board of Directors.* San Francisco: Mexican American Legal Defense and Education Fund.

Martinez, Vilma. 1984. Interview with author. 16 March.

Maslow, Abraham. 1954. *Motivation and Personality.* New York: Harper & Row.

Massey, Douglas S. 1979a. "Effects of Socioeconomic Factors on the Residential Segregation of Blacks and Spanish Americans in U.S. Urbanized Areas." *American Sociological Review* 44: 1015-1022.

Massey, Douglas S. 1979b. "Residential Segregation of Spanish Americans in United States Urbanized Areas." *Demography* 16: 553-563.

Mauco, Georges. 1984. *Les étrangers en France et le problème du racisme.* Paris: La pensée universelle.

McAllister, Ian, and Donley T. Studlar. 1984. "The Electoral Geography of Immigrant Groups in Britain." *Electoral Studies* 3: 139-150.

McCarthy, John D., and Mayer N. Zald. 1973. *The Trend of Social Movements in America: Professionalization and Resource Mobilization.* Morristown, NJ: General Learning.

McConnell, Grant. 1953. *The Decline of Agrarian Democracy.* Berkeley: University of California Press.

McConnell, Grant. 1966. *Private Power and American Democracy.* New York: Knopf.

McEvedy, C., and R. Jones. 1973. *Atlas of World Population History.* New York: Harmondsworth.

McFarland, Andrew S. 1983. "Public Interest Group Lobbies versus Minority Factions." In *Interest Group Politics*, ed. Allan Ciglar and Burdett Loomis. Washington: Congressional Quarterly Press.

McFarland, Andrew S. 1987. "Interest Groups and Theories of Power in America." *British Journal of Political Science* 17: 129-147.

McRae, K. 1984. *Conflict and Compromise in Multilingual Societies: Switzerland.* Waterloo, Canada: Wilfred Laurier University Press.

McRae, K. 1986. *Conflict and Compromise in Multilingual Societies: Belgium.* Waterloo, Canada: Wilfrid Laurier University Press.

McWhinney, Edward. 1979. *Quebec and the Constitution.* Toronto: University of Toronto Press.

Meier, August, Elliott Rudwick, and Francis L. Broderick, eds. 1967. *Black Protest Thought in the Twentieth Century.* Indianapolis: Bobbs-Merrill.

Merhländer, Ursula, et al. 1979. *Situation der ausländischen Arbeitnehmer und ihrer Familienangehörigen in der Bundesrepublik Deutschland.* Bonn, Germany: Friedrich-Ebert Stiftung.

Merhländer, Ursula, et al. 1981. *Situation der ausländischen Arbeitnehmer und ihrer Familienangehörigen in der Bundesrepublik Deutschland: Repräsentativuntersuchung.* Bonn, Germany: Bundesministerium für Arbeit und Sozialordnung..

Merrit, William T. 1985. "Testimony by President William T. Merrit, National Association of Black Social Workers." In Committee on Labor and Human Resources, U.S. Senate, *Barriers to Adoption.* Washington: Government Printing Office.

Merton, Robert K. 1938. "Social Structure and Anomie." *American Sociological Review* 3: 672-682.

Merton, Robert. 1949. *On Theoretical Sociology.* New York: Free Press.

Merton, Robert K. 1968. *Social Theory and Social Structure.* New York: Free Press.

Messina, Anthony M. 1985. "Race and Party Competition in Britain: Policy Formation in the Post-Consensus Period." *Parliamentary Affairs* 38: 423-436.

Messina, Anthony M. 1987. "Mediating Race Relations: British Community Relations Councils Revisited." *Ethnic and Racial Studies* 10: 186-202.

Messina, Anthony M. 1989a. "Anti-Immigrant Illiberalism and the 'New' Ethnic and Racial Minorities in Western Europe." *Patterns of Prejudice* 23: 17-31.

Messina, Anthony M. 1989b. *Race and Party Competition in Britain.* London: Oxford University (Clarendon) Press.

Mexican American Legal Defense and Education Fund (MALDEF). 1982a. "Anheuser-Busch Grant Spurs Leadership, Citizenship." *MALDEF*, Fall/Winter, 1.

Mexican American Legal Defense and Education Fund. 1982b. "MALDEF Dinners: Success in Los Angeles." *MALDEF*, Fall/Winter, 5.

Mexican American Legal Defense and Education Fund. 1982c. "Some Corporate Friends." *MALDEF*, Spring/Summer, 8.

Mexican American Legal Defense and Education Fund. 1983. "Federal Budget Unfair to Latinas." *MALDEF*, Spring/Summer, 2.

Milbrath, Lester W., and M. L. Goel. 1977. *Political Participation*. Chicago: Rand McNally.

Miller, Arthur H., Patricia Gurin, Gerald Gurin, and Oksana Malanchuk. 1981. "Group Consciousness and Political Participation." *American Journal of Political Science* 25: 494-511.

Miller, Mark. 1981. *Foreign Workers in Europe: An Emerging Political Force*. New York: Praeger.

Miller, Mark. 1986. "Policy Ad-hocracy: The Paucity of Coordinated Perspectives and Policies." *The Annals of the American Academy of Political and Social Science* 485: 64-75.

Miller, Mark, and Philip L. Martin. 1982. *Administering Foreign Worker Programs: Lessons from Europe*. New York: Praeger.

Minces, Juliette. 1973. *Les travailleurs étrangers en France*. Paris: Editions du seuil.

Minderhedennota. 1983. Hand. II, 1982-1983, 16102, nrs. 20-21.

Moe, Terry. 1980. *The Organization of Interests*. Chicago: University of Chicago Press.

Monreal, Gregorio. 1985. "Annotations Regarding Basque Traditional Political Thought in the Sixteenth Century." In *Basque Politics: A Case Study in Ethnic Nationalism*, ed. William A. Douglas. Reno, Nevada: Associated Faculty Press and Basque Studies Program, University of Nevada.

Mora, Magdalena, and Adelaida R. Del Castillo, eds. 1980. *Mexican Women in the United States: Struggles Past and Present*. Occasional Paper no. 2, Los Angeles: University of California Chicano Studies Research Center.

Morris, Raymond N., and C. Michael Lanphier. 1977. *Three Scales of Inequality: Perspectives on French-English Relations*. Don Mills, Canada: Longman Canada.

Moulin, Jean-Pierre. 1985. *Enquête sur la France multiraciale*. Paris: Calmann-Lévy.

Moynihan, Daniel Patrick. 1973. *The Politics of a Guaranteed Income: The Nixon Administration and the Family Assistance Plan*. New York: Random House.

Moynihan, Daniel Patrick. 1986. *Family and Nation*. San Diego: Harcourt Brace Jovanovich.

Muller, Edward N. 1972. "A Test of a Partial Theory of Potential for Political Violence." *American Political Science Review* 66: 928-959.

Mundt, Robert J., and Peggy Heilig. 1982. "District Representation: Demands and Effects in the Urban South." *Journal of Politics* 44: 1035-1048.

Murguía, Edward. 1975. *Assimilation, Colonialism and the Mexican People*. Austin: University of Texas Press.

Murphy, Raymond. 1982. "Power and Autonomy in the Sociology of Education." *Theory and Society* 11: 179-203.

Murray, Richard, and Arnold Vedlitz. 1978. "Racial Voting Patterns in the South: An Analysis of Mayoral Elections from 1960 to 1977 in Five Cities." *The Annals of the American Academy of Political and Social Science* 438: 29-39.

Muus, P. J. 1987. *Migration, Minorities and Policy in the Netherlands: Recent Trends and Developments. Report for the Continuous Reporting System on Migration (SOPEMI) of the Organization for Economic Co-Operation and Development (OECD)*. Amsterdam: University of Amsterdam Press.

Myrdal, Gunnar. 1944. *The American Dilemma*. New York: Harper & Row.

Nairn, Tom. 1981. *The Breakup of Britain*. London: Verso.

National Coalition to End Racism in America's Child Care System. 1984. *Newsletter*. Taylor, Michigan.

National Council of La Raza. 1984a. "Council Appreciates Corporate Assistance." Seventh Annual Conference Program.

National Council of La Raza. 1984b. "GM's John McNulty, Cong. Garcia Among Those to be Honored at 1984 National Conference." *El Noticiario* 3: 1-2.

National Council of La Raza. 1984c. "Seventh Annual NCLR Conference to Focus on Hispanic Leadership." *El Noticiario* 3: 1-3.

National Council of La Raza. 1985a. "NCLR Conference Focus: Hispanic Groups/Private Sector Cooperation." *El Noticiario* 4: 2.

National Council of La Raza. 1985b. "Policy Analysis Update." *El Noticiario* 4: 4.

NCLR (see National Council of La Raza).

Nelson, Candace, and Marta Tienda. 1985. "The Structuring of Hispanic Ethnicity: Historical and Contemporary Perspectives." *Ethnic and Racial Studies* 8: 49-74.

Nelson, William. 1987. "Cleveland: The Evolution of Black Political Power." In *The New Black Politics*, ed. Michael Preston, Lenneal Henderson, and Paul Puryear. Second edition. New York: Longman.

Nelson, William, and Winston Van Horne. 1974. "Black Elected Administrators: The Trials of Office." *Public Administration Review*, 34: 526-533.

Nelson, William, and Philip Meranto. 1977. *Electing Black Mayors*. Columbus: Ohio State University Press.

New York Times. 1976. "Bilingual Danger." *New York Times*, November 22.

New York Times. 1985. *New York Times*, March 10.

Nimni, Ephraim. 1989. "Marx, Engels and the National Question." *Science and Society* 53: 297-326.

Nordlinger, Eric. 1981. *On the Autonomy of the Democratic State.* Cambridge, England: Cambridge University Press.

Norton, Philip. 1984a. *The British Polity.* New York: Longman.

Norton, Philip. ed. 1984b. *Law and Order in British Politics.* Hampshire, England: Gower.

Nuestro. 1982a. "Corporate Money for Organizations . . . Who Gives It? . . . Where Does It Go?" *Nuestro* 6: 27-31.

Nuestro. 1982b. "The Movement's Organization Man." *Nuestro* 6: 22-24, 62-64.

Oates, Stephen. 1982. *Let the Trumpets Sound: The Life of Martin Luther King, Jr.* New York: New American Library.

O'Connor, Karen, and L. Epstein. 1984. "A Legal Voice for the Chicano Community: The Activities of the Mexican-American Legal and Educational Fund." *Social Science Quarterly* 15: 245-267.

OECD (See Organization for Economic Cooperation and Development)

Office of Population and Census Surveys (OPCS) 1986. "Labor Force Survey 1985: Ethnic Group and Country of Birth." *OPCS Monitor*, Ref. LFS 86/2 & PP1 86/3, issued 11-12-86.

Olsen, Marvin E. 1970. "Social and Political Participation of Blacks." *American Sociological Review* 35: 628-697.

Olson, Mancur. 1965. *The Logic of Collective Action.* Cambridge, MA: Harvard University Press.

OPCS (See Office of Population and Census Surveys)

Organization for Economic Cooperation and Development. 1973. *Manpower Policy in France.* Paris: OECD.

Organization for Economic Cooperation and Development. 1986. Continuous Reporting System on Migration. *SOPEMI.* Paris: OECD.

O'Rourke, Timothy J. 1982. "Constitutional and Statutory Challenges to Local At-Large Elections." *University of Richmond Law Review* 17: 39-98.

Orren, Karen. 1976. "Corporate Power and the Slums: Is Big Business a Paper Tiger?" In *Theoretical Perspectives on Urban Politics*, ed. Willis D. Hawley et al. Englewood Cliffs, NJ: Prentice Hall.

Ousely, H. 1984. "Local Authority Race Initiatives." In *Local Socialism? Labor Councils and New Left Alternatives*, ed. M. Boddy and C. Fudge. London: Macmillan.

Owens Smith, J. 1987. *The Politics of Racial Inequality.* Westport, CT: Greenwood.

Ozawa, Martha N., and William T. Alpert. 1984. "The Distributive Effects of Survivor Insurance Benefits and Public Assistance." *Social Service Review* 58: 603-621.

Paddison, Ronan. 1983. *The Fragmented State: The Political Geography of Power.* New York: St. Martin's.

Padilla, Felix M. 1984. "On the Nature of Latino Ethnicity." *Social Science Quarterly* 65: 651-664.

Padilla, Felix M. 1985. *Latino Ethnic Consciousness.* Notre Dame: University of Notre Dame Press.

Panorámica. 1984. Bilbao: Basque Government, Department of Statistics.

Park, Robert. 1921. *Old World Traits Transplanted.* New York: Harper.

Park, Robert, and Ernest Burgess. 1921. *An Introduction to the Science of Sociology.* Chicago: University of Chicago Press.

Patterson, James T. 1986. *America's Struggle against Poverty: 1900-1985.* Cambridge, MA: Harvard University Press.

Paulston, Christina Bratt. 1980. *Bilingual Education: Theories and Issues.* Rowley, MA: Newbury House.

Payne, Stanley. 1985. "Navarra and Basque Nationalism." In *Basque Politics: A Case Study in Ethnic Nationalism*, ed. William Douglass. Reno: Basque Studies Program Occasional Papers Series, no. 2.

Penninx, M. J. A. 1981. "The Contours of a General Minorities Policy." *Planning and Development in the Netherlands* 13: 5-26.

Penninx, R. 1979. "Towards a General Ethnic Minorities Policy?" In Netherlands Scientific Council for Government policy, *Ethnic Minorities* 17.

Pennix, R. 1986. "International Migration in Western Europe since 1973: Developments, Mechanisms and Controls." *International Migration Review* 20: 951-972.

Perotti, Antonio. 1985. *L'immigration en France depuis 1900.* Paris: Centre d'information et d'études sur les migrations.

Perry, Huey, and Alfred Stokes. 1987. "Politics and Power in the Sunbelt: Mayor Morial of New Orleans." In *The New Black Politics*, ed. Michael Preston, Lenneal Henderson, and Paul Puryear. Second edition. New York: Longman.

Peterson, Paul E., and Paul Kantor. 1977. "Political Parties and Citizen Participation in English City Politics." *Comparative Politics* 8: 197-217.

Petras, Elizabeth. 1981. "The Global Market in the Modern World Economy." In *Global Trends in Migration: Theory and Research on International Population Movements*, ed. M. Kritz, C. Keely, and S. Tomasi. Staten Island, NY: Center for Migration Studies.

Pinard, M., and R. Hamilton 1984. "Les québecois votent non: Le sens et al portée du vote." In *Comportement électoral au Québec*, ed. Jean Crête. Chicoutimi, Canada: Gaeton Morin.

Piore, Michael. 1979. *Birds of Passage: Migrant Labor and Industrial Societies.* New York: Cambridge University Press.

Piven, Francis Fox, and Richard Cloward. 1971. *Regulating the Poor: The Functions of Public Welfare.* New York: Random House.

Piven, Frances Fox, and Richard A. Cloward. 1977. *Poor People's Movements.* New York: Pantheon Books.

Piven, Frances Fox, and Richard A. Cloward. 1982. *The New Class War: Reagan's Attack on the Welfare State and Its Consequences.* New York: Random House.

Portes, Alejandro. 1976. "Determinants of the Brain Drain." *International Migration Review* 10: 489-504.

Portes, Alejandro, and John Walton. 1981. *Labor, Class and the International System.* New York: Academic.

Portes, Alejandro, and Rafael Mozo. 1985. "The Political Adaptation Process of Cubans and Other Ethnic Minorities in the United States: A Preliminary Analysis." *International Migration Review* 19: 35-63.

Power, Jonathan. 1979. *Migrant Workers in Western Europe and the United States.* New York: Pergamon.

Prashar, Usha, and Stan Nicholas. 1986. *Routes or Roadblocks?* London: The Runnymede Trust.

President's Commission on Foreign Languages and International Studies. 1979. *Strength Through Wisdom: A Critique of U.S. Capability.* Washington: Government Printing Office.

Preston, Michael. 1987. "The Election of Harold Washington: An Examination of the SES Model in the 1983 Chicago Mayoral Election." In *The New Black Politics*, ed. Michael Preston, Lenneal Henderson, and Paul Puryear. New York: Longman.

Prost, Antoine. 1966. "L'immigration en France depuis cent ans." *Esprit* 348: 532-545.

Przeworski, Adam, and Henry Tuene. 1970. *The Logic of Comparative Social Inquiry.* New York: Wiley.

Rae, Douglas, et al. 1981. *Equalities.* Cambridge, MA: Harvard University Press.

Rainwater, Lee, and William L. Yancey. 1967. *The Moynihan Report and the Politics of Controversy.* Cambridge, MA: M.I.T. Press

Ramdin, Ron. 1987. *The Making of the Black Working Class in Britain.* Aldershot, England: Gower.

Rath, J. 1983. "The Enfranchisement of Immigrants in Practice: Turkish and Moroccan Islands in the Fairway of Dutch Politics." *Netherlands' Journal of Sociology* 19: 151-180.

Rath, J. 1988a. "Mobilization of Ethnicity in Dutch Politics." In *Lost Illusions, Caribbean Minorities in Britain and the Netherlands*, ed. M. Cross and H. B. Entzinger. London: Routledge.

Rath, J. 1988b. "Political Action of Immigrants in the Netherlands: Class or Ethnicity?" *European Journal of Political Research* 16: 623-644.

Rawlings, Colin, and Michael Thrasher. 1985. *The 1985 County Council Election Results in England: A Statistical Digest*. Plymouth, England: Plymouth Polytechnic.

Rawlings, Colin, and Michael Thrasher. 1986. *The 1986 Metropolitan Borough Election Results*. Plymouth, England: Plymouth Polytechnic.

Reed, Evelyn. 1970. "Women: Caste, Class or Oppressed Sex?" *Problems of Women's Liberation*. New York: Pathfinder.

Rees, Tom. 1979. "The United Kingdom." In *The Politics of Migration Policies*, ed. Daniel Kubat. New York: Center for Migration Studies.

Reich, Michael. 1981. *Racial Inequality*. Princeton: Princeton University Press.

Reimann, Horst, and Helga Reimann. 1979. "Federal Republic of Germany." In *International Labor Migration in Europe*, ed. Ronald Krane. New York: Praeger.

Reinhard, M., A. Armengaud, and J. Dupaquier. 1968. *Histoire générale de la population mondiale*. Paris: Montchrestien.

Remba, Oded. 1973. "Income Inequality in Israel: Ethnic Aspects." In *Israel: Social Structure and Changes*, ed. M. Curtis and M. S. Chertoff. New Brunswick, NJ: Transaction.

Research and Intelligence Unit. 1986. *London Borough Council Elections, 8 May 1986*. London: London Residuary Body.

Rich, Wilbur. 1987. "Coleman Young and Detroit Politics." In *The New Black Politics*, ed. Michael Preston, Lenneal Henderson, and Paul Puryear. Second edition. New York: Longman.

Richardson, Bill. 1986. "Hispanic American Concerns." *Foreign Policy* 60: 30-39.

Richmond, Anthony H. 1988. *Immigration and Ethnic Conflict*. London: Macmillan.

Riker, William, and Peter Ordeshook. 1973. *An Introduction to Positive Political Theory*. Englewood Cliffs, NJ: Prentice Hall.

Rist, Ray. 1978. *Guestworkers in Germany: The Prospects for Pluralism*. New York: Praeger.

Robinson, Robert V., and Jonathan Kelley. 1979. "Class as Conceived by Marx and Dahrendorf: Effects on Income Inequality and Politics in the United States and Great Britain." *American Sociological Review* 44: 38-58.

Robinson, Theodore, and Thomas Dye. 1978. "Reformism and Black Representation on City Councils." *Social Science Quarterly* 58: 133-141.

Rochefort, David A. 1986. *American Social Welfare Policy: Dynamics of Formulation and Change*. Boulder, CO: Westview.

Rodriguez, Richard. 1982. *Hunger of Memory: The Education of Richard Rodriguez, An Autobiography*. Boston: David R. Godine.

Rogers, Rosemarie, ed. 1985. *Guests Come to Stay*. Boulder, CO: Westview.

Rokkan, Stein, and Derek Urwin, eds. 1982. *The Politics of Territorial Identity: Studies in European Regionalism*. London: Sage.

Rose, E. J. B., et al. 1969. *Colour and Citizenship*. London: Oxford University Press.

Rose, Richard, ed. 1974. *Lessons from America*. New York: Halstead.

Rose, Richard 1976. "On the Priorities of Citizenship in the Deep South and Northern Ireland." *Journal of Politics* 38: 247-291.

Rosenberg, Morris. 1981. "The Self-Concept: Social Product and Social Force." In *Social Psychology: Sociological Perspectives*, ed. Morris Rosenberg and Ralph H. Turner. New York: Basic.

Ross, Jeffrey, and Ann Baker Cottrell. 1980. *The Mobilization of Collective Identity: Comparative Perspectives*. Lanham, MD: University Press of America.

Rothschild, Joseph. 1981. *Ethnopolitics: A Conceptual Framework*. New York: Columbia University Press.

Rudolph, Joseph R., and Robert J. Thompson, eds. 1989. *Ethnoterritorial Politics, Policy, and the Western World*. Boulder, CO: Lynne Rienner.

Runciman, W. G. 1966. *Relative Deprivation and Social Justice*. Berkeley: University of California Press.

Safran, William. 1984. "The French Left and Ethnic Pluralism," *Ethnic and Racial Studies* 7: 447-461.

Safran, William. 1985. "The Mitterrand Regime and Its Policies of Ethnocultural Accommodation." *Comparative Politics* 18: 41-63.

Safran, William. 1989a. "The French State and Ethnic Minority Cultures: Policy Dimensions and Problems." In *Ethnoterritorial Politics, Policy, and the Western World*, ed. Joseph R. Rudolph, Jr. and Robert J. Thompson. Boulder, CO, and London: Lynne Rienner.

Safran, William. 1989b. "Immigration and Immigrants in the USA and France: Some Comparisons." *Revue Française d'Études Américaines* 41: 303-313.

Safran, William. 1989c. "Minorities, Ethnics, and Aliens: Pluralist Politics in the Fifth Republic." In *Policy-Making in France from de Gaulle to Mitterrand*, ed. Paul Godt. London and New York: Pinter.

Saggar, S. 1987. "The Rediscovery of Race in London: Developments in Local Government in the 1980s." Paper presented at the Political Studies Association, Annual Conference, Aberdeen, Scotland.

San Miguel, Guadelupe, Jr. 1984. "Conflict and Controversy in the Evolution of Bilingual Education in the United States: An Interpretation." *Social Science Quarterly* 65: 505-518.

Sartori, Giovanni. 1968. "Political Development and Political Engineering." In *Public Policy*, vol. 17, ed. John D. Montgomery and Albert O. Hirschman. Cambridge, MA: Harvard University Press.

Sauvy, Alfred. 1946. "Evaluation des besoins de l'immigration française." *Population* 1.

Scanzoni, John H. 1971. *The Black Family in Modern Society*. Boston: Allyn and Bacon.

Scarman, Lord. 1981. *The Brixton Disorders: 10-12 April 1981*. Presented to Parliament by the Secretary of State for the Home Department. London: Her Majesty's Stationery Office.

Schaar, John H. 1981. *Legitimacy in the Modern State*. New Brunswick, NJ: Transaction.

Schain, Martin. 1987. "The National Front in France and the Construction of Political Legitimacy." *West European Politics* 10: 229-252.

Schattschneider, E. E. 1935. *Politics, Pressures and the Tariff*. Englewood Cliffs, NJ: Prentice Hall.

Schattschneider, E. E. 1960. *The Semisovereign People*. New York: Holt, Rinehart & Winston.

Schattschneider, E. E. 1975. *The Semisovereign People*. Hinsdale, IL: Dryden.

Schlesinger, Arthur M., Jr. 1983. *The Almanac of American History*. New York: Bramhall House.

Schlozman, Kay Lehman, and Sidney Verba. 1979. *Insult to Injury: Unemployment, Class and Political Response*. Cambridge, MA: Harvard University Press.

Schmitt, Karl. 1974. *Mexico and the United States*. New York: Wiley.

Schmitter, Barbara. 1984. "Sending States and Immigrant Minorities--the Case of Italy." *Comparative Studies in Society and History* 26: 325-334.

Schnapper, Dominique. 1985/86. "L'Opinion publique et les travailleurs immigrés." *Tocqueville Review* 7: 251-266.

Schnapper, Dominique. 1987. "Unité nationale et particularismes culturels," *Commentaire* 38: 361-365.

Schneider, Susan Gilbert. 1976. *Revolution, Reaction or Reform: The 1974 Bilingual Education Act*. New York: Las Americas.

Schoen, Douglas E. 1977. *Enoch Powell and the Powellites*. New York: St. Martin's.

Schorr, Alvin. 1986. *Common Decency: Domestic Policies after Reagan*. New Haven: Yale University Press.

Segall, Marshall H. 1976. *Human Behavior and Public Policy: A Political Psychology*. New York: Pergamon.

Semyonov, Moshe, and Vered Kraus. 1983. "Gender, Ethnicity and Income Inequality: The Israel Experience." *International Journal of Comparative Sociology* 24: 258-272.

Sewell, William H., and Robert M. Hauser. 1975. *Education, Occupation and Earning: Achievement in the Early Career*. New York: Academic.

Shakeshaft, Charol. 1984. "Her Land on the Frontier." Paper presented at the Berkshire Conference of Women Historians, Smith College.

Shakti. 1986. "The Asian Voice, May 1986." *Shakti,* September, 13-15.

Shingles, Richard D. 1979. "College as a Source of Black Alienation." *Journal of Black Studies* 9: 267-290.

Shingles, Richard D. 1981. "Black Consciousness and Political Participation: The Missing Link." *American Political Science Review* 75: 76-91.

Shingles, Richard D. 1986. "The Black Gender Gap: Double Jeopardy and Politicization." Paper presented at the annual meetings of the Midwest Political Science Association, Chicago.

Shingles, Richard D. 1987a. "New Measures of Subjective Political Efficacy and Political Trust." National Election Studies Report on the 1987 NES Pilot Study.

Shingles, Richard D. 1987b. "Relative Deprivation and the Inclination to Protest." National Science Foundation Report for Grant No. SES-8419793.

Sierra, Christine M. 1982. "The Political Transformation of a Minority Organization: The Council of La Raza, 1965-1980." Ph.D. dissertation. Stanford University.

Simon, Herbert. 1985. "Human Nature and Politics: The Dialogue of Psychology with Political Science." *American Political Science Review* 79: 293-304.

Simon, Rita J., and Howard Alstein. 1981. *Transracial Adoption.* Lexington, MA: Lexington Books.

Simons, Janet. 1986. "Coors Turns Boycotters into Buyers." *Advertising Age* 57: 42-47.

Smiley, Donald V. 1977. "French-English Relations in Canada and Consociational Democracy." In *Ethnic Conflict in the Western World,* ed. Milton J. Esman. Ithaca: Cornell University Press.

Smith, James, and Finis Welch. 1978. *Closing the Gap: Forty Years of Economic Progress for Blacks.* R-3330-DOL. Santa Monica, CA: Rand.

Smith, Lee. 1981. "The Unsentimental Corporate Giver." *Fortune* 21: 121-134.

SOFRES. 1987. *L'État de l'opinion.* Paris: Seuil.

Solé, Robert. 1987. "Mettre les beurs à la table d'honneur," *Le Monde,* May 20.

SOPEMI (Continuous Reporting System on Migration). 1985. Paris: OECD.

Sowell, Thomas. 1983. *The Economics and Politics of Race: An International Perspective.* New York: Morrow.

Spengler, J. J. 1938. *France Faces Depopulation.* Durham: Duke University Press.

Spengler, Joseph J. 1979. *France Faces Depopulation: Postlude Edition, 1936-1976.* Durham: Duke University Press.

Staples, Robert. 1978. *The Black Family: Essays and Studies.* Second edition. Belmont, CA: Wadsworth.

Stasi, Bernard. 1984. *Immigration: Une chance pour la France*. Paris: Laffont.

Steinberg, Steven. 1981. *The Ethnic Myth*. New York: Antheum.

Steiner, Stan. 1968. *The New Indians*. New York: Delta.

Stockman, David. 1986. *The Triumph of Politics: The Inside Story of the Reagan Revolution*. New York: Harper & Row.

Stone, John. 1985. *Racial Conflict in Contemporary Society*. Cambridge, MA: Harvard University Press.

Studlar, Donley. 1977. "Social Context and Attitudes toward Coloured Immigrants." *British Journal of Sociology* 28: 169-184.

Studlar, Donley. 1978. "Policy Voting in Britain: The Coloured Immigration Issue in the 1964, 1966, and 1970 Elections." *American Political Science Review* 72: 46-64.

Studlar, Donley. 1980. "Elite Responsiveness or Elite Autonomy: British Immigration Policy Reconsidered." *Ethnic and Racial Studies* 3: 207-223.

Studlar, Donley. 1985. "'Waiting for the Catastrophe': Race and the Political Agenda in Britain." *Patterns of Prejudice* 19: 3-15.

Studlar, Donley. 1988. "Nonwhite Policy Preferences, Political Participation, and the Political Agenda in Britain." In *Race, Government, and Politics in Britain*, ed. Zig Layton-Henry and Paul Rich. London: Macmillan.

Studlar, Donley, and Susan Welch. 1987. "Understanding the Iron Law of Andrarchy: The Effects of Candidate Gender on Voting for Local Office in Scotland." *Comparative Political Studies* 20: 174-181.

Sundquist, James L. 1968. *Politics and Policy: The Eisenhower, Kennedy and Johnson Years*. Washington: Brookings Institution.

Sundquist, James L. 1986. "Has America Lost Its Social Conscience--and How Will It Get It Back?" *Political Science Quarterly* 101: 513-533.

Suttles, Gerald. 1972. *The Social Construction of Communities*. Chicago: University of Chicago Press.

Taebel, Delbert. 1978. "Minority Representation on City Councils: The Impact of Structure on Blacks and Hispanics." *Social Science Quarterly* 59: 142-152.

Tannahill, J. A. 1958. *European Voluntary Workers in Britain*. Manchester, England: Manchester University Press.

Tapinos, Georges. 1975. *L'immigration étrangère en France, 1946-1973*. Paris: Presses Universitaires de France.

Thomas, Robert D., and Richard W. Murray. 1986. "Applying the Voting Rights Act in Houston: Federal Intervention or Local Political Determination?" *Publius* 16: 81-96.

Tibon-Cornillot, Michel. 1984. "Le défi de l'immigration maghrébine." *Politique Aujourd'hui* 4: 41.

Tienda, Marta, and Lisa J. Niedert. 1985. "Language, Education, and the Socioeconomic Achievement of Hispanic-Origin Men." In *The Mexican*

American Experience, ed. Rodolfo O. de la Garza et al. Austin: University of Texas Press.

Tilly, Charles 1978. *From Mobilization to Revolution*. New York: Randon House.

Time. 1980. "Battle over Bilingualism." *Time*, September 8.

Time. 1987. "Our Time Has Come." *Time*, June 1.

Titmuss, Richard M. 1968. *Commitment to Welfare*. New York: Pantheon.

Titmuss, Richard M. 1974. *Social Policy*. New York: Pantheon.

Tocqueville, Alexis de. 1956. *Democracy in America*. New York: The New American Library.

Tufte, Edward R. 1978. *Political Control of the Economy*. Princeton: Princeton University Press.

Turner, Jonathan, and Edna Bonacich. 1980. "Toward a Composite Theory of Middleman Minorities." *Ethnicity* 7: 144-158.

Tyree, Andrea, Moshe Semyonov, and Robert Hodge. 1979. "Gaps and Glissandos: Inequality, Economic Development and Social Mobility in 24 Countries." *American Sociological Review* 44: 410-424.

U.S. Bureau of Census. 1959-1984. "Current Population Reports," Series P-60.

U.S. Department of Labor, Employment Standards Administration. 1982. "Black Lung Benefits Act: Annual Report on Administration of the Act During Calendar Year 1981."

Verba, Sidney, and Norman H. Nie. 1972. *Participation in America*. New York: Harper & Row.

Verbunt, Gilles. 1985. "France." In *European Immigration Policy: A Comparative Study*, ed. Tomas Hammar. Cambridge, England: Cambridge University Press.

Wagner, Stephen T. 1981. "The Historical Background of Bilingualism and Biculturalism in the United States." In *The New Bilingualism: An American Dilemma*, ed. Martin Ridge. Los Angeles: University of Southern California Press.

Wall, Wendy L. 1984. "Companies Changing the Way They Make Charitable Donations." *Wall Street Journal*, June 21.

Waller, Robert. 1983. *The Almanac of British Politics*. London: Croom Helm.

Wallraff, Gunter. 1985. *Ganz Unten*. Cologne, Germany: Kiepenheuer & Witsch.

Wallraff, Gunter. 1987. *Lowest of the Low*. London: Pluto Press.

Walzer, Michael. 1982. "Pluralism in Political Perspective." In *The Politics of Ethnicity*, ed. Michael Walzer, Edward T. Kantowicz, John Higham, and Mona Harrington. Cambridge, MA: The Belknap Press of Harvard University.

Ward, R., and R. Jenkins, eds. 1984. *Ethnic Communities in Business: Strategies for Economic Survival*. Cambridge, MA: Cambridge University Press.

Waxman, Chaim L. 1983. *The Stigma of Poverty: A Critique of Poverty Theories and Policies*. New York: Pergamon.

Weber, Max. 1947. *The Theory of Social and Economic Organization*. Talcott Parsons and A. M. Henderson translators and editors. New York: Free Press.

Weems, Luther. 1978. "Black Community Research Needs: Methods, Models and Modalities." In *Social Research and the Black Community: Selected Issues and Priorities*, ed. Lawrence E. Gary. Washington: Institute for Urban Affairs and Research, Howard University.

Welch, Susan, and John R. Hibbing. 1984. "Hispanic Representation in the United States Congress." *Social Science Quarterly* 65: 328-335.

Welch, Susan, Janet Clark, Robert Darcy, and Margery M. Ambrosius. 1985. "The Effect of Candidate Gender on Electoral Outcomes in State Legislative Races." *Western Political Quarterly* 38: 464-475.

Welch, Susan, and Donley Studlar. 1985. "The Impact of Race on Political Behaviour in Britain." *British Journal of Political Science* 15: 458-467.

Welch, Susan, and Donley Studlar. 1988. "The Effects of Candidate Gender on Voting for Local Office in England." *British Journal of Political Science* 18: 273-280.

Whisler, Kurt. 1983. "How Hispanic Organizations Have Fared with the Cutbacks: A Survey." *Caminos* 3: 54-55.

White, John. 1985. *Black Leadership in America: 1985-1968*. New York: Longman.

Wihtol de Wenden, Catherine. 1978. *Les immigrés dans la cité: La représentation des immigrés dans la vie publique en Europe*. Paris: Documentation Française.

Wihtol de Wenden, Catherine, ed. 1988a. *La Citoyenneté et les changements de structures social et nationale de la population française*. Paris: Fondation Diderot.

Wihtol de Wenden, Catherine. 1988b. *Les immigrés et la politique: Cent cinquante ans d'évolution*. Paris: Presses de la Fondation Nationale des Sciences Politiques.

Wilensky, Harold L. 1975. *The Welfare State and Equality*. Berkeley: University of California Press.

Wilensky, Harold L. 1983. "Political Legitimacy and Consensus: Missing Variables in the Assessment of Social Policy." In *Evaluating the Welfare State: Social and Political Perspectives*, ed. S. E. Spiro and E. Yuchtman-Yaar. New York: Academic.

Williams, Eddie N. 1982. "Black Political Progress in the 1970s: The Electoral Arena." In *The New Black Politics*, ed. Michael B. Preston. New York: Longman.

Wilpert, Czarina. 1980. *Die Zukunft der zweite Generation*. Koenigstein, Germany: Verlay Anton Hain.

Wilson, K., and Alejandro Portes. 1980. "Immigrant Enclaves: An Analysis of the Labor Market Experience of Cubans in Miami." *American Journal of Sociology* 86: 295-315.

Wilson, William Julius. 1987. *The Truly Disadvantaged*. Chicago: University of Chicago Press.

Wise, Jennings C. 1971. *The Red Man in the New World Drama*. New York: Macmillan.

Woehrling, J. 1985. "Minority Cultural and Linguistic Rights and Equality Rights in the 'Canadian Charter of Rights and Freedoms.'" *McGill Law Journal* 31: 50-92.

Yalden, Maxwell F. 1981. "The Bilingual Experience in Canada." In *The New Bilingualism: An American Dilemma*, ed. Martin Ridge. Los Angeles: University of Southern California Press.

Young, G. 1984. "Local Authorities and Racial Disadvantage: Report of the Conference Organized by the CRE." London.

Young, K. 1985. "Racial Disadvantage." In *Between Center and Loyalty*, ed. G. Jones, et al. London: Gower.

Yrizar, Pedro de. 1973. "Los Dialectos y Variedades de la Lengua Vasca: Estudio Lingüístico-Demográfico." *Separata del Boletín de la Real Sociedad Vascongada de los Amigos del País* 29: 77-78.

Zarinski, Raphael. 1989. "Ethnic Extremism among Ethnonational Minorities in Western Europe: Dimensions, Causes, and International Responses." *Comparative Politics* 21: 253-272.

Zenner, Walter. 1982. "Arabic-Speaking Immigrants in North America as Middleman Minorities." *Ethnic and Racial Studies* 5: 457-76.

Index

Contributors and Editors

Robert P. Clark is Professor of Government at George Mason University, where he has taught since 1977. He has published numerous articles and he is the author of three books on Basque affairs, the most recent of which, *Negotiating with ETA: Obstacles to Peace in the Basque Country 1975-1988*, was published in 1990 by the University of Nevada Press.

Richard L. Engstrom is Research Professor of Political Science at the University of New Orleans. His research on electoral systems has appeared in the *American Political Science Review, Journal of Politics, Social Science Quarterly, Electoral Studies*, and other journals. He is currently working on a book on minority vote dilution with Michael D. McDonald.

Roy Fitzgerald is currently an associate in the litigation department of the law firm of Gunster, Yoakley and Stewart, P.A., West Palm Beach, Florida. He received a B.A., M.A., J.D., and Ph.D. from the State University of New York at Buffalo.

Luis R. Fraga is Associate Professor of Political Science at Stanford University. His research interests are in the area of the management of ethnic and racial conflict, urban politics, and educational policy. He has published in the *Journal of Politics, Urban Affairs Quarterly, The Western Political Quarterly,* and *West European Politics*. In 1989-90, he was a Fellow at the Center for Advanced Study in the Behavioral Sciences.

Gary P. Freeman is Associate Professor of Government at the University of Texas at Austin. He is the author of numerous articles on immigration and social policy and the book *Immigrant Labor and Racial Conflict in Industrial*

Societies. He is currently working on a comparative study of Australian and American immigration policy.

D. John Grove is Associate Professor at the Graduate School of International Studies at the University of Denver. He is the author of *Global Inequality and Ethnic Change: A Seven Nation Study*, and he is currently working on a comparative study of inequality and nationalism.

Barbara Schmitter Heisler is Associate Professor of Sociology and Anthropology at Gettysburg College. She has published numerous articles on immigration in Western Europe and, along with Martin O. Heisler, co-edited "From Foreign Workers to Settlers? Transnational Migration and the Emergence of New Minorities," a volume of *The Annals of the American Academy of Political and Social Science.* Her current research project focuses on urban poverty, immigration, and citizenship in Germany, The Netherlands, and the United Kingdom.

Marilyn Hoskin is Dean of Natural and Social Sciences and Professor of Political Science at the State University of New York College at Buffalo. She has written in the area of political socialization and presidential support as well as that of immigration and is the author of *The Political Involvement of Adolescents* and *New Immigrants and Democratic Society.* She has also contributed to numerous journals and edited books.

Gary Klass is Associate Professor of Political Science at Illinois State University, where he teaches courses in American public policy and research methods. He is the author of several publications on comparative and American social welfare policy.

J. A. Laponce is Professor of Political Science at the University of British Columbia. He is the author of numerous articles and *The Protection of Minorities* and *Languages and Their Territories.* He is currently working on a comparative study of ethnic federalism.

Michael D. McDonald is Associate Professor and Director of Graduate Studies in Political Science at the State University of New York at Binghamton. His areas of interest are legislative politics and representation. His work on electoral systems and the election of minorities and women has appeared in the *American Political Science Review*, the *Journal of Politics*, and elsewhere.

Anthony M. Messina is Associate Professor of Political Science at Tufts University. He has published numerous journal articles on the politics of race and immigration in Britain and Western Europe and he is the author of *Race and*

Party Competition in Britain. His current research focuses on the political consequences of consensus politics in Britain and West Germany between 1945 and 1989.

Isidro D. Ortiz is Associate Professor of Mexican American Studies at San Diego State University. He is the co-editor of *Chicano Studies: A Multidisciplinary Approach.* He has also published articles and book chapters on diverse aspects of Chicano and Latino politics. The experiences of Latinos in American politics are the foci of his current research.

Jan Rath is a cultural anthropologist at the Institute for Sociology of Law at the Catholic University of Nijmegen, The Netherlands. He is the author of a number of journal articles and book chapters on the sociology and politics of race and ethnic relations and he has written *Minorization: The Social Construction of 'Ethnic Minorities.'* He is currently involved in a comparative project on the reaction of host societies to the institutionalization of Islam.

Laurie A. Rhodebeck is Assistant Professor of Political Science at the State University of New York at Buffalo. Her research interests focus on public opinion and voting behavior in American politics and the refinement of survey research methods. Her published work includes articles on the role of reference groups in structuring mass political behavior, the development of age-specific political identities, and the stability of racial prejudice among white Americans.

William Safran is Professor of Political Science at the University of Colorado, Boulder and vice-president for the Research Committee on Politics and Ethnicity of the International Political Science Association. His publications include *Veto-Group Politics, The French Polity,* and he is the co-author of *Ideology and Politics: The Socialist Party of France* and *Politics in Western Europe.* He has contributed chapters to 14 books and numerous articles on various aspects of French and West European politics.

Shamit Saggar is Lecturer in Politics at Queen Mary and Westfield College, University of London. He is a specialist on the politics of race in contemporary Britain and other advanced industrial democracies and, in addition to his numerous articles, he has authored *Race and Public Policy* and *Race and Politics in Britain.* He is currently working on a comparative study involving Britain, Canada, Australia, and the United States.

Ronald J. Schmidt is Professor of Political Science at California State University, Long Beach. He specializes in domestic public policy and minority politics in the United States, and he is currently writing a book on cultural pluralism and the politics of language in the United States.

358

Richard D. Shingles is Associate Professor of Political Science at Virginia Polytechnic Institute and State University. He is the author of various publications on race and gender relations, political participation and political ideology. Work for his forthcoming book, *The Politics of Race and Gender: Parallels in the Political Thought and Action of Female, African, Mexican and Native-Americans*, has been sponsored by a Humanities grant from VPISU and a MacArthur Foundation Fellowship awarded by the Joint Center for Political and Economic Studies.

Donley T. Studlar is Professor of Political Science at Oklahoma State University. He is the co-editor of *Dilemmas of Change in British Politics* and *Political Economy: Public Policies in the United States and Britain* and the author of numerous articles on race and politics in Britain. His Ph.D. dissertation on the latter subject was awarded the first Samuel H. Beer Prize of the British Politics Group.

Susan Welch is Professor of Political Science and Dean of the College of Liberal Arts at Penn State University. She has published widely on women and minorities, including *Black Americans' Views of Racial Equality* which was published in 1991 by Cambridge University Press.

Frederick D. Wright is Director of the African-American Studies Program at the University of Notre Dame. He specializes in American politics, and the subfields of Black and Southern politics. His articles have appeared in *Publius: The Journal of Federalism*, the *Journal of the Inter-denominational Theology Center*, and an edited volume, *Blacks in Southern Politics*.